Fundamentals of Criminal Advocacy

Based upon the authors' following treatises—SUCCESSFUL TECHNIQUES FOR CRIMINAL TRIALS; HANDLING NARCOTIC AND DRUG CASES; INVESTIGATION AND PREPARATION OF CRIMINAL CASES; DEFENDING BUSINESS AND WHITE COLLAR CRIMES; AND CRIMES OF VIOLENCE: HOMICIDE AND ASSAULT

F. Lee Bailey
of The Massachusetts and United States Supreme Court Bars

Henry B. Rothblatt
Member of New York, California, District of Columbia, and Florida Bars
Adjunct Professor of Law, New York Law School

1974

LCP BW

THE LAWYERS CO-OPERATIVE PUBLISHING CO.
Rochester, New York 14603

BANCROFT-WHITNEY CO.
San Francisco, California 94107

Library of Congress Catalog Card Number 73-90861

DEDICATION

To future trial lawyers, with the hope that this work will sharpen the tools of advocacy and inspire the highest standards in trials of criminal cases.

FOREWORD

by F. Lee Bailey and Henry B. Rothblatt

A well-seasoned lawyer has an obligation to his young colleagues to pass on to them the knowledge and insights he has gathered over his years of practice. Years of courtroom experience provide an attorney with a perspective and a sense of the law which cannot be acquired in any classroom or law library.

While acknowledging the value of practical experience for students, most law schools until recently have made little attempt to meet the need of the student for a taste of the legal contests he will be waging as an attorney. For the most part these needs for guidance and experience in practice have been met by attorneys such as us who are the natural source of information and advice for the novice.

Based upon several of the authors' treatises in the Criminal Law Library series, this volume is actually an elaborate map which will take any careful reader safely through the hazardous and poorly-marked roads of the criminal trial system. All phases of the trial are treated. We guide you from the moment you receive an initial phone call from your client. We tell you how to win in the politics of plea bargaining. We explain how to draft and argue pre-trial motions effectively. And we tell you how to take advantage of the discovery opportunities offered by evidentiary hearings.

An in-depth examination of the trial process is the heart of this book. We tell you how to conduct a voir dire examination and how to present an effective opening statement. The sections concerning the art of cross-examination of prosecution witnesses should be especially helpful. They will help you to understand the purposes of cross-examination and show you how to set reasonable goals for the defense during this crucial part of a trial. This book also contains sections concerning the presentation of the defense and the summation. The best of the trial techniques we have mastered in our years of practice are here.

Our thanks to Earl Kellet, Esq., Jonathan M. Purver, Esq., and Joseph Marticelli, Esq., of the Lawyers Co-operative Publishing Company, whose patience and aid were crucial to the creation of this volume.

Special thanks to Emma Alden Rothblatt, Herb Altman, and Henrietta Santo for their help and suggestions.

Our appreciation to Melanie Martin and Sharon Haddock for their advice and assistance in the preparation of this manuscript.

Our thanks to our associates Joseph Seijas, Stephan Peskin, Rocco Vignola, Stanley Zinner, Andrew Zweben, Gerald Alch, Colin W. Gillis, John Albert Johnson, and Dr. Frederic J. Barnett.

Special appreciation goes to Rose Ruiz, Robert Gladstone, Andrew Ferber, Deborah Sabel, Mattie Lee Alexander, Terry Stoltz, and Judith T. LaMagra.

F. LEE BAILEY

HENRY B. ROTHBLATT

TABLE OF CONTENTS

CHAPTER TWO

GENERAL PRINCIPLES OF INVESTIGATION

CHAPTER THREE

INITIAL CONTACTS WITH CLIENT AND INTERVIEW

CHAPTER SIX

SELECTION AND PREPARATION OF EXPERT WITNESSES

CHAPTER TWELVE

CROSS-EXAMINATION

CHAPTER EIGHTEEN

HOW TO HANDLE PREJUDICIAL CONDUCT OF TRIAL JUDGE

CHAPTER NINETEEN

THE CHARGE TO THE JURY

CHAPTER TWENTY ONE

JUDGMENT AND SENTENCE

CHAPTER ONE

ARRAIGNMENT, BAIL AND PLEA

A. INITIAL CONSIDERATIONS

§ 1. In general

Your client has been arrested. Usually, he will be arraigned on the complaint the day after the arrest. The arraignment consists of reading the charge in the complaint to the defendant. If you appear, the court will consider a date convenient to all parties for a preliminary hearing.[1]

If your client was just arrested at the time of your initial retention you must obtain the basic information such as the name, address and telephone number both of the caller and of the defendant, the time and place of the arrest, and the place where the defendant is being held. You must also

1. **Annotation:** Right of motorist stopped by police officers for traffic offense to be informed at that time of his federal constitutional rights under Miranda v Arizona. 25 ALR3d 1076.

find out who, if anyone, is willing to pay the premium for a bailbond and to furnish security for it in the event you take the case and are able to arrange for bail.[2]

If you decide to take the case, try to contact the defendant by telephone. Advise him as to when you expect to arrive at the place where he is being held and tell him not to answer any questions until you arrive there. Also advise him to object to appearing in a lineup or to any physical examination or examination of his hair or blood and to refuse to take part in any lie detection tests.

Find out whether the defendant has been mistreated in any fashion and ask him who should be called with regard to the furnishing of bail. Inform the authorities that the defendant is not to be exhibited for identification, placed in a lineup or to be subjected to any other form of test or inspection. Ascertain the complete name, rank and number of the investigating officer and find out where he can generally be reached.

B. ARRAIGNMENT

§ 2. In general

Arraignment and plea in criminal cases are essential to due process of law guaranteed by the Fourteenth Amendment to the Federal Constitution.[3] The term "arraignment" is used to describe the procedure that precedes the making

2. **Annotation:** Amount of attorneys' compensation in absence of contract or statute fixing amount. 56 ALR2d 13 at page 201.

3. Hack v State, 141 Wis 346, 124 NW 492.

Annotations: Accused's right to assistance of counsel at or prior to arraignment. 5 ALR3d 1269.

Delay in taking before magistrate or denial of opportunity to give bail as supporting action for false imprisonment. 98 ALR2d 966.

Right of prosecution to writ of certiorari in criminal case. 91 ALR2d 1095.

Determination in extradition proceedings, or on habeas corpus in such proceedings, whether crime is charged. 40 ALR2d 1151.

Admissibility of confession as affected by delay in arraignment of prisoner. 19 ALR2d 1331.

Right of accused to bill of particulars. 5 ALR2d 444.

of a plea.[4] The purpose and necessity of an arraignment are to fix the identity of the accused, to inform him of the charge against him, and to give him an opportunity to plead.[5]

Under federal law, arraignment is sine qua non to the trial itself because it is the preliminary stage where the accused is informed of the indictment and pleads to it, thereby formulating the issue to be tried.[6]

Statutes specifying the time for arraignment in particular cases must, of course, be followed. In the absence of a statute the accused must ordinarily be arraigned before impaneling and swearing the jury,[7] or at least before the introduction of evidence.[8]

Whether it is necessary to arraign the accused and give him an opportunity to plead after the indictment or information has been amended usually depends on the materiality of the amendment.[9] If the indictment or information has been materially changed, the accused should not be put on trial without rearraignment.[10] The mere correction of a

4. Johnson v United States, 225 US 405, 56 L Ed 1142, 32 S Ct 748.

5. Thomas v State, 255 Ala 632, 53 So 2d 340; State v Trabbold, 47 Del 391, 91 A2d 537; Ex parte Livingston, 116 Fla 640, 156 So 612; People v Terry, 366 Ill 520, 9 NE2d 322; Dunn v Commonwealth (Ky) 350 SW2d 709; State v Barnett, 193 Minn 336, 258 NW 508; United States v Aurandt, 15 NM 292, 107 P 1064; Sharer v State, 40 Okla Crim 420, 269 P 511.

See also, to the same effect, State v Barnes, 4 Conn Cir 464, 234 A2d 649; McCuan v State, 196 Kan 457, 413 P2d 69 (appearance before magistrate is not an arraignment); Commonwealth v Phelan, 427 Pa 265, 234 A2d 540, cert den 391 US 920, 20 L Ed 2d 657, 88 S Ct 1803.

6. Hamilton v Alabama, 368 US 52, 7 L Ed 2d 114, 82 S Ct 157 (referring to Rules 10, 11, Fed Rules of Crim Proc).

7. State v Ward, 48 Ark 36, 2 SW 191.

8. Disney v Commonwealth, 9 Ky LR 413, 5 SW 360; Steen v State, 92 Tex Crim 99, 242 SW 1047; State v Thompson, 58 Wash 2d 598, 364 P2d 527, cert den 370 US 945, 8 L Ed 2d 811, 82 S Ct 1590, reh den 371 US 855, 9 L Ed 2d 94, 83 S Ct 50.

And see State v Harrison (Mo) 29 SW2d 63, wherein the accused was arraigned after the prosecutor had made his opening statements to the jury.

9. State v Hurd, 5 Wash 2d 308, 105 P2d 59.

10. Thomas v State, 255 Ala 632, 53 So 2d 340; Hanley v Zenoff, 81 Nev 9,

clerical or other immaterial error in the accusation, however, does not require a second arraignment and plea.[11]

§ 3. Waiver of arraignment

An arraignment, not being a part of a trial by jury, may ordinarily be waived.[12] However, a waiver will not be effective unless the accused knows the nature of the charge against him and has a full opportunity to defend himself.[13]

Quite a few cases in different jurisdictions recognize that the accused can waive his right to arraignment in misdemeanor trials,[14] and in some jurisdictions and cases, the right may be waived even when the charge is for a felony.[15]

§ 4. Mode and sufficiency of waiving arraignment

The power to waive an arraignment must be exercised by

398 P2d 241; State v Hurd, 5 Wash 2d 308, 105 P2d 59.

11. State v Dargatz, 244 Mo 218, 148 SW 889; State v Foley, 44 Mont 311, 120 P 225; Rasmussen v State, 63 Wis 1, 22 NW 835.

12. Eckels v State, 153 Tex Crim 402, 220 SW2d 175.

Annotation: Right to waive indictment, information, or other formal accusation. 56 ALR2d 837.

13. Garland v Washington, 232 US 642, 58 L Ed 772, 34 S Ct 456.

14. Hayden v State, 55 Ark 342, 18 SW 239; Frank v State, 142 Ga 741, 83 SE 645, error den 235 US 694, 59 L Ed 429, 35 S Ct 208; Pines v District Court of Woodbury County, 233 Iowa 1284, 10 NW2d 574; State v Cruse, 112 Kan 486, 212 P 81; Bishoff v Commonwealth, 123 Ky 340, 96 SW 538; State v Rasberry, 113 La 651, 37 So 545; People v Weeks, 165 Mich 362, 130 NW 697; State v Bowman (Mo) 213 SW 97; State v Klasner, 19 NM 474, 145 P 679; People v Osterhout (NY) 34 Hun 260; Wescoat v State, 47 Ohio App 266, 17 Ohio L Abs 299, 191 NE 816; Phillips v State (Okla Crim) 267 P2d 167; State v Brock, 61 SC 141, 39 SE 359; State v Reddington, 7 SD 368, 64 NW 170; State v Prouty, 94 Vt 359, 111 A 559; State v Straub, 16 Wash 111, 47 P 227; Hack v State, 141 Wis 346, 124 NW 492.

15. Garland v Washington, 232 US 642, 58 L Ed 772, 34 S Ct 456; Beaty v United States (CA4 NC) 203 F2d 652; State v Trabbold, 47 Del 391, 91 A2d 537; Padgett v State, 117 Fla 75, 157 So 186; Mitchell v State, 22 Ga 211; Kelly v People, 132 Ill 363, 24 NE 56; Rogers v State, 211 Ind 47, 5 NE2d 509; State v Winstrand, 37 Iowa 110; State v Glave, 51 Kan 330, 33 P 8; State v Robinson, 36 La Ann 873; People v McHale (Sup) 15 NYS 496; Ingham v State, 35 Ohio App 311, 172 NE 401; Ex parte Robinson, 56 Okla Crim 404, 41 P2d 127.

the accused in person or with his express consent.[16] Where the right of the accused to waive an arraignment is recognized, an express waiver in open court is, of course, sufficient.[17] An arraignment may also be waived in a less formal manner, such as by the voluntary entry of a plea,[18] or by announcing readiness for trial.[19]

The accused is not denied due process when it is determined that he has waived his right to arraignment by failing to object and proceeding to trial. Thus one can waive arraignment by going to trial without objection,[20] or by silence, at least in all except capital cases, if the accused

16. Wells v Terrell, 121 Ga 368, 49 SE 319; State v McMichael, 50 La Ann 428, 23 So 992.

17. Tarver v State, 95 Ga 222, 21 SE 381; Bishoff v Commonwealth, 123 Ky 340, 96 SW 538; State v Rasberry, 113 La 651, 37 So 545.

18. Paris v State, 36 Ala 232; Moore v State, 51 Ark 130, 10 SW 22; Bassett v State, 44 Fla 12, 33 So 262; Harris v State, 11 Ga App 137, 74 SE 895; Fitzpatrick v People, 98 Ill 259; Meyers v State, 156 Ind 388, 59 NE 1052; State v Winstrand, 37 Iowa 110; State v Rasberry, 113 La 651, 37 So 545; State v Weeden, 133 Mo 70, 34 SW 473; Goodin v State, 16 Ohio St 344.

Arraignment may be waived by filing a demurrer or a special plea. Kincade v State, 14 Ga App 544, 81 SE 910.

Arraignment may be waived by pleading not guilty. Utterback v Commonwealth, 105 Ky 723, 49 SW 479; State v O'Kelley, 258 Mo 345, 167 SW 980; State v Walton, 50 Or 142, 91 P 490.

19. Williams v State, 227 Ark 228, 297 SW2d 771; Hall v State, 136 Fla 644, 187 So 392; Blanton v State, 233 Ind 51, 115 NE2d 122, reh den 233 Ind 56, 116 NE2d 631, later app 234 Ind 142, 124 NE2d 382, cert den 350 US 850, 100 L Ed 756, 76 S Ct 90; State v Trams, 189 Kan 393, 369 P2d 223; State v Vallo (Mo) 33 SW2d 899; Tanner v State (Okla Crim) 381 P2d 888.

20. Beaty v United States (CA4 NC) 203 F2d 652; State v Trabbold, 47 Del 391, 91 A2d 537; Harvey v State, 232 Ind 574, 114 NE2d 457; Re Bundy, 144 Kan 64, 58 P2d 80; Cravens v Commonwealth (Ky) 262 SW2d 466; State v Jacobs, 195 La 281, 196 So 347; Ayala v State, 226 Md 488, 174 A2d 160; State ex rel. Williams v Rigg, 256 Minn 568, 99 NW2d 450, cert den 363 US 814, 4 L Ed 2d 1155, 80 S Ct 1252; Lowe v State, 201 Miss 618, 30 So 2d 53; State v O'Kelley, 258 Mo 345, 167 SW 980; Maher v State, 144 Neb 463, 13 NW2d 641, cert den 323 US 757, 89 L Ed 606, 65 S Ct 91; State v Renner, 34 NM 154, 279 P 66; Cincinnati v Strasburger, 79 Ohio App 424, 35 Ohio Ops 207, 47 Ohio L Abs 293, 72 NE2d 393, app dismd 147 Ohio St 535, 34 Ohio Ops 425, 72 NE2d 266; State v Harvey, 117 Or 466, 242 P 440; State v Mayfield, 235 SC 11, 109 SE2d 716, cert den 363 US 846, 4 L Ed 2d 1728, 80 S Ct 1616, reh den 364 US 857, 5 L Ed 2d 81, 81 S Ct 36; State v Reddington, 7 SD 368, 64 NW 170; State v Straub, 16 Wash 111, 47 P 227.

is fully informed as to the charge and is not otherwise prejudiced in the trial of the case by the omission of that formality.[21]

C. BAIL AND RECOGNIZANCE

§ 5. In general

At the time of the arraignment the court will fix bail. Attempt to obtain low bail! Before the arraignment, confer with the assistant prosecutor in charge of arraignments in the Magistrate's Court and try to obtain his consent to a low bail. At the arraignment explain to the court all the favorable factors concerning the defendant: his good prior record, his marital status, number of children he has, his employment situation and how long he has held his position. State every reason why the accused is not likely to flee the jurisdiction but will face the charge in the complaint. The Judge will then fix bail and postpone the preliminary hearing to an adjourned date.[22]

In some jurisdictions, the Magistrate does not have the power to fix bail where the defendant is charged with a felony or some serious misdemenors and has been previously convicted of a felony or serious misdemeanors. You generally must then make application for bail to a Judge of the Court having jurisdiction in the trial of felony cases.

In order to obtain the most favorable possible bail terms you must, as noted, be prepared to supply the Court with all information relevant to establishing that your client is not likely to jump bail. If you were retained at the time of the preliminary hearing and you cannot adequately advise the Court in this regard, seek to have the arraignment put

21. Garland v Washington, 232 US 642, 58 L Ed 772, 34 S Ct 456; Theis v State, 45 Ga App 364, 164 SE 456; Price v State, 53 Okla Crim 353, 12 P2d 249; Hack v State, 141 Wis 346, 124 NW 492.

22. **Annotations:** Dismissal or vacation of indictment as terminating liability or obligation of surety on bail bond. 18 ALR3d 1354.

Death of principal as exoneration, defense, or ground for relief, of sureties on bail or appearance bond. 63 ALR2d 830.

over for an hour or two. Have your client, or one of his relatives, fill out a questionaire similar to the one following to assist you in pressing for the setting of a reasonable bail or a discharge on your client's own recognizance or a conditional release.

Bail Questionnaire

Name: ____________ Age: ________

Address: ____________

Length of time at this address?____________

What type of housing is this (public housing, apartment house, rooming house, etc.)____________

Previous address:____________

Length of time at that address?____________

Employment: ______________________ ______________________

Nature of Job Employer's name

If student, set forth name of school, class and class rank.

____

Employer's address:____________

Length of time employed by this employer?____________

Salary (indicate whether weekly, monthly, etc.)________

Previous Employment:

______________________ ______________________

Nature of job Employer's name

Employer's address: ________ Number ________ Street ________ City ________ State

Dates of employment

____________ to ____________

If unemployed: Length of time unemployed?____________

Do you receive unemployment compensation?

If so, how much?____________

Do you own your own home? (value)____________

automobile? (value)____________

bank accounts?

(name and address of bank,

and amounts in account)____________

other property of value?

(Nature of property, value?)____________

Other sources of income?____________

______________________ ____________

Type of income Amount

______________________ ____________

Type of Income Amount

Liabilities:
bank debts? (Set forth the names and addresses of banks and amounts)____________________

____________________ ____________________

debts on instalment purchases (set forth names of sellers, and amounts)____________________

other debts (Amount:)____________________

Names of dependents ____________________ Amounts contributed to ____________________ their support____________________

If you receive public assistance or welfare payments, amount ____________________

Previous Criminal Record (including pending charges):

Arrests____________ ____________________ ____________________

Date Charge Outcome

What members of your family do you live with?____________________

Illnesses or debilitating physical disabilities:

____

Does anyone in your immediate family have such an illness or disability?____________________

§ 6. Nature of bail

Courts will usually accept as bail either a surety bond posted by a licensed bonding company, a real property bond or cash or negotiable securities. The surety bond is the most expensive, albeit the most common, form of bail as the other types will be returned when the defendant has met all of his obligations to appear. However, he will not recover all amounts paid as premiums to a surety company.

Unless your client is a properous businessman there may be some risk in having him post cash bail or a property bond if bail has been fixed in a substantial amount. The danger is that the prosecutor or court personnel might infer that your client is somehow linked to organized crime. Such rumors have often found their way to the ears of potential jurors.

D. NATURE, PURPOSE AND NECESSITY OF PLEA

§ 7. In general

As a general rule, due process of law requires that an

accused shall plead or be ordered to plead, or in a proper case that a plea of not guilty be filed for him, before his trial can rightfully proceed.[23]

A plea is not a mere formality.[24] The purpose of the plea is to make an issue.[25]

Accordingly, there can be no trial on the merits in a criminal case until the accused has pleaded not guilty or such plea has been entered for him by the court.[26]

Generally, the accused has an absolute right to an opportunity to plead.[27] The fact that the accused did plead, or at least was furnished an opportunity to plead, must appear affirmatively in the record.[28] This requirement as to the record is not a matter merely of form; it is a matter of substance.[29] If, however, a plea is actually made at the proper time, a failure to make a record thereof is not fatal, since the trial court may order the entry of the plea nunc pro tunc.[30]

§ 8. Who may make plea

Some jurisdictions have required that in felony cases the

23. Crain v United States, 162 US 625, 40 L Ed 1097, 16 S Ct 952. But see Garland v Washington, 232 US 642, 58 L Ed 772, 34 S Ct 456.

24. People v Moore, 21 Ill App 2d 9, 157 NE2d 94.

25. State v Poynter, 34 Idaho 504, 205 P 561, 208 P 871; United States v Aurandt, 15 NM 292, 107 P 1064.

26. Sexton v State, 29 Ala App 336, 196 So 742, cert den 239 Ala 662, 196 So 746.

27. Hamilton v State, 147 Ala 110, 41 So 940; Territory v Brash, 3 Ariz 141, 32 P 260; Long v People, 102 Ill 331; Weaver v State, 83 Ind 289; State v Preston, 107 La 521, 32 So 67; Salfner v State, 84 Md 299, 35 A 885; State v Llewellyn, 93 Mo App 469, 67 SW 677; Territory v Gonzales, 13 NM 94, 79 P 705; State v Cunningham, 94 NC 824.

28. Bowen v State, 98 Ala 83, 12 So 808; Wright v People, 22 Colo 143, 43 P 1021; Warrace v State, 27 Fla 362, 8 So 748; Bowen v State, 108 Ind 411, 9 NE 378; State v Wilson, 42 Kan 587, 22 P 622; Hendrickson v Commonwealth, 23 Ky LR 1191, 64 SW 954; Hanson v State, 43 Ohio St 376, 1 NE 136; Lynch v State, 99 Tenn 124, 41 SW 348; Noble v State, 50 Tex Crim 581, 99 SW 996; State v Moore, 57 W Va 146, 49 SE 1015.

29. State v Walton, 50 Or 142, 91 P 490.

30. State v Donahue, 75 Or 409, 144 P 755, 5 ALR 1121, adhered to on reh 75 Or 420, 147 P 548, 5 ALR 1126.

Purpose of a plea is to make an issue. Plea entering is a matter of substance.

accused must plead in person,[31] while in misdemeanor cases this may be done by an attorney[32] even in the accused's absence,[33] at least where the accused has authorized the plea to be made.[34] Other cases make the distinction that a plea of guilty must be entered by the accused in person,[35] while a plea of not guilty may be entered by an attorney.[36] According to some decisions, even a plea of guilty may be made by an attorney for the accused where the accused is present and indicates his approval or acquiescence in the plea.[37]

In no event may the attorney enter a plea of guilty for the accused where he is not authorized to do so.[38]

§ 9. Waiver; failure or refusal to make plea

There is some authority to the effect that the accused

31. Julian v United States (CA6 Mich) 236 F2d 155; Thomas v State, 255 Ala 632, 53 So 2d 340; Dale v City Court of Merced, 105 Cal App 2d 602, 234 P2d 110; People v Smith, 6 Ill 2d 414, 129 NE2d 164; State v Richardson, 223 Ind 557, 63 NE2d 195; State v Walton, 50 Or 142, 91 P 490; Sperry v Commonwealth, 36 Va (9 Leigh) 623; State v Foley, 131 W Va 326, 47 SE2d 40.

32. Warren v State, 19 Ark 214; Dale v City Court of Merced, 105 Cal App 2d 602, 234 P2d 110; Bogle v State, 155 Miss 612, 125 So 99; People v Welsh, 88 App Div 65, 84 NYS 703.

33. Dale v City Court of Merced, 105 Cal App 2d 602, 234 P2d 110; Mahoney v State, 197 Ind 335, 149 NE 444.

34. Territory v Cook, 7 NM 248, 33 P 1022.

35. Nahas v State, 199 Ind 117, 155 NE 259; Johnson v Commonwealth, 254 Ky 775, 72 SW2d 472.

36. Dale v City Court of Merced, 105 Cal App 2d 602, 234 P2d 110; Bogle v State, 155 Miss 612, 125 So 99.

The theory behind this is that a plea of not guilty cannot injure the accused. People v Bowman, 81 Cal 566, 22 P 917.

37. Garland v Washington, 232 US 642, 58 L Ed 772, 34 S Ct 456; Brown v United States (CA8 Mo) 182 F2d 933; United States v Denniston (CA2 NY) 89 F2d 696, 110 ALR 1296, cert den 301 US 709, 81 L Ed 1362, 57 S Ct 943; United States v Bentvena (DC NY) 193 F Supp 485; Marler v People, 139 Colo 23, 336 P2d 101; Re Morelli (App) 76 Ohio L Abs 501, 148 NE2d 96; State ex rel. Burkhamer v Adams, 143 W Va 557, 103 SE2d 777, cert den 358 US 869, 3 L Ed 2d 101, 79 S Ct 102.

38. People v Rogers, 56 Cal 2d 301, 14 Cal Rptr 660, 363 P2d 892.

may waive his right to plead,[39] but he must do this in person and his attorney cannot, under any circumstances, waive the accused's right to an opportunity to plead.[40]

The general rule is that one who stands mute on arraignment in legal effect pleads not guilty.[41] By standing mute on arraignment, the defendant in a criminal prosecution does not permit the truth of the essential allegations, as charged, to stand admitted, in a manner comparable to their filing of pleas of nolo contendere, and the allegations of facts in support of the information must be proved, at least prima facie, by the state before a finding of guilty can be made.[42]

E. NEGOTIATIONS FOR A PLEA

§ 10. Generally

Most criminal cases are disposed of by pleas of guilty. Virtually all the pleas are part of an arrangement or "bargain" with the prosecuting authority. You must understand the subtleties and possible pitfalls of "bargaining" in order to represent your client properly.

It has lately become fashionable to attack the plea bargaining system insofar as it forces the defendant to forfeit the rights he would normally have at trial. In fact, the plea bargaining process can work greatly to the advantage of your client if you are capable of bargaining effectively in his behalf. These facts can then be translated into power for your side of the bargaining process. The more anxious the prosecutor is to obtain a plea of guilty, the

39. Bryans v State, 34 Ga 323; Commonwealth v McKenna, 125 Mass 397; People v Bradner, 107 NY 1, 13 NE 87; State v Brock, 61 SC 141, 39 SE 359; State v Reddington, 7 SD 368, 64 NW 170.

40. State v Walton, 50 Or 142, 91 P 490.

41. Wood v United States, 75 App DC 274, 128 F2d 265, 141 ALR 1318; State v Early, 211 NC 189, 189 SE 668.

42. State v Hughes, 3 Conn Cir 181, 209 A2d 872, 14 ALR3d 1166, certif den 152 Conn 745, 209 A2d 189.

greater the advantage of the defendant in the bargaining process.

In order to gain a good bargaining position, you must be able to determine and exploit the weaknesses of the prosecution's case, as well as his incentives for seeking to negotiate a plea.

§ 11. Incentives for the prosecutor

A plea bargain is an exchange of a guilty plea for the benefit of the defendant. The prosecution offers the defendant an opportunity to receive a lighter sentence than he otherwise might receive. Such an arrangement may benefit the prosecution in various ways. A plea provides him with a conviction for his record without the necessity of a trial. It often aids him in keeping the court's calendar up to date. His case against the defendant may have some weaknesses which would make a trial difficult for the prosecutor.

You should only agree to a guilty plea when conditions are of maximum benefit to your client. The time and expense of a trial are often so taxing on the state that you will find the closer the trial date comes, the more inclined the prosecutor will be to agree to a plea for the defendant. Plea bargaining allows the prosecutor to do justice to the victim, the defendant, and the state. The process gives him flexibility in sentencing which may otherwise be lacking.

§ 12. Advising your client

It is your duty to encourage your client to plead guilty if you are convinced he has no chance of acquittal. It is pointless to proceed to trial if the proof of guilt is overwhelming and your chances of impeaching or discrediting prosecution witnesses is slim. If your client resists such suggestions, assure him that you will defend him energetically if he elects to trial. Exercise particular caution never to appear to coerce or threaten your client regarding his decision to plead or go to trial.

In advising your client of the possible advantages of pleading, consider also the following:

1. merits of your legal defenses;

2. effectiveness of your factual defenses;

3. effectiveness of the prosecution's case;

4. availability and effectiveness of your client as a witness;

5. publicity surrounding the case;

6. nature of the crime and the likelihood of it engendering hostility toward your client;

7. ability and effectiveness of the prosecutor likely to try the case;

8. attitude of the potential judge;

9. likelihood of obtaining a favorable plea;

10. possibility of obtaining a commitment regarding the sentence;

11. attitude of the judge who would impose the sentence after a plea;

12. consequences for your client of a guilty plea;

13. possibility that your client may want to protect another person, such as a spouse, who could technically be prosecuted for the same incident.

Make sure your client is aware of all the consequences of the plea, such as possible fines or period of imprisonment and any statutory forfeitures or civil disabilities. He may lose the right to public employment or military service, his voter's rights, driver's license, or license to engage in a particular occupation or business. There may be the possibility of deportation or registration under various local criminal registration regulations.

Your client may be too anxious to accept a prosecution offer against your advice. The desire may be motivated by pressures external to the case and unrelated to your client's bargaining position. It is your role to protect your client's legal rights and to use all your influence to dissuade him from yielding. If you cannot effectively guide your client, you should remove yourself from the case.

§ 13. Know relevant facts concerning client

While negotiating with the prosecutor you must be aware of the mitigating factors and circumstances which support your argument for a reduced charge and sentence. All the factors relevant in a sentencing process are relevant to plea bargaining. These include favorable information about the defendant's family and employment background; future employment prospects; his youth and/or lack of any previous criminal record; the defendant's addiction to narcotics as a cause for the crime; the willingness of the defendant to join available treatment programs and to cooperate with the authorities.

§ 14. Thoroughly analyze the law and investigate the case

Before beginning the bargaining process, you must thoroughly investigate the case and analyze the law. Your investigation of all the facts surrounding the commission of the crime will provide you with all possible defense theories and may disclose possible areas which would make an eventual conviction less certain. You may uncover a legal defense or a key witness you did not know existed.

Before serious bargaining, familiarize yourself with all the possibilities available to your client, including all the lesser offenses to the crime charged and the sentences they carry.

§ 15. Negotiating with the prosecutor

In talking informally with the prosecutor, you must maintain a position of strength. Give him enough information to let him know he does not have an open and shut case without revealing your defense theories to him. Point out the weaknesses in his case. Maintain that you do not hesitate to go to trial but that it is in the interest of the prosecutor for the defendant to plead to a lesser crime.

The prosecution may be interested in the cooperation of the defendant in an ongoing investigation or prosecution. If such an arrangement yields no worthwhile information to the court, explain that it is not the fault of the defendant that what he knows already may be known or considered trivial by the police.[43] A client with some experience in such areas may, in fact, recommend to you an early plea when he is anxious to exchange information in return for a plea.

§ 16. The sentence

In exchange for a plea of guilty, the defendant will generally receive leniency in sentencing in one of several ways.

The charge in the indictment may be reduced to a lesser offense providing for a lesser punishment.

Numerous counts of a multi-count indictment may be dismissed. This is frequently coupled with the acceptance of a plea to a count providing less punishment than that the most serious counts of the indictment.

In some jurisdictions, the judge has broad sentencing discretion. You should attempt to seek a favorable sentencing recommendation from the prosecutor. In some situations, the same end is accomplished merely by having the

43. Involvement of a trial judge in the bargaining process must be carefully handled. The Court of Appeals for the D.C. Circuit recently laid down guidelines for federal trial judges within its jurisdiction who become involved in plea bargaining. First, in any prospective non-jury case, the prosecutor shall not inform the judge that the defendant has offered to plead guilty.

Second, once a trial judge has received information that a guilty plea has been offered, the judge should excuse himself or insist upon a jury trial.

prosecutor refrain from making an unfavorable recommendation.

Make certain that any plea will cover all pending charges. If a plea to a lesser offense contained in one indictment cannot be taken in satisfaction of all pending indictments, seek the prosecution's agreement to the dismissal of other pending charges on a *nolle prosequi.*

In some jurisdictions which impose additional punishment for multiple offenders, the prosecution has discretion with regard to such additional punishment. In such instances, press the prosecution to agree not to seek multiple offender treatment.

§ 17. When to conduct negotiations formally

You will probably conduct plea negotiations informally, but if there has been a great deal of publicity surrounding your client's case, you should conduct yourself very formally. In such cases, have all exchanges in writing, forcing the prosecution and the judge to respond by written order and, if possible, by written statement in explanation of the order.

§ 18. Inspection of statements and documents

During negotiations, do not hesitate to request inspection of witnesses' statements, police and laboratory reports, and other vital documents which will help you analyze the prosecution's case. If plea negotiations fail, you still should have discovered a great deal about the prosecution's case.

§ 19. Enforcing the bargain

In *Santobello v New York,*[44] the Supreme Court held that "when a plea of guilty rests in any significant degree on a promise or agreement of the prosecutor . . . such a promise must be fulfilled."[45] The court remanded the case

44. 404 US 257, 30 L Ed 2d 427, 92 S Ct 495.

45. 30 L Ed 2d at page 433.

to the lower court to determine whether the bargain should be specifically enforced or the defendant given an opportunity to withdraw his plea.[46]

In *United States ex rel. Culbreath v Rundle,*[47] the court held that if a judge ultimately determines that he cannot accept the government's recommendation as to sentence, the defendant should be permitted to withdraw his plea.[48] Thus, you can be assured that a bargain agreed upon will be enforced or the defendant will be afforded the chance to withdraw the plea.

§ 20. Constitutionality of plea bargaining

Plea bargaining has been described as unfair and inaccurate;[49] its constitutionality has been challenged.[50] Jurists have referred to it as a necessary evil below the dignity of the court.[51] In spite of these alleged evils, the practice flourishes and will continue to flourish.

The United States Supreme Court has upheld the Constitutionality of plea bargaining. In Brady v United States,[52] the court said, "We cannot hold that it is unconstitutional for the State to extend a benefit to a defendant who in turn extends a substantial benefit to the State. . ."[53]

The American Bar Association recommends the imposition of leniency on those defendants who choose to enter a plea of guilty.[54]

46. 30 L Ed 2d at page 433.

47. (CA3) 466 F2d 730.

48. 466 F2d at page 735.

49. 4 Crim L Bull 201 (1968); 83 Harv L Rev 1387 (1970); 49 BUL Rev 514 (1969).

50. 83 Harv L Rev 1387 (1970).

51. 56 Minn L Rev 718 (1972).

52. 397 US 742, 25 L Ed 2d 747, 90 S Ct 1463.

53. 397 US 742 at page 753, 25 L Ed 2d 747.

54. In § 1.8 of their Approved Standards Relating to pleas of Guilty (1968), they isolate the considerations legitimizing this process: § 1.8 Consideration of plea in final disposition.

(a) It is proper for the court to grant charge and sentence concessions to defendants who enter a plea of guilty or nolo contendere when the interest of the public in the effective administration of criminal justice would thereby be served. Among the considerations which are appropriate in determining this question are:

F. PLEA OF NOT GUILTY

§ 21. In general

There are several types of pleas: pleas to the jurisdiction; pleas in bar; pleas of not guilty; pleas in abatement; pleas of former jeopardy; pleas of *nolo contendere;* and pleas of guilty.[55] For the student, greatest attention will be focused on the pleas of not guilty and guilty.

A plea of not guilty denies and controverts the existence of every fact essential to constitute the crime charged[56] or to establish the accused's guilt.[57] It places in issue all matters implicit in the accused's denial of guilt[58] and every material allegation of the indictment or information.[59]

Specifically, the plea of not guilty puts in issue the

(i) that the defendant by his plea has aided in ensuring the prompt and certain application of correctional measures to him;

(ii) that the defendant has acknowledged his guilt and shown a willingness to assume responsibility for his conduct;

(iii) that the concessions will make possible alternative correctional measures which are better adapted to achieving rehabilitative, protective, deterrent or other purposes of correctional treatment, or will prevent undue harm to the defendant from the form of conviction;

(iv) that the defendant has made public trial unnecessary when there are good reasons for not having the case dealt with in a public trial;

(v) that the defendant has given or offered cooperation when such cooperation has resulted or may result in the successful prosecution of other offenders engaged in equally serious or more serious criminal conduct;

(vi) that the defendant by his plea has aided in avoiding delay (including delay due to crowded dockets) in the disposition of other cases and thereby has increased the probability of prompt and certain application of correctional measures to other offenders.

(b) The court should not impose upon a defendant any sentence in excess of that which would be justified by any of the rehabilitative, protective, deterrent or other purposes of the criminal law because the defendant has chosen to require the prosecution to prove his guilt or *nolo contendere.*

55. For a discussion of the significance and use of each, see Bailey and Rothblatt, Successful Techniques for Criminal Trials §§ 47–52.

56. State v Golden, 67 Idaho 497, 186 P2d 485.

57. Demonia v State, 69 Ga App 862, 27 SE2d 101.

58. People v Aquilante, 208 Cal App 2d 530, 25 Cal Rptr 344.

59. United States v De Angelo (CA3 NJ) 138 F2d 466; People v James, 59 Cal App 2d 121, 138 P2d 30; State v Baker, 246 Iowa 215, 66 NW2d 303;

commission of the crime charged,[60] the question of intent[61] or guilty knowledge,[62] the question of venue,[63] and the truthfulness of a statement in the indictment that certain facts were unknown to the grand jurors.[64]

Under a plea of not guilty, the accused may avail himself of any defense that is not required to be specially pleaded[65] or that is not raised by appropriate motion,[66] such as the defense of entrapment[67] or the statute of limitations.[68]

G. PLEA OF GUILTY

§ 22. In general

A plea of guilty is a formal criminal pleading,[69] and the minutes of a plea of guilty are regarded in law as an official court document.[70]

Generally, the accused has the right to plead guilty,[71]

Rounds v Commonwealth, 282 Ky 657, 139 SW2d 736; Overton v State, 78 Nev 198, 370 P2d 677.

60. Floyd v State, 182 Ga 549, 186 SE 556; People v Pratt, 251 Mich 243, 231 NW 564.

61. State v Baker, 246 Iowa 215, 66 NW2d 303.

62. People v Everhardt, 104 NY 591, 11 NE 62.

63. Anderson v Commonwealth (Ky) 349 SW2d 826; State v Smith, 57 Mont 563, 190 P 107; Ex parte Millsap, 29 Okla 472, 118 P 135; State v Casey, 108 Or 386, 213 P 771, motion den 108 Or 418, 217 P 632.

64. People v Hunt, 251 Ill 446, 96 NE 220.

65. Bandy v State, 102 Ohio St 384, 131 NE 499, 21 ALR 594.

66. Henderson v United States (CA5 Fla) 237 F2d 169, 61 ALR2d 666.

67. Sorrells v United States, 287 US 435, 77 L Ed 413, 53 S Ct 210, 86 ALR 249; Henderson v United States (CA5 Fla) 237 F2d 169, 61 ALR2d 666; State v Marquardt, 139 Conn 1, 89 A2d 219, 31 ALR2d 1206.

68. State v Landis, 177 Tenn 304, 145 SW2d 1032.

69. Bankey v Sanford (DC Ga) 74 F Supp 756, affd (CA5) 165 F2d 788, cert den 333 US 847, 92 L Ed 1130, 68 S Ct 649.

70. People v Elfe, 34 Misc 2d 206, 228 NYS2d 220.

Practice Aids: 7 Am Jur Trials 477, Homicide § 80.

71. Arrington v State, 35 Ala App 205, 45 So 2d 9; Canada v State, 144 Fla 633, 198 So 220; Harshman v State, 232 Ind 618, 115 NE2d 501; People v Coates, 337 Mich 56, 59 NW2d 83, cert den 346 US 840, 98 L Ed 361, 74 S Ct 64; State v Hardy, 339 Mo 897, 98 SW2d 593; Kissinger v State, 147 Neb 983, 25 NW2d 829;

and, when not prohibited by statute, may do so even in a capital case.[72] The accused may even plead guilty despite the advice of his attorney, if he is mentally competent to enter a plea.[73] On the other hand, statutory requirements of a plea of guilty must be complied with and the record should show that all requirements have been satisfied.[74]

The judge of a trial court may not enter into a binding agreement with a prisoner to excuse him from the penalties of his crime if he pleads guilty.[75] An agreement whereby the prosecuting attorney promises the performance of certain acts in consideration of the filing of a plea of guilty is not binding on the court, the plea generally being treated as an ordinary plea of guilty.[76] There is authority, however, to the effect that pleas of guilty based upon a promise of prosecuting officials to recommend a specific sentence, which promise is intentionally or unintentionally breached by the promisor, should be set aside.[77]

§ 23. Voluntary nature of plea

A plea of guilty must be entirely voluntary,[78] and before accepting a plea of guilty, it is the duty of the court to

Feig v Bromberger, 19 Misc 2d 703, 74 NYS2d 307; Williams v State, 89 Okla Crim 95, 205 P2d 524; State ex rel. Baker v Jameson, 72 SD 638, 38 NW2d 441.

72. Strickland v State, 199 Ga 792, 35 SE2d 463; Johnson v State, 79 Okla Crim 363, 155 P2d 259; State v Sewell, 69 SD 494, 12 NW2d 198; State v Brown, 60 Wyo 379, 151 P2d 950.

73. State v Dodd, 70 Wash 2d 513, 424 P2d 302, cert den 387 US 948, 18 L Ed 2d 1338, 87 S Ct 2086.

See also Rule 11, Fed Rules of Crim Proc.

74. People v Sturdy, 235 Cal App 2d 306, 45 Cal Rptr 203.

75. Richardson v Commonwealth, 131 Va 802, 109 SE 460.

76. State v Wyckoff (Iowa) 107 NW 420; State v Kring, 8 Mo App 597; Maxwell v Turner, 20 Utah 2d 163, 435 P2d 287.

77. Darnell v Timpani, 68 Wash 2d 666, 414 P2d 782.

78. Canada v State, 144 Fla 633, 198 So 220; State v Bastedo, 253 Iowa 103, 111 NW2d 255; Pool v Commonwealth, 301 Ky 531, 192 SW2d 490; Rogers v State, 243 Miss 219, 136 So 2d 331; State v McBane, 128 Mont 369, 275 P2d 218; Re Application of Kinnison (Okla Crim) 335 P2d 645; Huffman v Alexander, 197 Or 283, 251 P2d 87, reh den 197 Or 331, 253 P2d 289; Pennington v Smith, 35 Wash 2d 267, 212 P2d 811.

satisfy itself of the voluntary character of the plea.[79] To be voluntary, a plea of guilty must be freely, unequivocally, intelligently and understandingly made in open court by the accused with full knowledge of his legal and constitutional rights and of the consequences of his act. It cannot be the product of or induced by coercive threat, fear, persuasion, promise, or deception.[80] In determining whether a plea of guilty is voluntary, the sole inquiry should be whether the plea was made under such circumstances as to constitute it reliable and trustworthy evidence of the accused's guilt of the offense with which he was charged.[81]

The plea must be made intelligently and understandingly[82] by one competent to know the consequences,[83] and must not be induced by fear, misapprehension, persuasion, promises, inadvertence, ignorance,[84] or fraud.[85] There is no due process of law where a guilty plea is obtained by coercion[86] or by deception[87] or a trick.[88]

79. State v Jennings, 104 Ariz 3, 448 P2d 59, on reh 104 Ariz 159, 449 P2d 938; State v Waldron, 273 Minn 57, 139 NW2d 785; Cresci v State, 36 Wis 2d 287, 152 NW2d 893.

In determining whether a plea of guilty is voluntary, the court's sound discretion exercised in cases on an individual basis is better than to mandate a uniform procedure that might become a purely ritualistic device. People v Nixon, 21 NY2d 338, 287 NYS2d 659, 234 NE2d 687, cert den 393 US 1067, 21 L Ed 2d 709, 89 S Ct 721.

80. Woods v Rhay, 68 Wash 2d 601, 414 P2d 601, cert den 385 US 905, 17 L Ed 135, 87 S Ct 215.

81. Application of Buccheri, 6 Ariz App 196, 431 P2d 91.

82. State v Jones, 267 Minn 421, 127 NW2d 153.

83. Canada v State, 144 Fla. 633, 198 So 220; Cassidy v State, 201 Ind 311, 168 NE 18, 66 ALR 622, disapproved on other grounds Schmittler v State, 228 Ind 450, 93 NE2d 184, ovrld on other grounds State v Lindsey, 231 Ind 126, 106 NE2d 230; Pool v Commonwealth, 301 Ky 531, 192 SW2d 490; Rogers v State, 243 Miss 219, 136 So 2d 331; State v McBane, 128 Mont 369, 275 P2d 218; Re Application of Kinnison (Okla Crim) 335 P2d 645; Huffman v Alexander, 197 Or 283, 251 P2d 87, reh den 197 Or 331, 253 P2d 289.

84. Rubenstein v State (Fla) 50 So 2d 708; Pool v Commonwealth, 301 Ky 531, 192 SW2d 490; State v Jones, 267 Minn 421, 127 NW2d 153; Rogers v State, 243 Miss 219, 136 So 2d 331; State v McBane, 128 Mont 369, 275 P2d 218; Re Application of Kinnison (Okla Crim) 335 P2d 645; Huffman v Alexander, 197 Or 283, 251 P2d 87, reh den 197 Or 331, 253 P2d 289.

85. Re Ernst, 179 Wis 646, 192 NW 65, 30 ALR 681.

86. Pennington v Smith, 35 Wash 2d 267, 212 P2d 811.

A plea of guilty is not rendered involuntary by the fact that it was partly induced by the possibility that a more serious charge might be prosecuted.[89]

The Federal Rules of Criminal Procedure expressly provide that the court shall not accept a plea of guilty without first determining that the plea is made voluntarily.[90] And in federal prosecutions the failure to advise an accused of his right to counsel will invalidate a plea of guilty even in the absence of a showing of prejudice.[91]

H. WITHDRAWING OR CHANGING A PLEA

§ 24. In general

A person who enters a plea to an accusation in a criminal case does not always have the right to withdraw the plea[92] in order to file a different plea[93] or to interpose objections which should have been raised before entering the plea.[94]

Good cause must be shown for a change of plea[95] and where it is plain that substantial justice will not be promoted, and that substantial rights of the accused will not be prejudicated, the application for leave to withdraw the

87. Palmer v Ashe, 342 US 134, 96 L Ed 154, 72 S Ct 191, conformed to Commonwealth ex rel. Palmer v Ashe (Pa) 86 A2d 61.

88. Pennsylvania ex rel. Herman v Claudy, 350 US 116, 100 L Ed 126, 76 S Ct 223.

89. Parrott v Haugh (Iowa) 158 NW2d 766.

90. Rule 11, Fed Rules of Crim Proc. Any noncompliance with Rule 11 of the Fed Rules of Crim Proc is reversible error.

See McCarthy v United States, 394 US 459, 22 L Ed 418, 89 S Ct 1166.

91. United States ex rel. Durocher v La Vallee (CA2 NY) 330 F2d 303, cert den 377 US 998, 12 L Ed 2d 1048, 84 S Ct 1921.

92. State v Dison, 162 La 437, 110 So 642; State v Henspeter, 199 Minn 359, 271 NW 700; State v Dickerson, 72 NJ Super 459, 179 A2d 33.

93. Gleckman v United States (CA8 Minn) 16 F2d 670; State v McNeal, 304 Mo 119, 262 SW 1025.

94. State v McNeal, supra.

95. People v McDowell, 204 Cal App 2d 734, 22 Cal Rptr 646.

plea should be denied.[96] In the absence of a statute otherwise providing, the granting or refusing of leave to withdraw a plea in a criminal case rests in the sound discretion of the trial court,[97] subject to review for abuse of discretion.[98]

§ 25. Withdrawal of guilty plea

In the absence of a statute stating differently, the defendant's right to withdraw a guilty plea is not absolute.[99] It is within the discretion of the trial court to permit the plea to be withdrawn,[1] even in capital cases.[2] It has been broadly stated that the court's discretion should always be exercised in favor of innocence and liberty,[3] but the refusal of the court to allow withdrawal of a plea of guilty will not be interfered with except on a very clear showing of fraud or other irregularity preventing the accused from obtaining justice.[4]

As in other cases of discretionary power, no general rule can be laid down as to when an accused will be permitted to withdraw his plea of guilty. The decision in each case

96. Hunter v State, 3 Okla Crim 533, 107 P 444.

97. People v Brooks, 72 Cal App 2d 657, 165 P2d 51; Abshier v People, 87 Colo 507, 289 P 1081; State v Nichols, 167 Kan 565, 207 P2d 469; People v Goldman, 245 Mich 578, 223 NW 124; Coan v Hilton, 91 NH 489, 23 A2d 369; State v Lee Lim, 79 Utah 68, 7 P2d 825; La Fave v State, 233 Wis 432, 289 NW 670.

98. Dean v Maxwell, 174 Ohio St 193, 22 Ohio Ops 2d 144, 187 NE2d 884, 5 ALR3d 1263.

99. Everett v United States, 119 App DC 336 F2d 979; United States v Denniston (CA2 NY) 89 F2d 696, 110 ALR 1296, cert den 301 US 709, 81 L Ed 1362, 57 S Ct 943; State v Nichols, 167 Kan 565, 207 P2d 469; People v Bencheck, 360 Mich 430, 104 NW2d 191; State v Jones, 234 Minn 438, 48 NW2d 662; Coan v Hilton, 91 NH 489, 23 A2d 369; State v Crandall, 225 NC 148, 33 SE2d 861; State v Virgi, 84 Ohio App 15, 39 Ohio Ops 16, 51 Ohio L Abs 431, 81 NE2d 295; Commonwealth v Phelan, 427 Pa 265, 234 A2d 540, cert den 391 US 920, 20 L Ed 2d 657, 88 S Ct 1803.

1. Everett v United States, 119 App DC 60, 336 F2d 979; Verberg v State, 137 Ala 73, 34 So 848.

2. State v Hill, 81 W Va 676, 95 SE 21, 6 ALR 687.

3. Lambert v State, 245 Miss 227, 147 So 2d 480; Henning v State, 184 Tenn 508, 201 SW2d 669.

4. State v Baforo, 146 Wash 312, 262 P 964; State v Reppin, 35 Wis 2d 377, 151 NW2d 9.

must depend to a great extent on the particular circumstances.[5]

§ 26. Withdrawal of plea of not guilty

It is discretionary with the court to permit or deny the withdrawal of a plea of not guilty[6] to allow a different plea to be entered[7] or a motion to quash to be filed.[8] It is not a matter of right with the accused,[9] and the trial court's ruling on an application for permission to change a plea of not guilty will not be disturbed on appeal except for abuse of discretion.[10]

Leave to a defendant to file a special plea in bar after a plea of not guilty has been entered should be denied where the matters set forth therein are mere matters of defense determinable under the general issue.[11] No abuse of discretion is involved in refusing to permit a defendant to change his plea of "not guilty" to "not guilty by reason of insanity," where it appears that the original plea was not ignorantly induced or made through motives of hope or fear unduly operating upon his volition.[12]

§ 27. Federal courts

The Federal Rule of Criminal Procedure applicable to

5. Jordan v State (Fla App) 107 So 2d 56; Pittman v State, 198 Miss 797, 23 So 2d 685; Jurgenson v State, 166 Neb 111, 88 NW2d 129; State v Virgi, 84 Ohio App 15, 39 Ohio Ops 16, 51 Ohio L Abs 431, 81 NE2d 295; La Fave v State, 233 Wis 432, 289 NW 670.

6. State v Powers, 239 Iowa 430, 30 NW2d 476, cert den 340 US 838, 95 L Ed 615, 71 S Ct 23.

7. People v Northcott, 209 Cal 639, 289 P 634, 70 ALR 806.

8. People v Turner, 260 Ill 84, 102 NE 1036.

9. Commonwealth v Tucker, 189 Mass 457, 76 NE 127.

10. Tomlinson v United States, 68 App DC 106, 93 F2d 652, 114 ALR 1315, cert den 303 US 642, 82 L Ed 1102, 58 S Ct 645, cert den 303 US 646, 82 L Ed 1107, 58 S Ct 645.

11. United States v Murdock, 284 US 141, 76 L Ed 210, 52 S Ct 63, 82 ALR 1376, ovrld on other grounds Murphy v Waterfront Com. of New York Harbor, 378 US 52, 12 L Ed 2d 678, 84 S Ct 1594, motion to retax costs den 379 US 898, 13 L Ed 2d 174, 85 S Ct 183.

12. People v Northcott, 209 Cal 639, 289 P 634, 70 ALR 806.

withdrawal of pleas after sentence in a criminal case, in providing that motions to withdraw a plea of guilty or nolo contendere may be made only "before sentence is imposed or imposition of sentence is suspended," adds the qualification that after sentence has been imposed the court may set aside a judgment of conviction and permit the defendant to withdraw his guilty or nolo contendere plea if such action is required "to correct manifest injustice."[13] A motion to withdraw a plea of guilty, under this Federal Rule, is addressed to the trial court's discretion[14] and its ruling on such a motion will be reversed only if its discretion was abused.[15]

No "manifest injustice," for purposes of the Rule, is shown by proof that the accused, in entering his plea of guilty or nolo contendere, did so in the expectation that he would receive a less severe sentence than that actually imposed.[16] It has, however, been recognized that "manifest injustice" may flow from conduct of the prosecution improperly inducing the accused to expect lenient punishment,[17] or from the accused's misunderstanding, reasonably

13. See Rule 32(d), Fed Rules of Crim Proc.

14. United States v Ford (CA4 Md) 363 F2d 375; United States v Washington (CA3 Pa) 341 F2d 277, 9 ALR3d 448, cert den 382 US 850, 15 L Ed 2d 89, 86 S Ct 96, reh den 382 US 933, 15 L Ed 2d 346, 86 S Ct 317.

15. Friedman v United States (CA8 Iowa) 200 F2d 690, cert den 345 US 926, 97 L Ed 1357, 73 S Ct 784, reh den 345 US 961, 97 L Ed 1381, 73 S Ct 937 (denial of motion to withdraw plea of guilty held proper); United States v Shneer (CA3 Pa) 194 F2d 598 (denial of motion to withdraw plea of nolo contendere held proper); Smith v United States (CA6 Mich) 180 F2d 851 (denial of motion to withdraw plea of guilty held proper); United States v Searle (CA7 Ill) 180 F2d 209 (denial of motion to withdraw plea of guilty held proper); Mitchell v United States (CA5 La) 179 F2d 305 (denial of motion to withdraw plea of guilty held proper); Stidham v United States (CA8 Mo) 170 F2d 294 (denial of motion to withdraw plea of guilty held proper); United States v Harris (CA2 NY) 160 F2d 507 (denial of motions to withdraw pleas of guilty held proper).

16. United States v Parrino (CA2 NY) 212 F2d 919, cert den 348 US 840, 99 L Ed 663, 75 S Ct 46; Collins v United States (CA8 Mo) 211 F2d 789; United States v Shailer (CA2 Vt) 202 F2d 590, cert den 347 US 947, 98 L Ed 1094, 74 S Ct 646; Friedman v United States (CA8 Iowa) 200 F2d 690, cert den 345 US 926, 97 L Ed 1357, 73 S Ct 784, reh den 345 US 961, 97 L Ed 1381, 73 S Ct 837; United States v Shneer (CA3 Pa) 194 F2d 598; United States v Searle (CA7 Ill) 180 F2d 209.

17. United States v Parrino (CA2

entertained, of the trial judge's remarks, regarding the severity of the sentence that might be imposed.[18]

The Federal Rules of Criminal Procedure do not impose any limitation on the withdrawal of a guilty plea before sentence is imposed,[19] but a motion to withdraw a plea after sentence under the Federal Rule must be so denominated, and must be conditioned on a showing of manifest injustice.[20]

Before sentencing, the inconvenience to court and prosecution resulting from a change of plea is ordinarily slight as compared to protecting the right of the accused to trial by jury. But if a plea of guilty could be retracted with ease after sentence, the accused might be encouraged to plead guilty to test the weight of potential punishment, and withdraw the plea if the sentence were unexpectedly severe.[21]

NY) 212 F2d 919, cert den 348 US 840, 99 L Ed 663, 75 S Ct 46; United States v Sehon Chinn (DC W Va) 74 F Supp 189, affd (CA4) 163 F2d 876.

18. United States v Parrino (CA2 NY) 212 F2d 919, cert den 348 US 840, 99 L Ed 663, 75 S Ct 46; United States v Lias (CA4 W Va) 173 F2d 685.

19. See Rule 32(d), Fed Rules of Crim Proc.

20. Kadwell v United States (CA9 Nev) 315 F2d 667.

21. Kadwell v United States, supra.

See Stidham v United States (CA8 Mo) 170 F2d 294, stating that one seeking to withdraw a plea of guilty under the federal rule must, at the time motion for leave to withdraw the plea is made, state some reason why the judgment should not stand against him, and that reason must amount to a fraud or an imposition on him, or a misrepresentation of his legal right.

CHAPTER TWO

GENERAL PRINCIPLES OF INVESTIGATION

A. INTRODUCTION

§ 28. Investigate thoroughly

Hard evidence, rather than abstract legal arguments is what decides most criminal cases. You must be fully in command of the facts in order to be fully in command of a case. Do not let the prosecution surprise you by any of its evidence.

The value of proper investigation is not limited to the trial itself. It may help you obtain for your client a favorable bail or convince the prosecutor to drop or reduce charges. Good investigation will make negotiating a plea easier. It may well aid in getting a light or suspended sentence for your client in the event of a conviction.

§ 29. Defense investigation and police investigation: a comparison

Criminal investigation is, of course, fundamentally, a police function. When the police fail to prevent crime they must assume the responsibility for the detection and apprehension of the criminal.

With every modern method of investigating crime available to him, the police investigator has many advantages over the defense investigator. He is on the scene at the outset. Large numbers of officers assist him. He has modern police laboratories and many otherwise confidential records are available for his use.

However, by their very nature, police investigatory procedures are conducted on an "assembly-line" basis. Whether or not all good leads are followed up depends upon the available manpower, the press of other business, and the disposition and/or personal prejudices of the officer on the case. These considerations point to the need for adequate investigation by the defense.

§ 30. Have a theory of defense

A proper defense investigation is limited only by the time and resources at your command. The investigation will perforce be selective. In other words, you must have a theory for your defense, and you must investigate facts material to this theory.

§ 31. Be prepared to alter your theory

At the same time you must avoid becoming unalterably committed to your theory. In the search for facts, you must be alert both to those which do not support your theory as well as to those facts which suggest a better theory.

§ 32. Defense advantages over the prosecution

The advantage to the defense is that while the prosecution must prove each and every element of the crime, the defense need overcome only one. It is desirable but not necessary for the defense to establish that some other person committed the crime. All you need establish is that the case against the defendant is deficient in some important respect.

§ 33. Be familiar with police investigation methods

Be completely familiar with police investigative methods. Such familiarity will help you plan your own investigation. Knowing what is ordinary to a police investigation will enable you, in cross-examining law enforcement officers, to take advantage of any deviation from accepted police investigative methods.

§ 34. Evidence is more convincing than technique

You will be no more effective in court than the evidence you can affirmatively present and the manner in which you can demolish the prosecution's case. Evidence which has been overlooked, improperly obtained or handled can never be retrieved no matter how much technical skill you bring to your task. Many attorneys lose cases because they are unaware that the police have mishandled evidence. You can lose a case if you don't know the principles of proper defense investigation or if you don't know how to examine potential witnesses with tact and intelligence.

While scientific aids have played an expanding role in modern investigation, criminal investigation is still basically an art. You cannot learn investigation from books or lectures alone. Study, practice and self-analysis are the only means of learning the difficult techniques of interrogation and surveillance.

Unless you have been an investigator or law enforcement officer, you probably have seldom had the opportunity to follow the investigation as a somewhat abstract procedure.

B. CATEGORIES AND PRIORITIES OF INVESTIGATION

§ 35. General categories of investigation procedure

Investigative techniques can be divided into these four general categories:

1. The collection, preservation, processing, and presentation of physical evidence.

2. Interviews with the defendant, witnesses, complainants, and the police.

3. Records, private and public.

4. Surveillance in its various forms.

Rarely will you ever be called upon to use all of these categories, but you should understand each if you hope to provide comprehensive representation for your clients.

§ 36. Go to the most likely sources of information first

First, establish a rational set of priorities. To do this, you must study the broad outlines of the case. Obviously, the two most likely sources of information are the investigating officers and the defendant. Use these two resources at the outset of the case.

§ 37 Speed is usually essential

Speed is often essential in the investigation of a particular case. Physical facts change and useful evidence may be discarded. Witnesses may become forgetful or they may disappear. (Persons in marginal social classes are highly mobile; they may leave suddenly without any trace.)

Further, people become more difficult to locate as they blend quickly back into the neighborhood after witnessing an offense or an arrest. If and when they are found again, they may be useless as witnesses. Persons in marginal economic circumstances rarely keep diaries or deskbooks; they are likely to forget events with the passage of time, particularly if they were observers of the happenings rather than direct participants. For such reasons, speed will usually be an essential element of any successful investigation.

§ 38. Concentrate first on sources which are perishable, mobile, or changeable

In establishing an order of priorities, you should concentrate first on those things which are either perishable, mobile, or changeable. Investigate quickly those witnesses likely to be mobile and those who are likely to forget if they are not interviewed soon. Bear in mind that many persons are susceptible to official suggestion; the framework of the questions often gives shape to the form of the answers. For example, more people will describe someone as tall if they are asked directly whether he was tall or short than would so answer if they are simply asked to describe his height. It is in your client's interests for you to question such witnesses in a fair manner before the police question them and possibly influence them in a way unhelpful to your client.

See witnesses quickly even if the police have already questioned them. You will find that often they will have had the opportunity to recall events or circumstances previously overlooked. Also, the police may overlook a productive line of questioning that does not agree with their theory of the case.

§ 39. Investigate witnesses client thinks are essential to his defense

To determine the order of priority in interviewing witnesses, attempt to reach early in the investigation any and all witnesses whom the client says can help him, either by furnishing him with an alibi or in any other way.

Seek out such witnesses and interview them even if you feel that they will not provide useful information. You may be wrong about their usefulness. Every client is entitled at the very least, to the small comfort of knowing that his own lawyer does not disbelieve him without a fair inquiry. Remember, the failure to look for witnesses named by a defendant is the most frequent ground of post-conviction attacks against the competence of trial counsel.

§ 40. Thoroughly question client

The complete, intensive questioning of the client himself is of great importance. He is the one person, among all those to be interviewed, who knows absolutely whether he is guilty or innocent.

The initial interview with the client is also important for

the opportunity it provides for you to furnish advice to him about his legal rights. You can also learn what, if anything, he has told the police, and what the circumstances surrounding the police interrogation were. If your client has either already been charged, is a prime suspect, or is the object of a police search, notify the police that you have been retained and that you desire not to have your client interrogated in your absence.

§ 41. Visit the site of any important event relating to the case

Whether or not you use an investigator, it usually will pay you to inspect the site of any important event in the case. This is especially true with respect to the site of the offense, the arrest, and of any search and seizure of your client. You will find that while looking for specific items, you will perceive others whose significance might escape anyone else's notice—items which add new dimensions to the case.

On any such visit you should try to accomplish the following: 1) ascertain whether any physical changes have affected the scene since the time of the events in question; and 2) make a diagram of the scene, using approximate measurements for later use during trial. If you do this, you will find it of assistance when a witness testifies falsely as to matters of spatial relations. On motions to suppress evidence allegedly illegally obtained it is invaluable. (It is often crucial for you to know whether a particular door opened in or out.)

When possible, visit the site at the same time of day as the events in question took place. It may become important to know, for example, whether a police officer could have made a particular observation at night with the aid of light from a nearby light pole. You should attempt to distinguish objects from a similar distance with the aid of such light. Also, you should question people living in the area to determine whether or not the light was in working order on the night in question.

§ 42. Miscellaneous sources of information

In your defense investigation you will not have access to all of the records and files utilized by the police. However, many miscellaneous sources of information are available to you. Among the most useful to keep in mind are police reports, logs, and dockets; in a death case, the medical examiner's files or the coroner's transcript and report; newspaper files and photographs; U. S. Weather Bureau records; relevant records maintained by business concerns, such as time-clock cards and invoices, etc.; and hospital, prison, and court records.

Other profitable sources of information are the records of telephone calls and telegrams. Information on file in credit bureaus can often provide key information and can be of assistance as to issues of notice.

Resort may also be had to records of various sorts—from schools, courts, military services, unions, social security agencies, welfare departments or services, family physicians, hospital admissions offices, etc.

C. ADVANTAGES OF RETAINING A PROFESSIONAL INVESTIGATOR

§ 43. Hired investigators save time and have access to sources that you may not know of

The question of whether you should hire an investigator or conduct the investigation yourself is usually determined by the available financial resources. An investigator is recommended wherever practicable.

A good investigator often has sources of information which are unavailable to all but the most experienced criminal lawyers. These include contacts with community leaders, police, prison, court and probation officials; and contacts with other professional fact-gatherers, such as newsmen, social workers, and politicians.

§ 44. A hired investigator can be called to testify

You can call on an investigator to testify if stories given by witnesses at the trial conflict with previous versions they gave you. Also, if you need photographs for the defense, someone besides you should have taken them. The photographer can testify to provide a foundation for the admission of pictures into evidence when the prosecutor refuses to stipulate to their accuracy.

§ 45. Work closely with a hired investigator

If a private investigator is retained, you must work closely with him. Familiarize him with the nature and theory of your planned defense. Unless you have supreme confidence in the investigator, you must channel his efforts carefully. You must take pains to make sure he turns up information which is relevant to the defense. In criminal matters the most interesting matters are often the most useless, and it is up to you to remain vigilant against irrelevancies.

D. SURVEILLANCE

§ 46. When to engage in surveillance—factors to be considered

Surveillance is a technique equally available to the defense investigator as it is to the police. Everyone is permitted to look and observe. However, proper surveillance—that is, the kind which can avoid detection and achieve significant results—usually requires a trained, professional investigator.

§ 47. Watch for evidence illegally obtained by police surveillance

The police frequently conduct surveillance through the use of electronic eavesdropping equipment and other technological devices. The use of such devices frequently violates the constitutional rights of the accused. You should always attempt to ascertain whether such devices were used, and, if so, when. It is possible that the police obtained such information prior to the date of a court order allowing them to use electronic eavesdropping equipment. In such a case, the evidence obtained is inadmissible.

§ 48. Proper use of electronic surveillance devices

You may properly use electronic devices in certain situations. For example, anyone may record a telephone conversation with the consent of one of the parties. It is perfectly proper for you or your investigator to wear a concealed microphone while interrogating certain witnesses whom you have reason to believe may later change their version of certain incidents.

§ 49. No investigator should rely on memory alone

Finally, no matter how effective an investigation has been, the facts ascertained may later have to be reproduced in court. The mass of detail in a major case is so overwhelming that points which do not seem essential may be forgotten. Many of these points will become important when the case is tried. Few investigators can successfully rely upon their memories to retain those points.

Each fact obtained by the investigator should be recorded by him as soon as possible. It should then be made a part of his more permanent records. By the time of trial, all information should be indexed and cross-indexed in such a manner as will permit instant accessibility to any desired item of information.

§ 50. Summary

This introductory chapter has indicated the wide range of knowledge necessary to you as a defense investigator. In summary, you must know how to:

a. Gain respect, inspire confidence, and maintain good will;

b. Master the techniques and methods of obtaining evidence and statements from clients, victims, witnesses, and informants;

c. Detect discrepancies or lack of good faith in interviews and interrogations;

d. Take notes and make diagrams and sketches;

e. Connect every interval of time and action;

f. Substantiate all facts with statements of witnesses or items of evidence;

g. Collect and preserve evidence;

h. Determine what evidence is admissible in criminal trials;

i. Use scientific means of developing physical evidence;

j. Call upon chemists, fingerprint technicians, photographers, ballisticians, or other technicians for assistance;

k. Take and preserve written statements that will be admissible as evidence;

l. If the investigator is not an attorney, he must know how to testify in court;

m. Make complete reports of activities;

n. Familiarize yourself with particular court procedures.

CHAPTER THREE

INITIAL CONTACTS WITH CLIENT AND INTERVIEW

A. BASIC WARNINGS

§ 51. Initial client interview
§ 52. Do not talk extensively with client on the phone
§ 53. Tell your client to speak with no one
§ 54. An early interview is best
§ 55. Speak to arresting officer in charge
§ 56. Insist the police note your visits
§ 57. Find out the precise nature of the charges
§ 58. Clearly establish the respective roles of attorney and client
§ 59. Warn your client to speak and write nothing
§ 60. Warn against possible police efforts to undermine his confidence in you

B. ELICITING THE FACTS

§ 61. Nature of the interview
§ 62. Obtain details of the arrest
§ 63. The client's story may change with time
§ 64. Let no inconsistencies slip by
§ 65. Urge client strongly to take you into his confidence
§ 66. Establish rapport before you take interview notes
§ 67. Use a disinterested interpreter
§ 68. Calm a nervous client by allowing him to talk freely
§ 69. Avoid much cross-examination at first
§ 70. Have the client write out his version of the facts
§ 71. Don't make early predictions

A. BASIC WARNINGS

§ 51. Initial client interview

The most important discussion you will ever have with your client in a criminal case will be the initial interview. Your client's first judgment of you may be indelible, and it can influence all future dealings you have with him. It will establish whether or not your attorney-client relationship is to be grounded on mutual confidence, trust, and respect.

§ 52. Do not talk extensively with client on the phone

The nature of this first interview with the client will be governed by the circumstances of the case. For example, if the client telephones you immediately upon his arrest, he should be asked to reveal nothing except his location. Do not discuss any additional details at that time. Your client should be strictly enjoined from signing anything or discussing anything with anybody, including relatives and friends, until you or your associate, properly identified, visit him.

§ 53. Tell your client to speak with no one

Tell your client that it is imperative that he not talk to anyone. An arrest is an emotionally disturbing experience, and many persons often seem to have a compelling urge to seek relief from inner agitation by telling all that they know. Whether your client has until now been a normal and intelligent person or a hardened criminal, this urge to talk and explain may overwhelm him. You must make sure that he guards against this natural human tendency.

§ 54. An early interview is best

Even if he is free from this impulse to talk, an arrested

person is almost certainly bound to be subjected to other forms of pressure. Until he is lodged in jail he remains in the custody of the police. Though legally forbidden to interrogate him without prior warnings of rights and presence or waiver of counsel, the police may nevertheless on a wide variety of pretexts interrogate him.

If for no other reason it is of the utmost urgency for you to interview your client without delay, regardless of who summoned you. An early interview will not only warn and advise the defendant, but will permit him to talk to his own lawyer rather than someone else, if he has to yield to his urge to "tell all."

Once a person in custody requests counsel, all interrogation must be halted until his attorney appears. If you do not appear you place an absolute bar on lawful interrogation. However, your appearance at this time will forestall later police claims of a voluntary waiver by your client of his rights.

§ 55. Speak to arresting officer in charge

When you learn where your client is being held, the first thing you should do is telephone the precinct or office and speak either to the person who made the arrest or to the officer in charge. Advise him that you have been retained and that, save for the taking of his pedigree, you do not want your client questioned. Make arrangements during this conversation to meet with your client as soon as possible.

§ 56. Insist the police note your visits

When you appear insist that your presence be noted so that a record is made of the time and date of your visit.

§ 57. Find out the precise nature of the charges

Often, in the course of locating a client in custody (or in checking on the status of a client who is the subject of a police search) you will speak to a precinct desk officer or to some investigating officer. In these conversations ask the specific charge against the defendant. Try to ascertain any other charges being considered. It is very helpful if you find out the precise nature of the charge and the elements thereof at the time of the first interview.

The most important and obvious function of the initial interview with a client is to obtain information which will allow you to begin the investigation. The information gathered during the client interviews will be used as a basis for almost every phase of the preparation of the trial.

§ 58. Clearly establish the respective roles of attorney and client

Settle the respective roles that you and your client will play in the defense at the outset of the initial interview. In regard to the client, advise him of his rights to have a trial at which he contests guilt, to have a jury trial, to testify in his own defense, to be present, and to have counsel present at every judicial proceeding in his case. Inform him that you will present every defense that the law permits to protect his rights, and that none of his rights will be waived without his express consent. As to your position as his attorney, make it clear that you alone will control the strategy of the defense, decide what legal points are to be raised, determine what witnesses to call, engage in whatever discussions you deem necessary with the prosecutor.

§ 59. Warn your client to speak and write nothing

As soon as you meet your client, advise him again to say or write nothing to the police except with your consent. Make the reasons for this warning clear to your client. Only when he is made to realize that harmless or irrelevant remarks may rise to plague him at the trial will he remain quiet. Tell him, for example, that a signature may become the standard of comparison with contested writing, or that fellow prisoners may seek information from him as a means of obtaining favorable consideration for their own cases.

§ 60. Warn against possible police efforts to undermine his confidence in you

Warn your client about common police stratagems. Police occasionally tell persons suspected of a crime that their attorneys only want them to remain silent to ensure that there will be a trial and a higher fee or that they have nothing to fear if they are innocent. Warn your client to be on guard against any effort by the police to make him talk while you are absent.

B. ELICITING THE FACTS

§ 61. Nature of the interview

The nature of the interview with the client will, of course, be affected by the nature of the case and the surrounding circumstances. A jailhouse interview with a person having a long criminal record will markedly differ from one held in your office with a corporation executive accused of a "white collar" crime.

§ 62. Obtain details of the arrest

If your client has already been arrested when you first see him, obtain a full account of the facts of the case including details about the arrest, his confinement through the moment of the interview, names and addresses of all persons who may have had a significant part in any of these matters, etc.

Ascertain all of the circumstances of the arrest. Was your client informed that he was being arrested? . . . of his right to remain silent? . . . to be represented by counsel? . . . that anything he might say could be used against him? Did such warnings precede the start of questioning? Did the police search him or the apartment or the car in which he was arrested? If so, was a warrant exhibited? Did the police confiscate any property found on his person or on the premises? Were others arrested with him? Did any of them say anything in his presence? Was he interrogated? Did he appear in a line-up? Under what circumstances was the line-up held? Was he asked to speak and make gestures? These questions are vital and you must insist that your client give you every detail he can remember.

You should also ask at this first interview about any previous difficulties your client may have had with the law. Ask about his prior employment, about any relatives and friends who might assist in obtaining bail. Any uncompleted business concerning your fee should be discussed.

§ 63. The client's story may change with time

Even though the client may still be overwrought at the time of this interview and his memory somewhat inaccurate, you should try to obtain from him an account of what happened. An early recital even under such circumstances may guarantee your receiving an unvarnished tale. The longer a person remains in custody, the more likely he is to absorb ideas from fellow prisoners or guards as to how he should alter his story in order to absolve himself from or lessen the gravity of the charge placed against him. These ideas are frequently irrelevant and outdated and they often create hazards which complicate later preparation and trial.

§ 64. Let no inconsistencies slip by

The client must be urged to give a full account of what he knows about the case. Cross-examine him about inconsistencies and lapses of memory in his story. It should be verified by comparing it with other available evidence. If your client objects to this treatment from his own attorney, remind him that the prosecutor will be far rougher and that inconsistencies developed on cross-examination at trial will be disastrous by comparison.

§ 65. Urge client strongly to take you into his confidence

Tell your client in the strongest possible terms that you expect him to tell you the whole and exact truth. Stress the nature of the attorney-client privilege. Explain that adequate representation is impossible unless you are aware of every fact which the prosecution might find. In listening to his story, you must make certain that your client does not sense on your part any moral disapproval of his actions, for if he does, he will naturally tend to hide the most incriminating facts from you. Accordingly, it is necessary for you to avoid any overt reaction to anything your client reveals to you.

If your client is not responding, and you believe that he either is having difficulty communicating or is concealing information, direct your efforts toward reducing his tensions and fears. The simplest way to do this is to tell the client that you are going to help him and that you need information.

If your client does not grasp the relevance of your questions, and so fails properly to respond to them, explain the reason for the questions. Patience is necessary when the client is operating under stress.

§ 66. Establish rapport before you take interview notes

It is good practice to talk to your client for a few minutes before you begin to take notes. This will establish rapport. A good impression of competence and interest can be shown by summarizing orally important points of what the client told you at the same time that you are writing them down. Also, ask him clarifying questions. Avoid long periods of writing in silence (except as a tactic to unnerve the client when you believe that he is lying to you). Write down in detail what the client tells you.

These notes will later serve to refresh your memory as well as your client's. They may even be admissible at trial, if the prosecution seeks to create the impression that your client's trial testimony is a recent fabrication. In some cases it is worthwhile to read your notes to your client at the end of the interview and to have him read, sign and date them.

§ 67. Use a disinterested interpreter

If your client has difficulty with English, avoid the use of an interpreter who is connected with the police or the prosecutor's office. A disinterested interpreter is preferable to a member of the defendant's family. A defendant will often be ashamed to tell the truth in front of a friend or relative. Social service agencies will often be able to provide qualified interpreters. If no other reasonable choice is available, use a friend or relative, but preferably one to whom the defendant does not have close emotional ties.

§ 68. Calm a nervous client by allowing him to talk freely

If your client is having difficulty in answering your questions, let him tell his story in his own words without interruption. This should serve to put him at ease.

This will give you a collection of unsolicited details on which to cross-examine him later if you suspect untruth. It will also show you something about how your client's mind works, his intelligence and verbal ability. Do not ask questions which may be above your client's level of comprehension.

§ 69. Avoid much cross-examination at first

Once the client has told you his story, ask specific questions to determine if all of the legal elements of the charge against him have been established in his version of the incident. Unless you feel that the client is obviously lying and unless you feel a need to do so for purposes of effective defense investigation, you ought not to cross-examine much in the initial interview. A more propitious time for cross-examining your client would be after independent investigative efforts and after the attorney-client relationship has had a little more time to solidify.

In subsequent interviews, the client should be increasingly cross-examined, in a fashion which may range all the way from a mild expression of surprise to open incredulity and derision. Your best judgment of what is necessary not only to preserve the lawyer-client relationship but also to get at the truth will determine how far you should go. Criminal clients often lie to their lawyers. If your client is to be saved from himself, he must be confronted with inconsistencies in his story, or between his story and other information obtained by you since these can be expected to be exposed at trial.

§ 70. Have the client write out his version of the facts

If your client is not yet in custody or has been arrested and is out on bail, have him put his version of the facts in writing. This will serve several purposes. He will be less likely to forget important details at this stage, and will also be discouraged from later changing his story. His statement will give you a basis from which to work. It is also good practice to have your client write out his autobiography including his employment record, schooling, position in the community and the like. This not only may prove useful at trial, but it also may provide information to a probation officer to lay the foundation for a plea for clemency to a court.

§ 71. Don't make early predictions

The attorney should never commit himself as early as the first interview to a decision of what he hopes to accomplish for his client. Rarely will anything be factually certain at so early a stage. Indeed, your client himself may well be less aware of the facts than he thinks. Attorneys who make predictions at early stages open the door to many difficulties. Avoid the temptation to make a favorable prediction based upon your client's version of the facts.

Instead assure him of your interest and your guarantee to do your best work in his behalf.

§ 72. Office interviews

Give your client your complete attention if the first interview takes place in your office. Instruct your secretary or the switchboard operator to hold all except the most urgent calls. If you take a call, excuse yourself for doing so. Your client has a problem which is important to him; try to give him all the time he needs.

A calm atmosphere will help your client relax and make it easier for him to give you all relevant information. The client interview should not be conducted in the presence of third persons except when absolutely necessary. The only exceptions to this are those times when you must have a secretary present to transcribe the conversation or an interpreter. Remember that third persons interfere with the attorney-client relationship and may inhibit the full disclosure of all essential facts. And, perhaps more important, the presence of third persons may prevent a later claim that the attorney-client interview constituted a privileged communication.

§ 73. Adapt interview technique to the client's personality

Adapt your interviewing technique to the various types of clients—some are loquacious, others shy or defensive. If your client is talkative, let him tell his own story initially without interruption. You may be tempted from time to time to voice personal opinions in response to his remarks, but you should try to avoid doing so because this will merely invite defensive remarks and inhibit the interview altogether.

CHAPTER FOUR

LOCATING FACT WITNESSES

C. VITAL STATISTICS

A. TRACING MISSING WITNESSES

§ 74. Using an investigator

One of the major tasks of the defense investigator is the locating of fact witnesses. You must decide at the outset whether to undertake personally the task of locating and interviewing witnesses, or whether to hire a private investigator or a skip-tracing specialist.

For those cases in which the investigation is of great importance, calling for skills not ordinarily possessed by an attorney, a professional investigator should be retained.

On the other hand, there may be sound reasons to justify your close personal involvement in the locating and interviewing of witnesses. You are apt to be better acquainted with the issues than an outside investigator; hence, you may be better equipped to conduct the investigation so as to resolve those issues to your client's advantages wherever possible. Also, bear in mind that you will learn much from personal contact. By talking to witnesses yourself, you can judge their friendliness to your side of the case, determine their usefulness as witnesses and make other decisions based on personal observation regarding their appearance, manner of speaking, etc.[1]

1. **Practice Aids:** Suppression or fabrication of papers or evidence. 7 Am Jur 2d, ATTORNEYS AT LAW § 27.

Annotation: Fabrication or suppression of evidence as ground of disciplinary action against attorney. 40 ALR3d 169.

§ 75. Turn to client

The first source to which the investigator should turn is the client. Ask him the names of all witnesses, both friendly and hostile, whom he can identify either by name, description or otherwise. You should interview witnesses to the occurrence as quickly as possible. Their identities may often be obtained not only from the defendant but also from the prosecutor's office, the police and reporters. Informal chats with prosecutors and police officers often yield the names of potential witnesses (whom the investigator might not otherwise have discovered).

§ 76. Canvass the area of the crime

In canvassing, the investigator should speak to everyone in the neighboring area who had a chance to observe the events. Attempt to speak to persons normally in the area at about the time of day of the event in question.

§ 77. Keep files

The greatest problem involved in the locating of witnesses is usually the finding of a known person whose present whereabouts are unknown. There are many ways of locating such persons. First of all, the defense investigator should prepare separate files for all missing witnesses. Into such a file he should place all available information pertaining to such persons, along with descriptions, dates, and notes of all investigative methods used and procedures followed. Such a file will be of great help, for, if all information with reference to the identity of witnesses is systematically kept up-to-date and complete, the data will suggest more specific approaches to discovering the witnesses' present whereabouts.

§ 78. Finding a missing witness

In tracing a missing witness the best initial procedure is to try to reach him by telephone. Always be extremely polite in inquiring about a missing witness. Speak in a slow and quiet manner. Make the person on the other end of the telephone aware that you have a problem and need his assistance.

Timing is very important to effective telephone inquiries. Contacts who are interrupted at a very busy time in their day will not be as cooperative as they might have been had they been called at a more opportune time.

§ 79. Identify yourself

You should always identify yourself at the beginning of any conversation. While the identification may not have any meaning to the person called, he will be more at ease if he feels that the caller is not trying to conceal his identity.

At times you will encounter a situation in which friends, former neighbors, or former employers of the missing witness are either unable or are unwilling to give you any information. Sometimes this happens because such persons may be too lazy to think hard about your problem; oftentimes, it is because of an unwillingness to become involved. In such situations, you may find the use of a pretext helpful. The simplest, and yet one of the most effective devices is to call and assume the role of an old friend of the witness who has just arrived in town. You may thus be able to secure information which you might not ordinarily have received.

When you go out into the field in search of a missing witness, you should always identify yourself at the outset. Be forthright if the interviewee is friendly and responsive. If, however, he is hostile, you may find it necessary to fabricate a cover story. However, as a word of caution, you must never represent yourself to be a policeman or other law enforcement officer, nor should you attempt in any way to defraud the person being interviewed.

§ 80. Language problems

In the event you are seeking to find a missing witness

and in so doing are interviewing several of his neighbors who speak a foreign language, it is advisable to conduct the interview in English. This is true even if you speak the language spoken by the person being interviewed. One good reason for this is that you may be able to obtain more information by listening to what they say to one another in their own language when they are unaware that you can understand them.

B. SOURCES OF INFORMATION

§ 81. Newspapers

Newspaper "morgues" often provide useful information. Newspaper files contain photographs as well as clippings. They are almost always indexed by subject as well as by name.

In addition, those newspaper reporters and photographers who were assigned to the crime are frequently reliable sources of information; sometimes they may be able to furnish leads to witnesses.

If all else fails, the field investigator can resort to the tactic of posting a notice on a building or fence in the immediate vicinity of the place where the alleged crime or the arrest took place. Such notices should request witnesses, or persons having knowledge about witnesses, to contact the attorney. Sometimes it will help to offer a reward.

Another means of locating witnesses is by placing announcements in the classified sections of local newspapers, or broadcasting over the radio, with potential witnesses being directed to contact the attorney. In determining whether to make some offer of reward you should bear in mind that a witness may be discredited in court if the prosecutor can show that the witness accepted money to testify.[2] The response to this kind of advertising is notori-

2. **Practice Aids:** Cross-examination of witness to show financial interest as bias. Am Jur, WITNESSES (1st ed § 721).

ously poor, and as a procedure it is recommended only as a last resort.

§ 82. Telephone records

When the name of the missing witness is known, the first step in an investigation into his present whereabouts is to check the telephone company records. This must be done by telephone in order to obtain the most current information available. Since the regular alphabetical telephone directories are published by the local telephone company once a year, they become obsolete very quickly. Furthermore, information contained in the regular alphabetical telephone directory for a city may have been compiled long before the date of publication.

When checking with the information operator or the telephone directory, take care to look up the name under spellings similar to the one he has.

If the witness' last name is an unusual one, the investigator should contact all persons listed with such names. The chances are that persons with such unusual names are either related or acquainted with each other.

If the defense investigator has reason to believe that there is a telephone at the particular address but the number cannot be secured from information, assume that the telephone has an unlisted number. In this case, the business officer at the telephone company should be contacted directly and the representative advised that an attorney wishes to speak with the subscriber on a matter of importance. In such cases, the telephone company policy will usually contact the subscriber, and advise him that an attorney wishes to make telephone contact with him.

Many telephone companies keep records by street address as well as by name. Therefore, always check with the information operator or the business office in order to ascertain whether there is a telephone listed at the witness' last known address. If the answer is negative, inquiries should be made regarding the telephone number of the residence nearest his last known address. When this number has been secured, the investigator can call the party at that number to seek information regarding the witness.

§ 83. Post office

Officials of the post office will not reveal forwarding addresses to law enforcement officers. However, the defense investigator can resort to the registered mail to obtain such information. This can be accomplished by mailing a registered letter to the witness' last known address to be delivered only to the addressee. If a return receipt is requested and returned, it will show the address to which the letter was delivered. When using this device the envelope should contain some information or legend which will intrigue the witness to reduce the possibility of his rejecting the letter.

When regular mail sent to the witness at his last known address is returned, the face of the envelope should be carefully studied to see if the mailman has made the notations prescribed by postal regulations. Many times mail which is returned and marked "not here" has been so marked by the witness himself. However, if the witness has actually moved, the mailman will use a rubber stamp, placing his initials nearby and making a notation such as "Move—No Order," "Unknown," or "Not At This Address."

If regular mail sent to the witness is not returned, and if it is evident that he is no longer residing at that address, he nonetheless probably left a forwarding address with the post office. On first class mail, there is no provision for a sender to receive any notification of this address even if the letter is forwarded several times. To ascertain the forwarding addresses comply with the postal regulation which permits the sender to be informed of the addressee's new address under certain circumstances.

In order to take advantage of this section of the postal regulations, send a letter marked "Third Class Mail" with postage affixed at the third class rate. The words "Return

Requested" must be typed on the face of the envelope. Finally, only printed matter may be inserted in the envelope. That should be either a business announcement or a business card. If these rules are adhered to, the mailman will not deliver the letter to the addressee if the forwarding address is available. Instead, he will indicate the addressee's complete forwarding address on the face of the envelope and the letter will be returned to the sender for additional postage due for the special handling.

If the last known address of a missing witness is a small town in which mail is handled by rural route delivery, a letter may be sent to the local mailman in order to obtain positive verification of the address. Following is a sample of such a letter:

_______________, 19_______

Mail Carrier
Rural Route _______ [number]
_______________ [city], _______________ [state]

Dear Sir:

On the bottom of this letter would you kindly note whether or not you would be able to deliver a package to _______________ [name of missing witness], Rural Route _______ [number], _______________ [town], _______________ [state].

Thank you.

Very truly yours,

____

This letter can be typed on regular stationery. Enclose a self-addressed, stamped envelope.

The money order delivery service of the Western Union Telegraph Company may also be utilized to locate a missing witness. This service delivers certified checks in any desired amount to designated persons.

This method is useful in those cases in which defense counsel suspects that the missing witness is avoiding contact by staying with friends or relatives.

Send a check to the missing witness in care of his friends or relatives, and request a "report delivery" order. The telegraph company will then attempt to deliver the check to the missing witness. After delivery has been made, a report containing the time and place of delivery is made to the sender of the check. The message agent will merely advise the friend or relative that he has a money order for delivery to the addressee only. He will not disclose the amount, which should be only ten cents. The justification for the small amount may be contained in the message accompanying the money order. For example, the following message may be used:

---------------, 19-------

Dear ---------------:

It is imperative that I discuss an important matter with you as soon as possible. Please contact me at ---------------. I have enclosed a money order for 10¢, which you should use to reach me by telephone so that we may discuss this matter. If it is a toll call and the charge is more than 10¢, please call me person-to-person collect. My telephone number is ---------------.

Very truly yours,

----

§ 84. Begin at last known address

The field investigation for a missing witness should begin at his last known address. Although the witness may continue to avoid the defense attorney even at his home, a check with neighbors, residents, and local businessmen in the area may well bring forth the information needed to make contact with the witness. Children playing in the area, as well as newspaper delivery boys and route salesmen, are also good sources of information. Although mailmen are prohibited from giving information regarding patrons on their route, they are permitted to give information regarding events observed by them during the course of their duties.

Always attempt to secure the name of the landlord or manager at the witness' last known residence. These persons will usually possess information which neighbors and others lack.

§ 85. School records

If the missing witness has a school-age child, check with the schools in the neighborhood to find out which one the child attended. Generally, the records kept by the school will show the new address of the parent, even though the child has transferred to another school. At the very least, you should be able to obtain the name and address of the new school at which the child is registered, since the former school is required to forward the scholastic records to the new school. You can then check with the new school to obtain the parent's present address.

§ 86. Utility companies

The local gas and electric utility is another source of information concerning missing witnesses. Since a subscriber who moves to another home in the same community must transfer his account with the utility company, a record of his new address should be on file. If you furnish the utility company with an address, you can learn if a named person is a subscriber at that address. Generally, no other information is available to the public.

§ 87. Tracing through financial obligations

Missing witnesses may often be traced through their financial obligations. Whenever credit is extended to a person, much information about him is assembled. The party extending credit will usually have files showing the home and business address of the obligor, as well as his occupation, income, personal assets and other data relating tc his present circumstances. Information of this kind is compiled whether one has purchased insurance, bought a car on time-payment plan, or obtained a credit card. Most persons have some such financial ties, and if you are able to determine who may have extended credit to the missing person you may be able to get hold of valuable information. To this end you can have a retail credit agency investigate and report on the present whereabouts of the witness;

"tracer" and "skip" reports are frequently available, as are Dun and Bradstreet financial reports.

Bail bondsmen, building and loan associations, insurance companies, insurance brokers, local banks are other sources of information. They accumulate data on the financial responsibility of individuals; on occasion they may possess information counsel needs to locate a missing witness.

Banks are especially good as a source for information for the witness' banking connection, and it may be possible to examine current checks which he has cashed and thereby determine his present whereabouts.

If the witness is known to have taken an extended trip, he may have purchased traveler's checks, in which case a record of his home address should be on file at the place where the checks were issued.

A witness known to be active in the trading of stocks and bonds may be located with a minimum of time and effort as comprehensive records are kept when securities are bought and sold.

Income tax records will not be available to an attorney attempting to trace a missing witness. However, if the witness owns property, an examination may be made of the assessment lists to discover to what address the tax bills are sent. The county assessor maintains an index to assessed property, by city, by block and lot number. An address is all that is needed to determine to whom the property is assessed. An alphabetical file by names is also maintained by the assessor.

§ 88. Hobbies

Another means of locating elusive witnesses may be through investigating their known hobbies and spare-time pursuits. For example, a person interested in books may sometimes be traced through his public library card. Applicants for a library card must give their home address, and character references are usually required.

Motorboats, sailboats, thoroughbred animals, racing cars, private planes, and the like must generally be registered in the name of the owner; hunting and fishing permits must usually be obtained from a public agency. Such records are often a source of useful information.

The names of chess and bridge players, skiers, hikers, philatelists, photographers, coin collectors, etc., can be checked through various official and semi-official membership rolls. If the witness belongs to a lodge, club, fraternal organization, or any other social group that meets regularly, other members may be able to supply you with information you need if you approach them properly.

§ 89. Documents

Among those documents which can be used to trace missing witnesses are birth certificates, school and college records, scholastic achievement records, marriage records, parenthood records, employment records, civil service examination and civic employment records, permit and license records, public health records, divorce records, voting registration records, property registration records, inheritance records, criminal fine and penalty records, civil litigation records, military service and discharge records, social security and public pension records, passport records, and finally, death records, estate records, and burial records.

§ 90. Department of motor vehicles

If the witness' full name is known, the files of the Department of Motor Vehicles provides excellent information. All states have alphabetical records of all driver's licenses issued which give previous addresses as well as age, marital status, and a physical description of the driver.

Most states file automobile registration records by owner's name including any known nicknames, even if the operator's license search proves negative.

§ 91. County courthouse

Searches at the county courthouse may also prove productive, if the witness is known to have been listed as either plaintiff or defendant in a lawsuit. If he was listed as the plaintiff in any action, his residence address as well as the name of his attorney will usually be found. If a defendant, his address will usually be shown on an affidavit of service.

§ 92. Marriage license applications

If the missing witness is known to be married, he or she can sometimes be located by examination of marriage license applications. These applications will contain his or her address, names and addresses of parents, identifications of the intended spouse, date and place of birth, and other useful information. These records are indexed both alphabetically and chronologically, under the names of both bride and groom. Many states also have a statewide alphabetical-chronological index.

§ 93. Law enforcement agencies

Records of law enforcement agencies are another source of information. Although some police records are confidential, much information is available if you follow the procedure prescribed by the agency. A search of "mug books," modus operandi files, and other special records may prove to be helpful in locating a witness.

Another source for you to consider is accident investigation reports. These identify both parties and witnesses. Most police agencies index them alphabetically as well as by time and location. These reports are commonly open to the public.

§ 94. Close relatives

If it appears that the witness is not merely avoiding you but is actually missing, you should consider the feasibility (through a close relative of the missing person) of invoking the investigative powers of the missing persons bureau. If the case is within its jurisdiction, this bureau will teletype a missing persons report to various police groups and municipal and state agencies, will also alert hospitals and other places to which one might go or be taken in case of emergency, and in some cases will circularize a photograph of the missing person in key areas.

If your client is a ghetto resident, you should have a member of his family or a friend accompany you on any search of the neighborhood. The defense investigator, if such is done, will avoid being thought of as a detective or finance company representative and is likely to meet with a better response.

§ 95. Profession

If the missing person is a member of a profession, he can usually be located through the applicable directory. All professional persons are either licensed or certified. Public records are kept as to lawyers, engineers, public accountants, architects, doctors, registered nurses, osteopaths, optometrists, dentists, and veterinarians. A home or business address may be ascertained from a check of these records.

Licensing provisions also govern various skilled trades and semi-professional occupations, such as surveyors, real estate brokers, seamen, barbers, and the like. Some public body is charged with maintaining records on such categories which may prove to be useful in locating a witness.

Where a missing witness is a teacher, he can sometimes be located by examination of the records kept by school administration agencies. At both the state and local level, boards of education maintain complete records on all teachers which show the teacher's name, address, academic background, and name of school at which employed. Similar records are kept by teacher's associations in most states. Other clues to his whereabouts may be found in the Directory of American Scholars.

If the missing witness is connected professionally with a sport, his name, address, and other personal data will be found in the records of the supervising commission or association. For example, a state racing commission will maintain information on employees and officials, jockeys, trainers, stablehands, and others.

If the witness is known to be connected with one of the armed services, military records available locally should be checked for his name and address. There is a military locator service at all armed forces installations that can supply appropriate information. Although it is sometimes necessary to identify the post to which the serviceman is attached, a check of all military installations for a particular area can readily be made. If the serviceman is known to be an officer, his name should also be listed in one of the officer registers maintained by the Army, Navy, Air Force, and Marine Corps. These publications will also provide a great deal of background information on the witness.

C. VITAL STATISTICS

§ 96. Inspecting the records: the right to inspect

Public records contain much relevant information useful to you in the location of witnesses and in the investigation of a criminal case.[3] Data concerning birth, marriage, divorce, death, education, real property, licensing, and registration may save countless hours of individual interviews. Records also serve as a reference to confirm or discount information from allegedly reliable sources.

Generally, public records and documents are open for

3. For a detailed discussion of the right to inspect public records, see 66 Am Jur 2d, RECORDS AND RECORDING LAWS §§ 12–46.

Practice Aids: Techniques and methods of locating public records are treated in 2 Am Jur Trials 409, LOCATING PUBLIC RECORDS.

public inspection. However, not all records, documents, and writing possessed by the government are made available to the public. In some cases, particularly where communications are made in confidence to officials, public interest may require secrecy.

In some states, writings are regarded as a "public writing" only if they fulfill two requirements: 1.) they must be "official documents," and 2.) they must be "the written act, or records of acts," of public officials.

The most difficulty will be found in examining records of official reports made by agencies of state and the federal governments. The bases for keeping such records secret are usually found in statute.[4]

Mandamus is available where inspection is arbitrarily barred.[5]

§ 97. The right to copy

The right to inspect public records commonly carries with it the right to make copies; without the right to copy the records, the right to inspect them would be practically valueless. Thus, a statute providing that certain records will be open to inspection of any person during reasonable business hours is construed as granting a reasonable right to copy the records as well as to examine them. The right to examine and copy records is frequently granted by decisions that hold that persons engaged in the business of searching records are entitled to access to the records.[6]

It is understood that reasonable conditions may be imposed with respect to the right to inspect public records, and the right to inspect implies that those exercising it shall not take possession of the registry or monopolize the

4. **Practice Aids:** 23 Am Jur 2d, DEPOSITIONS AND DISCOVERY §§ 173–177.

5. **Practice Aids:** For enforcement, by mandamus, of the right to inspect public records, see 52 Am Jur 2d, MANDAMUS §§ 201–206.

6. **Practice Aids:** 66 Am Jur 2d, RECORDS AND RECORDING LAWS § 82.

record books so as to interfere unduly with the work of the office or with the exercise of the right by others.

Where custodians are required to furnish copies of records in their offices, there is no duty to make copies unless there has been a proper demand and the tender of the fees provided by statute for the performance of the duty. In the absence of statute, the general practice is that any person or corporation has a right to inspect and make abstracts of public records without the payment of a fee.

§ 98. Birth records

Birth certificates are prepared by physicians or hospital authorities. They are usually filed in the central vital statistics office of the state, county, or city in which the birth occurred. Information contained in these certificates can be obtained by requesting certified copies of the original records.

§ 99. Death records

For every death an official certificate should be recorded at the place where the death occurred. These certificates are prepared by physicians, funeral directors, coroners, medical examiners, hospital authorities, or other professional attendants, and are currently filed in the central office of the registrar, division, or bureau of vital statistics, which may be centralized on a state, county, city, or district level. Information contained in death certificates is useful for various purposes. You may obtain the information you desire by requesting a certified copy of the original record.

Information to be found on death certificates often includes the names of the decedent's parents, the decedent's birthplace, occupation, age, and attending physician, as well as the date and cause of death. Other information which can be extremely useful such as the decedent's last address, the place of burial, and the name of the person supplying this information to the registrar and the name of the undertaker are often listed on the death certificate.

A copy of the death certificate may usually be obtained by writing to the vital statistics office in the place where the death occurred. The letter, with money order enclosed, should state the purpose for which the copy is needed, since the type of copy issued may vary depending on the purpose for which it is to be used.

By inquiring at the cemetery where the deceased is buried, you may find the names of the persons, if any, who have arranged for care of the burial plot. From these persons you can very often get further information about the decedent.

§ 100. Marriage records

Information supplied from the copy of a marriage license on file will often supply useful leads in tracking the parties to the marriage. For example, the clergyman who performs the ceremony will sign the certificate before it is filed.

Marriage license certificates also list the names of the parents of the applicant as well as the applicant's dates of birth and occupations, residence, and whether they had been previously wed.

§ 101. Summary

The techniques discussed in this chapter should aid you in locating prosecution witnesses as well as prospective defense witnesses.

A talk with the arresting officers and those who investigated the case may yield names of prospective prosecution witnesses. You can also obtain information from conversations with members of the prosecutor's staff.

CHAPTER FIVE

INTERVIEWING AND PREPARING WITNESSES

D. KINDS OF WITNESSES

E. PROBING TESTIMONY

F. VICTIMS AS WITNESSES

G. RECORD OF INTERVIEW

H. STATEMENTS

A. INTRODUCTION

§ 102. Attorney should conduct interview himself

The defense attorney can locate witnesses himself or leave the job to a non-lawyer investigator, but the defense attorney should conduct interviews himself.

Effective preparation for trial involves more than the investigation of the facts and preparation of law. It also includes a study of the personality and history of each individual involved in the case, including your client, witnesses on both sides, and the prosecutor. Only you can do these things effectively, since you will be trying the case. Therefore, don't leave an interview of witnesses to others. Do it yourself. There is no other way you can effectively coordinate all the information to be assembled.

§ 103. Necessity of speed

Begin locating and interviewing witnesses as soon as possible after being retained. A passage of time can severely affect the ability of witnesses to remember events. Failure to quickly interview witnesses can often turn friendly ones into unwilling or hostile witnesses. Also, physical evidence may undergo change or injury.

Often, facts appear strange and frequently seem improbable. In these cases the surrounding circumstances can make the facts probable or believable. However, you are not just seeking bare facts from a witness. You must also find out how and why the witness remembers the facts and why the facts occurred. When you have this information, check it with other witnesses. Also, check the existence of the surrounding circumstances for they may be even more improbable than the fact itself.

§ 104. Investigative function of the interview

In addition to helping uncover all pertinent facts, the interview should enable you to foresee the testimony particular witnesses are likely to give at trial and to discover in advance any information that might discredit or disqualify the witness or render his testimony objectionable.

Never promise a witness a reward or compensation for an interview or for his testimony. The fact that a witness is paid for his time or testimony can be brought up on cross examination with disastrous effect.

Expert witnesses are, of course, excepted from this general rule. An expert or specialist may be paid, not for his testimony, but for the loss of time from his special field and for the time and effort spent in analyzing and studying the subject matter. You can discuss the matter of compensation with the expert in these terms.[1]

An interview is an informal questioning to learn facts. A successful investigation of crime requires that you be able to learn, through personal questioning, what the person interviewed observed through his five senses. Each person interviewed is presumed to have information that may aid you. Effective interviewing requires that you make full use

1. **Practice Aids:** For a discussion of the rules governing compensation of witnesses, generally, see Am Jur, Witnesses (1st ed §§ 874–885).

of all the knowledge of human nature you have, in order that the witness discloses all he knows about the subject in question. If an individual does not possess any knowledge of the crime, the interview should establish that fact. Pertinent negative evidence is as much a part of a complete investigation as is positive information.

§ 105. Reliability of witness' observations: some caveats

When you interview make sure all the important facts in the case are covered and that the particular witness is speaking the truth. As far as truthfulness is concerned there are two dangers to guard against. These are, that the witness' intelligence or powers of observations are such that even though he wants to be truthful, his evidence is of little value, or, that he is deliberately lying.

Witnesses to the same event frequently differ in their accounts. This could result from one or both of the mentioned dangers. Never make the mistake of accepting a witness' statements as a reflection of the actual facts as they occurred. Even the most astute witness is capable of making mistakes in his perception of an event through any of the five senses.

The best way to guard against mistakes is to obtain descriptions of the particular event from as many people as possible. The comparison of several statements should enable you to determine the correct facts. When there is only one witness to an event, this method, of course, cannot be used. Instead, use your knowledge of human nature and of such emotions as fear, terror, pain, or hatred, that produce mistakes in perception. Be cautious in accepting a witness' account of an event even in ordinary circumstances.

Versions by different witnesses of the same event often appear contradictory. It is part of your task in an interview to guide the questioning to separate fact from fancy, and to assist the witness in recalling actual facts.

Always be alert to the possibility that the person you are

interviewing may be psychologically incapable of giving an accurate answer.

Color-blindness, deafness, or other physical handicaps unknown to the witness, may have resulted in faulty perception. The observation of the witness may have been affected by strong emotions.

A witness' age and sex must be taken into consideration. Children are easily led into making incorrect statements, since they tend to agree with the questioner. Some people often respond with what they regard as the required or desired answer to a question. Statements by persons whose age and conduct give an impression of senility cannot be given much credence.

Alcoholics and psychotics often make statements of pure fancy which give them a feeling of importance. Moreover, many psychotics appear perfectly normal to the inexperienced interviewer.

Be wary of the interested witness whose version of the incident is slanted to favor the prosecutor's or the victim's side of the case.

B. TIME AND PLACE OF INTERVIEW

§ 106. Order of interview

When you are ready to interview witnesses, compile a list of those witnesses already located. (Add other witnesses to the list as soon as they are located.) List witnesses according to their anticipated reaction to you, with friendly witnesses listed before disinterested, unwilling and hostile witnesses.

Try to interview friendly witnesses first since they are usually more willing to submit to lengthy periods of intensive questioning. These interviews are usually very productive and don't involve great effort on your part. In addition, they can provide valuable ammunition for the later interviews you conduct with hostile or reluctant witnesses.

§ 107. Preparing for the interview

Prepare properly for a good interview. Be familiar with the facts of the case and know as much as possible about the witness to be interviewed. Prepare your questions for the witness.

The extent of preparation for an interview will depend, among other things, on whether the witness is friendly or hostile. The friendly witness is helpful, has no objection to probing questions, and may be interviewed on several different occasions. The hostile witness, however, is often closemouthed and may only be available for one interview. Therefore, to properly interview a hostile witness, a list of questions to be asked should be prepared prior to the interview.

The preparation of background information on a witness is advisable if you have some reason to believe that he will be reluctant or hostile. An investigation of the witness will often suggest some method of approach that would otherwise have gone unnoticed.

Thorough preparation is particularly important if a signed statement is to be taken. There may only be one opportunity to take such a statement. And, having once taken it, you cannot return to ask a question you forgot in the first interview.

Sometimes preparation of a map or diagram is necessary after a witness interview has begun. Always be prepared for such an eventuality. Be equipped with the necessary materials, including photographs of the place in which the witness made any of his observations. If you are adequately prepared, you will be better able to assist the witness to communicate more effectively or explain more clearly what may be a very complicated matter. You might, in this way, also help jog his memory and enable him to give a more complete and accurate story. Devices of this kind can be used subsequently on examination or cross examination if properly identified and authenticated. Magnetic or chalk blackboards like those commonly used in trial work may also be employed in the interview of a witness.

§ 108. Interview only one witness at a time

Never interview witnesses in a group. If you do, one witness, in telling his version of the incident, may unconsciously transmit it to another witness who hears him. Witnesses in a group tend to compare notes and to make their stories correspond, which may or may not be in your interest.

Even if two or more persons are planning to make the same statement to you, their statements should be taken separately. Only one of the statements may be admissible under applicable rules of evidence.

§ 109. Appointments

Make advance appointments with friendly witnesses but not with hostile ones. When it is possible to interview a hostile witness without an appointment made in advance, do so. If interviewed spontaneously, he will not have had time to prepare a slanted version of his story. Further, the potentially hostile witness who is contacted in advance may well arrange not to be available whenever he is wanted for the interview.

§ 110. Where to hold the interview

There are no fixed rules on where to hold an interview, but there are many advantages to conducting interviews in your office. You have a psychological advantage there as well as the tools for recording or reproducing the witness' statement for his signature.

Interview the witness where there are no members of his family or friends present to distract him. A witness' reactions often reveal whether or not he is telling the truth. If possible, seat him where you can easily observe him. Often an interview in their own home gives some subjects a feeling of security and importance which enables them to effectively conceal or disguise their reactions. This is less easy to do in an attorney's office.

A friendly witness won't usually object to being interviewed in your office, and, in fact, may even enjoy the experience. However, the hostile witness may resent such a procedure and be more closemouthed than ever. There are certain hostile witnesses, though, who may be more cooperative in an atmosphere which is new to them.

The witness' place of employment may be a good place for an interview. Ask the witness being interviewed in his office to find a quiet and private place. If the witness is under pressure to return to his work, he may wish to divulge all his information as quickly as possible. However, these interviews risk incurring his resentment at being called away from his work. You may also have to contend with such distractions as telephone calls, customers, or other employees. Further, the witness' place of employment may be totally unsuited for an interview.

The witness' home may well be the best place for the interview. If interruptions can be kept to a minimum, the home setting is advantageous in that the witness is more relaxed and perhaps more helpful and cooperative. In fact, some individuals may be made so nervous and ill at ease at the prospect of the interview that they cannot give a satisfactory statement unless the interview is conducted at their home.

Some witnesses are less likely to refuse an interview if you offer to see them at their office or at home during the evening. Your main consideration in the conduct of interviews is the amount of information you can obtain. Do not permit false dignity to interfere with this consideration by insisting that all witnesses come to your office regardless of the inconvenience caused them.

C. QUESTIONING

§ 111. Manner of conducting interview

Witnesses are neither the property of the prosecution nor of the defense. They are free and independent people.

Always bear that in mind. When you ask a witness to grant you an interview and to testify, you are usually asking him to give his time and energy on a matter from which he has nothing to gain. While this might not be so with the friendly witness, he should be treated with the same consideration accorded any other witness. Your job is to keep witnesses friendly and removed from temptation.

To this end, use a physician's warm manner when interviewing witnesses. There is no reason to incur a witness' anger or to have him harbor resentment toward you. Prospective witnesses are much more likely to talk openly with you if treated as equals.

§ 112. Various witnesses

Use the utmost tact and friendliness with witnesses. Even with the friendly witness, who will usually make himself available to you for interviewing, mold your examination to his temperament and intellect. That presupposes that you have the perception to evaluate the personality of the individual you interview. Every witness must be treated differently. No one method works successfully with all witnesses. Dull and unimaginative witnesses require that questions be put slowly and in simple terms. Talkative and impulsive ones must be held in check, yet not rudely nor too frequently subdued lest you offend their sensibilities. Meticulous people yield precise facts. However, these witnesses often answer only the exact questions asked and may not give information not strictly asked for. Be sure to ask such persons whether they observed or heard or know anything about the events in question not covered by your questions.

The interviewer must also be wary of an opinionated witness who answers questions with his interpretation of the facts rather than his observation. Unless you are firm in your search for the facts, you risk accepting conclusions and interpretations in place of the facts. Should you do that, your witness is sure to fall apart under skillful cross-examination.

The interviewer should be tactful in his questioning, particularly if he has reason to believe a witness is either holding back information or not telling the truth. There is a danger of losing the witness completely if you make him aware of your suspicions. He must be drawn out slowly and handled intelligently in order to elicit the true facts.

One or more of the persons interviewed may become suspects later in the investigation. Be careful during any interview not to reveal pertinent facts about the crime under investigation to the person being interviewed. The interview should be a pleasant one, but you cannot permit the witness to turn it into an interrogation of the investigator.

The witness must be questioned in a way that a complete and detailed statement of what he saw, heard, and did is obtained. In short, the statement should contain everything the witness knows about the crime. Don't take anything for granted. The continuity of the story or the chain of evidence should be as complete as possible. It pays to employ the old newspaper axiom, "Who did What, When, Where, Why, and How?"

Interviewing is an art in much the same way that examination or cross-examination is an art. It requires the application of equal skill and ability. The art demands that you be a good student of human nature and possess the ability to make a tactful remark or apply subtle pressure with perfect timing.

While you must be friendly and even sympathetic to the witness during the interview, always remember that a good interview is essentially an adversary proceeding.

§ 113. Tips to the attorney

Conduct the interview in layman's language. At trial many witnesses have successfully repudiated signed statements given during the course of an interview on the ground that the language used was clearly not theirs or that they did not understand a particular term or word contained in the statement.

Convey the impression that you have no personal interest in the matter, that you are merely seeking information. Be tactful, impartial, patient, sympathetic, and a good listener. Even if you are thoroughly familiar with the facts of the case, approach the witness as if you only have general information and want to learn the full, detailed story of the crime.

Never bully or argue with a witness. Elicit information in a casual and informal manner. Always be in full control of your reason and emotions. Your attitude toward the witness and your reaction to his answers must be considered from a tactical point of view. If you press your questioning more forcefully, do it only as a preplanned tactic rather than as a reaction to the witness' personality.

Ask questions of witnesses even when you already know the answers to them. This device will help you determine the honesty of a particular witness' answers. Compare his attitude and demeanor when he answers questions to which you don't know the answer in advance. An unexplained change in his ease in answering, in his tone of voice, or in his manner may suggest evasion or untruthfulness on the part of the witness.

Don't ask leading questions. An intelligent witness will see the desired answer and may be insulted. The answers given to leading questions are not reliable. Further, the use of leading questions conveys information to the witness you may not want him to know.

§ 114. Beginning the interview

At the outset of an interview, introduce yourself to the witness and explain the purpose of the interview to him. Follow this by a casual conversation designed to promote a common ground for discussion and to develop some mutual interest. A friendly and informal manner will keep the witness comfortable and relaxed. Do not flourish notebooks or documents until you have gained the witness' confidence and have determined whether he is friendly or hostile.

§ 115. The basic approaches

Use direct and indirect approaches. The indirect approach is a discussion carried on in conversational tone which permits the witness to talk without having to answer direct questions. The direct approach consists of direct questioning. Use of the interrogation technique, or a forceful direct approach, often succeeds when the witness fears retribution from a criminal, desires to protect a friend or relative, is impudent, or, for other reasons, is unwilling to cooperate with you.

Make use of the indirect approach when dealing with lying, unreliable witnesses. Allow them to set forth their version of the events in full. They may, through contradictions or denial, trip themselves into an admission by which the true facts can be obtained. When interviewing shy or nervous people, you may have to get your information piecemeal. Interview these people in their normal environment and be as casual and calm as possible. Allow the talkative person to speak freely and to use his own expressions, but confine him to the subject by appropriate questions.

When witnesses pretend to know nothing about a crime, ask many questions, any one of which, if answered, will refute their claim that they know nothing at all. Disinterested witnesses may divulge more information if their personal interest can be aroused by an indirect approach. Always attempt to put uneducated witnesses at ease and help them express themselves as best they can without putting words in their mouths. Flattery is often successful when alcoholics or braggarts are interviewed.

§ 116. The interview

After chatting informally with a witness, ask some preliminary questions. These should be designed to further help break the ice and help you evaluate the witness. He should, in this preliminary questioning, promptly disclose by his answers whether he will be friendly and cooperative, reluctant, or hostile.

Your questioning about the crime should begin with a search for such factual and incontrovertible matters as time, date, place, weather conditions, etc. Thus, with the comfortable assurance that only accurate information is being sought, the interview should proceed on a more leisurely basis into the details of the crime investigated. If the witness suddenly becomes reluctant or apprehensive during the interview, revert to noncontroversial matters.

When the interview is under way, always allow the witness to make an initial statement in narrative form. This statement may be fairly long if the witness is friendly, or relatively short or nonexistent in the case of a hostile witness. In any event, ask him to state the events he observed in the order in which the events occurred. Don't interrupt him during this account, for the continuity of his story may be broken if his attention is diverted.

At the end of his narrative ask questions designed to obtain a more complete account and to clarify any ambiguities in his story. Explore any area of possible misunderstanding in order to leave no doubt as to the exact nature of the witness' trial testimony.

As noted, witnesses to an unusual incident tend to state their conclusions or reactions to the incident rather than the underlying facts. In questioning, probe beneath superficial evaluations for evidence with evidentiary value which can furnish leads.

If you like, you can return to important matters in the questioning so that they will have been repeated for emphasis. A significant admission by the witness may be strengthened by reiteration. However, this is always done at the risk of possible modification, explanation, or outright retraction, if the witness realizes the emphasis being placed on the particular point raised.

Remain in absolute control of the interview at all times. Be careful not to elicit false information through improper questioning. You can permit digression or discussion of matters seemingly unrelated to the crime to put the witness at ease, but don't permit him to become evasive. If he should become so evasive that the purpose of the interview is obscured, reorient the interview by more formal questioning, by taking notes, or by sheer aggressiveness.

Your attitude and demeanor will directly affect the success or failure of the interview. Unless a special situation presents itself, be friendly, yet businesslike. Try to lead the witness into becoming talkative, then direct the conversation to the investigation. Avoid both a clash of personalities and acts of undue familiarity. Never use profanity or violent expressions such as "kill," "steal," "confess," or "murder." Do not relate improbable stories and avoid such distracting mannerisms as pacing the floor or fumbling with objects.

§ 117. Assisting with descriptions

An experienced interviewer learns to provide certain indexes to help witnesses describe persons and things. For example, the eye-level method of determining height may be used as a standard. You can get an estimate of height by asking a witness to tell how far another person's eyes were above or below his own. Speed is difficult to estimate accurately. Even opinions based on long experience may be subject to influence by noise, light, weather, and other conditions.

Age is difficult for witnesses to judge because of differences among individuals. If you use selected individuals for comparison, choose them carefully. In strange situations or those involving unusual circumstances, the witness may have no standards or associations on which to base his judgment and may be unable to utilize the standards you present for comparison. A detailed review or reconstruction of events can sometimes help the witness recall events, but be careful to avoid confusing the actual event with the reconstruction.

§ 118. Testing the witness' senses and perception

You will find it valuable during the course of an interview to test the witness' ability to accurately judge speed, direction or distance. The testing of his eyesight or sense of smell, color, or hearing may also be indicated. While it isn't usually feasible to test each of these abilities, some tests can be performed discreetly.

Test a witness' sense of time by asking him to estimate the passage of a specified time, such as two minutes, without looking at his watch. Most witnesses have a tendency to greatly exaggerate the passage of time, particularly when they are under emotional or physical stress. Therefore, question witnesses closely about time lapses.

Caution friendly witnesses that very few people can accurately estimate the passage of time under such circumstances. If the witness is hostile, note any exaggerations about the lapse of time for possible use on cross-examination.

If you have any doubt about the witness' ability to hear, you can test it by deliberately speaking in a low voice during part of the interview. If the witness has difficulty hearing you, ask him whether or not he wears a hearing aid. If he does, ask him whether or not he was wearing it at the time of the occurrence in question.

Ask whether or not he wears glasses, and, if so, whether he is farsighted or nearsighted. Try to discover whether he wears glasses regularly or merely on occasion and whether or not he was wearing his glasses at the time of the occurrence.

In those cases in which color perception plays a large role, witnesses may be questioned about colorblindness. Do not, however, attempt to test them through deception, i.e., referring to a red object as gray. You will only arouse their enmity and mistrust. You can buy simple devices for checking vision and color blindness in medical supply stores. In view of the hostility aroused when a witness is asked to submit to such testing, weigh the danger of antagonizing the witness against the degree of necessity of discovering information about his vision and his color perception.

A witness' sense of direction may be tested by directing him to "point in a southerly direction," or to "point in the direction of the courthouse." If weakness appears, and the witness is a friendly one, he should be given appropriate instructions with maps or diagrams. If the witness is a hostile witness, note his weakness for future reference in cross-examination.

D. KINDS OF WITNESSES

§ 119. In general

Interview procedures should be tailored to each individual witness. It is possible to classify witnesses by type and indicate the particular techniques most likely to succeed with each type, but broad classifications are merely guidelines, and general guidelines must be modified to fit the personality of specific witnesses. In other words, your attitude must change with each witness and you must aim to make each reveal as much as he knows to you while keeping his friendship.

The climate of an interview can often change during the course of the interview. Be sensitive to any change in the witness' attitude and alert in modifying your approach in dealing with him. It is also necessary during the course of an interview to continuously evaluate the witness' mannerisms and emotional state in terms of the information being developed. A witness' mannerisms will often convey important information to the alert interviewer.

The witness' manner while he relates his story or answers questions may indicate that he is not telling the truth or is concealing information. Evasiveness, hesitation, or unwillingness to discuss situations may signify a lack of cooperation.

The alert interviewer must also consider the relationship of the witness' body movements to his emotional state. A dry mouth indicated by the wetting of the lips, fidgeting, or vague movements of the hands may indicate nervousness or deception. A "cold sweat" or pale face may indicate fear. A slight gasp, holding the breath, or an unsteady voice may indicate that your knowledge shocked the witness.

You can observe the pumping of the heart by the pulse in the subject's neck. A ruddy or flushed face may be an indication of anger or embarrassment, not necessarily guilt. It may also indicate that the matter under discussion is of vital importance or that some information is being withheld. Although not all such symptoms are necessarily valid indications of the witness' emotions and may be a manifestation of his physical condition or health, they are often related to his emotional state.

§ 120. The friendly witness

A friendly or willing witness will usually be eager to tell his version of the events in question. While this is the easiest type of witness to question, he should not be taken for granted. Deal affirmatively with friendly witnesses in order to keep them friendly through the trial. From time to time a friendly witness can become an unwilling or even a hostile witness. This change can be the result of events over which you have no control. There are two basic ways to guard against such a development.

The first method is to get a signed statement from the friendly witness as soon as possible. Whether he swears to his statement is not too important. A sworn statement, of course, can be the foundation for a perjury indictment. But a signed statement, witnessed by a third party, is just as good a deterrent to a change in his testimony, and can be used with equal effectiveness. The second method of guarding against change in attitude is to take the friendly witness into your confidence and keep him informed of your progress. Do this only with great discretion. If a witness does go over to the prosecution, you don't want him taking knowledge of your defense plans with him.

The friendly witness is often anxious to please you. This can create problems. In his desire to give you the answer he thinks you want to hear, he may be willing to stretch the truth. This can result from a desire to be helpful or from a deep desire to keep your client out of jail. A friendly witness can also stretch the truth out of a subconscious desire to be liked. He may feel he can achieve this goal by telling you what he thinks you want to know rather than what he really knows. This type of friendly witness is most dangerous on the stand. There is usually no similarity between his direct testimony and his statements under cross-examination.

Therefore, in preparing a friendly or willing witness, avoid leading questions. Don't indicate the answers you want to hear. The easier you make it for a friendly witness to give you what he thinks is the right answer, the less likely you are to get the truth.

§ 121. The unwilling or uncooperative witness

Imagination and ingenuity are the keys to dealing with the unwilling or uncooperative witness. They often have information of great value to the defense of the case. A witness' unwillingness to testify may be based on a number of reasons. For example, he may feel close to the victim, or may have a real or imaginary fear of reprisal, or he simply may not want to become involved and go through the time and trouble of making a court appearance.

Many inhabitants of rural areas are inclined to be close-mouthed and taciturn when interviewed. Wives are often reluctant to answer questions in the absence of their husbands. Other persons may refuse to cooperate with the defense investigator because of their relationship with the person they suspect of being the actual culprit.

When a witness is uncooperative and there appears to be no readily understandable reason for his conduct, you should consider him a possible suspect. Guilt will sometimes close the mouth of an apparently innocent witness and further investigation may reveal him to be the actual culprit.

If you believe that a witness possesses information important to the defense, your problem becomes one of identifying the cause of his lack of cooperation. Use your client and friendly witnesses to learn all you can about the unwilling witness. Your inquiry, for this purpose, should cover his personality, interests, personal friends, ambitions and hobbies. Try to discover the witness' motivation. Even if you cannot discover his motivation with complete assuredness, you should be in a position to make an educated guess about it.

If a witness is personally friendly toward you or your client, but fears reprisal from some source if he cooperates with you, a direct approach to him might be best. If, on the other hand, he harbors a grudge against you, it might be better to approach him through an intermediary with whom he is friendly.

If an unwilling witness agrees to see you but warns that he will not testify, interview him on his terms. In talking with him, make it clear that you are seeking information only and are not there to persuade him to change his mind about testifying. You may get valuable information which you may be able to corroborate with someone else's testimony. If no information is obtained, you will at least have established personal contact, which you may be able to utilize at some later stage in the case. In the course of preparation, many things can change, and among them are those factors which make for an unwilling witness.

If an unwilling witness insists that he will not speak to you about the case, do not try an approach based on his sense of decency, social responsibility, or civic duty. This approach won't be effective since it doesn't attack the cause of the witness' decision not to cooperate. It sometimes pays to suggest that the witness' attitude is the result of cowardice and a lack of courage. Be cautious with such an approach, however, and use it only on those fearful witnesses who also display an air of bravado.

If a witness fears retaliation, stress the fact that if he were hurt in any way it would be tantamount to an expression of guilt by the true culprit. Once the witness' statement is made, the culprit would no longer have any reason to interfere with him. If "involvement" is feared, make every effort to convince the witness of the importance of his testimony and the little inconvenience he's likely to experience.

You might also tell a witness who doesn't want to get involved that the interview might reveal that he can add little to the information you already have. If that is the case, you would no longer trouble him. However, explain that if he refuses to submit to an interview, you may have no choice later but to subpoena him as a witness, in which case he would be inconvenienced and his involvement would be a matter of public attention.

When reluctance to give information is due to national origin and regional habits it can generally be overcome with the aid of a person of the same origin. Someone who understands the witness' native tongue and customs can be of great help.

In these situations, you or your local assistant should attempt to discover the witness' motivation. If it is simply a reluctance to talk to strangers, the local assistant should be able to overcome any resistance. If the defendant comes from the same background as the witness, stress the fact that you are helping him and that to do so you need the assistance of other persons of the same background. In other words, appeal to the witness' sense of national or regional pride.

The questioning of a wife who is hesitant because of her husband's absence may easily be postponed until her husband can be present. However, encourage her to tell her own story and not to lean on him for assistance.

§ 122. The hostile witness

The most troublesome of all witnesses is one who is hostile. Not only is he uncooperative but often he has a desire to harm you and your client's case. If possible, don't interview hostile witnesses. There is always a possibility that time and changed circumstances will make him friendly or less hostile.

If you believe an interview is necessary, always have a third person present. If you fail to take that precaution, you may later be faced with the charge of corrupt conduct with regard to the witness.

Investigate the hostile witness as you did the unwilling witness. Discover his motivations and weaknesses. Check all hostile witnesses, whether you decide to interview them or not, to see whether or not they have an arrest or criminal record. You can do this through private inquiries and a personal check of court records in the vicinity. Discovery of this type of evidence should be sought by motions. Always inquire about criminal records at the preliminary hearings. This information can be a great help during cross-examination at the trial.

If the hostile witness agrees to an interview and your investigation has not found an approach that will change his attitude toward you, interview him for every inconsistency or contradiction in his story for later use at the trial.

If possible, obtain a signed statement. If the hostile witness refuses to sign, but acknowledges that his statement is correct, both you and the third person there should certify that fact. Then sign the statement yourselves as witnesses. Check all statements made by a hostile witness to news media so that you can call the reporter to impeach him if the witness changes his story.

§ 123. The prosecution witness

Witnesses do not belong to one party to a litigation. You have the right to interview any witness or prospective witness who may have information pertinent to your client's case.

This right is recognized by the Canons of Professional Ethics. They provide that a lawyer may properly interview any witness or prospective witness for the opposing side in any civil or criminal action without the consent of opposing counsel or party.[2] Many laymen don't understand this, however, and witnesses, including complainants, who have given incriminating information to the police or prosecutor believe they belong to the prosecution. Explain to witnesses interviewed that this is not the case and that they have as much obligation as a citizen to talk to you as to the prosecutor. Further, if they do not do so, the trial will be unfair. Of course, no witness has an actual obligation to talk to either the prosecution or to you. Do not suggest that he has. However, his moral obligation to tell what he knows to both sides must be brought home to him.

If a potential witness continues in his refusal to speak to you, ask him whether he has received instructions from the prosecutor's office or from a police officer not to speak to you. If he indicates that this is the case, or if you aren't satisfied with his denial, contact the prosecutor. Advise him of the requirements of the Canons and inform him that by giving such instructions to the witness he violated your client's Constitutional rights.[3]

If you are unsatisfied by the prosecutor's response, seek

2. Canon 39 of the Canons of Professional Ethics of the American Bar Association states: "A lawyer may properly interview any witness or prospective witness for the opposing side in any civil or criminal action without the consent of opposing counsel or party. In doing so, however, he should scrupulously avoid any suggestion calculated to induce the witness to suppress or deviate from the truth, or in any degree to affect his free and untrammeled conduct when appearing at the trial or on the witness stand." [Am Jur 2d Desk Book, Document 91.]

3. Gregory v United States, 369 F2d 185 (DC Cir, 1966).

an order in the trial court requiring the prosecutor to show cause:

1. Why the charges against your client should not be dismissed with prejudice, on the ground that the prosecutor has unconstitutionally interfered with the preparation of the defense and that there is no way of ascertaining how much harm has been done, or of correcting the wrong at this stage; in the alternative,

2. Why the prosecutor should not be ordered to identify all witnesses to whom he gave such instructions, so that they may be brought before the court and instructed that they are free to speak to the defense.

§ 124. Codefendants

When questioning codefendants, find out first whether or not they are represented by an attorney. If so, courtesy dictates that you contact their lawyer for permission to interview his clients. Direct the interview of a codefendant toward any information he has given the authorities. If he admits guilt, find out whether or not he intends to testify for the prosecution and implicate the defendant. If he denies his guilt, find out what he knows about the crime and what his defense is. Your tactics relating to severance and jury trial or waiver will hinge on the answers to these inquiries.

§ 125. Child witnesses

Interviews with child witnesses require special techniques and skills. You may have to spend a significant amount of your time gaining the child's confidence and friendship. Many children are reluctant to discuss matters openly with strangers.

You may be able to separate truth from imagination in a child's story. While some children are exceptionally accurate in their ability to narrate facts, others tend to fantasize as a matter of course. When a child is unable to distinguish fact from fantasy in his own mind, even if you ask him if he knows the difference between right and wrong and truth and falsehood, his affirmative answer does not constitute a guarantee that his story is factual.

A number of preliminary questions should be put to the child to determine the truthfulness of his statements. These questions should cover a wide range in order to disclose those areas in which his flights of fancy are likely to occur.

This line of questioning reveals that the child is truthful about his own academic abilities but that he tends to exaggerate his physical abilities. In other areas he seems to be factual but somewhat evasive. Armed with this knowledge you should be able to interview the child, exercising extreme care in those areas in which he is most likely to fantasize.

It is useful to have an adult present when a child's statement is to be taken. Otherwise, even a signed statement is of little use if the child changes his testimony.[4]

Teenage witnesses usually prove to be good observers. Many of them, however, will have a tendency to either exaggerate or romanticize a situation.

§ 126. The untruthful witness

There is no foolproof technique to discover when a witness is lying or to prevent him from lying. If you are faced with a pretrial plan of deception on the part of certain witnesses, it can only be exposed, if at all, by a detailed and meticulous interview. The question then, is one of the depth of your perception and your skill in questioning.

In any such confrontation you will have certain important advantages. You will inevitably be calmer than the

4. **Practice Aids:** Competency of children as witnesses, see Am Jur, Witnesses (1st ed §§ 129 et seq.).

Qualifying an infant witness to testify. 6 Am Jur Proof of Facts 333, 338, Infants.

Annotation: Admissibility of deposition of child of tender years. 30 ALR2d 771.

witness, since he is the one attempting to deceive. Further, you should, at the time of the interview, be familiar with the case. You will know what is probably true and what is most likely false. Each witness interviewed should yield pieces of a story which when fitted into place will form a part of a mosaic. The mosaic will take form and shape in your mind long before the last section is in place. Consequently, you should be on your guard when confronted with a story which does not fit into the pattern of others you have been told.

You, of course, can ask questions. The witness cannot. By questioning thoroughly you can arrive at points the witness has not considered, and on which he has not consulted his accomplices: At this point contradictions should appear. You should be able to investigate these contradictions and piece together the entire fabric of falsehood created by the witness. To reach this goal you must take full advantage of the superiority of your situation. Question freely and record every reply.

If you believe that your client has been falsely accused, attempt to find the actual culprit. Even if you cannot fully establish his guilt you will help your client's chances of gaining an acquittal by presenting a reasonable theory that someone else committed the crime. All this being so, a false alibi by an untruthful witness is the most serious obstacle you will have to overcome.

E. PROBING TESTIMONY

§ 127. Difficult alibis

The most difficult false alibis to attack are those in which the truth has been told about all of the incidents, but the date or time has been changed. For example, if the crime was committed on a Thursday afternoon, the real culprit may tell you that he was then at a meeting when in fact the meeting took place on Wednesday afternoon. However, all the details supplied by other witnesses will corroborate the alibi.

If you suspect this kind of alibi, carefully question the witness about his activities during the period immediately before and after the crime. Attack the date, not the incidents of the alibi. Since all the incidents related will actually have taken place, it will be useless to attempt to challenge the alibi itself. Such a line of questioning would only serve to establish the truthfulness of the story. Thus, aim your attack at incidents before and after the alibi events.

§ 128. Take statements early

You should proceed on the assumption that every statement made by a witness might be false. False statements crop up even in the most apparently innocent interview. Find out if a witness has some motive for not speaking truthfully. Motives may be found in the personal relationship of witness and client, witness and victim, or even of witness and the alleged crime itself. Discover whether any witness stands to gain or lose from the results either of your investigations or of police investigation.

If the witness has some connection with the crime, you must mistrust everything he says. Verify all his statements. Spare no trouble to ascertain the witness' point of view. Witnesses almost always betray themselves, if only by word.

The untruthful witness who is trying to inculpate your client to protect the real culprit will often give himself away unknowingly. He may, for instance, attribute bad qualities to your client while not saying anything truly contemptible about him. While apparently trying not to injure the client, however, he will often let slip a very grave accusation about him. Such conduct should make you suspicious about such a witness.

§ 129. Test a suspicious witness

Test the suspicious witness. Question him, for example, about something of which you are certain and which, if untrue, would tend to establish your client's guilt. The witness' answer will help you to judge his truthfulness.

§ 130. Some witnesses exaggerate

Witnesses to an exciting event will often tend to exaggerate the facts as they retell the event. As a result, a car which was going 75 miles per hour will be reported as going "at least 90." A man 6 feet tall will be described as a giant. A night on which light rain was falling will be described as "stormy," and the pavement at the time "slick as ice," though it may be no more slippery than any other paved street when wet.

§ 131. The prejudiced witness

A witness prejudiced against your client will often make improbable statements which reveal his hostility. Do not discourage such a witness during the interview. The time to attack the witness is during cross-examination at the trial.

Not every witness who tells an obvious lie should be challenged. Caution only those untruthful witnesses who will appear for the defense. If the witness is a hostile witness, encourage him to make wild statements. The more absurd his opinion, the more effective it will be to confront him with it at the trial.

§ 132. Witnesses who memorize

Sometimes a witness will memorize his story. Such a story may either be a part of a conspiracy to inculpate your client or it may merely be an attempt by a nervous witness to get his story "down pat." Protect yourself against memorized stories by having all witnesses tell their versions at least twice during the interview.

If a witness has memorized his story, he will not only use the same words each time he tells the story but he will also repeat the same tonal inflection. Try to discover the reason for the memorization. If the witness seems afraid, tell him you know he has memorized. He may break down and reveal a plot against your client. If, however, the witness seems to be a strong-willed person, you should not confront him. Instead, use other investigative methods to discover if he is part of a conspiracy. Use your knowledge of his memorization to attack on cross-examination. You can impress a jury by memorizing the witness' story yourself and reciting it with him as he testifies.

F. VICTIMS AS WITNESSES

§ 133. The victim

Most victims are reluctant to discuss a case with defense counsel. To obtain an interview you must impress the victim with the need for fairness. The prosecutor sometimes will be of assistance in arranging such an interview.

§ 134. Interview victims cautiously

Do not interview the victim at all until you have spoken with most of the other witnesses. Become familiar with most of the key facts before this interview, which should not be held unless you either want specific information or need to find out something about the victim's frame of mind. Since the victim will probably have to testify at some preliminary stage in the proceedings, interview him only if you need information which you will not be able to acquire at that time.

Always interview victims in the presence of some third person to protect yourself against charges of harassment and undue influence. Your goal will determine the manner in which you conduct the interview.

§ 135. Obtain an accurate account

A victim's memory of the surrounding circumstances of a crime, particularly if it was one involving violence, is apt to be partial and imperfect. Therefore, try to fix the crime in the context of the circumstances existing before, during and after the crime.

§ 136. Investigate the victim's character and reputation

Discover all you can about the victim's reputation before interviewing him. Is he a man of good character? Is he apt to be prejudiced against your client because of religious, racial, national origin or any other grounds? Such information will help you to judge the victim's credibility during the course of the interview. It will also tell you if the victim has any reason for unfairly implicating your client.

§ 137. Avoid possibly psychologically injuring the subject

While the possibility of such damage is often overestimated, avoid the usual techniques of interrogation as much as possible.

Always avoid grilling, coercing, or giving advice. These techniques—characteristic of tactics employed by police—may induce possible trauma in the child victim.

Begin the interview by asking about tangible things. Don't ask probing, emotional questions until the interviewee is at ease. Remember that rapid, abrupt, or demanding questions easily destroy rapport.

G. RECORD OF INTERVIEW

§ 138. Recording devices: help or hindrance

Consider the use of a voice recorder during the interview. Recorders furnish observable proof of the fairness of the interview and questioning, and eliminate the possibility of a witness' claim that he did not read his statement. More important, recordings can be used very effectively in jury trials. The sound of a witness' voice has far greater impact on the jury than a mere reading of the transcript of his testimony or interview. A recorded interview contains all the color and shadowing of speech of the witness and discloses the full emotional content of what was said.

It is often possible to obtain a recorded statement from a witness who refuses to sign a written statement. Many witnesses are sensitive about signing anything that looks like a document, but will permit the recording of their voices, perhaps not fully realizing that a properly taken and presented recorded statement is as effective and legally binding as a written statement. They know or should be told that a voice recording will be a faithful reproduction of the entire conversation. They know that a handwritten statement often omits portions unfavorable to the taker of the statement, may not be in the exact words of the speaking party, and can be slanted.

A recording is also advantageous in interviewing a non-English speaking witness. Make use of an interpreter during this kind of interview, identifying him by name and address at the outset. The recording will preserve the witness' original remarks and can be of value if the witness later asserts that his remarks were not properly translated.

If a voice recorder is used during an interview, it is advisable to follow a prescribed procedure. Begin by identifying yourself and the witness, and state the date, place, and time of the interview. Then have the witness state his name, address, and place of employment. You should then describe the make and model of the recording equipment.

Once the interview has begun, don't stop or interrupt the recording device unless the witness has completed his statement or until the end of the particular belt, disc, or tape is reached. This safeguards against a prosecutor's attempt to discredit the record on the grounds that it doesn't contain the entire statement of the witness by virtue of the fact that the recording device was turned off at a point during the interview, thereby omitting some all-important remark. Keep the microphone "open" during the entire interview, even if there is an interruption. If the witness suddenly has to attend to some urgent business, state so, in order to explain the period of silence that follows.

You must, of course, remember that your own words are also being recorded. Avoid any hint of overreaching, deception, or distortion.

Most interviews require at least two or three discs or tapes to obtain a complete statement. This means that each disc, belt, or tape should be brought to a close with the statement that what the witness has said will be played back to him. Then state: "This is the end of belt No. ______. Mr. ____________________, has your statement so far been true and complete and correct?"

At the end of the recorded interview, ask the witness whether or not his remarks have been played back to him, whether or not the answers he has given are true and complete, whether or not he understands them, and whether or not there is any need for clarification or addition.

After you remove the record from the machine, have the witness sign it in ink or crayon. Explain that this is done to identify the disc or tape rather than to authenticate his statement.

It is also advisable to keep proper service records of all your recording equipment. These records can be useful in establishing that particular equipment was in good working order at the time a recording was made.

Recording devices are now small enough to permit surreptitious recordings of a witness' voice. These recordings, when admissible, are particularly effective as a means of discrediting or impeaching hostile witnesses.

There are many drawbacks to the practice of recording witness interviews surreptitiously. Recording instruments do not usually have a sufficiently long playing time to permit recording of the entire interview. Further, the witness might move around in a manner that would prevent the recorder from picking up everything he says.

Defense attorneys should consider all the pros and cons before deciding whether to attempt to record a particular interview. The idea of a recording will assure some witnesses and frighten others. A shy or timid witness may be even more reticent in the presence of a recording device and develop "stage fright." With other witnesses, all of the preparation involved in setting up an interview in comfortable, relaxed surroundings may have been in vain after the recorder is introduced. Its presence, in such cases, can result in a strained and formal atmosphere.

Witnesses pressed for time may consent to an interview because the presence of a recorder eliminates the time usually consumed by the writing, transcription, and signing of a statement. It ensures that only a small amount of time will be taken up by the interview.

The best procedure for deciding the advisability of its use may well be to begin an interview without mention of a recorder. When you feel you have learned enough about the witness to predict his reaction, you can then decide whether he should be asked for permission to record the balance of the interview.

§ 139. Warnings about recording devices

To avoid the possibility of being accused of manipulation, record on those devices with which it is most difficult to tamper. The relative ease with which the tapes of magnetic devices can be altered or rearranged renders them inappropriate for use in interviews.

§ 140. Admissibility

Although there has been some criticism of the use of recordings in evidence in the past, it is now almost universally held that sound recordings made by the defense, if related to otherwise competent evidence, are admissible so long as a proper foundation is laid. This is true even if the witness' statement was recorded without his knowledge.[5]

A proper foundation for the admission of a recording usually includes:

1. A showing that the recording device was capable of taking the witness' statement.
2. A showing that the operator of the device was competent to record the interview.
3. A showing of the authenticity and correctness of the recording.
4. A showing that no changes, additions, or deletions have been made.
5. A showing of the manner of preservation of the recording.
6. Identification of the interviewer, the person interviewed, and any other person taking part.
7. A showing that the statement was elicited without improper inducement.[6]

5. Admissibility of Recording of Oral Confession in Criminal Case. Jones on Evidence § 399.

Sound Recording as Demonstrative Evidence. Belli, Modern Trials § 175.

Tape Recording of Conference between Plaintiff and Persons Representing Defendant Secretly Made by Plaintiff Subject to Discovery. 7 Defense LJ p 263.

Practice Aids: Admissibility of phonographic reproductions of sound in evidence, see 29 Am Jur 2d, EVIDENCE § 436.

Annotations: Admissibility of sound recordings in evidence. 58 ALR2d 1024.

Refreshment of recollection by use of memoranda or other writings. 82 ALR2d 473 at page 589.

6. The presence of irrelevant, incompetent, immaterial, or obscene matter in a recording, even though it cannot be segregated from the material matter, will not ordinarily bar it from evidence so long as the objectionable portions are not prejudicial. Paulson v Scott (1951) 260 Wis 141, 50 NW2d 376, 31 ALR2d 706.

It is proper to replay a recording at the trial to give the jury an opportunity to compare the voice said to be that of the witness on the recording with his voice as they hear it from the witness stand, and to convince the jury that there has been no dubbing. People v Grace (1958) 166 Cal App 2d 68, 332 P2d 811.

The fact that a recording may not reproduce an entire conversation, or may be indistinct or inaudible in part, does not of itself require its exclusion; however, the recording will be rejected if it is so inaudible and indistinct that the jury must speculate as to what was said. State v Slater (1950) 36 Wash 2d 357, 218 P2d 329.

§ 141. Transcripts of the recording

The use in evidence of typewritten transcripts of sound recordings has been objected to as a violation of the best evidence rule. Generally, however, typewritten transcripts are admitted in evidence if their accuracy and reliability are clearly established, and if the original recording is produced for purposes of comparison.[7] If you decide at some point to transcribe a recording, do it in a way that will establish its authenticity and accuracy. A suggested form of authorization follows:

I ...., do hereby certify that on ...., 19........, at the hour of ...., at the home of ...., I personally interviewed and took the statement of ....

I further certify that the statements given by Mr. .... were stated by him to be the truth to the best of his knowledge and belief, and that the statements given by him were recorded on .... *(make, model, and serial number)* equipment and that the original belts, *(or tapes, wires, or discs)* .... in number, were used to prepare the foregoing attached .... *(number)* pages, and that these pages constitute a complete, truthful, and correct transcription of the statements as given by Mr. .... without erasure, alteration, deletion or addition.

I further certify that the taking of said recorded statement was with the consent of Mr. ...., and that he was present during the entire recording of the interview and statement.

I further certify that I have listened to the original recording and have compared it to the above transcribed copy, and find it to be an exact record of our conversation.

....

....

Notary Public

I ...., do hereby certify that I have listened to the original record of the conversation and statement taking place between Mr. .... and Mr. ...., and that the statement I have transcribed is a complete, true, and accurate record of the entire conversation contained thereon, without alteration, addition, or deletion.

....

Date

7. 58 ALR2d 1024 at page 1042.

H. STATEMENTS

§ 142. Notes of interview

Always take complete notes of an interview. Most witnesses will not object to this. Do not permit the taking of notes to interfere with your purpose of eliciting information. If the witness is reluctant to divulge information while you are taking notes, write them up as soon as possible after the interview while all the information is fresh in your mind. Include in your notes the date, time and place of the interview, identity of the witness interviewed and the names and addresses of all other persons present. Summarize all the information obtained from the witness.

§ 143. The statement

Witnesses' statements are often crucial. Since they crystallize the witnesses' oral testimony, they are particularly important in the event a witness later changes his story.

Cooperative when first questioned, many persons because of fear, friendship, or other considerations, later decide to change their version of what happened. If the witness' information is at all relevant, try to get it down in writing over the signature of the witness.

§ 144. Obtain statements of hostile witnesses and victims

Try to obtain statements from everyone you can, even from uncooperative and hostile witnesses and from a victim. If their stories are unfavorable to your client, they will still be bound by them once they are written down. If you later turn up evidence putting their tales into question, their signed statements will be a safeguard against their switching to a more convenient story.

§ 145. Avoid using printed forms

The best statement is one signed by the witness. The worst, which should be avoided at all costs, is the practice of taking statements on printed forms. Most jurors will conclude that the use of such forms is proof that the statement was not actually taken from the witness.

§ 146. Inadmissible evidence in statements

If a friendly witness gives you a statement which may be offered in evidence, it should not contain any inadmissible evidence. However, if the statement is that of a hostile witness and is to be used as a means of impeaching his testimony, it may be offered against him notwithstanding the fact that certain language in it will not be allowed to go to the jury.

Similar reasoning applies if the witness makes some prejudicial reference to the race or religious background of the defendant. Before giving his statement, a friendly witness should be cautioned that such remarks will weaken the value of his testimony. The statement of a hostile witness, on the other hand, should include anything and everything that suggests bias or prejudice. This may be used to discredit his testimony.

§ 147. How to take a statement

A signed statement should usually be taken in the following manner:

1. Indicate in the heading the date and place where the statement is being taken.
2. Set forth the witness' name and address, such as "I, John Doe, residing at 101 Main Street, Newtown. . . ."
3. Set forth your name and capacity, if you took the statement, and those of any witnesses, such as ". . . I am making this statement to Peter Poe, attorney for defendant Richard Roe, in the presence of Bill Boe and Saul Soe. . . ."
4. Include a declaration by the witness that he has been advised of his rights, especially wherever it is possible that the statement might incriminate him, such as any sort of admission of wrongdoing. For

instance, "I am making this statement of my own free will. I have been advised that I do not have to make a statement, and that any statement made by me may be used against me."

5. The body of the statement should usually contain a chronological recital of the incidents being investigated and the witness' part in it. It should resemble as closely as possible the witness' manner of speech. Grammatical errors should not be corrected; the witness should not be coached; however, he may be asked questions for purposes of clarity and to help bring out desired information. The statement may be either in narrative form (in which the subject is permitted to talk freely while his words are taken down) or written out in his own hand.

To indicate your fairness, the statement should reflect facts favorable to the witness. Read the statement back to the witness before he signs it and allow him to make corrections and additions to it. Have the witness initial each such change. This will not only prevent a later claim of alteration but will also serve to demonstrate the voluntary nature of the statement. Number each page of the statement; it is a good idea to have the witness initial each page to prevent a later claim that pages were inserted or removed. The last paragraph of the statement should read approximately as follows:

> "I have read this statement of ______ pages and signed and numbered each page and initialed all corrections. I have made this statement freely and voluntarily. No promises were made to induce me to sign this statement, and no one has threatened or coerced me in any manner to obtain this statement. It is the truth."

Have the witness sign the statement in ink. If others are present, have them sign their names and addresses both as witnesses to the statement itself and to the signature of the witness. Keep witnesses' statements locked in a file cabinet or safe. You should be prepared to testify that any statement has been in your possession from the time it was made until the time of its use at trial, thereby establishing as a fact that no other persons had access to it and that there was no opportunity for anyone to tamper with it.

I. SELECTION, PREPARATION AND PRESENTATION OF NON-EXPERTS

§ 148. In general

The preparation of fact witnesses is an entirely different phase of your pretrial activities from the interviewing of all potential witnesses. Once familiarized with the facts of the case, you must then familiarize your witnesses with their roles in the case.

You must have an integrated theory of defense. With good preparation you can present the most effective defense possible for your client. Organize your evidence tightly so you can present your theory cohesively at trial.

§ 149. Should you demand a jury?

After you have interviewed all of the potential witnesses and analyzed all the relevant physical evidence, evaluate the effectiveness of your defense at trial. You must know both the strengths and weaknesses not only of your own, but also of the prosecution's case.

In most cases a jury trial is best. It is far easier to create a reasonable doubt in the mind of at least one juror than in the mind of one judge. However, do not choose a jury trial if you think your client and witnesses, because they may lack persuasiveness and be coarse in appearance and manner of speech, would poorly impress a jury. Trial judges usually pay less attention to such human weaknesses. If you think the obverse holds true, that the prosecution's witnesses will make a poorer appearance than the defense witnesses, you should, of course, insist on a jury.

In most jurisdictions you will, before trial, be able to ascertain the name of the trial judge. In part, your decision as to whether to waive a jury will depend upon your familiarity with the trial judge. What is his reputation for fairness? What is his attitude toward the criminal defendant? What about his willingness to acquit a defendant if the prosecution's evidence is weak? In reaching your decision, you must also study the background and personalities of your client and his witnesses and also consider the applicable facts and the law.

If you believe that the defense witnesses will be unconvincing and the prosecution's case is powerful, consider the negotiation of a plea. Only do so, however, if you are satisfied of your client's guilt and if your client is willing publicly to admit his guilt in exchange for a plea.

§ 150. Selection of witnesses

Since defense witnesses are usually scarce, you should select as witnesses only those who can materially support your theory of defense and who will increase the jury's favorable attitude toward the defendant. Both judge and jurors identify a defendant with his witnesses. A witness is testifying for the defendant and will appear to be vouching for him. Hence, the demeanor of defense witnesses is important. Their apparent honesty, likeability or good judgment will cause the jury to react favorably to the defendant. Contrarily, the seemingly dishonest or disreputable defense witness may well lead the jury to view the defendant negatively.

You must weigh the value of each witness against his likely impact on the jury. If possible call personable witnesses to testify on even minor points. Reject shifty or abrasive witnesses if their testimony is merely cumulative.

§ 151. Preparing fact witnesses

During the interview, you want to get a witness to reveal all pertinent facts. In preparing a witness for trial, on the other hand, you want to focus on specific testimony with the view of how best to present it at this stage. You must inform the witness rather than be informed by him.

Review the facts, explain your theory of defense, and show the witness just where his testimony fits into the overall picture. Your witnesses will have more confidence and be able to testify with greater effectiveness if they are aware of their particular place in the defense.

Familiarize the witness with the procedures of trial. Explain the purposes of direct examination and cross examination. Tell him about the trial so that he feels at ease when he takes his place in the witness chair. You can often calm the anxieties of nervous witnesses by having them observe parts of some other trial.

§ 152. Preparation of key defense witnesses

In addition to the general preparation, examine all key defense witnesses individually in the same manner as will be done in court. While you can conduct both the direct and the cross examination, more realistic preparation is achieved if the cross examination is conducted by one of your associates.

During this mock cross examination confront each witness with every challenging question you can possibly anticipate. Do this with the badgering and disbelieving attitude the prosecutor is apt to have. Tell each witness that if he can withstand such mock cross examination, he will be able to testify at trial without fear.

Warn the witness that a little nervousness is natural and will be accepted by the jury.

Before the mock cross examination, brief each witness about the prosecutor's pet habits or idiosyncrasies. If he asks questions in an irritating manner, if he points a finger to disparage a witness, or if he has any other mannerisms designed to make a witness feel ill at ease and uncomfortable, try to prepare your witness for them.

Alert each witness in advance of the kind of questions with which the prosecutor may try to trap him. Explain how to answer such questions. For example, if a witness is asked if he discussed his testimony in advance with the defense counsel, make sure he does not deny it. Explain that there is nothing improper about this practice since it is an accepted part of our system of criminal justice.

If asked if he is being paid for his testimony, tell each witness not to conceal the fact if he has been paid the statutory witness fee. If he is asked about special dates, times, and places, tell him not to hesitate to say so if he does not remember.

Caution witnesses not to answer questions unless they fully understand them. Many witnesses are afraid to ask that a question be repeated. Caution your witnesses further not to permit themselves to be rushed. Tell them to let the judge know if at any time they do not hear a question or if they become confused about dates or facts.

In order for a jury to make a correct and wise decision, it must have all the evidence put before it in a truthful manner. Tell your witnesses that while they take an oath to tell nothing but the truth, there are two ways to tell the truth. One is in a halting, stumbling, hesitant manner, which raises doubts in the jury's mind. The other is in a confident, straightforward manner which makes the jury have more faith in what a witness is saying.

§ 153. Rules for witnesses

It is good practice to make your witnesses familiar with some of the basic rules of testifying. Not all of these rules will apply to each witness, of course, but they are reliable guidelines. You should impress upon your witness the desirability of:

1. Standing upright when taking the oath and saying "I do" in a clear voice.

2. Dressing conservatively and wearing clean clothes.

3. Revisiting the scene of the alleged crime (if applicable to his testimony) to familiarize himself with it prior to trial.

4. Avoiding the memorizing of his testimony.

5. Talking toward the jurors and looking at them most of the time; speaking to them frankly and openly as to a friend or neighbor, in a tone of voice sufficiently clear and loud enough so that the farthest juror can hear the testimony.

6. Listening carefully to all questions. (Impress on your witness the fact that no matter how nice the prosecutor may seem, he is trying to destroy the witness.)

7. Being serious both on and off the stand. Make sure your witness understands that his demeanor can be observed by jurors any place in the courthouse.

8. In the event of answering a question incorrectly, tell your witness he should correct himself immediately.

9. Clarifying at once an answer of his that may be unclear.

10. Explaining his answers if it seems necessary to do so rather than to stick with a simple "yes" or "no". But make sure he understands to answer only the question asked and not to volunteer information.

11. Remaining polite, even under the most intensive cross examination, and at all times avoid appearing to be a cocky witness or a "wise guy."

12. Becoming silent at once if the judge interrupts or if the prosecutor interposes an objection.

13. Avoiding any mannerisms which the jury may interpret as signs of nervousness or falsity. (The mock examination should reveal a witness' offensive mannerisms.)

14. Not looking at defense counsel for answers; and trying not to seem overly partisan.

15. Avoiding the use of technical language. The witness should be instructed that the jury should be able to follow and understand everything he has to say.

J. SPECIFIC WITNESSES

§ 154. The defendant

In order to decide whether to put the defendant on the witness stand, you should ask yourself such questions as these: How strong is the prosecution's case? What are the strengths of your defense without the defendant's testimony? Does the defendant have a criminal record? What are his appearance and attitude? Is he likely to withstand cross examination well? How will the jury react to him?

If you decide to put the defendant on the stand, prepare him with special care, for his testimony will be scrutinized more carefully than anyone else's. If your client takes the stand, he *must* be able to convince the jury of his innocence.

Your client should be the last witness to testify in order to benefit from observing the other witnesses. If all other witnesses precede him to the stand he can then explain inconsistencies, if any, in the presentation of the defense. Try to make your client understand the possible advantages of being last.

Tell your client the theory of the defense and the place each witness will occupy in it. The client should know in advance what to anticipate at each stage of the trial. Most of the "witness" rules discussed earlier apply especially to the defendant. Subject him to an intensive mock cross examination.

Your investigation should have turned up all statements made by the defendant to the authorities. The defendant should not be permitted to testify unless he can explain *all* such statements. Remember, in some jurisdictions an admission which has been suppressed as involuntary may nevertheless be used by the prosecution for impeachment purposes.

Help the defendant find ways to convey to the jury that he is a likeable and honest person. If the defendant is in custody, arrange for him to wear civilian clothes during the trial. He is entitled to present himself in a dignified manner, and this includes the right to be tried wearing civilian clothes.[8] Insist that your client be permitted a haircut if he needs one and the opportunity to shave daily during the trial.

§ 155. Codefendants

Give special attention to the stories of codefendants. Never represent a codefendant if there is any chance either of a conflict of interest or a conflict of testimony. If such conflict exists, move for a severance and do not call that codefendant as a witness.

If there is to be a joint trial, work out strategy with the other defense attorneys. Call a codefendant as a witness only if he is presentable and likeable and can offer testimony vital to your defense.

The jury will tend to identify your client with his codefendants. If a codefendant appears to be a criminal type or has a bad reputation, your client will suffer no matter how well the codefendant does on the stand. If his testimony clashes with your theory of defense, the jury is apt to regard both your client and the codefendant as liars. If his testimony supports your theory, the jury may believe that your client and the codefendant planned to agree on a lie.

§ 156. Alibi witnesses

Alibi witnesses are most difficult to prepare. This is because they are the most vulnerable to cross examination, even when they are telling the truth. Never call someone to testify as an alibi witness if you know that his testimony is not true. However, do not shy away from an alibi defense merely because there is no corroboration for his testimony or because a special relationship exists between him and your client.

8. United States ex rel. Diamond v Social Service Dept. 263 F Supp 971 (FD Pa).

Maintaining false alibis to meet a false charge is the way many defendants end up in prison. If the prosecution can establish the falsity of an alibi (either through cross examination or through a showing that the witness was somewhere else) he can gravely injure the defense. Many jurors regard a false alibi as an admission of guilt.

If the prosecutor makes a practice of cross examining every defense witness in great detail, you should merely examine the alibi witness on the essentials of his story. Then let the cross examination confirm the truth of the testimony by bringing out the witness' reason for remembering the events or by corroboration of the events. If, however, you are unable to predict the prosecutor's tactics, you should elicit this information yourself on direct examination.

The alibi witness should be able to give a specific reason for remembering the particular date involved. If the reason for his recollection of the date is a special event, such as a birthday or anniversary, make sure the witness has some official record or certificate to corroborate the date.

The best possible alibi witness is the disinterested person who can place the defendant somewhere else at the time in question. If you can produce such a witness, have him bring in whatever records he can to support his testimony. For example, a record of the delivery will be kept by a delivery man, of the trip by a taxi driver, of a sale by a clerk, etc.

§ 157. Character witnesses

Usually the defendant's character is not an issue in a case unless he himself makes it one. You must then take care in deciding whether or not to use any character witness. Using such witnesses sometimes backfires because it may allow the prosecutor the chance to smear your client through character witnesses of his own.

However, evidence of a defendant's good character can

create a reasonable doubt of his guilt, even where there could otherwise be no such doubt.[9] Use character witnesses who are prominent persons if there is no great likelihood that their testimony will be effectively rebutted.

Use character witnesses to establish the defendant as one who would not be likely to commit the crime in question. For example, in a larceny prosecution you need to establish your client's reputation for honesty but not for chastity or sobriety.[10]

The character witness should be prepared to explain the basis of his knowledge of your client's reputation. He can use negative evidence to do this. That is, the witness can testify that he has lived in the same neighborhood (or worked alongside him, or has been his minister, etc.) as the defendant for many years and has never heard anything said against him.

During the cross examination, the prosecutor may ask a character witness if he has ever heard particular rumors or reports derogatory to the defendant's reputation. This type of cross examination is effective in attacking the witness' credibility. You should make sure that such inquiry is limited to whether or not the witness has heard such rumors or reports. He cannot be made to answer whether he knows of a particular act of misconduct by the defendant.[11]

If your character witnesses are open to any such attack, do not put them on the stand. They can only harm the defense by admitting that rumors of your client's misconduct have come to their attention.

If you decide to offer character testimony, obtain the most prominent persons possible and, within the rules of the trial court, introduce as many as you can.

9. Edgington v United States, 164 US 361, 41 L Ed 467, 17 S Ct 72; People v Trimarchi, 231 NY 263, 131 NE 910; People v Conrow, 200 NY 356, 93 NE 943.

10. Practice Aids: 29 Am Jur 2d, EVIDENCE §§ 336–351.

11. Michelson v United States, 335 US 469, 93 L Ed 168, 69 S Ct 213.

CHAPTER SIX

SELECTION AND PREPARATION OF EXPERT WITNESSES

I. HYPOTHETICAL QUESTION

J. REPORTS

A. INTRODUCTION

§ 158. In general

Defense attorneys lag far behind prosecutors in making full use of expert testimony. Personal knowledge of the effectiveness of police laboratories has oriented prosecutors toward the use of experts. Unfortunately, and to their disadvantage, defense attorneys often tend to think of expert witnesses only in connection with an insanity defense.

To do the most effective job for your client, you must seek whatever specialized assistance is available to you. Expert testimony can be of critical importance in your presentation of the defense. An expert witness can help clarify, and in some instances, determine the facts of a case.

Frequently, an expert can demonstrate that witnesses could not actually have seen something they honestly believe they observed, or that the cause of a physical happening was other than the apparent cause. He can identify, explain, and describe such occurrences as hit and run accidents, not personally observed by him.

Areas in which you can profitably have recourse to an expert witness are unlimited. The sciences are not the only field in which expert knowledge can be used to your client's advantage. Anyone commanding special or peculiar knowledge rarely possessed by the layman can qualify as an expert.

§ 159. Know when an expert can help you

Orient your thinking to the use of expert witnesses. That is, be alert for circumstances in which an expert can be of use. Consider the use of an expert by an alert counsel defending a client charged with burglary. During the course of interviewing witnesses, counsel learned that the thief had carried off a portable color television set holding it by a handle in his right hand. Questioning of the defendant revealed that he had recurrent pains in his right elbow. He declared that he never carried a heavy object in his right hand. An orthopedist called upon by counsel examined the defendant. The orthopedist determined that, due to the disability, the defendant could not possibly have carried an object as heavy as the television set. After a conference the prosecutor dropped the charges against the counsel's client.

§ 160. Use the expert whether he testifies or not

When appropriate, call experts into cases in an advisory capacity to assist in completing your factual investigation. This should be done whether or not they will ultimately be called on to testify at trial.

§ 161. Call on experts early in the case

Many experts are reluctant to testify. If, however, you believe an expert's knowledge and advice can be helpful to you, bring him into the case anyway. Do this at as early a stage as possible. Too often an expert is hindered in his work by a passage of time and the resulting destruction of evidence.

As a general rule, experts may not be subpoenaed to give their opinions. They may declare a fee and refuse to testify. Experts can, however, be compelled to testify on any pertinent facts in a case of which they have personal knowledge.

§ 162. How to select an expert witness

The selection of an expert is a problem only when you have a number of experts from which to make a selection. This is the usual case. Your choice in the selection of experts will be extensive if you use the suggested sources for locating experts.

§ 163. Consider the availability, cost, and ability

When selecting an expert, consider his stature in his field, his availability, the cost of his services, and his ability to organize ideas and express them clearly.

If you use the expert only to assist in the investigative phases of the case, your primary concerns are his ability and qualifications. If you also plan to use him as a witness, try to anticipate his probable effect on the jury, bearing in mind his demeanor, his ability to communicate, and whether or not he is likely to impress others as an honest and fair person.

If you believe you are likely to deal with a jury with parochial attitudes, try to obtain a local expert, even if he is less qualified than some one from another area. Often jurors with insular attitudes distrust the outsider who comes into their midst as an "expert."

B. FEES

§ 164. The expense factor in hiring expert witnesses; rules of the court

When hiring an expert witness, consider the expense. Examine the rules of the court in this regard. Various statutes and court rules provide for payments to cover the fees of expert witnesses in certain cases. Generally, the more serious the crime charged, the more likely provision for the payment of this expense exists. If no statute or rules cover your case, consider moving for an order to obtain payment. In the alternative, consider moving for a dismissal on the grounds that your client's constitutional rights have been impaired. The "equal protection" clause of the 14th Amendment of the Constitution is violated when only the prosecution and wealthy defendants are able to have recourse to expert witnesses.

§ 165. Payment of fees for testimony

While an expert is entitled to be reimbursed for the time he expends on a case, it is unethical to pay him to testify in a favorable manner. Since most cross-examinations of defense experts cover the amount of their fee, avoid the impression that your expert is merely a hired witness. Never offer a fee contingent upon an acquittal. Such an arrangement will completely demolish your expert's credibility.

Make it clear to the expert witness that he has been retained by your client. Do not obligate yourself personally to pay his fee. It is good practice to have your expert witnesses paid in advance. It will make the witness more relaxed and deter the prosecution from hinting at a possible contingent fee arrangement.

§ 166. Determining the amount of the fee

Medical experts should be paid on a retainer fee basis, unless they are receiving a fee fixed by the court and paid out of public funds. An expert's fee usually depends upon the amount of time he is expected to spend in preparing the case and testifying, his office expenses and materials to be used in the case, the financial sacrifice involved in his actual attendance at the trial, his customary fees if he has had experience in testifying in court, and the amount of responsibility he is expected to assume. His fee should also include an allowance for traveling time to and from court. Some experts charge by the day or by the hour regardless of whether they are doing office work or court work.

C. QUALIFICATIONS

§ 167. Background and experience are important to impress the jury

The particular problem for which expert help is needed

may ultimately be resolved by the question of whether or not the jury believes your expert witness or the prosecutor's expert witness. The jury will, in part, be persuaded by the contrast between the impressiveness of the background and experience of the particular witnesses.

Juries prefer the expert witness with the greatest formal education and practical experience. They are also impressed that a particular witness has had books and articles published in his field of expertise.

§ 168. The "professional" expert witness

Some persons derive all or most of their income from testifying as experts at trials. If possible, do not use these witnesses. A relentless prosecutor can easily destroy their credibility on cross-examination. Jurors will come to believe that such witnesses will testify to anything on behalf of anyone who is willing to pay their price.

This rule does not apply to someone whose status as an expert almost inevitably leads to court appearances, such as an examiner of questioned documents. The qualifications of such experts are generally better the more often they have appeared to testify.

If the expert you call on has had extensive experience as a witness, try to determine the general reaction of the bench and bar to him. Your client can suffer both at trial and on appeal if the expert you select suffers from a poor reputation for honesty or ability.

§ 169. Preparing yourself to deal with the expert

While preparing your defense, you must prepare both your expert witness and yourself. Familiarize yourself with the expert's area of expertise in order to determine intelligently how best to present his testimony at trial. Such familiarity will also enable you to handle the cross-examination of the prosecutor's witnesses.

Have any expert you retain on behalf of your client explain those technical matters which you find difficult. He should also be able to supply you with a good reading list in the area or with the appropriate reading materials themselves.

§ 170. Research thoroughly the background of the prosecution's experts

If you know the name of the prosecution's expert witness in advance, obtain, read, and index everything he has written on the particular subject. You can completely demolish his testimony if, on cross-examination, you can confront him with his own prior statements which actually or apparently conflict with any part of his testimony on direct or cross-examination.

D. DEVELOPING TESTIMONY

§ 171. When unsure of yourself study transcripts of relevant testimony from other trials

If you feel unsure of your ability to successfully handle some phase of expert testimony, obtain transcripts of trials with similar testimony. Read and analyze the transcripts looking for points well handled by defense counsel and points poorly handled. Devise your own strategy to avoid any pitfalls into which other defense attorneys have fallen.

§ 172. How to deal with evidentiary problems

As part of your pre-trial work, familiarize yourself with the law applicable to the evidence. Often, it will only be after a thorough researching of the law that your need for an expert witness will become apparent. Research all evidentiary problems concerning the admissibility of any expert witness' testimony. In addition, devise ways to examine an expert so the evidence you want to introduce through him is legally admissible. Since the prosecutor will probably make some objections when your expert begins to testify, have some pertinent citations ready for quick reference in order to prevent obstruction of your expert's testimony by these tactics.

§ 173. Interview the expert early in the case

Have a personal interview with your expert in order to obtain the maximum benefits from him. Avoid telephone interviews or a correspondence carried on through the mail.

Your first meeting with the expert should take place as far in advance of trial as is possible. It is neither practical nor considerate to call upon an expert shortly before a trial and expect him to be prepared to testify. He needs enough time to arrange his working schedule. Furthermore, an early interview may disclose information of which neither you nor your client were previously aware. Such information can provide your investigation with new leads and may even result in a dismissal of the charges against your client or the negotiation of a favorable plea.

§ 174. The expert should be asked to view your problem impartially

The expert's job in the initial meeting is to apply the principles of his particular field to your problem and render an impartial opinion. Do not attempt to influence an expert with suggestions. In the long run he can only be of value to you if his opinion is absolutely objective. Encourage him, however, to express any honest doubts he may harbor about the problem.

It will not be possible to elicit a preliminary opinion from all experts at your first meeting with them. Some will first have to do independent investigation before offering opinions; others will have to interview your client. Some experts will have to analyze the available physical evidence.

Obtain full biographical information from the expert at the first meeting. Fully explain your tentative theory of defense and what you hope to prove through him. Ask the expert for his opinion about how best to present your available evidence to aid the defense. Expert witnesses with previous experience in testifying at criminal trials can often provide useful trial hints. They are often also capable of pointing out the weaknesses or foibles of the potential prosecution expert witnesses which you may be able to use profitably at trial.

In familiarizing the scientific or technical expert with the background of the case, do not concern him with the background of the individual. His concerns are only physical facts and items of evidence.

The information you provide must give him a basis for evaluating the physical facts and for reconstructing the crime. Eyewitness accounts are generally worthless for these purposes and may tend to prejudice him. Occasionally, however, facts which can be established by eye witnesses aid in interpretation. Exclude irrelevant accounts from your recitation of the facts to the expert.

§ 175. Familiarize yourself with technical language

During your first meeting with the witness, begin to familiarize yourself with the technical language of his field so you can conduct proper direct and cross-examination. The expert can also suggest how to phrase technical terms to make them understandable to the jury.

§ 176. Determine the expert's suitability as a possible witness

It is also important to determine at the outset whether or not the expert is qualified to be a witness in the particular case. In order to establish his qualifications, subject the expert to extensive questioning on his special knowledge. Have him submit in advance a written resume of his educational background and experience.

§ 177. Study the expert's background thoroughly

Inquire about any teaching position, school connection, or position with a government agency that the expert may have had. Find out about any books, articles, special research papers, or other literature he has written which qualify him to speak as an authority on the particular subject at issue. In addition, note the expert's affiliations with particular organizations, societies, hospitals, institutions, and similar bodies.

§ 178. Prepare a questionnaire on qualifications

Prepare a questionnaire for the expert to fill out that you can put to use in qualifying him during his direct examination. Such questionnaires are simple to make up and should cover the expert's educational background, teaching, and professional experience, authorship, honors received, and his membership in professional organizations and societies.

§ 179. Utilizing the expert for investigation

Experts are often of great assistance during the investigative stages and traditionally have not been fully utilized by defense attorneys at this stage. Many investigators are more conscious of people and their statements than of the physical evidence and physical facts surrounding the event. The evidence can be damaged, lost, or contaminated. The early use of an expert can be of greatest assistance in preserving evidence.

Little purpose is served if you come to an expert long after a crime with inadequate information in the hope that he can reconstruct and interpret the happening.

§ 180. Using more than one expert

After consulting one expert you may feel you need an additional expert in the same field. In certain circumstances, for example, the information obtained by the first expert may be inadmissible because of hearsay or under some other exclusionary evidentiary rule. You must then obtain a second expert witness who is able to testify.

At other times, the expertise of the first expert may not cover the entire problem you consulted him about and you may want a second expert to supplement his testimony. You may wish to impress the jury by the number of distinguished experts who can testify on behalf of your client. This would naturally have to be within the limits of applicable court rules on the number of expert witnesses who may be called to testify to the same issue.

Expert witnesses can be sensitive to inquiry on their qualifications. Two experts can often be troublesome. It may be wise, in the event you decide that you need an additional expert, to leave his selection to your first expert. Even if you yourself decide on the identity of the second expert, consider the advisability of permitting the first expert to call to retain his services.

An approach through the first expert can often facilitate better cooperation between the experts. If you retain a second expert on your own, the first expert may feel slighted or believe you consider him inadequate. The result can color his interpretation of the evidence or may adversely affect him on the stand by making him less confident and, so, less believable.

If you decide to use two or more expert witnesses for a particular problem, or an expert witness and an expert consultant, confer with them together prior to trial. A joint conference will allow you to clear up any contradictions in their views. A joint conference will encourage the experts to offer helpful suggestions to each other about recent developments in their field which bear on the problem at hand.

§ 181. Consultation with the prosecution's experts

It may prove helpful to arrange a conference between your expert witnesses and those of the prosecution. Do so if you believe it may help limit the issues by means of a stipulation as to the existence of certain facts. Do not seek to arrange a conference unless you are reasonably certain it will be productive.

Attend any such conference yourself as a guard against inadvertent disclosure of fact or theory by your experts. Although they have extensive knowledge of a particular subject, they are not trained in the law and may not realize the legal significance of what they know and what they are stipulating to.

Unless you are using the consultation as a means of discovering the thinking of the prosecution's experts, a better way to arrive at the stipulation may be to have one of your experts prepare with you a written statement of what he thinks can be stipulated. Submit the statement to the prosecution's expert, who can review it and indicate those portions of the statement with which he agrees. This tactic can save both time and money.

E. ADMISSIBILITY OF EXPERT TESTIMONY

§ 182. In general

The opinions of expert witnesses are admitted into evidence on the theory that they are necessary to justice. Normally, the following three questions arise when a witness is called as an expert:

1. Is the subject on which he is to testify one upon which the court can receive the opinion of an expert?
2. What qualifications are necessary to enable an expert witness to testify on the subject?
3. Does the witness meet these qualifications?

The trial court answers these questions in its own discretion;[1] its discretion in this regard is rarely interfered with on appeal.

1. Jones v Tucker, 41 NH 547.

§ 183. When an expert may or may not state his conclusion

Expert testimony is generally admitted in two classes of cases:

(a) those cases in which the facts from which the jury must draw its conclusion are not common knowledge, but particularly within the knowledge of experts. In these cases, the facts may be stated by the expert, but it is improper for him to relate his conclusion;

(b) those cases in which the conclusions to be drawn, as well as the facts, depend on expert knowledge not within the range of ordinary training or intelligence. In this class of cases, the expert can testify on the facts and then give his conclusion. The jury is free to accept or reject that conclusion.[2]

As an example of the first class of cases, you may retain an artist to draw a composite sketch of the suspect from descriptions given by the witnesses. This, incidentally, is good practice if your client does not resemble the descriptions originally given. The artist may testify that the witnesses agreed that the composite picture resembled the person they saw. The artist-witness cannot, however, testify that this picture does not resemble your client. The jury is perfectly capable of reaching this conclusion without outside assistance.

In the second class of cases, a handwriting expert may examine a questioned signature and the signature of the defendant. He can relate facts on the similarities and differences in writing. He can also state his conclusion that the signatures were not made by the same hand. His conclusion is admissible because the average juror does not have the training necessary to reach a conclusion.

The fact that some people are more knowledgeable than others by virtue of their training does not enable them to state an opinion to the jury. Let us look at a case in which

2. Dougherty v Milliken, 163 NY 527, 57 NE 757.

the defense claims that the accused had suffered an epileptic attack and has no recollection of committing the crime. If the expert called on by the prosecution is a physician, it would not be proper for him to testify that certain acts of concealment after the crime indicate recollection of having committed it. He cannot state that the acts of concealment are inconsistent with the defense claim because the jury is competent to draw this conclusion. Further, the defendant is severely prejudiced by having such a conclusion come from an expert.[3]

An expert opinion can be based on records which are of the type customarily and reasonably relied upon by experts in the field. These records need not be introduced into evidence; the right of confrontation is satisfied by the presence of the expert for cross-examination.[4]

F. MANNER OF TESTIFYING

§ 184. The expert on the stand

Many of the general rules regarding preparation of lay witnesses apply to expert witnesses with equal effect. Either of the two may have nervous mannerisms or an argumentative or hostile nature. It is your job to make the expert feel comfortable and relaxed on the witness stand. See to it that he comes across to the jury as a knowledgeable, honest and impartial witness.

§ 185. Caution your expert to be calm

Caution your expert against appearing to be overconfident and arrogant. Advise him to listen to the prosecutor's cross-examination in full before he answers. When faced with expert witnesses who reach contradictory conclusions, jurors tend to believe the one who maintains his dignity

3. People v Barber, 115 NY 475, 22 NE 182; People v Higgins, 5 NY2d 607, 159 NE2d 179.

4. United States v Williams (CA5 Tex) 447 F2d 1285, cert den 405 US 954, 31 L Ed 2d 231, 92 S Ct 1168, reh den 405 US 1048, 31 L Ed 2d 591, 92 S Ct 1308.

and seems calm and unruffled. The excitable expert who insults his questioner and who openly resents any implication that he may be wrong will not usually impress jurors with his ability. Also, jurors who might have difficulty following the intricacies of testimony on a complex, technical point may view demonstrations of exasperation by a witness as a sign that the prosecutor has uncovered some flaw in his reasoning or logic.

§ 186. Using technical language

Both you and your experts must be prepared to use technical language. Familiarize yourself with the technical jargon of the particular field in order to be sure that testimony given in these terms is understood by the jurors.

During direct examination of your expert witnesses, do not allow any technical term to come into the record without an explanation. If basic language is being used, have the expert explain the technical terms involved. Jurors enjoy hearing and learning technical terms if they can fully understand their meaning.

While cross-examining the prosecution's witnesses, use your knowledge of the technical terms in the field. Your familiarity with the terms will cause the jurors to regard you as somewhat of an expert who can deal with other experts at their level. The impression created will help you when you present your final argument, once again using as many basic, non-technical terms as possible.

§ 187. The witness must know rules of evidence

The expert witness will generally understand his role in the case better than the lay witness. If, however, he lacks previous courtroom experience, he must be made to understand the rules of evidence as they relate to the manner in which he must present his testimony.

Caution the expert to confine his testimony to statements

of the facts. He should give opinions about the facts only when requested by counsel or the court.

The expert should appear to be impartial throughout his testimony. It is his function to persuade the jury of certain facts, but the responsibility for gaining an acquittal does not rest on his shoulders.

§ 188. Preparing for direct and cross-examination

Prepare for a logical and orderly examination. While you need not prepare an expert with mock direct and cross-examination as you should with key lay witnesses, you should put all key questions you intend to ask at trial to your expert witness prior to the trial. Do this in the exact form and order in which you intend to ask the questions at trial. This prevents surprise and helps prepare the witness.

Correct him if he uses such phrases as "as far as I know," "to the best of my knowledge," or "it would seem that." These phrases open the door to possible demolition of the witness on cross-examination by the prosecutor's contention that they are indications of doubt.

§ 189. Tell your expert how to react to objections

Caution your expert that the prosecutor may object to portions of his testimony. Tell him that if this happens, he must not answer until the court makes a ruling on the objection.

§ 190. Witness should not correct your pronunciation

The witness should also be cautioned against correcting your pronunciation of technical terms. (While he should do so in private meetings with you, a correction on the stand will cause the jury to suspect your competence.) The witness should, of course, feel free to correct the prosecutor's pronunciation.

G. CROSS-EXAMINATION

§ 191. Prepare expert to defend his qualifications

The witness must be prepared to have his qualifications and his premises and conclusions thoroughly challenged on cross-examination. This experience is likely to be a horrible one to an expert witness without previous courtroom experience. He will be uneasy explaining his conclusions to a skeptical lawyer who is not listening to be convinced. Such a witness needs guidance.

If your witness has been published, review his writings and discuss with him any real or seeming contradictions between the writings and his testimony. He should be prepared to explain any such contradiction.

§ 192. Inform the expert about the manner of prosecution

Learn as much as you can about the prosecutor's methods and manner of cross-examination and prepare your expert to meet them. Inform him of some of the standard tricks of cross-examination and how to meet them. For example, a prosecutor may try to discredit the answer to a hypothetical question by asking your witness which facts he could omit from the question which would still allow him to reach the same opinion. In answering this question the witness should state that he would not omit anything.

The expert should not deny that he consulted with you about the case. He can answer such questions confidently and without hedging lest the jurors infer that there is something improper about the consultations. The expert should also be made aware of the possibility that he will be asked whether he is familiar with fictitious persons or nonexistent texts.

§ 193. Expert must give responsive answers

Tell your witness that the court insists on responsive

answers. He must concentrate on the gist of the question put to him and avoid giving an impression of evasiveness by picking at words irrelevant to the point of the question. If he doubts the meaning of a question have him ask for clarification or preface his answer with the phrase, "If I understand you correctly. . . ."

Caution the witness that objections will be taken if he is unresponsive. He must "stick to the question" and avoid lecturing. Interruptions and requests to have his answers stricken from the record will only serve to confuse him and will interrupt the continuity of his testimony.

§ 194. Caution expert not to distort information

The witness' duty to be responsive does not impose an obligation to give distorted information. If he cannot give a categorical answer, he should state so. He has the right to say that a "yes" or a "no" answer would be misleading. If the prosecution allows him to give only a partial or truncated answer, be alert to the necessity for fuller explanation on a redirect examination.

§ 195. Inform expert of all the facts

Inform your expert of all of the facts in the case before trial. Let him decide which are relevant and which are not. Do not let your witness be confronted on cross-examination with a new fact of which you neglected to inform him because you thought it unimportant.

Don't place your witness in the uncomfortable position of having to render a spur of the moment opinion on its importance.

Inform your expert about any dispute between your version of the facts and that of the prosecutor. The prosecutor is bound to ask your expert during cross-examination whether his opinion would be different if one or another of the underlying facts were altered. Your witness should be prepared to answer.

H. MEDICAL EXPERTS

§ 196. Why the medical witness may be reluctant to testify

Medical experts sometimes hesitate to testify in court. The courtroom setting often seems repugnant to them. They expect to be respectfully heard when their opinions are sought by colleagues or patients. They do not usually take orders from anyone. At trial everything is changed and they are not permitted to question witnesses to ascertain facts of medical importance. They are denied the right to express their opinions freely and in their own way, even though they are sworn to tell the truth.

In court, experts are told when to speak and when to stop talking. They may be required to give an opinion on a hypothetical statement of facts which they believe gives only a distorted picture of the case and they are not permitted to amend it. Rather than having their views received with respect and deference, they are likely on cross-examination to have them ridiculed, misstated, and twisted into absurdities. Their intelligence and professional competence will in all likelihood be questioned, and even their integrity may be impugned.

§ 197. Convince medical experts that their testimony is crucial

Convince physicians that their fears of court are overplayed and that justice requires their presence at trial. It is generally easier to convince an expert physician to testify at a criminal trial than it is to get him to testify in a civil case, such as malpractice, during which you may be attempting to establish the negligence of another physician. Hopefully, as medical schools continue to stress courses in forensic medicine the dimensions of this problem will shrink.

§ 198. Use of models and charts

Do not expect juries to be able to visualize those parts of

the anatomy involved in the expert's testimony. When you offer anatomical testimony as a part of the defense, confer with your experts about possibly using models and charts to demonstrate the body's organic system and to highlight the areas which are the subject of testimony.[5]

In a homicide prosecution, you should not use charts to illustrate the anatomy of the deceased as they may only serve to sicken the jury. However, you may use them if the purpose is to illustrate that the prosecution is mistaken in its attribution of the cause of death.

In introducing charts and models, ask the witness whether he could better communicate his knowledge other than with words. The witness can truthfully say, "I can show it to the jury as I show it to my students at medical school to explain the parts affected. I have brought here some of these parts, not of dead people, but models, which will clearly indicate what I mean."

§ 199. Preparation of medical witness for trial

The medical witness should be informed (as is the case in most jurisdictions) that he will not be able to use medical books or articles during the direct examination. Warn him not to quote from a book or article or to directly quote a book as authority for his opinion. Direct quotes can be very damaging to him on cross-examination if the prosecutor can find an inconsistency in the text on that point.

Tell your witness to answer forthrightly if he is being compensated for his appearance and to reveal the exact amount of compensation if the prosecutor inquires.[6] Eva-

5. **Practice Aids:** Foundation for admission of skeletal model. 7 Am Jur Proof of Facts 601, 614, Maps, Diagrams, and Models.

6. Expert Witness Fees. 43 Criminal LJ pp 777–783.

Expert Testimony and Compensation for Expert Witness. Forensic Sciences J vol 2 no 1 p 73.

Expert Witnesses Fees—Protection for Indigent Party. 48 Northwestern ULR pp 106–112.

Cost of Expert in Civil Litigation. 2 Syracuse LR pp 324–329.

Agreements as to Fees or Compensation of Expert Witnesses. Jones on Evidence § 879.

Practice Aids: Compensation for

sive replies such as "I guess so," "I believe so," or "that depends on how long you keep me here" will only invite further questions as to how much the compensation will increase if he testifies for an hour more or fifteen minutes more. His reply should reflect his realization that he is being reimbursed for the time he has spent away from patients and consultations. The jury may well believe that the compensation was little enough for his time and trouble.

Your medical expert should be prepared to sustain his findings against attacks based upon seemingly contradictory findings of other experts and opinions reported in medical literature. He must be able to reasonably explain the difference between the body of facts upon which his findings are based and those facts which cause other experts to arrive at contradictory conclusions.

When your preparation of the expert is concluded, it should be impossible for you to ask your expert witness a question on direct examination to which you do not already know his answer.

If your expert witness is to testify on cause of death or injury, make clear to him the differences between legal cause (reasonable certainty) and the pure, fixed criteria which amount to medical cause.[7]

§ 200. Caution witness not to show bias

Caution your medical expert not to show any bias during the cross-examination. He should be prepared to testify truthfully on the number of times he has appeared as an expert medical witness, and should completely repudiate any implication that his fee in the case is dependent upon an acquittal.

expert witnesses, see Am Jur, Witnesses (1st ed §§ 880 et seq.).

7. **Annotations:** Necessity, in homicide prosecution, of expert medical testimony to show cause of death. 31 ALR2d 693.

Admissibility of opinion evidence as to cause of death, disease or injury. 136 ALR 965 at page 967, 66 ALR2d 1082, at page 1087.

§ 201. Witness should never disparage other medical opinion

Your expert should never disparage the opinion given by another doctor. While he should be prepared to disagree with another medical witness, he should never condemn another medical expert. This tends to arouse jury sympathy toward the other doctor. Even if he believes that the prosecution's expert is a fraud, he himself should not become involved in showing the fraud. Let him merely advise you how to expose the fraud, leaving you the actual task of exposure.

I. HYPOTHETICAL QUESTION

§ 202. The hypothetical question may be useful

The hypothetical question is used to place before a jury the opinion of an expert who does not have personal knowledge of the facts on which his opinion is based. While some jurisdictions require a hypothetical question, others permit experts to state their opinions and reasons without prior specification of the data on which they are based, leaving that for cross-examination. Those jurisdictions not requiring the use of a hypothetical question usually permit one to be asked if counsel so desires.

The use of a hypothetical question may be desirable even if you are not required to use it. It will permit you to state the underlying hypotheses to the jury before the prosecution does.

The hypothetical question can be based on any theory reasonably deduced from the evidence. It must, however, select and present the facts fairly and may not assume facts not already proven.[8]

In answering the hypothetical question, the expert must

8. **Practice Aids:** Hypothetical questions to expert with no personal knowledge of facts. 6 Am Jur Proof of Facts 159, 165, Hypothetical Questions.

accept as true every fact contained in the question. The jury, however, can be instructed to disregard the witness' answer if the evidence does not establish the truth of all the facts stipulated in the question.

If you decide to use a hypothetical question, you must present the facts to the jury in a logical pattern. The question should include all the essential facts in the case and yet not be long and confusing.

If you want to use a hypothetical question at trial, familiarize your expert with its mode and function. He must understand the premise underlying the use of the hypothetical question and understand that the evidence mentioned in the question is assumed to be true.

Caution your expert not to question or interrupt you during trial while you ask the hypothetical question. He should not ask, for example, for information about matters already included in the question. He should not ask whether a particular test has been performed or what the results of the test were. Nor should he raise questions concerning the presence or absence of specific signs, symptoms, or other indications of a condition.

Interruptions of this kind will dilute the effectiveness of the hypothetical question. A witness' emphasis on certain matters which are already in evidence but separated by him from the question can cause the jury to view the question with suspicion. They may even doubt its entire validity. Further, the singling out of various matters makes them choice targets for cross-examination.

These problems can be avoided if you obtain expert help in the preparation of the question. In framing the question, try to avoid probable objections by the prosecutor. Objections will have the effect of confusing the jury on the exact nature of the question.

Include conflicting evidence in the question. This allows the expert to select the evidence he finds credible and base his opinion on it. The question should seem fair and balanced. If the jury believes that the question is too defense-oriented, it will simply ignore the witness' answer. You may, however, exclude facts introduced by the prosecution if they conflict with evidence you introduced for the defense.

§ 203. Procedure when asking hypothetical question

When you ask an expert a hypothetical question, employ the following procedure:

1. introduce and qualify the witness;
2. let the witness give his factual testimony, if he has knowledge of the facts;
3. begin the question by asking the witness to assume certain facts as true [premise of the question];
4. conclude the question by first asking the witness if he has an opinion on a certain point, assuming that the given facts are true; and secondly, by asking him, after he has given an affirmative answer, to give his opinion on the point;
5. after he has stated his opinion, ask him to give his reasons for it.

While you should have prepared the hypothetical question carefully, do not read it to the witness. If you do, the jury will feel that you and your expert witness are merely reciting a prepared script. If you must use the exact wording of scientific information or of prior testimony, weave the written material into the body of the question without other prepared aids.

The question should be put in a straightforward manner without either excessive dramatic emotion or a dull monotone. The jury should be left with the feeling that the facts of the case have not been distorted and that the question fairly reflects the facts they have heard placed into evidence.

In answering the question the expert should present (and you should elicit) the logic behind the answer and those scientific facts supporting it. This detailed answer should contain the heart of your defense. It should detail the pivotal points of your defense and explain them.

Ask the witness for a certain or a reasonably certain answer. If this cannot be done, ask the witness whether in his opinion it is probable that a state of events existed. As a last resort you can ask the witness whether it is possible that the state of facts existed. Bear in mind, however, that some jurisdictions require that the answer, in order to be admissible, be couched in terms of certainty or reasonable certainty.

You increase the effectiveness of the hypothetical question if you give a copy of the question to the witness well in advance of trial and then allude to that fact at trial.

J. REPORTS

§ 204. Obtain a report from your expert before trial

Whether or not your expert testifies in answer to a hypothetical question, it is vital that the expert give you a detailed report setting forth the facts and his findings in writing prior to trial. The report should be dated and signed.

The expert's report will help you to prepare well the case for trial, and it can be of assistance at trial. Prepare copies in advance of trial for yourself, the witness, the prosecutor, and the court. Also, have an additional copy marked for identification that you can later seek to have admitted into evidence.

After the witness has identified the report, you may question him with reference to it. In a non-jury trial the court will be able to use the report to follow testimony referring to charts, equations, graphs, illustrations, etc. If trial is held before a jury, have the materials blown up for viewing by the jury.

It is unlikely that the report itself will be received as

substantive evidence in a jury trial. Its use, however, will ensure that no information elicited from the expert is omitted by error. The report will also help the expert organize his testimony. It will increase the expert's confidence because of the ready accessibility to his report, and it will impress on the jury the care with which the expert reached his conclusion.

CHAPTER SEVEN

PRE-TRIAL MOTIONS AND PROCEEDINGS

A. INTRODUCTION

§ 205. In general

As a general rule, discovery in criminal cases is much more limited than it is in civil cases. You must therefore develop the technique of viewing pretrial motions in their proper perspective. Whether or not a particular motion is ostensibly made to discover information, you must keep its discovery potential in mind.

All motions made during the course of a trial should

have the objectives of obtaining the relief requested and discovering information. Additionally, each motion must contain a sufficient record to justify the granting of the relief, so that if necessary, it can be sustained on appeal.

If you are moving for relief on several legal grounds, your motion should include them all. To simply move to dismiss the indictment is meaningless, as a denial of the motion will offer no basis for review. It is not the function of a trial judge or appellate court to review the record for you. Since appellate courts usually review motions only on the specific grounds stated, it is best to keep the grounds as general as possible. A statement such as "I move to dismiss the indictment because it fails to state a crime," will fulfil the purpose. Do not specify more than is absolutely necessary.

You should exercise care before lumping requests for various relief together in one motion. In certain jurisdictions motions for alternative relief may be denied in their totality if any ground exists for denial.

B. THE PRELIMINARY HEARING

§ 206. In general

The general purpose of a preliminary hearing is to determine whether there is sufficient evidence to hold a defendant for further proceedings.[1] As far as you are concerned, however, the preliminary hearing should play the equally important function of revealing the nature and strength of the prosecution's case against your client. At the preliminary hearing the prosecution will normally present only the minimal amount of evidence it feels is necessary to establish a prima facie case. It is your job to

1. Preliminary hearing. 4 Wharton's Criminal Law and Procedure § 1619.

Practice Aids: Nature and purpose of preliminary hearing. 21 Am Jur 2d, Criminal Law §§ 443, 444.

Annotation: Duty to advise accused as to right to assistance of counsel. 3 ALR2d 1003 at page 1032.

obtain complete disclosure of all the relevant facts from the witnesses who appear.

§ 207. Waiver

Your initial consideration with regard to a preliminary hearing is whether it should be held at all.[2] If, after commencing your investigation you find that the evidence against your client is strong and that you will probably not learn anything new at the hearing, you should consider waiving the hearing.

If, however, it appears that the prosecution's case is not too strong or that your client is unable to give you a clear account of the incident or that you are encountering difficulty in locating witnesses, a preliminary hearing is desirable and should be held.

Keep in mind that a preliminary hearing will perpetuate the testimony of witnesses. Therefore, hostile witnesses can hurt you even if they die or otherwise become unavailable.[3] Furthermore, if a witness has been severely cross-examined, he may identify himself with the prosecution and resist later interviews. On the other hand, a preliminary hearing offers you an opportunity to examine a witness before he has been carefully prepared by the prosecution. You can often make effective use of the hearing minutes for impeachment purposes at trial.

You should consider the possibility of calling friendly witnesses if the particular jurisdiction allows you to do so. This can serve to perpetuate their case and solidify their emotional link to the defense.

2. **Practice Aids:** Waiver of preliminary hearing, see 21 Am Jur 2d, Criminal Law § 446.

Annotation: Defendant's plea to indictment or information as waiver of lack of preliminary examination. 116 ALR 550.

3. **Annotations:** Use in criminal case of testimony given on preliminary examination, by witness not available at present trial. 15 ALR 495, 79 ALR 1392, 122 ALR 425, 159 ALR 1240.

Claim of privilege by a witness as justifying the use in criminal case of his testimony given on a former trial or preliminary examination. 45 ALR2d 1354.

§ 208. Conducting the hearing

At the preliminary hearing prosecution witnesses will often be more hostile to your client than they will at later stages in the proceeding. This is because they will still be emotionally involved and unable to think clearly. This offers you the opportunity to elicit inconsistent statements which may be used for impeachment purposes at trial. In attempting to get such statements you will have to resist the natural inclination of the court to shorten or limit the hearing.

Most prosecution witnesses will be anxious to testify in order to further their concepts of justice. This anxiety to reveal the entire story will often result in the divulgence of information helpful to your client. The usual rules of evidence apply at preliminary hearings. It will often be advantageous for you to allow hearsay evidence to come in without objection. You will thereby obtain more information to help you prepare for the trial. You can always object to the hearsay testimony when it is later given at trial.

If the prosecution's case is obviously weak from the outset and should be dismissed for lack of evidence, vigorously object to the introduction of all inadmissible evidence. Always object to a child testifying under oath and insist on the right to a voir dire examination on the child's competency to take the oath.

If the child's testimony is not offered under oath it will not be perpetuated. Most attorneys will ask children on the voir dire whether they are aware of the difference between lying and telling the truth. Children can usually answer such questions easily. Instead, ask the child to distinguish between a lie and a fib. This will have a disarming effect and the answer will often serve to disqualify the child from testifying under oath.

If a prosecution witness' testimony is sketchy or indefinite and you believe that you will probably try to highlight its flaws at the eventual trial, do not pinpoint its flaws at the preliminary hearing. Instead, you should ask the witness whether he has told everything he knows, everything he observed and said, and whether he desires to add anything to his testimony. Thus, any possible gaps will be closed and the witness will find it difficult to add to or change his testimony at trial.

In considering the discovery nature of the preliminary hearing you should take advantage of everything which is offered. If a prosecution witness rambles and gives unresponsive answers, do not object and move to strike his answers. Let the witness continue stumbling. This may lead to new information and reveal further sources of inquiry on cross-examination. You should, however, press your questions so that the answers you receive are responsive.

Do not cross-examine favorable witnesses harshly. Avoid the risk of having him change his testimony in a way which can hurt your client's cause. You also want to avoid having the witness develop an animosity toward you or your client. You should highlight any portions of the testimony of prosecution witnesses which are favorable to or consistent with the defense. This will prevent such witnesses from successfully changing their testimony at trial.

§ 209. Information to be obtained at the preliminary hearing—checklist

Among those items of information which you should obtain, if possible, from the witnesses at the preliminary hearing are the following:

1. The witness' name and address and whether he has ever been known by another name.
2. The general background of the witness, including his place of birth and the names and addresses of close relatives.
3. The witness' marital history, including the num-

ber of marriages, number of children, and places of marriages and divorces.

4. A complete description of what occurred at the scene of the alleged crime.

Permit the witness to narrate his own account of the occurrence before tying him down to particulars. Obtain the names and addresses of all other persons present, as well as a complete physical description of the place of the incident.

5. The full employment record of the witness.

6. Whether the witness has ever been convicted of a crime, and if so, the nature of the crime and the time and place of conviction.

7. All information obtainable concerning the witness' conversations and statements relative to the alleged crime.

Obtain the names of detectives and the assistant district attorney the witness spoke to, the substance of these conversations, and the nature and details of statements signed by the witness, as well as information as to statements of accomplices and codefendants.

8. Whether the witness has related everything that took place and everything he saw and heard concerning the alleged crime, and whether he has anything to add to what he has stated.

§ 210. Motions to be made at the close of the hearing

After the prosecution has rested at the preliminary hearing the following motions should be made:

1. Motion to dismiss vague, indefinite charge. The complaint or affidavit charging the defendant with the crime must be drawn with as much particularity as an information of indictment.[4] If the complaint is vague

4. **Practice Aid:** Sufficiency of complaint. 21 Am Jur 2d, Criminal Law § 441.

and indefinite the defendant has the right to move to dismiss it for being insufficient in law.

2. Motion to dismiss for failure of proof. This motion should be made substantially in the following manner: "I move to dismiss the charge on the ground that there has been insufficient evidence produced to establish that a crime has been committed, and insufficient evidence produced to establish satisfactory cause to believe that the defendant is guilty of such crime."

3. Motion to reduce original charge to lesser charge (e.g., reduce from felony to misdemeanor). "I move to dismiss the charge of—*[robbery]* and request that in lieu of such charge the defendant be charged with the crime of—*[simple assault].*"

C. MOTIONS ADDRESSED TO INFORMATION OR INDICTMENT

§ 211. Motions addressed to the indictment or information

Part of your job is to ensure that your clients are not convicted on defective indictments or informations. The indictment or information will often not charge any offense. At other times a vital element may be missing from the charge. You must closely examine the indictment or information to detect any defects which are present.

§ 212. Motions to quash, set aside or dismiss

A motion to quash, set aside or dismiss an indictment is based upon a deformity which must have occurred in the finding, indorsement or presentation of the indictment.[5] There are many such defects possible. For example, you may discover that someone not permitted by law to be present was in fact with the grand jury during its consider-

5. 4 Wharton's Criminal Law and Procedure pp 706–717 §§ 1853–1864; 1 Orfield, Criminal Procedure Under the Federal Rules pp 427 et seq §§ 6:61 et seq.

ation of the indictment.[6] On other occasions you may find that the evidence presented to the grand jury was illegal or insufficient[7] or that your client's constitutional rights were violated by his appearance before the grand jury as a witness.[8] Therefore, you must always investigate the availability of the motion.

A motion addressed to the indictment will be denied if there are vital unresolved questions of fact. Such questions will not be resolved on a preliminary motion.[9] However, if you can demonstrate the indisputable falsity of the evidence before the grand jury, or if the prosecutor concedes its falsity, the indictment will be dismissed.

You must be thoroughly familiar with the history of the case as a successive indictment which charges the same crime and will afford the basis for quashing all prior indictment.[10] A motion may also be addressed against the indictment if the indictment has not been brought to trial within the statutory period (usually the next successive term of court) without any fault on the part of your client.

§ 213. Demurrer

A demurrer to an indictment or information is the criminal counterpart of a civil motion for judgment on the pleadings. A demurrer raises only those objections which appear on the face of the indictment.[11] If you demur to the

6. **Annotation:** Presence in grand jury room of person other than grand juror as affecting indictment. 4 ALR2d 392.

7. Illegal, incompetent, and insufficient evidence as ground for objection to grand jury proceedings. 4 Wharton's Criminal Law and Procedure p 701 § 1852.

8. **Annotation:** Privilege against self-incrimination as to testimony before grand jury. 38 ALR2d 225 at page 295.

9. **Annotations:** Quashing indictment for lack of insufficiency of evidence before grand jury. 59 ALR 567.

Competency or sufficiency of evidence before grand jury as affecting validity of indictment or conviction in Federal Court. 100 L Ed 404.

10. **Annotation:** Pleading waiver, estoppel, and res judicata. 120 ALR 8 at page 132.

11. **Practice Aids:** Demurrer as means of raising objection to indictment or information. 41 Am Jur 2d, Indictments and Informations §§ 287–290.

indictment all of the allegations of the indictment or information as well as those facts which may reasonably be implied therefrom will be regarded as true.[12]

A demurrer can usually be interposed only before a defendant pleads to the charge. You must therefore examine the charge carefully before you permit your client to plead. If at the time your client is arraigned to plead to the charges you have not yet had time to study it, request an adjournment for that purpose. The right to demur is absolute and, hence may be interposed after the withdrawal of a plea. Similarly, you may interpose a demurrer on behalf of your client after the making of other motions but before the entry of a plea to the charge.

The specific grounds for a demurrer to the information or indictment will usually appear in a statute, and you should examine the charge with the statute in mind.[13] The common grounds of demurrer are: (1) lack of jurisdiction in the grand jury to issue the indictment; (2) improper form; (3) charging of more than one crime in the information or indictment; (4) insufficiency of the facts alleged; and (5) the inclusion of justification, excuse, or a bar to prosecution in the charge itself.

§ 214. Lack of jurisdiction in the grand jury

In order to demur on the ground that the grand jury lacked jurisdiction to indict, the lack of jurisdiction must appear on the face of the indictment itself.[14] You cannot resort to the grand jury minutes to establish the lack of jurisdiction.[15] However, if resort to such minutes will estab-

12. **Annotation:** Power of court to pass on competency, legality, or sufficiency of evidence on which indictment is based. 31 ALR 1479.

13. **Practice Aids:** Particular grounds for demurrer, see 41 Am Jur 2d, Indictments and Informations §§ 288–290.

14. **Practice Aids:** Jurisdiction of grand jury, generally, see 41 Am Jur 2d, Indictments and Informations § 14.

15. **Practice Aids:** Right of accused to minutes of grand jury, see 21 Am Jur 2d, Criminal Law § 331.

lish the lack of jurisdiction, make a motion to set aside the indictment.

If a careful reading of the charge indicates that the crime alleged took place in another jurisdiction, you may demur to the charge. Such a motion or plea would be the proper remedy.

§ 215. Improper form of charge

The indictment or information serves the function of placing the defendant on notice of the exact nature of the crime charged. As such, it must conform to certain standards. Examine the charge to make certain that it properly sets forth the name of the court which has jurisdiction, the title of the action, the names of the parties,[16] and a plain and concise statement of the acts constituting the crime.[17] In addition, the charge should be signed by the district attorney.[18]

Informations and indictments are defective when they contain too little information.[19] Verbosity, on the other hand, will not afford you a basis for attack if the indictment or information contains a statement of the acts which

16. Allegation of parties to offense. 4 Wharton's Criminal Law and Procedure, pp 610–615 §§ 1789–1792.

Annotation: Amendment of indictment or information with respect to name or capacity of person alleged to have been victim of crime as ground for continuance. 85 ALR2d 1204.

17. Naming or designing offense in charge. 4 Wharton's Criminal Law and Procedure, p 568 § 1770.

Annotations: Error in naming the offense covered by allegations of specific facts in complaint, indictment, or information. 121 ALR 1088.

Power to amend indictment. 7 ALR 1516 at page 1535, 68 ALR 931.

18. Signatures as requisites of charge. 4 Wharton's Criminal Law and Procedure pp 539, 543 §§ 1751, 1754.

Practice Aids: Signature by prosecuting attorney or deputy as requisite in charge, see 41 Am Jur 2d, Indictments and Informations §§ 58, 59.

Annotation: Power of assistant or deputy prosecuting or district attorney to file information, or to sign or prosecute it in his own name. 80 ALR2d 1067.

19. Practice Aids: Charging the offense, see 41 Am Jur 2d, Indictments and Informations §§ 66–158.

constitute the crime.[20] If the charge contains a statement as to your client's prior criminal record, you should demur to it unless the prior record affects or is an element of the crime charged.[21] In such event the failure to set forth a statement of such prior criminal record will furnish a basis for demurrer.

§ 216. Misjoinder of offenses

It is generally improper for an indictment or information to charge more than one crime. It is vital that you demur in the event of misjoinder since a failure to object to a misjoinder can result in a waiver.[22]

§ 217. Insufficiency of the facts alleged

Your failure to demur to the indictment on the ground that the facts stated do not constitute a crime will not amount to a waiver. You may interpose this objection at the trial itself even in the absence of a previous motion on this ground.

Whether to demur or to await the developments presents a tactical question. If you believe that there is no way in which the defect can be cured, you should demur to the charge. If, however, the defect is one which is easily curable you should give serious consideration to holding the motion in abeyance until the time of trial. If the indictment is dismissed at that late stage there is less of a chance that your client will be reindicted.

As a general rule, the furnishing of a bill of particulars

20. **Annotation:** Error in naming offense covered by allegations of specific facts in complaint, indictment, or information. 121 ALR 1088.

21. **Annotation:** Chronological or procedural sequence of former convictions as affecting enhancement of penalty for subsequent offense under habitual criminal statutes. 24 ALR2d 1248 at page 1278.

22. **Practice Aids:** Joinder of offenses in charge, see 41 Am Jur 2d, Indictments and Informations §§ 209–231.

Annotation: Joinder in same indictment of defendant charged singly with one offense and codefendant charged jointly with him with another offense. 82 ALR 484.

by the prosecutor will not cure a defective charge.[23] The indictment or information must stand or fall on its own merits. However, when simple or short-form indictments or informations are used, a bill of particulars may, in some jurisdictions, cure the failure to allege sufficient facts.

§ 218. Justification, excuse or bar to prosecution on the face of the charge

Carefully examine the indictment or information to determine whether justification, excuse or a bar to prosecution appears on its face. If so, a demurrer will lie.[24] These defenses must plainly appear on the face of the charge since, as noted, all the allegations of the charge are deemed true for purposes of the demurrer.

§ 219. Should you demur?

The question of whether to demur should be examined from a tactical viewpoint. If the particular objection is one which will be waived by your failure to move, you should by all means demur.[25] If, on the other hand, the objection is not waived, the demurrer will give the prosecution an earlier opportunity to correct a defective charge.[26] Your

23. **Annotation:** Right of accused to bill of particulars. 5 ALR2d 444.

24. **Annotation:** Necessity in indictment or information of alleging facts relied upon to avoid effect of lapse of limitation period. 99 ALR 153.

25. **Practice Aids:** Waiver and cure of defects in indictment or information, see 41 Am Jur 2d, INDICTMENTS AND INFORMATIONS §§ 299–303.

See also 4 Wharton's Criminal Law and Procedure, pp 742–746 §§ 1881–1882.

26. Amendment of indictment or information. 4 Wharton's Criminal Law and Procedure pp 733–745 §§ 1876–1880.

Annotations: Finding or return of indictment or information within period of limitation as stopping running of limitation against prosecution. 90 ALR 452 at page 455.

Power of court to amend indictment. 7 ALR 1516, 68 ALR 928.

Necessity of arraignment or plea after amendment of indictment or information. 58 L Ed 772.

Decisions reviewable on direct appeal by United States under provisions of Criminal Appeals Act relating to rulings on indictments. 87 L Ed 191; 2 L Ed 2d 1805.

wiser alternative may be to wait until your client is on trial and in jeopardy before making your motion.

D. DEPOSITIONS TO PERPETUATE TESTIMONY

§ 220. In general

You will sometimes find it desirable to perpetuate the testimony of certain witnesses who, for one reason or another, may be unavailable to testify at trial. While there is no general provision for pretrial examination of parties or witnesses in criminal cases as a matter of course, provisions have been made for the taking of depositions under certain circumstances.[27] These provisions are creatures of statute and practice varies widely in different jurisdictions. Accordingly, you should carefully examine the statutory provisions in the jurisdiction in which the trial will be had.

There are two basic methods of taking depositions prior to trial. These are the conditional examination and the examination on commission. In federal courts, the clerk of the court is vested with authority to take depositions.

§ 221. The conditional examination

The basis for a conditional examination is generally a reasonable belief that the person you seek to examine will not be available to testify at trial. The reasons set forth in the statute are generally sickness or infirmity,[28] imminent departure from the jurisdiction,[29] or some other good cause.

In order for a deposition taken by conditional examina-

27. **Practice Aids:** Use of depositions in criminal cases, see 23 Am Jur 2d, Depositions and Discovery § 11; see also 5 Wharton's Criminal Law and Procedure §§ 2038–2040 pp 183–186.

28. **Practice Aids:** Proof of illness of witness as ground for introduction of deposition, see 4 Am Jur Proof of Facts 433, 446, Depositions.

29. **Annotation:** Construction of statute or rule admitting in evidence deposition of witness absent or distant from place of trial. 94 ALR2d 1172.

tion to be admissible into evidence at trial, the condition which created your right to take the examination (illness, infirmity, etc.) must continue up to the time of trial.[30]

The papers in support of an application for a conditional examination must be carefully drawn. In addition to showing the basis upon which the examination is sought, you should show that the testimony involved is both material and necessary. This motion should be made before the court in which the matter is pending, on notice to the district attorney. Check the statutory procedure carefully to determine whether the application may be made before the indictment is returned or whether it is available only after indictment.

The examination will usually be held before the judge who signed the order. The prosecutor has the right to be present and to cross-examine witnesses. Most statutes permit objections to be taken at trial when the deposition is finally read into evidence in the same manner as though the witness were being examined orally in court.

If you believe that objections to your questions may be sustained at trial, rephrase the same question several times in various ways in order to counter the basis of the anticipated objection. By so doing, you will increase the chances of getting the particular answer before the jury. Follow this procedure even if the prosecutor does not object to the original question at the conditional examination.

§ 222. The examination on commission

An examination on commission is appropriate in those cases in which the witness resides out of the jurisdiction and where it is unlikely that he will be in the jurisdiction at the time of trial.[31] Hence, an examination on condition

30. Wharton's Criminal Law and Procedure § 2039 p 184.

Annotation: Sufficiency of showing of grounds for admission of deposition in criminal case. 44 ALR2d 768.

31. Annotation: Construction of statute or rule admitting in evidence deposition of witness absent or distant from place of trial. 94 ALR2d 1172.

does not partake of the conditional nature of a conditional examination.

An examination on commission may only be held with notice to the prosecution. No prosecutor can request an examination on commission without affording you the opportunity to attend and to cross-examine the witness.

Some such examinations are conducted on written interrogatories. If this method is used, the proposed questions are submitted by one side to the other for settlement and the possible inclusion of cross-interrogatories. If you make the motion your affidavits should set forth the necessity for and the materiality of proposed deposition in great detail.

Most jurisdictions limit objections to the proposed questions to the sole ground of relevancy. You should carefully check the appropriate local statute to determine the proper manner and procedure in the conduct of an examination on commission.

§ 223. Some tactical considerations

There are many different rules concerning the right of the prosecutor to take depositions.[32] Most statutes do not differentiate between the prosecutor's right to take depositions and the defense's right to take them. However, in some states an examination on commission is only available in the first instance, to the defendant. However, under such statutes, once the defense avails itself of this procedure, it may then be used by the prosecution.

Therefore you should consider carefully before availing yourself of an examination on commission. If the examination is to be taken on commission, the prosecution will be informed of the nature of the testimony sought. Further, the prosecution will now have the door open for the taking of its own out-of-state testimony. The areas from which it may draw its proof are thus enlarged.

32. **Annotation:** Constitutionality of statute permitting state to take or use in evidence depositions in criminal case. 90 ALR 377.

These possible adverse consequences require you to proceed with great care when considering the taking of testimony by deposition.

§ 224. Motion to inspect grand jury minutes

Motions to inspect grand jury minutes are usually granted only if the motion is intended to secure information which will enable you to move to set aside the indictment as the result of some infirmity in the grand jury proceedings.[33] Your motion should be framed so as to make its purpose apparent.

Your moving papers should set forth your belief as to what transpired before the grand jury, together with the basis for the requested relief. Demonstrate that the motion is being made in good faith by showing a legitimate basis for your attack on the indictment.

One of the most common grounds for a motion to inspect grand jury minutes is that the legal evidence adduced before it was insufficient to warrant an indictment. For example, most sex crimes require that the testimony of the complaining witness be corroborated. Your investigation of the case may reveal that no evidence is available. Hence, the motion would be proper and if granted should lead to a dismissal of the indictment.

Exercise care in the preparation of your affidavits. You must strike a balance between showing enough to demonstrate that there is a valid legal basis for the motion and revealing information which might be useful to the prosecutor at trial.

§ 225. Motion for psychiatric examination

Your investigation of a case may lead you to believe that the charge is a result of the complainant's imagination, that the complainant is unable to distinguish fantasy from

33. **Practice Aids:** Defendant's right to disclosure of grand jury minutes. 21 Am Jur 2d, CRIMINAL LAW § 331.

reality or that he is a habitual liar. In such instances, and in others, it may be as important to determine the complainant's psychological makeup as it is to acquire such information about your client. In such instances you should move for a psychiatric examination of the complaining witness.

There is a clearly discernible trend toward ordering such examination particularly in cases involving sex offenses. In such cases it is clear that an inquiry into a complainant's social history and mental makeup is of paramount importance in ascertaining truthfulness of her allegations. Further, young children, especially those complaining of sexual assault, are prone to exaggeration and flights of fancy.

In drafting your requests for a psychiatric examination of the complainant, set forth the basis for your belief as to its necessity. Do not hesitate in so doing to resort to extrajudicial materials. Standard reference works in the areas of psychiatry, psychology and forensic psychology can be used to demonstrate the probability that such an examination will play a useful role in getting at the truth.

§ 226. Motion for continuance

A motion for continuance or adjournment can become desirable or necessary for many reasons. Trial judges are usually lenient in granting such motions if any sort of a showing of good cause is made.[34]

34. **Annotations:** Right to continuance because counsel is in attendance at another court. 112 ALR 593.

Effect of, and remedies for, exclusion of eligible class or classes of persons from jury list in criminal cases. 52 ALR 919 at page 930.

Amendment of indictment or information with respect to name or capacity of person alleged to have been victim of crime as ground for continuance. 85 ALR2d 1204.

Continuance of criminal case because of illness or death of counsel. 66 ALR2d 267.

Withdrawal or discharge of counsel in criminal case as ground for continuance. 66 ALR2d 298.

Continuance of criminal case because of illness of accused. 66 ALR2d 232.

Do not, however, make the mistake of requesting an adjournment without first requesting the prosecutor's consent. If the prosecutor objects or you fail to allege proper grounds a denial of the motion may result and you risk prejudicing the judge against you.

There are many legitimate reasons which can necessitate such a motion. Among such grounds are your unfinished investigation of the case, your inability to locate or the temporary unavailability of a key witness, prejudicial statements by the prosecutor to newspapers and inflamed public passions surrounding the case.[35]

The granting of a continuance is within the discretion of the trial judge.[36]

Unless you have been informally advised by the court that an oral application for a continuance will be granted, such motions should be made in writing and be supported by affidavits.[37] This is especially important if you are seeking the relief because of the unavailability of a witness.[38] In such a case your affidavit should set forth your exercise of diligence in attempting to locate him, your intent to have

35. Public hostility as ground for continuance. 5 Wharton's Criminal Law and Procedure p 21 § 1926.

Annotation: Hostile sentiment or prejudice as ground for continuance of criminal trial. 39 ALR2d 1314.

Practice Aids: Popular prejudice and excitement as ground for granting continuance. 17 Am Jur 2d, CONTINUANCE § 40.

36. **Practice Aids:** Discretion of court in granting continuance, see 17 Am Jur 2d, CONTINUANCE § 3.

Also 5 Wharton's Criminal Law and Procedure p 26 § 1930.

37. **Practice Aids:** Affidavit in support of motion for continuance. 17 Am Jur 2d, CONTINUANCE § 44.

Annotations: Continuance of criminal case because of illness or death of counsel. 66 ALR2d 267 at page 273.

Withdrawal or discharge of counsel in criminal case as ground for continuance. 66 ALR2d 298 at page 303.

Continuance of criminal case because of illness of accused. 66 ALR2d 232 at page 239.

38. **Practice Aids:** Absence of witnesses or evidence as ground for continuance, see 17 Am Jur 2d, CONTINUANCE §§ 29–32.

Annotations: Right to continuance to procure witness to alibi. 41 ALR 1530.

Right of accused to continuance because of absence of witness who is fugitive from justice. 42 ALR2d 1229.

him in court on a certain day,[39] and the materiality of his testimony.[40] In passing on such a motion, the trial judge will consider the gravity of the offense charged, the character of the evidence, the number and availability of witnesses, the nature of the defense, and all other germane circumstances. You must therefore frame your contentions accordingly. If possible make the motion with notice to, and the consent of, the prosecutor. While such consent is desirable, it is not always forthcoming.

If the prosecutor denies that a missing witness would testify as set forth in your affidavit, the court will probably still grant the continuance to the date requested. However, if the prosecutor admits that the witness would testify as set forth in your affidavit, the continuance will probably be denied. In such event, insist that he also admit the truth of the testimony. The trial judge will often grant the continuance if the prosecutor refuses to concede the truth of the testimony.

If a severance seems necessary your motion should be made prior to the commencement of trial.[41] The motion should be made as early as possible to avoid any contentions by the prosecutor that you have waived your rights in this regard.[42]

§ 227. Motion for severance

Motions for severance often become necessary in cases in which defendants have been jointly indicted.[43] Recent deci-

39. **Practice Aids:** Showing of ability to procure evidence, see 17 Am Jur 2d, CONTINUANCE § 31.

See also 5 Wharton's Criminal Law and Procedure p 14 § 1921.

40. **Practice Aids:** Showing as to character of testimony, see 17 Am Jur 2d, CONTINUANCE §§ 29–33.

41. **Practice Aids:** Time of demand for severance of prosecution, see Am Jur, TRIAL (1st ed § 64).

42. **Practice Aids:** Showing of diligence, see 17 Am Jur 2d, CONTINUANCE § 32.

See also 5 Wharton's Criminal Law and Procedure p 12 § 1921.

43. **Practice Aids:** Severance in criminal cases, see Am Jur, TRIAL (1st ed § 56).

Annotations: Right to severance where codefendant has incriminated himself. 54 ALR2d 830.

Rule 21(b), Federal Rules of Crimi-

sions with regard to the use of confessions by one defendant which implicate another have virtually mandated severances in such instances. Such motions, however, are still made necessary by many other factors,[44] such as the existence of antagonistic defenses among defendants,[45] the joinder of your client with defendants who have long criminal records, the use of a codefendant as a prosecution witness, the fact that a codefendant may be brought in court as a prisoner or manacled or the joinder of a person facing one charge with a codefendant who is being tried on that and many other charges.

Motions for severance are often sparingly granted. They are addressed to the court's discretion which will usually not be reversed in the absence of a showing that the trial would probably have had a different result had the severance been granted.

On a related point you should seek an election of counts or separate trials if your client is indicted on several counts (either for different crimes or for the same crime committed in a different way or through different means) and it does not appear from the indictment that the charges involve acts of a similar nature or are connected or parts of a common scheme or plan.

Your motion for a severance should allege every applicable ground. Set forth allegations of fact rather than the conclusions you draw therefrom. A motion for a severance should be made on notice to the prosecutor, giving him the opportunity to submit opposing papers.

E. PRETRIAL DISCOVERY

§ 228. In General

Pretrial discovery is the process by which the defense,

nal Procedure, relating to transfer, on defendant's motion, of prosecution for an offense committed in two or more districts or divisions. 86 ALR2d 1343 at page 1352.

44. Practice Aids: Grounds for severance in criminal prosecution, see Am Jur, TRIAL (1st ed § 59).

See also 5 Wharton's Criminal Law and Procedure p 58 § 1946.

45. Practice Aids: Antagonistic defenses as grounds of severance, see Am Jur, TRIAL (1st ed § 60).

for the purposes of preparing its case, gains access to certain information possessed by the prosecution. The criminal law offers only limited discovery tools to the defense attorney. In fact, when rules or statutes do not provide the defense with the right to discovery, a defendant is not usually entitled to inspect the evidence the prosecution possesses.[46] There are, however, persuasive arguments you can use to convince the court to order the discovery you seek.

From the defense point of view, discovery can be extremely helpful in preparing a case. Often your client may wrongly feel that it is not in his interest to be completely honest with you. He may keep parts of the truth from you or, through ignorance, he may limit certain statements or facts germain to the case. You should zealously use all possible discovery tools at your disposal in order to avoid having such a client destroy the possibility of a well-prepared defense.

Also, most criminal defendants are not people with unlimited financial resources. Your client may not be able to pay for lengthy investigative efforts or expert help from other professionals such as doctors or chemists. The prosecution, on the other hand, has theoretically unlimited use of the services of state investigators, policemen, F.B.I., and other state law enforcement agencies. Discovery is often the only method by which you can overcome this relative disadvantage to the resources of the prosecution. Also, potential witnesses are often more willing to talk with police or prosecution representatives than with investigators for the defense. Your only means of finding out what these witnesses know may be through discovery.

Prosecutors and others unfamiliar with or unsympath-

46. People ex rel. Lemon v Supreme Court of State, 245 NY 24, 156 NE 84, 52 ALR 200; People v Gatti, 167 Misc 545, 4 NYS2d 130; State v Goldberg, 261 NC 181, 134 SE2d 334, cert den 377 US 978 12 L Ed 2d 747, 84 S Ct 1884.

Annotation: Right of accused in state courts to inspection or disclosure of evidence in possession of prosecution. 7 ALR3d 8.

etic to the relative weakness of a criminal defendant in the judicial system may argue that broad discovery practices will lead to perjury by criminal defendants rather than to honest fact finding. This argument ignores the right of a defendant to a fair trial and the principle that the primary aim of the legal process is the establishment of truth.

In moving for pretrial discovery you should urge that a denial of this right to your client is a denial of due process under the fourteenth amendment.[47]

There is no ground in Common Law for a defendant to claim a right to pretrial discovery or inspection.[48] Courts were traditionally powerless to force the prosecution to disclose any of its case. Now, however, many courts claim an inherent power to compel discovery in the interests of justice.[49]

47. Right of discovery in criminal case.

Practice Aids: 23 Am Jur 2d, Depositions and Discovery §§ 307–323.

Annotation: Right of defense counsel to compel prosecuting attorney to disclose information as to prospective jurors. 78 ALR2d 309.

In Brady v Maryland, 373 US 83, 10 L Ed 2d 215, 83 S Ct 1194, the Supreme Court held that the suppression by the prosecution of evidence favorable to an accused upon request violates due process where the evidence is material either to guilt or to punishment, irrespective of the good faith of the prosecution.

Giles v Maryland, 386 US 66, 17 L Ed 2d 737, 87 S Ct 793, conformed to 245 Md 342, 227 A2d 745.

48. Shores v United States (CA8 Ark) 174 F2d 838, 11 ALR2d 635; United States v Singer (DC NY) 19 FRD 90; State ex rel. Helm v Superior Court of Cochise County, 90 Ariz 133, 367 P2d 6; State ex rel. Mahoney v Superior Court of Maricopa County, 78 Ariz 74, 275 P2d 887; State v Dorsey, 207 La 928, 22 So 2d 273; People v Johnson, 356 Mich 619, 97 NW2d 739; State ex rel. Robertson v Steele, 117 Minn 384, 135 NW 1128; Pinana v State, 76 Nev 274, 352 P2d 824; State v Goldberg, 261 NC 181, 134 SE2d 334, cert den 377 US 978, 12 L Ed 2d 747, 84 S Ct 1884; State v Lavallee, 122 Vt 75, 163 A2d 856.

49. United States v Rich, 6 Alaska 670 (photograph of piece of glass claimed to contain defendants' fingerprints); People v Gerold, 265 Ill 448, 107 NE 165 (books seized by state from county treasurer accused of withholding funds from successor in office); Sprinkle v State, 137 Miss 731, 102 So 844 (stenographically recorded dying declaration).

Annotation: Right of accused in state courts to inspection or disclosure of evidence in possession of prosecution. 7 ALR3d 8.

Practice Aids: 5 Am Jur Trials 331, 405, Excluding Illegally Obtained Evidence (judicial discovery procedures).

§ 229. State Courts

Generally, the rule of state courts is that pretrial discovery motions are addressed to the discretion of the court. The practice as developed is that discovery should be granted if the items sought are admissible as evidence and if denial of the motion would result in a failure of justice.[50]

The affidavits in support of your motion should be drawn carefully to show that the information you seek is necessary to the preparation of the defense. Avoid giving the impression you are on a fishing expedition.

The inherent power claimed by trial courts allows them broader discretion than Federal or State rules which permit discovery in specified instances. This discretion allows trial courts to allow discovery when a denial would cause great hardship to the defense in the preparation of its case. Even in situations in which your right to discovery is not specifically recognized by rule or statute, you must press for discovery essential to the preparation of your case.

The trend in state courts seems to be toward more liberal discovery practices.[51] You should note, however, that this trend will increase discovery for the prosecution as well as the defense.[52]

§ 230. Rule 16(b) Federal Rules

Rule 16 of the Federal Rules of Criminal Procedure

50. United States ex rel. Raymond v Illinois (CA7 Ill) 455 F2d 62 (prosecution's due process responsibility to disclose evidence is not discharged by disclosure to the defendant; disclosure must be made to defense counsel) cert den 409 US 885, 34 L Ed 2d 141, 93 S Ct 103; State v Patterson, 28 Ohio St 2d 181, 57 Ohio Ops 2d 422, 277 NE2d 201, (If trial judge finds that favorable evidence relevant either to the guilt or punishment of the defendant has been withheld, he must order the disclosure of the evidence) cert den 409 US 913, 34 L Ed 2d 174, 93 S Ct 242.

51. Dennis v United States, 384 US 855, 16 L Ed 2d 973, 86 S Ct 1840.

Proposed Amendments to Rules of Criminal Procedure for the United States District Courts (Committee on Rules of Practice and Procedure of the Judicial Conference of the United States), Proposed Amendment to Rule 16, 48 FRD 587 (1970); Rezneck, "The New Federal Rules of Criminal Procedure," 54 Geo LJ 1276 (1966); American Bar Association Standards Relating to Discovery and Procedure Before Trial (1969).

52. Advisory Committee Note to Proposed Amendments, 48 FRD 595.

provides a good discovery tool. According to Rule 16(b), upon a showing of reasonableness and materiality to the defense, the court may allow the inspection, copying, or photographing of all or part of books, papers, documents, tangible objects, buildings or places in the possession, custody or control of the government. The discovery is not limited to items obtained from the defendant or taken from others by seizure or process.[53] You should seek then all material in the hands of the government which is necessary to the preparation of the defense, from whatever source obtained. You need not seek designated documents.[54] However, you must draw your motion carefully to avoid denial on the basis that it is only a "fishing expedition".[55] The breadth of your request will be considered together with the statutory requirement of reasonableness.

In using this rule, you should allege that the widest latitude be given you in order to conform with the spirit of the rule.[56]

Under 16(b) you can now apply for discovery of information which may be used as part of your defense and also apply to discover information which will be used by the

53. United States v Crisona (DC NY) 271 F Supp 150.

54. United States v Reid (DC Ill) 43 FRD 520; United States v Bel-Mar Laboratories, Inc. (DC NY) 284 F Supp 875.

55. United States v Cobb (DC NY) 271 F Supp 159; United States v Louis Carreau, Inc. (DC NY) 42 FRD 408; United States v Van Allen (DC NY) 28 FRD 329.

This inherent difficulty has been acknowledged by the Advisory Committee and is the reason behind the proposed change in favor of discovery whenever the government intends to use the property as evidence at trial, or the property was obtained from or belongs to the defendant. 48 FRD at 602; American Bar Association, Standards Relating to Discovery and Procedure Before Trial § 2.1(a)(v) and Commentary, pp 68, 69 (1969). Indeed, the Committee suggests that "materiality" is shown by the fact that the government intends to use the evidence at trial. It is further suggested that Brady v Maryland, 373 US 83, 10 L Ed 2d 215, 83 S Ct 1194, makes materiality the only required showing, abrogating the additional demonstration of "reasonableness." 48 FRD at 602. Great weight can be added to your arguments in favor of discovery by utilization of such suggestions.

56. United States v Tanner (DC Ill) 279 F Supp 457.

prosecution.[57] The rule can be used to obtain discovery of statements of hostile co-defendants who will not tell you the contents of statements they made to the government.[58] You should move for production before trial of all photographs used in any pretrial identification of the defendant.[59]

When the government has names of persons whose testimony might be helpful to the preparation of the defense, they are obligated to furnish you with those names. This obligation exists quite apart from Rule 16(b).[60]

§ 231. Rule 16(a)-Federal Rules

Under Rule 16(a), the court may order the government to permit inspection and copying or photographing of your client's grand jury testimony, any written or oral statements made by him, and the results or reports of any physical or mental examinations or scientific tests or experiments made in connection with the case. You may obtain statements made to third persons, as well as those made to agents.[61] Under 16(a) you should argue an absolute right to the materials, and unlike Rule 16(b), you need not show reasonableness or materiality to the defense in a Rule 16(a) motion.[62] There is a proposed amendment to Rule 16(a) which would make such disclosure mandatory.[63]

57. United States v Zovluck (DC NY) 274 F Supp 385.

58. United States v Aadal (DC NY) 280 F Supp 859, affd (CA2) 407 F2d 381, cert den 395 US 967, 23 L Ed 2d 754, 89 S Ct 2114.

59. United States v Cranson (CA4 Va) 453 F2d 123, cert den 406 US 909, 31 L Ed 2d 821, 92 S Ct 1607.

60. United States ex rel. Meers v Wilkins (CA2 NY) 326 F2d 135.

61. United States v Black (DC Dist Col) 282 F Supp 35; United States v Lubomski (DC Ill) 277 F Supp 713.

62. United States v Projansky (DC NY) 44 FRD 550, cited with approval in United States v Isa (CA7 Ill) 413 F2d 244, later app 452 F2d 723; United States v Aadal (DC NY) 280 F Supp 859, affd (CA2) 407 F2d 381, cert den 395 US 967, 23 L Ed 2d 754, 89 S Ct 2114.

63. Insofar as the proposed amendment relates to scientific tests and examinations, the Advisory Committee has noted that mandatory disclosure thereof seems justified because 1) it is difficult to test expert testimony at trial without advance notice and preparation; 2) it is not likely that such evidence will be distorted or mis-

§ 232. Rule 17(c)-Federal Rules

Many see Rule 17(c) of the Federal Rules of Criminal Procedure as the equivalent of a subpoena duces tecum; a subpoena which compels production of documents or objects for use as evidence. When used properly, the rule is, in effect, an aid to discovery. The rule expedites trial by providing a time and place before trial for inspection of subpoenaed materials.

Rule 17(c) permits you to subpoena documentary evidence and objects. It allows the court to direct production of documents and objects before it prior to trial for inspection by parties and attorneys. You may subpoena materials into evidence but must only show that you issued the subpoena in good faith to obtain evidence.

When objects are taken from your client or seized from third persons, your right to examine them falls under Rule 16. However, 17(c) will provide you with an opportunity to inspect items received from third persons but not taken from them by seizure or process.[64]

Draw your subpoena clearly so that it does not appear that you are out fishing for anything you can get or that you are trying to obtain blanket production of all the prosecution's evidence. A subpoena which is drawn too broadly will probably be denied.[65]

used if disclosed prior to trial; 3) to the extent that a test may be favorable to the defense, its disclosure is mandated under the rule of Brady v Maryland, 373 US 83, 10 L Ed 2d 215, 83 S Ct 1194, 48 FRD at 603.

64. United States v Cohen (DC NY) 15 FRD 269.

In United States v Greater Blouse, Skirt & Neckwear Contractors' Asso. (DC NY) 177 F Supp 213, the court rejected the argument that the practice of using Rule 17(c) as an additional means of discovery was prohibited by the decision in Bowman Dairy Co. v United States, 341 US 214, 95 L Ed 879, 71 S Ct 675, and held that if a subpoena is directed toward a good faith effort to obtain evidence, there is no reason why such evidence may not be reached under Rule 17(c), even though not obtainable under Rule 16.

65. United States v Ward (DC NY) 120 F Supp 57, stating that the decision in Bowman Dairy Co. v United States, 341 US 214, 95 L Ed 879, 71 S Ct 675, supports the granting of pretrial inspection only to the extent

§ 233 Bill of Particulars

The purpose of a bill of particulars is to supplement the indictment. It should inform the defendant of the crime charged in order to allow the preparation of the defense, to protect against surprise, and to enable him to plead double jeopardy in case of a subsequent prosecution for the same offense.

However, if an indictment fails to allege any matter of substance, it is fatally defective and cannot be cured by a bill of particulars. Objections to defects may be waived without a timely motion. So move swiftly where there is the slightest question of clarity.

Under the provisions of Rule 7(f),[66] the granting of a bill of particulars is a matter for the court's discretion. You have a right to a bill if the language of the indictment is such that you may be surprised or unprepared at trial.[67]

The application will not necessarily be defeated by the fact that you may have the materials you request.

A bill of particulars is not a discovery tool, but it can be successfully used as a discovery device if you can obtain particularization as to names, places, dates and other items of information relevant to the charge.

In drawing your request for a bill, do not attempt to

that a good faith effort is made to obtain evidence; United States v Smith (DC Ill) 209 F Supp 907; United States v Frank (DC Dist Col) 23 FRD 145; United States v Louie Gim Hall (DC NY) 18 FRD 384.

See also United States v Hanlin (DC Mo) 29 FRD 481.

66. Rule 7(f), Fed Rules of Crim Proc.

See also 1 Arfield, Criminal Practice under the Federal Rules §§ 7:129 et seq.

67. Annotations: Right of accused to bill of particulars. 5 ALR2d 444.

Criminal liability for evasion of Federal income taxes. 86 L Ed 392 at page 408, DN III and IV supplemented 97 L Ed 66.

It was held defendant was entitled to a bill of particulars specifying date and location of each of the acts charged, where indictment stated time of commission as "on or about" a specific date, and the place of commission was given only as being within a certain federal court district, United States v Davis (DC Ga) 330 F Supp 899.

show evidentiary necessity of the information sought. Even if you feel the granting of the bill would serve some evidentiary function, direct your application only to the face of the indictment.

A bill of particulars should give you the particulars of every essential element of the crime charged. If a bill furnished to you is deficient, move to compel the prosecution to furnish the particulars ordered or, in the alternative, for a dismissal of the prosecution. Many state statutes require that a bill of particulars be furnished whenever it is sought.

§ 234. —State Courts

State courts are often reluctant to exercise their inherent power to require discovery and inspection of documents in the possession of the district attorney or the police. You may have to argue vigorously that the discovery is crucial if your client is to receive a fair trial with due process. There is little decisional law in this area and you may have to rely on Federal or out-of-state authority to support your request.

There is no uniform rule regarding the defendant's right to inspect his confessions or statements. It is the general view that the defendant has no absolute right to inspect his statements,[68] but on application addressed to the court's discretion,[69] the court may direct such inspection in the interests of justice.[70] The court will grant inspection to

68. People v Garner, 57 Cal 2d 135, 18 Cal Rptr 40, 367 P2d 680, cert den 370 US 929, 8 L Ed 2d 508, 82 S Ct 1571.

69. State v Thompson, 54 Wash 2d 100, 338 P2d 319.

70. State ex rel. Polley v Superior Court of Santa Cruz County, 81 Ariz 127, 302 P2d 263; Vance v Superior Court of San Diego County, 51 Cal 2d 92, 330 P2d 773; Powell v Superior Court of Los Angeles County, 48 Cal 2d 704, 312 P2d 698; State v Haas, 188 Md 63, 51 A2d 647; State v Superior Court, 106 NH 228, 208 A2d 832, 7 ALR3d 1; State v Cicenia, 6 NJ 296, 78 A2d 568, cert den 350 US 925, 100 L Ed 809, 76 S Ct 215.

In at least one jurisdiction this so-called "rule of discretion" has been embodied in a rule of court providing that the court "may" if the interests of justice so require order the prosecutor to permit the def. to inspect and

resolve factual questions before it or if the fundamental to requirements of the court demands it.[71]

Some states follow the rule that the defendant has an absolute right to pretrial examination of his written confession.[72] In other states, courts have discretionary power to allow you inspection or copying of recordings of your client or the transcriptions of those recordings.[73] You may be allowed inspection of other statements made by your client if he is unable to remember what he said.

Some traditional hurdles to obtaining copies of confessions have been eliminated by the Supreme Court decisions regarding voluntariness of confessions[74] and the requirement that persons in custody be advised of their rights.[75] Now the prosecution must inform you before trial if he intends to use a confession or a statement made to a district attorney or a police officer.

This notice requirement will serve to inform you of inculpatory statements which the prosecution intends to offer in evidence at trial. But the requirement does not cover other statements your client may have made, such as exculpatory statements the prosecution does not intend to use. Such statements may be valuable to the defense and should be sought with discovery tools.

copy or photo. state. or conf. which he made. State v Johnson, 28 NJ 133, 145 A2d 313.

71. While the defendant is entitled to inspect and copy his written confessions, there is no law under which oral statements made by him before trial may be ordered reduced to writing and submitted to him. State v Bickham 239 La 1094, 121 So 2d 207, cert den 364 US 874 5 L Ed 2d 98, 81 S Ct 123.

72. Cash v Superior Court of County of Santa Clara, 53 Cal 2d 72, 346 P2d 407.

73. State v Yoeman, 112 Ohio St 214, 147 NE 3; Davis v State, 99 Tex Crim 517, 270 SW 1022.

Annotation: Right of accused in state courts to inspection or disclosure of evidence in possession of prosecution. 7 ALR3d 8.

74. Escobedo v Illinois, 378 US 478, 12 L Ed 2d 977, 84 S Ct 1758.

75. Miranda v Arizona, 384 US 436, 16 L Ed 2d 694, 86 S Ct 1602, 10 ALR3d 974; Johnson v New Jersey, 384 US 719, 16 L Ed 2d 882, 86 S Ct 1772, reh den 385 US 890, 17 L Ed 2d 121, 87 S Ct 12.

§ 235. Statements and Confessions of Co-defendants

Under Federal Criminal Rule 16, you have access to statements by co-defendants or co-conspirators upon a showing of reasonableness and materiality.[76] In seeking discovery under this rule, argue that access to a co-defendants' statements is necessary for you to be able to determine whether or not to move for a severance.[77] This logic is the basis for the proposed amendment to Rule 16, which would require disclosure of such statements upon motion of the defendants.[78]

If there is no severance, you are still entitled to receive notice of exclusionary hearings. You can determine the content of a co-defendants' statements or confessions by participating in a hearing held to determine their validity.

Some liberal state rules contemplate your inspection of confessions or written statements of defendants or co-defendants.[79]

The prosecution will inform co-defendant's counsel of his clients' inculpatory statements which will be used at trial. If you are co-operating with co-defendant's counsel you can get copies of these statements.

If you are not cooperating with co-defendant's counsel, and if there is no severance, you are still entitled to receive notice of the exclusionary hearing. You can determine the content of a co-defendant's statements or confession by participating in a hearing held to determine their validity.

76. United States v Fassler (DC NY) 46 FRD 43; United States v Westmoreland (DC Ind) 41 FRD 419.

77. Bruton v United States, 391 US 123, 20 L Ed 2d 476, 88 S Ct 1620, later app (CA8 Mo) 416 F2d 310, cert den 397 US 1014, 25 L Ed 2d 428, 90 S Ct 1248.

Rule 14, Fed Rules of Crim Proc.

78. Proposed Amendments and Commentary thereto, 48 FRD at 588, 601.

But see United States v Edwards (DC NY) 42 FRD 605.

79. State v Minor, 54 Del 385, 177 A2d 215.

Annotation: Right of accused in state courts to inspection of disclosure of evidence in possession of prosecution. 7 ALR3d 8.

§ 236. Discovery of Witnesses Statements

Trial courts generally deny the defense discovery statements by prospective prosecution witnesses. However, the court does have broad discretion to relax this general rule.[80]

The Jencks Act[81] provides that statements or reports in the possession of the United States made by a prospective government witness to a government agent cannot be subpoenaed, discovered or inspected until the witness testifies on direct examination in a federal prosecution.[82] The Jencks Act does not provide you with a discovery device[83] but it does make such statements available to you for impeachment purposes at trial.[84] Pretrial motions for dis-

80. State v Reynolds, 41 NJ 163, 195 A2d 449, 1 ALR3d 1438, cert den 377 US 1000, 12 L Ed 2d 1050, 84 S Ct 1930, cert den 377 US 1000, 12 L Ed 2d 1050, 84 S Ct 1934, reh den 379 US 873, 13 L Ed 2d 801, 85 S Ct 22, reh den 379 US 893, 13 L Ed 2d 81, 85 S Ct 23.

81. 18 USCS § 3500.

This statute was enacted as the result of the decision in Jencks v United States, 353 US 657, 1 L Ed 2d 1103, 77 S Ct 1007, wherein it was held that the defense in a federal prosecution was entitled to obtain for impeachment purposes documents containing statements which had been made to government agents by government witnesses, where a sufficient foundation was established by the witnesses that their reports were of the events and activities related in their testimony, and that these statements were therefore to be turned over to the defense at the time of cross-examination if their contents related to the subject matter of the witness's direct testimony, and if a demand had been made for specific statements which had been written by the witnesses or if orally made as recorded by government agents.

82. Peek v United States (CA9 Wash) 321 F2d 934, 5 ALR3d 802, cert den 376 US 954, 11 L Ed 2d 973, 84 S Ct 973.

Practice Aids: The validity and construction of the Jencks Act is discussed generally in 29 Am Jur 2d, Evidence § 845.

83. Bullock v United States (CA6 Tenn) 265 F2d 683, cert den 360 US 909, 3 L Ed 2d 1260, 79 S Ct 1294; McAden v State, 155 Fla 523, 21 So 2d 33, cert den 326 US 723, 90 L Ed 429, 66 S Ct 28; State v Johnson, 28 NJ 133, 145 A2d 313; State ex rel. Byrne v Circuit Court for Dane County, 16 Wis 2d 197, 114 NW2d 114 (apparently involving statement of alleged victim of statutory rape).

A tape recording of the actual voices of the briber and the bribee, made when the alleged bribe money was being paid, was not a recital of a past occurrence by a prospective witness and was not within the general purview of 18 USCS § 3500. United States v Sopher (CA7 Ill) 362 F2d 523, cert den 385 US 928, 17 L Ed 2d 210, 87 S Ct 286.

84. Campbell v United States, 365 US 85, 5 L Ed 2d 428, 81 S Ct 421;

covery and inspection of these statements will be denied.[85]

§ 237. Government Reports and Memoranda-Federal

Reports, notes, and memoranda made by government agents during the course of their investigation have been held exempt from the discovery provisions of Rule 16.[86] The Federal Rules of Criminal Procedure,[87] however, provides for a pretrial conference upon motion by either party or upon the court's own motion. The conference can consider ". . . Such matters as will promote a fair and expeditious trial." The practice in many federal jurisdictions is that Jencks material be delivered to the defense during the pretrial conference. Other jurisdictions have their own version of the pretrial conference.[88] You should take advantage of discovery opportunities therein.[89]

Palermo v United States, 360 US 343, 3 L Ed 2d 1287, 79 S Ct 1217, reh den 361 US 855, 4 L Ed 2d 94, 80 S Ct 41; People v Rosario, 9 NY2d 286, 213 NYS2d 448, 173 NE2d 881, 7 ALR3d 174, cert den 368 US 866, 7 L Ed 2d 64, 82 S Ct 117.

Annotations: Right of defendant in criminal case to inspection of statement of prosecution's witness for purposes of cross-examination or impeachment. 7 ALR3d 181.

Validity and construction of Jencks Act (18 USC § 3500) as to defendant's right to production of statements and reports of government witnesses. 5 L Ed 2d 1014 at page 1021.

85. United States v Rothman (DC Pa) 179 F Supp 935 (holding that statute does not apply to pretrial motion for discovery and inspection of memoranda in government's files); United States v Woodner (DC NY) 24 FRD 33 (holding that defendant was not entitled to witness' statements upon pretrial motion for discovery and inspection).

Annotation: Validity and construction of Jencks Act (18 USC § 3500) as defendant's right to production of statements and reports of government witnesses. 5 L Ed 2d 1014 at page 1022.

86. Goldman v United States, 316 US 129, 86 L Ed 1322, 62 S Ct 993 (decided before adoption of Federal Criminal Rule 16), reh den 317 US 703, 87 L Ed 562, 63 S Ct 22, ovrld on other grounds Katz v United States, 389 US 347, 19 L Ed 2d 576, 88 S Ct 507; Mahone v State, 120 Ga App 234, 170 SE2d 48; State v Superior Court, 106 NH 228, 208 A2d 832, 7 ALR3d 1.

87. Rule 17.1, Fed Rules of Crim Proc.

88. Rezneck, The New Federal Rules of Criminal Procedure, 54 Geo LJ 1276, 1294–1299 (1966); Ogden v United States (CA9 Cal) 303 F2d 724, later app 323 F2d 818, cert den 376 US 973, 12 L Ed 2d 86, 84 S Ct 1137.

89. State ex rel. Rasmussen v Tahash, 272 Minn 539, 141 NW2d 3; State ex rel. Goodchild v Burke, 27 Wis 2d 244, 133 NW2d 753, cert den

§ 238. Investigative Reports

Government investigators often have in their files some summary of a statement taken from an accused, and they will hide such summaries behind the "work product" exemption. You could seek an in-camera inspection in which the court could excise any material which is in fact privileged.[90]

In many states courts,[91] defendants are entitled to a pretrial production of notes by investigating officers and of reports made from those notes.[92] It has been held that defendants are entitled to examine original notes made by police officers of oral statements given by prosecution witnesses, and to inspect and copy written statements made from such notes.[93]

§ 239. Discovery of Documents Obtained from Defendant and from Others

The defense has a right to discovery of items taken from your client and to documents belonging to him but taken by the prosecution from others. Your right to this discovery has been upheld under Federal Rule 16 and in the state courts. You should set forth in your motion the necessity of knowing the exact nature of the items taken.

In most states, in the absence of a statute conferring

384 US 1017, 16 L Ed 2d 1039, 86 S Ct 1941.

90. United v Curry (DC Ill) 278 F Supp 508, wherein an agent summarized defendant's prior incriminatory statements taken at the office of the Federal Bureau of Narcotics. On motion by defendant for pretrial discovery thereof, the court ordered an in-camera inspection to allow production of the requested material.

But see United States v Acarino (DC NY) 270 F Supp 526, holding a Bureau of Narcotics summarization report within the Rule 16(b) work products exception.

91. United States v Rothman (DC Pa) 179 F Supp 935 (investigating officers' "work product" consisting of notes or memoranda of interview with defendants); United States v Black (DC Ind) 6 FRD 270 (FBI report).

92. People v Renchie, 201 Cal App 2d 1, 19 Cal Rptr 734, holding that trial court erred in ruling that demand for such production came too late when made at trial.

93. Funk v Superior Court of County of Los Angeles, 52 Cal 2d 423, 340 P2d 593.

such a right, the defendant cannot inspect records and writings of prospective prosecution witnesses.[94] In some federal prosecutions, records and papers obtained through seizure or process by the government from persons other than the defendant are sometimes subject to discovery and inspection under Rule 16.

§ 240. The Prosecution's Right to Discovery

When you move for discovery, remember that you may be allowing the prosecution a similar right to discovery of materials you want to remain secret. Many jurisdictions do allow the prosecution some discovery. You should familiarize yourself with the relevant statute or rule in the jurisdiction.[95] A denial of the prosecution's right to discovery is usually rooted in a desire to safeguard the defendant's right against self-incrimination.[96] You should use this ground where necessary. A failure to do so may constitute a waiver of the objection.[97]

Federal Rules grant limited discovery.[98] The court may condition the defendant's discovery under 16(a)(2) (physical and mental examinations, scientific tests or experiments) or 16(b) (inspection of books, papers, documents, tangible objects or places). The condition may be that the defendant produce for the government similar items the defense intends to produce at trial and which are in his possession control of custody. The rule excludes "reports, memoranda, or other internal defense documents", but allows for production of scientific or medical reports.

Of course, if you do not seek discovery under Rule 16, this relief is not available to the government. Also, discov-

94. State v Lavallee, 122 Vt 75, 163 A2d 856.

95. See, generally, 76 Harv L Rev 838 (1963).

96. United States v Brown (DC NY) 179 F Supp 893; United States v Duncan (DC NY) 22 FRD 295.

97. McCain v Superior Court of County of Los Angeles, 184 Cal App 2d 813, 7 Cal Rptr 841, later app People v McCain, 199 Cal App 2d 756, 18 Cal Rptr 912.

98. Rule 16(c), Fed Rules of Crim Proc.

ery will be denied to the government if your Rule 16 motion is either limited to a request for statements made by your client or he seeks wider relief but the motion is denied or granted only as to such statements.

State statutes allowing the prosecution degrees of discovery have been upheld.[99] There seems to be a trend toward increasing discovery for the prosecution.[1]

§ 241. The Motion

Move for discovery only after you are thoroughly familiar with the charges, any search and seizure warrants and any other papers which are available to you. Your investigation should have given precise data concerning the discoverable items in the prosecutor's hands as well as how and when he obtained them. You will then be prepared to make an educated guess about the contents of his file. You must use your imagination to compile a list of objects he probably has. You must prepare a motion which is as specific as possible with regard to the items sought.

Send a certified or registered letter to the prosecutor requesting permission to inspect the items you seek in the motion. If your request is denied, attach a copy of your letter and the reply, if any, to your motion papers.

If you cannot reasonably guess the exact nature of the

99. People v Shulenberg, 279 App Div 1115, 112 NYS2d 374; State v Thayer, 124 Ohio St 1, 176 NE 656, 75 ALR 48; Jones v Superior Court of Nevada County, 58 Cal 2d 56, 22 Cal Rptr 879, 372 P2d 919, 96 ALR2d 1213.

See, generally, Comment, The Self-Incrimination Privilege; Barrier to Criminal Discovery, 51 Cal L Rev 135 (1963).

1. United States v Fratello (DC NY) 44 FRD 444.

See Advisory Committee Notes to Proposed Amendments, 48 FRD at 606–610. It is interesting to note that the Proposed Amendments contain one proposal which would grant the prosecution a right to discovery independent of any request by the defendant. Because many feel that such a grant would be constitutionally invalid, an alternate proposal was included which leaves the government's discovery rights conditional upon a defense request.

See also American Bar Association, Standards Relating to Discovery and Procedure Before Trial § 3.2 (1969).

objects in the prosecutor's possession, your best approach is to make a general application look as specific as possible and then argue that the interests of justice requires disclosure.

CHAPTER EIGHT

THE EXCLUSIONARY HEARING

E. THE HEARING

F. CONFESSIONS

A. PREPARATION

§ 242. Interviewing Client

A motion to exclude or suppress illegally obtained evidence is often crucial to the defense. The ensuing indentiary hearing gives you a unique opportunity to gain an advantage over the prosecution if you are well prepared.

Skillful interviewing of your client is necessary to prepare you for the hearing and for possible suppression motions. Your client may not understand the legal implications of events which occurred during his arrest. He cannot be expected to understand the essential facts in regard to search or wiretapping. He will probably not know if a valid warrant was employed or if probable cause existed.

Your client must be guided carefully through all the events surrounding his arrest, including any statements made to him by police officers during his arrest, detention, and interrogation. Impress your client with the importance of his revealing all the facts to you and that you cannot adequately defend him without these facts.

Before interviewing your client, familiarize yourself with the substantive law governing exclusion or suppression of evidence. Without this knowledge you cannot be sure you are asking all the proper questions. You may easily pass over important clues.

The client interview will acquaint you with the facts of the case and also give you the names and addresses of all potential witnesses whom you must, of course, interview.

During this interview, you should obtain a personal history of the defendant which will acquaint you with his age, educational background, intellectual capacity, health, emotional state, awareness of events, personality disorders, maturity, stability, suggestibility, criminal record, behavior patterns, literacy, and language comprehension.

§ 243. Questions for the Client

Generally, we suggest a program of questioning of the client similar to the following, with appropriate modification for the specific facts of your case.

1. When and where were you arrested?
2. What were you doing when arrested?
3. Were there any witnesses to the arrest? (If so, direct your questions to determine the witnesses' specific identity or to elicit sufficient information to be able to locate them.)
4. Had the police been watching you before the arrest? (If yes, to your knowledge for how long? Trace, in detail, what you did during the period the police were observing you?)
5. What did you do during the 24 hours before the arrest? (To be asked if the client has no knowledge of police observation.)
6. How many police officers were present at your arrest and who were they?
7. Exactly what did the police say to you at the time of arrest? (For example, the police may have made statements to your client including facts that they could only have learned through an illegal search and seizure or wiretap: they may also have elicited damag-

ing information before giving your client the requisite warnings.)

8. Exactly what did you say to the police at that time?

9. Were you given a warrant or other document by the police? If so, where is it?

10. Did the police mention a search or arrest warrant? If so, what did they say about it?

11. Did the police conduct a search?

§ 244. Specific Questions on Arrest in an Automobile

Once you have a general picture of the circumstances surrounding the arrest, your questioning should be specific. If the arrest took place in or near an automobile, ask the following:

1. Do you own the car? If not, who does?

2. Were you inside the car? Was the car moving or stopped? Where was it located?

If the client was inside the car:

3. Were you the driver?

4. Were there other passengers?

5. Were you carrying a driver's license?

6. What did you do when you first saw the police? Did you try to elude them? If you were driving did you drive faster or change direction?

7. Did you try to throw anything away or hide anything within police view?

8. List all items in the car.

9. Which of these items could be seen by someone from outside the car?

10. Were the police in uniform?

11. Did they ask to see your driver's license?

12. Did the police give any reason for stopping you? If so, what was it? Was it for a traffic offense or other violation?

13. Was a search made of the car? Were you present?

14. Did you protest the search?

15. Where did the police search? (Specify the various parts of the car that might prove to be hiding places, such as trunk, glove compartment, under seats, in seat cushions, and under fenders.)

16. Was anything found? If so, what and where?

17. Did the police take anything into their possession? If so, did they give you a receipt? Where is the receipt?

18. Were you shown a search or arrest warrant? Was one mentioned? When?

19. Were you told that you could refuse to allow the search?

20. Were you placed under arrest before the search was conducted?

21. Were you searched? If so, when in relation to the search of the car?

22. What was found as a result of the frisk?

23. Were force, threats, or weapons used to accomplish the search?

24. Did you make any admissions at this time? If so, to whom?

25. Were the admissions made after the police showed you the results of their search?

If the client was not in the car when arrested ask him:

26. How far from the car were you?

27. Did you leave the car before or after you saw the police?

28. Did you lead the police to the car?

29. If so, did you do so as a result of force or threats or of having received promises?

30. Was the car forced open by the police or did they use keys (same for glove compartment or any locked

portion of the car)? If keys were used, were they obtained by the use of force, threats, or promises?

§ 245. Specific Questions on Arrest in a Building

If the arrest took place in a building, the following questions are recommended:

1. Describe the building and the specific section you were in.
2. Whose premises were these?
3. What were you doing there?
4. How did the police gain entrance?
5. Did someone give them consent to enter? If so, who?
6. What was his connection with you and/or the premises?
7. Did you hear the person converse with the police?
8. What was the substance of their conversation?
9. Did the police identify themselves before entering?
10. Did they announce their purpose before entering?
11. Did the police break into the building or room?
12. Was a pass key used?
13. When they entered, were the police in uniform?
14. Where were you?
15. Did they show their weapons?
16. Was a search made?
17. Who was present?
18. Was a search warrant shown or discussed? If so, under what circumstances? Give details.
19. Were you told you could refuse to allow a search?
20. Describe the search. What building, rooms, closets, furniture, etc., were searched?
21. Were you under arrest or under restraint during the search?
22. Relate anything said by anyone, including yourself, during the search.

23. Did you have any illegal object in your possession or one which could connect you to a crime on the premises when the search was made?

24. How long did the search last?

25. Describe in detail the items taken from the premises by police. Was a receipt issued? Where is it?

26. Did you or anyone else admit ownership of any of these items?

27. Did you make any admissions to anyone during the search? If so, to whom?

28. Were the admissions made after the police showed you the results of their search?

29. Were you taken away by the police when they left the premises?

30. What did they say to you and you to them? Did they employ force, threats, or promises?

§ 246. Specific Questions Concerning Search of Person

If your client tells you he was searched at the time of arrest, use the following line of questions:

1. Describe the clothing you wore.
2. Where were the police and what were they doing when you first saw them?
3. Where had you come from and where were you going? Describe the route.
4. Was this route one you usually follow?
5. Who was with you?
6. Do you know of any other person who was stopped or arrested around the time you were?
7. Did an unusual incident occur immediately before the arrest? If so, were you in any way involved? Describe.
8. Describe the area in detail.
9. Describe the visibility.
10. Did you try to conceal or dispose of anything while in the view of the police?

11. What was said and done by the police before they began the search?

12. Were you carrying anything on your person that was illegal to possess or which tied you to a crime?

13. If so, was it visible or were there bulges, etc., suggesting the items were concealed on your person?

14. Did you attempt to flee or escape or did you make any sudden moves when approached by the police?

15. If sudden moves were made, describe the moves in detail. Did these moves appear threatening?

16. When the police approached, what exactly did they say to you?

17. Were you ever told you were under arrest?

18. If so, were you given a reason for the arrest?

19. Did you resist the arrest in any way? If so, describe.

20. Were force or threats used by the police?

21. When and where were you searched?

22. Detail the search of your person.

23. Did you consent to the search?

24. Describe anything you gave the police without being searched. Why did you do so?

25. Describe any resistance by you, against the search?

26. What was searched besides your person?

27. Describe everything taken from you by the police.

28. How long had you possessed these items and how long had you been carrying them before the search?

29. Where and from whom had you obtained these items?

30. Describe the acts and statements of the police. Was there anything said which would indicate that the police knew of these items and where they might be found before the search?

31. Who knew you had these items? Has he a criminal record or has he been recently in police custody?

32. Describe any statements you made concerning the items taken from you. Who was present who could have heard the statements?

33. After you were taken into custody, were you searched again? What was found?

34. What did you give the jailer?

Information obtained from the above questions should form a solid foundation for a thorough investigation into the propriety of the seizure of evidence. If you suspect that the police obtained statements from the client improperly, additional paths must be explored during the interview.

§ 247. Other Questions Concerning Arrest

In addition to questions directly relating to the preceding guideline, the following questions should be asked:

1. Describe the circumstances of the police approach.
2. Were you detained? What time was it?
3. Relate in detail everything said to you by the police.
4. Did the police tell you (a) that you were not required to answer their questions, (b) that if you desired to remain silent they could not question you, (c) that if you said anything it could be used against you in court, (d) and that you had a right to a lawyer?
5. Were you told that if you wanted a lawyer and could not afford one, a lawyer would be appointed for you?
6. Were you told that even if you answered some questions you could refuse to answer further questions?
7. When were these warnings given you and by whom?
8. Relate as precisely as possible the exact substance of these warnings.

9. What was your response? Did you understand what the police were telling you?

10. What steps did the police take to ensure that you understood the warnings?

11. Had you been asked any questions before the warnings were given? What answers did you give?

12. Did you make any statements before the warnings were given?

13. Describe the attitude of the police when giving the warnings. Was their attitude consistent with the substance of the warnings?

14. Were you given papers to sign? Was one a waiver? Did you sign? Describe papers in detail.

15. If you signed, did you understand what you were signing?

16. Were any threats, force, or promises used to make you sign?

17. Did the police attempt to find out whether you understood what you were signing?

18. Were you taken to a police station? How long after the arrest? More than one station? Describe.

19. Were you informed of the charges against you?

20. When and where were you booked? How do you know what time it was?

21. Did you actually see the police enter information in the ledger?

22. When were you taken before a judge or magistrate?

23. Were you photographed or fingerprinted? When?

24. Were you placed in a lineup? When? How many others in the lineup? Describe.

25. Were you taken to the scene of the crime?

26. Were you told you could make a phone call? Did you ask permission to do so? Response?

27. Did you ask for a lawyer? When did you ask? Whom did you ask? How often? Response?

28. Who conducted the interrogation?

29. Describe the room in which it was held.

30. While it was going on were you accused of the crime with which you are charged? Were you given an indication of the severity of the sentence?

31. Did the questions inform you of the facts of the crime?

32. Were the questions directed at revealing information or did you feel the police were trying to implicate you? Give details.

33. Describe your physical condition at the time of the arrest. At the time of questioning.

34. Do you take narcotics, barbiturates, alcohol? Are you an addict? When had you last taken drugs or alcohol?

35. When had you slept last?

36. Did you ask for anything or question the reason for your detention? Response?

37. Describe the way the police treated you. Were they courteous, did they feed you, allow you to sleep, provide toilet facilities, place you in solitary confinement?

38. Were you ill during your detention? When? Did you receive treatment?

39. Were you frightened? Why?

40. Did the police use force or threats? Describe. When? Who was present?

41. If force was used, were you examined by a prison doctor? Did you describe your injuries to him? Were they visible? What was his response and treatment?

42. Describe the injuries in detail.

43. Describe any threats of harm to others made by the police.

44. How long before you made a statement? Did force or threats occur?

45. Were you promised any benefits in return for your cooperation, such as

(a) leniency?

(b) immunity from prosecution?

(c) charge of a lesser offense or fewer charges?
(d) low bail?
(e) a "break" in the sentence?
(f) the refraining from prosecution of wife or close family or friends?
(g) permission to communicate with family or lawyer?
(h) better treatment?

46. Were you told the police possessed physical evidence linking you with the crime? Give details.

47. Were you told that any of your associates implicated you in the crime?

48. Were you shown written statements purporting to implicate you?

49. Did a purported witness to the offense identify you in your presence?

50. Describe any scientific evidence such as fingerprints or ballistics you were told would be used against you.

51. Relate any explanations of law made to you.

52. Were you told how long you might be held before you would be charged with a crime? If so, give substance.

53. Were you told you could not be charged or released on bail until you made a statement?

54. Did you submit to any tests? Describe the circumstances surrounding your submission and detail the procedures used in testing.

55. Were you given the results? When?

56. Did you submit to a lie detector test? Who was present? Describe the operator, the room, the equipment, the interview or interviews and the questions asked.

57. What was your physical and emotional state at that time?

58. Were you advised of the questions to be asked in advance?

59. Were there any interruptions? Noise?

60. What was the manner of your questioner?

61. How long did the procedure last?

62. What were you told about the accuracy of the lie detector?

63. What were you told of its use in courts?

64. Were you told that the machine showed you were lying?

65. Did you make any statements, written or oral, that might incriminate you? How many? Describe.

66. For how long a period had you refused to make the statement or statements you finally made?

67. Why did you admit what you had previously denied?

68. Who was present?

69. Did you sign a written statement? If more than one page did you sign each page? Who wrote or typed it? Are there copies?

70. Did you read it before signing? Did you make any corrections? If so, were these corrections initialed?

71. Was a rewording made of an oral statement? Did you receive a transcript? Did you sign it?

72. What, if anything, was omitted or added to the statements?

§ 248. Questions Concerning Counsel for the Defendant

When you suspect that your client has been deprived of counsel ask the following:

1. How long after your arrest did you see a lawyer? What was his name?

2. Were you able to consult privately with him? Where? How long? How often?

3. Were you questioned by the police before your first consultation?

4. Were you informed of your right to counsel or were you told you did not need a lawyer?

5. Describe your first appearance in court.

6. Did you have a lawyer then?

7. Did you enter a plea? What?

8. Were you told to plead even though counsel was not present?

9. Were you advised of your right to counsel by the court in a way you understood?

10. After this first appearance, did anyone from the police department or district attorney's office discuss the charges with you in absence of counsel? Describe.

11. Have you made appearances in court, since the first appearance, without counsel? Describe.

§ 249. Information to be Obtained in a Juvenile Case

If your client is a juvenile, the answers to the following questions should also be obtained:

1. Under what circumstance was your client interrogated? Who was present?

2. Were his parents present when he was interrogated?

3. Did he discuss the charges against him with anyone?

4. Was he able to consult with an adult before he was interrogated?

5. Did he have a hearing in the juvenile court?

If the hearing was conducted:

6. Was he represented by counsel?

7. Did he testify or enter a plea?

8. Did the judge question him?

9. If the judge did question him, was he advised of his rights?

10. Was there a Court reporter present? (If so, you should try to obtain a transcript.)

§ 250. Other Witnesses

The client interview should provide you with enough leads to help you locate persons who may have witnessed the police conducting a search or arresting your client.

Friends, neighbors, family could all be helpful. Anyone actually present during the arrest, search, or interrogation can provide valuable information and be an important part of your actual presentation at the hearing.

If you plan to have your client testify at the hearing, corroborative testimony can be crucially helpful to you, since without it the word of the accused may possibly have to stand alone against that of police officers.

The exclusionary hearing may give the prosecution a chance to examine your client before trial. For that reason, you may not want your client to testify. Also, the defendant may be a bad witness. He may be inarticulate or unconvincing. Or he may make damaging admissions on collateral matters that may be used to impeach him at trial. If other witnesses are available, you have more flexibility in deciding whether or not to have your client testify.

Locate your witnesses and interview them quickly, since time erases memories. Approach people considerately in order to overcome their natural inclination to stay aloof.

You must not lead witnesses during these interviews or you run the risk that subsequent testimony may seem contrived. A simple narrative by the witness will not be enough, however. Certain operative facts must be established to suppress or exclude evidence. A question and answer approach is best to direct the witness in these areas.

Record, transcribe, or reduce to statement form the interviews you have with the witness. An independent third party should be present to protect against a charge of suborning the testimony. When a witness tells you he cannot help you because he did not observe the occurrence or cannot remember details, take a statement from him to that effect. He can be readily impeached if he later testifies for the prosecution on those matters he says he cannot address.

§ 251. Hostile Witnesses

Hostile witnesses such as the crime victim, the arresting officer, the interrogator, or the informer may not be cooperative. Don't press these witnesses to sign statements or have their words transcribed or they may refuse to tell you anything. Obtaining some information from these witnesses is better than having nothing at all as a result of overzealous efforts to obtain records for impeachment purposes.

Approach hostile witnesses, other than law enforcement officers, in a friendly and open manner. Explain who you are and your obligations to your client and to the court. Notetaking should be handled carefully. Always ask permission before you begin. If the interview goes well, ask the witness to sign a statement. Confine questioning to matters of the arrest, search, confession, detention, identification, etc. The witness may unwittingly reveal information crucial to the issue of excluding and suppressing evidence.

Always interview policemen in court or in the stationhouse; never bother them at home. Approach an officer by telling him you need his information to decide whether or not to recommend that your client accept a plea. An informal talk with a law enforcement official is often a valuable discovery tool.

§ 252. Records

Court files will reveal whether or not an arrest or search warrant was issued. These are matters on record and you can obtain copies easily. Inspect the affidavits submitted to procure the warrant and the return which would note the article seized. Jail records will give you a list of articles taken from prisoners when admitted. You can inspect police records to find out time and place of arrest, the arresting officers, the booking and the period of detention prior to charge.

B. OTHER HELPFUL SOURCES OF INFORMATION

§ 253. The Preliminary Hearing

Discovery procedures which may be available in the particular jurisdiction can be helpful in preparing a motion to exclude evidence. The first of these tools which you should exploit is the preliminary hearing. Your aim in this hearing will be full disclosure. You must question skillfully in order to obtain as much information as possible from prosecution witnesses concerning confessions, searches, etc. Prosecution witnesses are often unprepared at the stage of the hearing, and without having to forewarn the prosecution you have an opportunity to examine these witnesses on evidence that might be subject to exclusion.

When a witness testifies on an identification, make sure you elicit all relevant information about the circumstances of the identification. Find out if photographs, a lineup, or a show up were used; the details of the lineup procedure; who was present; police comments; and how long it took to identify the accused.

Question witnesses thoroughly about their own background and possible criminal record. This information, even if not complete, will give you a good base for further investigation.

The prosecution will try to keep the scope of the hearing very narrow. They will want to reveal as little as possible to the defense. You must try to open up the proceeding. Seek information details for use in obtaining witnesses for further investigation.

Obtain from the witness any possible statements made by the defendant. Ask the witness to give you all written and oral statements he made concerning the case. The court may try to restrict your questioning to the issue of probable cause, so be careful in your exploration for discovery purposes. You may have to argue that illegally obtained evidence may not be used to show probable cause and that without the disputed evidence there is insufficient reason for holding the accused.

§ 254. Inspection of Clients' Statements

Do not miss any opportunity to inspect statements made by your client. The client may be confused and remember the statement imprecisely. You may need it for determining if a motion to suppress is warranted.

§ 255. Bill of Particulars and Grand Jury Minutes

The bill of particulars does not necessarily contain detailed evidence. It is possible, however, to request and obtain further particulars about the evidence seized. A successful motion to inspect Grand Jury minutes will make available to you testimony which might be used for impeachment purposes during the hearing on the motion to suppress.

§ 256. Inspection of Physical Evidence

A motion to inspect physical evidence may help in determining if the nature of the evidence is consistent with police version of the procedures used to search for it. Inspection of the evidence will give you a basis for determining whether or not to move to suppress.

C. HEARING AS A DISCOVERY TOOL

§ 257. In General

The hearing on a motion to suppress is an excellent discovery tool. An exclusionary hearing has a broader scope than a preliminary hearing and it will allow you to discover facts beyond the issues of the hearing. The hearing on the motion should give you enough facts to decide whether to proceed to trial or to recommend negotiating a sentence reduction in return for a plea of guilty.

D. THE MOTION

§ 258. When to Move

The proper time to move varies according to statute. Usually, a motion to suppress must be made with reasonable diligence after the commencement of the criminal action, or at least ten days before trial, or any time before trial.

The motion is returnable in the court in which the criminal action is pending unless another court is designated by statute. The motion should be in writing upon reasonable notice to the prosecution.

§ 259. Moving Papers

Your moving papers should request the suppression of all evidence illegally seized. Couch the motion in terms which are broad enough to include both the evidence seized and the secondary evidence obtained as a result of the first illegal action. Seek to suppress statements made at the time of an illegal search or arrest.

Do not be overly specific in alleging facts. You do not want to indicate the theory of your motion in advance of the hearing. And you want to maintain sufficient flexibility to conform to the proof as it becomes apparent.

§ 260. Advantages of a Motion

A suppression motion, whether it is successful or not, can often be most helpful. If your motion is successful, you may end prosecution of the case or you may limit the use of damaging evidence or testimony. Even if your motion is unsuccessful, it can still serve as an important discovery device helping you prepare your trial defense. Even unsuccessful motions can establish a record of testimony of prosecution witnesses and give you an opportunity to cross-examine them. The record can be used for impeachment purposes at trial and aid you in your further investigation in the case.

§ 261. Disadvantages of a Motion; withdrawal of motion

However, there are situations in which you should not move to suppress. When the evidence in question is exculpatory, you will not want it excluded. Another example of evidence you may not want excluded would be a statement which may be exculpatory on its face but which is not consistent with the true facts of the case. Also, evidence seized by the police may prove to be exculpatory if you have it subjected to possible scientific tests which would destroy the link between the evidence and your client.

If a witness failed to identify your client in a lineup or has denied recognizing your client in a lineup, you may want to wait until trial to bring this out.

In some cases, evidence can be less damaging with a trial jury than testimony about the evidence. A weapon used by your client may be innocuous looking and may limit the harm caused at trial by testimony about the use of the weapon.

You may decide to withdraw your motion if you are considering interposing a guilty plea to a lesser charge or if there is evidence of guilt beyond the evidence in question. To pursue the motion needlessly will then simply antagonize the court and the prosecutor.

§ 262. Finality of Motion

If a suppression hearing is unsuccessful, you can raise the issue again at trial if you have discovered new or additional evidence not previously available. If a motion to suppress is denied, you generally cannot appeal the denial until the conclusion of the trial. Most statutes permit a defendant to interpose a guilty plea upon the denial of a motion and thereafter to appeal the decision on the motion. Some statutes permit the prosecution to appeal the grant of a motion on a stipulation that the prosecution cannot prevail at trial without the use of evidence in question. An affirmance on appeal will automatically result in a dismissal of the indictment.

E. THE HEARING

§ 263. Generally

The hearing is held before a judge without a jury. The court is not bound by traditional rules of evidence and it may accept hearsay testimony, since the issue is often whether or not probable cause existed for the issuance of a warrant or for an arrest. The minutes of the hearing are part of the record on appeal, so make certain all testimony is recorded.

§ 264. Order of Proof

The question of who proceeds first at a hearing is not entirely settled. You should contend that the party with the ultimate burden of proof (usually the prosecution) should proceed first. You may, however, have to put a witness on the stand to establish a prima facie showing of illegality.

If the law clearly states that all you need do is present prima facie showing of illegality with the burden then resting on the prosecution to prove the validity of the seizure, put in only a perfunctory case and rely upon cross-examination.

Object to the use of any statement given by your client, in accordance with the procedural requirements of the particular jurisdiction. This may require a formal motion on papers or simply an objection at trial to be followed by a formal hearing.

§ 265. Burden of Proof

The prosecution sustains the burden of proof to establish a consent search,[1] as well as the legality of a warrantless

1. Bumper v North Carolina, 391 US 543, 20 L Ed 2d 797, 88 S Ct 1788.

search, arrest, or frisk. There is conflicting authority about the burden of proof regarding search or arrest made pursuant to a warrant. Some authority supports the position that such searches are presumptively valid.

It is unclear who sustains the burden of proof regarding the voluntariness of the confession. The Miranda Case places a "heavy burden" on the prosecution to establish a claimed waiver of rights, and it would seem to follow that the prosecution sustains the burden of proving a confession voluntary.[2] However, some jurisdictions require merely that voluntariness be shown by a preponderance of the evidence. In any event, it is clear that the ultimate burden of proof rests with the prosecution.

The prosecution must produce conclusive evidence at the hearing. It cannot rely solely upon attacks on the defendant's credibility. If the prosecution fails to call police officers who witnessed the event, it is subject to the presumption that such testimony would not rebut the defendants' claims.[3]

§ 266. Presence of Jury

Since the Supreme Court ruling on Jackson v Denno,[4] the judge must make a proper determination of the voluntariness of the confession, on the facts as well as the law, before permitting the jury to hear the confession. The court disallowed use of the so-called New York rule. Under the New York rule, unless the judge ruled the confession involuntary as a matter of law without resolving disputed matters of fact, he instructed the jury to disregard the statement if it found the statement to be involuntary.

Various jurisdictions are now allowed to make their own

2. People v Carbonaro, 21 NY2d 271, 287 NYS2d 385, 234 NE2d 433, remittitur amd 21 NY2d 971, 290 NYS2d 199, 237 NE2d 360; State v Davis, 73 Wash 2d 271, 438 P2d 185.

3. Sims v Georgia, 389 US 404, 19 L Ed 2d 634, 88 S Ct 523, conformed to 224 Ga 36, 159 SE2d 290; State v Davis, 73 Wash 2d 271, 438 P2d 185.

4. 378 US 368, 12 L Ed 2d 908, 84 S Ct 1774, 1 ALR3d 1205.

rule, as long as they comply with the procedural requirements of Jackson v Denno. A hearing can be held in the presence of the jury if there is no objection.[5] Before a jury can hear a confession, the judge must hold it involuntary in an unequivocal recorded statement. "The trial judge may not leave the issue for the jury when the evidence is in conflict."[6]

The federal statutes[7] and most state statutes require that a hearing on the voluntariness of a confession be held out of the presence of a jury.

§ 267. Identification Evidence

The procedure to follow at hearings to determine whether or not tainted identification can be validated upon some independent basis is not established by the Wade[8] and Gilbert[9] Cases. Some states require the state to inform the defendant of any identification testimony to be offered at trial and so have attempted to make these hearings part of the general pretrial suppression procedure.[10] This gives the defense the opportunity to move to exclude improper identification testimony.

The question of identification will usually be dealt with at trial. Any hearing should be held out of the presence of the jury.[11]

5. Pinto v Pierce, 389 US 31, 19 L Ed 2d 31, 88 S Ct 192, reh den 389 US 997, 19 L Ed 2d 499, 88 S Ct 462.

6. Sims v Georgia, 385 US 538, 17 L Ed 2d 593, 87 S Ct 639, conformed to 223 Ga 126, 153 SE2d 567, later app 223 Ga 465, 156 SE2d 65, revd on other grounds 389 US 404, 19 L Ed 2d 634, 88 S Ct 523, conformed to 224 Ga 36, 159 SE2d 290.

7. 18 USCS § 3201(a).

8. United States v Wade, 388 US 218, 18 L Ed 2d 1149, 87 S Ct 1926.

9. Gilbert v California, 388 US 263, 18 L Ed 1178, 87 S Ct 1951.

10. Louisiana Code of Criminal Procedure, Art 703; New York Criminal Procedure Law § 710.30.

11. Caples v United States (CA5 Miss) 391 F2d 1018.

People v Ballot, 20 NY2d 600, 286 NYS2d 1, 233 NE2d 103; Thompson v State (Okla Crim) 438 P2d 287.

For sample examinations during hearing, see Bailey and Rothblatt, Handling Narcotic and Drug Cases, § 217.

F. CONFESSIONS

§ 268. In general

As enunciated in the Miranda Case,[12] in a hearing to exclude statements or confessions, the prosecution must come forward with proof which demonstrates the voluntariness of the statement or a waiver of the rights. The failure to give warnings as set forth in the Miranda Case renders invalid any warning given during custodial interrogation. The prosecution will usually contend that the warnings were given or that the admissions were made by the defendant before he was taken into custody. You should seek to establish through cross-examination or direct evidence that the warnings, if given, were administered perfunctorily or under circumstances which render it unlikely that any waiver was freely or intelligently given.

Even after a waiver is given by the defendant, the interrogation must halt when the defendant indicates his unwillingness to continue or when he requests an attorney. Furthermore, the combination of circumstances may indicate the defendant's will was overborne.

Among the characteristics of your client which may have some bearing on your approach are the issue of voluntariness and the age and intelligence of the defendant, whether or not he was under the influence of narcotics,[13] and the length of interrogation. Also, consider the number of officers involved, the manner in which your client was treated, the representations and promises made to him,[14] and any physical mistreatment involved.[15]

12. 384 US 436, 16 L Ed 2d 694, 86 S Ct 1602, 10 ALR3d 974.

13. **Annotation:** Use or administration of drugs or narcotics as affecting admissibility of confession. 69 ALR2d 384.

14. **Annotation:** Whose promises are contemplated by rule excluding confession made under promise of immunity. 7 ALR 419.

Practice Aids: Use of promises to induce confession, see 29 Am Jur 2d, Evidence §§ 558 et seq.

15. **Annotation:** Right of accused to show body to jury as evidence of violence by police in securing confession. 72 ALR2d 1322.

Only resort to implications of actual physical mistreatment if you stand a fair chance of proving it. Most judges react unfavorably to such claims and few such claims are sustained as bases for the exclusion of admissions.

Check appropriate records to help you establish the defendant's mental condition and his ability to communicate. Public school records, medical and hospital reports, police records, social and welfare workers' reports, military records should all be helpful.

Police records should corroborate your clients' statements about when he was booked, when he was removed from his cell for questioning, the identity of the questioning officers, and the lengths of the periods of interrogation. If a claim of physical abuse is made you can check with the jail physician to determine whether he examined your client.

CHAPTER NINE

WEIGHT AND SUFFICIENCY OF EVIDENCE

A. INTRODUCTION

§ 269. In general; reasonable doubt

A person who is accused of a crime has the right to insist that before he can be found guilty, there must be some substantial evidence upon every fact essential to the establishment of his guilt, and that this evidence shall be weighed by the jury and found sufficient to prove the case.[1]

1. Hoke v United States, 227 US 308, 57 L Ed 523, 33 S Ct 281; Ex parte Grimmett, 228 Ala 1, 152 So 263; McAllister v State, 17 Ala 434;

While the law prescribes certain rules for the guidance of juries in dealing with the evidence in criminal cases, it accords the juries full and unrestricted power to determine those facts which are proved and those which are not

Fendley v State, 182 Ark 1185, 30 SW2d 852; People v Townsend, 11 Ill 2d 30, 141 NE2d 729, 69 ALR2d 371, cert den 355 US 850, 2 L Ed 2d 60, 78 S Ct 76, reh den 355 US 886, 2 L Ed 2d 116, 78 S Ct 152, cert den 358 US 887, 3 L Ed 2d 115, 79 S Ct 128; Christie v Commonwealth, 193 Ky 799, 237 SW 660, 24 ALR 599; State v Gleim, 17 Mont 17, 41 P 998; Pumphrey v State, 84 Neb 636, 122 NW 19; State v Douglas, 26 Nev 196, 65 P 802; State v Lapointe, 81 NH 227, 123 A 692, 31 ALR 1212; Andrews v State, 64 Tex Crim 2, 141 SW 220.

Annotations: Admissibility of prosecution evidence on issue of consent, that rape victim was a virgin, absent defense attack on her chastity. 35 ALR3d 1452.

Withholding or suppression of evidence by prosecution in criminal case as vitiating conviction. 34 ALR3d 16.

Attorney-client privilege as affected by its assertion as to communications, or transmission of evidence, relating to crime already committed. 16 ALR3d 1029.

Admissibility, in criminal prosecution, of evidence secured by mechanical or electronic eavesdropping device. 97 ALR2d 1283.

Homicide: presumption of deliberation or premeditation from the circumstances attending the killing. 96 ALR2d 1435.

Corroboration of accomplice witness by objective evidence authenticated by same accomplice. 96 ALR2d 1185.

Kidnapping by fraud or false pretenses. 95 ALR2d 450 at page 455.

Criminal offense predicated upon indecent exposure. 94 ALR2d 1353 at pages 1358–1384.

Sufficiency of proof, through one witness, to support conviction under 18 USC § 1001, relating to falsifying or concealing fact, or making false or fraudulent statements, etc., in matter within jurisdiction of any United States department or agency. 93 ALR2d 730.

Maintainability of burglary charge, where entry into building is made with consent. 93 ALR2d 531.

Criminal offense of bomb hoax or making false report as to planting of explosive. 93 ALR2d 304.

Admissibility and probative effect of testimony that motor vehicle was going "fast" or the like. 92 ALR2d 1391 at pages 1393 and 1399.

Criminal liability in connection with application for, or receipt of, public relief or welfare payments. 92 ALR2d 421 at pages 429–443.

Criminal conspiracies as to gambling. 91 ALR2d 1148 at page 1178.

Criminal conspiracies as to gambling. 91 ALR2d 1148 at page 1180.

Evidence of acquisition or possession of money, source of which is not traced, as admissible against defendant in criminal case. 91 ALR2d 1046.

What constitutes "possession" of a narcotic drug proscribed by § 2 of the Uniform Narcotic Drug Act. 91 ALR2d 810.

Rape by fraud or impersonation. 91 ALR2d 591 at page 592.

Validity, construction, and effect of statutes establishing shoplifting as

proved,[2] where there is substantial evidence tending to establish them,[3] or the evidence pro and con is conflicting and is not controlled by some fact or circumstance so clearly and fully established as to leave no possible doubt of its existence and of such character as makes it necessar-

specific criminal offense. 90 ALR2d 811.

Perjury or false swearing as contempt. 89 ALR2d 1258 at pages 1322 and 1323.

Homicide: identification of victim as person named in indictment or information. 86 ALR2d 722.

Federal Constitution as affecting admissibility of evidence obtained by illegal search and seizure. 84 ALR2d 959.

Propriety, in trial of criminal case, of use of skeleton or model of human body or part. 83 ALR2d 1097.

What constitutes offense of official oppression. 83 ALR2d 1007 at pages 1009 and 1014.

Sufficiency of showing that burglary was committed at night. 82 ALR2d 643.

Validity, construction, and effect of statutes or regulations making possession of fish or game, or of specified hunting or fishing equipment, prima facie evidence of violation. 81 ALR2d 1093 at pages 1095 and 1103.

Burglary or breaking and entering of motor vehicle. 79 ALR2d 286 at page 289.

Prosecutrix in incest case as accomplice or victim. 74 ALR2d 705.

What constitutes offense of unlawful assembly. 71 ALR2d 875.

Intercourse accomplished under pretext of medical treatment as rape. 70 ALR2d 824.

Failure or refusal to obey police officer's order to move on, on street, as disorderly conduct. 65 ALR2d 1152 at page 1154.

Criminal responsibility of one other than driver at time of accident, under "hit-and-run" statute. 62 ALR2d 1130 at page 1131.

Validity and construction of Federal Bank Robbery Act. 59 ALR2d 946 at page 986.

Admissibility and permissible use, in malicious prosecution action, of documentary evidence showing that prior criminal proceedings against instant plaintiff were terminated in his favor. 57 ALR2d 1086.

Validity and construction of National Motor Vehicle Theft Act. 56 ALR2d 1309 at page 1365.

Entrapment to commit offense against laws regulating sales of liquor. 55 ALR2d 1322 at page 1379.

What amounts as to reckless driving of motor vehicle within statute making such a criminal offense. 52 ALR2d 1337.

Construction and effect of statutes making solicitation to commit crime a substantive offense. 51 ALR2d 953 at pages 958 and 959.

Modern status of rule governing admissibility of evidence obtained by unlawful search and seizure. 50 ALR2d 531.

Bribery in athletic contests. 49 ALR2d 1234 at page 1236.

Forgery: use of fictitious or assumed name. 49 ALR2d 852 at page 876.

Inference or presumption that owner of motor vehicle was its driver at time of traffic, driving, or parking offense. 49 ALR2d 456.

Pregnancy as element of abortion or homicide based thereon. 46 ALR2d 1393 at page 1404.

ily rule the whole case.[4] The matter of venue may always be proved by direct evidence,[5] but it may also be proved by circumstantial evidence or it may be inferred from the circumstances.[6] The proof is sufficient if, from all the facts and circumstances introduced in evidence, venue may be fairly and reasonably inferred.[7]

In a criminal prosecution, in order to warrant a conviction, the prosecution is required, in the discharge of the burden imposed upon it of establishing by proof all the essential elements of the crime with which the defendant is charged in the indictment, to establish beyond a reasonable

Sufficiency of showing of grounds for admission of deposition in criminal case. 44 ALR2d 768.

Determination, in extradition proceedings, or on habeas corpus in such proceedings, whether a crime is charged. 40 ALR2d 1151 at page 1158.

Mode of establishing that information obtained by illegal wire tapping has or has not led to evidence introduced by prosecution. 28 ALR2d 1055.

Requiring submission to physical examination or test as violation of constitutional rights. 25 ALR2d 1407.

Inference of malice or intent to kill where killing is by blow without weapon. 22 ALR2d 854.

Admissibility, in prosecution for bribery or accepting bribe of evidence tending to show the commission of other bribery or acceptance of bribe. 20 ALR2d 1012 at page 1035.

Question as to who are accomplices, within rule requiring corroboration of their testimony, as one of law or fact. 19 ALR2d 1352 at page 1358.

2. State v Kidwell, 62 W Va 466, 59 SE 494.

3. Ex parte Grimmett, 228 Ala 1, 152 So 263; Fendley v State, 182 Ark 1185, 30 SW2d 852; State v Coomer, 105 Vt 175, 163 A 585, 94 ALR 1038; State v Kidwell, 62 W Va 466, 59 SE 494.

Annotation: Conviction of criminal offense without evidence as denial of due process of law. 80 ALR2d 1362.

4. Ex parte Grimmett, 228 Ala 1, 152 So 263; State v Coomer, 105 Vt 175, 163 A 585, 94 ALR 1038; State v Kidwell, 62 W Va 466, 59 SE 494.

5. People v Aggie, 37 Cal App 2d 110, 98 P2d 806; State v Johnson, 189 Kan 571, 370 P2d 107.

6. People v Cavanaugh, 44 Cal 2d 252, 282 P2d 53, cert den 350 US 950, 100 L Ed 828, 76 S Ct 325; People v Mayfield, 196 Cal App 2d 72, 16 Cal Rptr 261; Hancock v State, 196 Ga 351, 26 SE2d 760, 147 ALR 1042; State v Johnson, 189 Kan 571, 370 P2d 107; Nix v State, 20 Okla Crim 373, 202 P 1042, 26 ALR 1053; Smazal v State, 31 Wis 2d 360, 142 NW2d 808.

7. People v Billingsley, 59 Cal App 2d Supp 845, 139 P2d 362; State v Johnson, 189 Kan 571, 370 P2d 107; People v Hetenyi, 304 NY 80, 106 NE2d 20; Woody v State, 10 Okla Crim 322, 136 P 430.

doubt that the accused is guilty of that crime, and in the absence of such a degree of proof of the defendant's guilt, he is entitled to an acquittal.[8]

"Reasonable doubt" is a term well understood but difficult to define.[9] There is no exact test by which it can be determined with certainty whether a doubt entertained in any given case is reasonable or otherwise; what would be reasonable to one person might be otherwise to another. Hence, whatever explanations may be given to the phrase, its meaning practically must depend very largely upon the character of the mind of the person acting.[10]

In some jurisdictions "reasonable doubt" is defined by statute and some courts take the view that such a statutory definition does not exclude the giving of correct additional definitions amplifying the statutory definition.[11] Others take the position that in view of such a statute, the trial judge, in defining reasonable doubt, should merely follow the language of the statute.[12]

8. Holt v United States, 218 US 245, 54 L Ed 1021, 31 S Ct 2; Billeci v United States, 87 App DC 274, 184 F2d 394, 24 ALR2d 881; Letcher v State, 159 Ala 59, 48 So 805; State v Schweitzer, 57 Conn 532, 18 A 787; Lombardo v State (Fla) 55 So 2d 914; Mitchell v State, 22 Ga 211; State v Sullivan, 34 Idaho 68, 199 P 647, 17 ALR 902; Carlton v People, 150 Ill 181, 37 NE 244; Green v State, 204 Ind 349, 184 NE 183, 87 ALR 1251; State v Wagner, 207 Iowa 224, 222 NW 407, 61 ALR 882; Commonwealth v Polian, 288 Mass 494, 193 NE 68, 96 ALR 615; McComb City v Hill, 100 Miss 193, 56 So 346; State v Hickam, 95 Mo 322, 8 SW 252; Schultz v State, 88 Neb 613, 130 NW 105; State v Lapointe, 81 NH 227, 123 A 692, 31 ALR 1212; State v Bartlett, 43 NH 224; People v Reese, 258 NY 89, 179 NE 305, 79 ALR 1329; State v Falkner, 182 NC 793, 108 SE 756, 17 ALR 986; State v Miclau, 167 Ohio St 38, 4 Ohio Ops 2d 6, 146 NE2d 293 (statutory requirement); Columbus v Hohman (App) 75 Ohio L Abs 417, 144 NE2d 296; Blake v State, 12 Okla Crim 549, 160 P 30; State v Campbell, 95 RI 370, 187 A2d 543, 6 ALR3d 499; State v Bundy, 24 SC 439; State v Hudson, 128 W Va 655, 37 SE2d 553, 163 ALR 1265; Stecher v State, 202 Wis 25, 231 NW 168, 70 ALR 203; Hollywood v State, 19 Wyo 493, 120 P 471, reh den 19 Wyo 522, 122 P 588.

9. People v Ahrling, 279 Ill 70, 116 NE 764; Hiller v State, 116 Neb 582, 218 NW 386, 58 ALR 1322.

10. Burt v State, 72 Miss 408, 16 So 342.

11. McGoon v State, 39 Ohio App 212, 10 Ohio L Abs 175, 177 NE 238.

12. Jolly v Commonwealth, 110 Ky 190, 61 SW 49; State v Williamson, 22 Utah 248, 62 P 1022; State v Eldredge, 45 Wyo 488, 21 P2d 545.

§ 270. Circumstantial evidence

In criminal prosecutions a resort to circumstantial evidence is, in the very nature of things, a necessity. Crimes are usually committed in secret and under conditions where concealment is highly probable, and to require direct testimony would, in many cases, result in freeing criminals and would deny proper protection to society.[13]

Whether or not one aids or abets another in the commission of a crime may be determined by circumstances as well as by direct evidence.[14]

§ 271. Character evidence

The decisions have broken away from the earlier view that evidence of a defendant's previous good character has weight only in cases in which there is doubt as to his guilt. It is now generally agreed that evidence of the defendant's established reputation for good character, if it is relevant to the issue, may alone create a reasonable doubt in the minds of the jury as to the defendant's guilt, where without it the other evidence may be convincing.[15] The fact that an innocent person may sometimes be placed in a position

13. Hickory v United States, 151 US 303, 38 L Ed 170, 14 S Ct 334; Commonwealth v Webster, 59 Mass (5 Cush) 295; State v Stiwinter, 211 NC 278, 189 SE 868; State v Johnson, 11 Wis 2d 130, 104 NW2d 379.

Annotation: Conviction of perjury where one or more of elements is established solely by circumstantial evidence. 88 ALR2d 852.

14. Brown v Commonwealth, 130 Va 733, 107 SE 809, 16 ALR 1039.

15. Edington v United States, 164 US 361, 41 L Ed 467, 17 S Ct 72; White v United States, 164 US 100, 41 L Ed 365, 17 S Ct 38; Bird City Equity Mercantile Exchange v United States (CA10 Kan) 338 F2d 790; Perara v United States (CA8 Ark) 235 F 515, 10 ALR 1; Scott v State, 105 Ala 57, 16 So 925; Springfield v State, 96 Ala 81, 11 So 250; Singh v State, 35 Ariz 432, 280 P 672, 67 ALR 129; Daniels v State, 18 Del (2 Penn) 586, 48 A 196; State v Dowell, 47 Idaho 457, 276 P 39, 68 ALR 1061; Wagner v State, 107 Ind 71, 7 NE 896; State v Lindley, 51 Iowa 343, 1 NW 484; Allen v Commonwealth, 134 Ky 110, 119 SW 795; Commonwealth v Leonard, 140 Mass 473, 4 NE 96; People v Garbutt, 17 Mich 9; Latimer v State, 55 Neb 609, 76 NW 207; State v Lang, 87 NJL 508, 94 A 631, 10 ALR 4; People v Roach, 215 NY 592, 109 NE 618; People v Gilbert, 199 NY 10, 92 NE 85; Commonwealth v Harmon, 199 Pa 521, 49 A 217; State v Barth, 25 SC 175; State v Harris, 58 Utah 331, 199 P 145; State v Daley, 53 Vt

in which evidence of his previous good reputation may be the only evidence with which he can oppose a criminal charge has been assigned as a reason for the modern rule.[16]

The later rule is not to be understood as supporting the proposition that evidence of good character outweighs, as a matter of law, all other evidence or raises a reasonable doubt of the defendant's guilt irrespective of the conclusiveness of the incriminating evidence. It goes no further than to require the probability of innocence arising from proof of good character to be considered in all cases in which such evidence is admissible.[17] Ultimately, proof of character or reputation must be considered by the jury in connection with all the other testimony and not independently thereof, and the guilt or innocence of the defendant must be determined from all the testimony.[18]

§ 272. Flight of accused

The flight of a person after a crime has been committed and before his arrest is a circumstance to be considered with the other circumstances of the case in determining his guilt or innocence.[19] The probative value of such evidence is to indicate a consciousness of guilt, and such evidence is to be considered by the jury and given such weight as they

442; State v Moyer, 58 W Va 146, 52 SE 30.

16. Shropshire v State, 81 Ga 589, 8 SE 450.

17. State v McGuire, 84 Conn 470, 80 A 761; Wagner v State, 107 Ind 71, 7 NE 896; State v Northrup, 48 Iowa 583; Cupps v State, 120 Wis 504, 97 NW 210, same result reached on reh 120 Wis 532, 98 NW 546.

18. Scott v State, 105 Ala 57, 16 So 925; Springfield v State, 96 Ala 81, 11 So 250; Singh v State, 35 Ariz 432, 280 P 672, 67 ALR 129; State v McGuire, 84 Conn 470, 80 A 761; State v Dowell, 47 Idaho 457, 276 P 39, 68 ALR 1061; People v Drwal, 27 Ill 2d 184, 188 NE2d 688; Wagner v State, 107 Ind 71, 7 NE 896; State v Hodge, 252 Iowa 449, 105 NW2d 613, app dismd and cert den 368 US 402, 7 L Ed 2d 394, 82 S Ct 437; State v Crisman, 244 Iowa 590, 57 NW2d 207; State v Harris, 58 Utah 331, 199 P 145.

19. Allen v United States, 164 US 492, 41 L Ed 528, 17 S Ct 154; People v Wong Ah Ngow, 54 Cal 151; People v Stanley, 47 Cal 113 (dictum); State v Woodruff, 47 Kan 151, 27 P 842; Grand Rapids v Williams, 112 Mich 247, 70 NW 547; Thorp v State, 59 Tex Crim 517, 129 SW 607; State v Taylor, 70 Vt 1, 39 A 447.

deem proper in connection with the other pertinent and material facts and circumstances in the case.[20]

§ 273. Possession of stolen property

The courts are agreed that when proper foundation is laid, the prosecution may, as a part of its evidence tending to prove the defendant's complicity in the crime charged, show his possession of stolen property or the proceeds thereof.

The view has been taken that possession of recently stolen property raises a presumption that the possessor stole it, and that this presumption becomes conclusive unless it is overcome or refuted by the circumstance of the taking or possession or by proof reasonably satisfactory that such possession was innocently or honestly acquired, where no evidence is introduced as to the defendant's good character.[21] Other courts however, have held that the single circumstance of possession of recently stolen property is not sufficient to sustain a conviction.[22] In any event if there is a presumption of guilt from possession of stolen property, it has been said to be one of fact to be found by the jury, and not a legal one.[23]

§ 274. Admissions or concessions by defendant or his attorney

As a general proposition, an accused's admission of incriminating facts not amounting to a confession, if uncorro-

20. Alberty v United States, 162 US 499, 40 L Ed 1051, 16 S Ct 864; Hickory v United States, 160 US 408, 40 L Ed 474, 16 S Ct 327; Commonwealth v Madeiros, 255 Mass 304, 151 NE 297, 47 ALR 962; Jenkins v Commonwealth, 132 Va 692, 111 SE 101, 25 ALR 882.

21. State v Moore, 101 Mo 316, 14 SW 182.

Annotation: Thief as accomplice of one charged with receiving stolen property, or vice versa, within rule requiring corroboration or cautionary instruction. 53 ALR2d 817.

22. People v Cline, 83 Cal 374, 23 P 391; State v Duncan, 7 Wash 336, 35 P 117, ovrld on other grounds State v Gifford, 19 Wash 464, 53 P 709.

23. Gravitt v State, 114 Ga 841, 40 SE 1003; Stockman v State, 24 Tex App 387, 6 SW 298.

borated by any other evidence, is not sufficient to sustain a conviction.[24] What the rule that an uncorroborated admission does not support a conviction really means is that the admission without corroboration is not sufficient evidence of the facts admitted.

The corroboration requirement applies to mere admissions, at least where the admission is made after the fact to an official charged with investigating the possibility of wrongdoing, and the statement embraces an element vital to the prosecution's case.[25] The need for corroboration extends beyond complete and conscious admission of guilt (a strict confession) to admissions of specific facts, which have the same possibilities for error as confessions. In that respect, exculpatory statements do not differ from other admissions of incriminating facts; they too must be corroborated.[26]

It is generally held that any concession, admission, or statement by a defendant's attorney in a criminal case obviates the necessity of the introduction of evidence by the prosecution on the point. Nevertheless, the prosecution is not precluded from introducing such evidence.[27]

§ 275. Lie detectors and truth serums

It would appear, at least in the absence of stipulation,

24. United States v Calderon, 348 US 160, 99 L Ed 202, 75 S Ct 186; Warszower v United States, 312 US 342, 85 L Ed 876, 61 S Ct 603; State v Romo, 66 Ariz 174, 185 P2d 757; People v Cullen, 37 Cal 2d 614, 234 P2d 1; Adams v State, 153 Fla 68, 13 So 2d 610; Jeffries v State, 92 Ga App 483, 88 SE2d 713; People v Rogers, 415 Ill 343, 114 NE2d 398; State v Cardwell, 90 Kan 606, 135 P 597; State v Jones, 150 Me 242, 108 A2d 261; State v Cooper, 358 Mo 269, 214 SW2d 19; Vanderheiden v State, 156 Neb 735, 57 NW2d 761; State v Bates, 76 SD 23, 71 NW2d 641; East v State, 146 Tex Crim 396, 175 SW2d 603; State v Bestolas, 155 Wash 212, 283 P 687; Konopisos v State, 26 Wyo 350, 185 P 355.

25. Smith v United States, 348 US 147, 99 L Ed 192, 75 S Ct 194.

26. Opper v United States, 348 US 84, 99 L Ed 101, 75 S Ct 158, 45 ALR2d 1308.

27. Godwin v State (Sup) 24 Del (1 Boyce) 173, 74 A 1101; People v Miller, 278 Ill 490, 116 NE 131; State v Wood, 99 Vt 490, 134 A 697, 48 ALR 985.

that the courts almost uniformly reject the results of lie detector tests when offered in evidence for the purpose of establishing the guilt or innocence of one accused of a crime, whether the accused or the prosecution seeks its introduction.[28]

The reason most commonly assigned for the exclusion of such evidence is the contention that the lie detector has not as yet attained scientific acceptance as a reliable and accurate means of ascertaining truth or deception.[29]

Truth serum tests occupy much the same position as lie detector tests, and no court has as yet recognized the admissibility of the results of such tests.[30]

The results of truth serum tests are not admissible in criminal trial, since such tests have not attained sufficient scientific recognition of dependability and reliability.[31]

§ 276. Expert testimony

Whether or not a witness is qualified to testify as an expert is generally a matter which falls within the discretion of the trial judge. His exercise of discretion in this regard will seldom be interfered with.[32] If your expert witness has outstanding qualifications, do not accept an

28. People v Jones, 52 Cal 2d 636, 343 P2d 577, cert den 361 US 926, 4 L Ed 2d 350, 80 S Ct 364; State v Chang, 46 Hawaii 22, 374 P2d 5; People v Boney, 28 Ill 2d 505, 192 NE2d 920; People v Davis, 343 Mich 348, 72 NW2d 269; State v Driver, 38 NJ 255, 183 A2d 655; Stape v Civil Service Com. 404 Pa 354, 172 A2d 161.

Skolnick, Scientific Theory and Scientific Evidence: An Analysis of Lie-Detection. 70 Yale LJ 694, April 1961.

29. Le Fevre v State, 242 Wis 416, 8 NW2d 288 (offer by defendant); State v Bohner, 210 Wis 651, 246 NW 314, 86 ALR 611 (offer by defendant).

30. State v Cypher, 92 Idaho 159, 438 P2d 904; People v Myers, 35 Ill 2d 311, 220 NE2d 297, cert den 385 US 1019, 17 L Ed 2d 557, 87 S Ct 752 (murder trial); Sallee v Ashlock (Ky) 438 SW2d 538.

31. Merritt v Commonwealth (Ky) 386 SW2d 727.

32. **Annotations:** Expert testimony as to modus operandi of criminals with respect to particular types of crimes. 100 ALR2d 1433.

Necessity, in homicide prosecution, of expert medical testimony to show cause of death. 31 ALR2d 693.

Expert evidence to identify gun from which bullet or cartridge was fired. 26 ALR2d 892.

offer by the prosecutor to stipulate as to his expertise. You have a right to have the jury hear his qualifications. If the witness is licensed, certified or the recipient of certain honors in his field, ask him to explain the significance of them to the jury. Impress the jury with the fact that the witness is well thought of and is of high standing within his profession or field of expertise. The witness should also be asked to name and describe his published works within his field.

If possible establish that your witness was either trained or employed by some agency of law enforcement or that he has, in the past, been consulted by or been a witness for the prosecution in criminal cases. In rural or provincial areas it is often preferable to use a local expert if a qualified one is available. Outsiders may be looked upon with suspicion.

To the greatest extent possible the witness' testimony should be delivered in terms which can be readily understood by the jury. This takes careful preparation. All technical terms should be explained.[33]

Depending upon the rules of the particular jurisdiction, the witness' answer may be to a hypothetical question or may be based upon all or some of the evidence on the case. The hypothetical question is of assistance when the expert's opinion is based upon facts of which he does not have personal knowledge. You must, however, furnish a basis in evidence for all facts narrated in the hypothetical question or it will become objectionable.

Do not load the facts in your question. The prosecutor's cross-examinations will attempt to show that the expert's answer would have been different if other facts were included. Your witness may seem intransigent if he adheres to his position in the face of other facts in the case. It is best to include such facts in the question.

33. See Bailey and Rothblatt, Investigation and Preparation of Criminal Cases §§ 188 et seq.

There is a trend in some jurisdictions to permit the expert to give his opinion based upon the evidence in the case. This method leaves to cross-examination the question of precisely which facts were considered by the expert.

After answering a question calling for his opinion, ask the witness if he has just considered his answer or if he had previously been informed of the facts. His testimony should indicate that you had asked him to study the facts, to assume that they were true, and to formulate an opinion based upon them. He should then identify both the statement of facts which you prepared for him and the report which he prepared based upon those facts. At this point you can offer the expert's report in evidence. Even if it is not admitted into evidence, you can use the report to further question the witness.

Expert witnesses are often able to prepare maps, charts, photographs, or other types of visual aids which can be of assistance. Such exhibits will also impress the jury with the care taken by the expert.[34]

B. CONFESSIONS

§ 277. In general

While verbal admissions of an accused on trial for crime must be cautiously received, it is the rule that free, voluntary, and deliberate confessions of guilt are entitled to great weight.[35] In fact, a confession has been termed as the highest and most satisfactory proof of guilt.[36] Thus, even verbal confessions where they are deliberately made and

34. See Bailey and Rothblatt, The Investigation and Preparation of Criminal Cases §§ 155 et seq.

35. Wilson v United States, 162 US 613, 40 L Ed 1090, 16 S Ct 895.

36. Sparf v United States, 156 US 51, 39 L Ed 343, 15 S Ct 273; Hopt v Utah, 110 US 574, 28 L Ed 262, 4 S Ct 202; People v Popescue, 345 Ill 142, 177 NE 739, 77 ALR 1199; Commonwealth v Knapp, 26 Mass (9 Pick) 496.

precisely identified, often afford very satisfactory evidence.[37]

On the other hand, the view has been taken that a confession is in reality, the weakest and most suspicious of all testimony.[38]

The weight of a confession is always to be determined by the jury,[39] and the jury in weighing the confession should act with great caution.[40]

§ 278. Corroboration

The general rule is well settled in this country that a naked extrajudicial confession of guilt by one accused of crime, uncorroborated by any other evidence, is not sufficient to warrant or sustain a conviction.[41]

37. Beckwith v Bean, 98 US 266, 25 L Ed 124.

See State v Roland, 336 Mo 563, 79 SW2d 1050, 102 ALR 601, stating that confessions possess considerable probative value.

38. Collins v Commonwealth, 123 Va 815, 96 SE 826.

39. Matthews v State, 55 Ala 187; People v Gukouski, 250 Ill 231, 95 NE 153; Ellis v State, 65 Miss 44, 3 So 188; State v Sherman, 35 Mont 512, 90 P 981; Berry v State, 4 Okla Crim 202, 111 P 676; 81 P 234; Espitia v State, 199 Tenn 696, 288 SW2d 731; Carr v State, 24 Tex App 562, 7 SW 328.

Annotation: Use or administration of drugs or narcotics as affecting admissibility of confession. 69 ALR2d 384 at page 385.

40. Wilson v United States, 162 US 613, 40 L Ed 1090, 16 S Ct 895; Sparf v United States, 156 US 51, 39 L Ed 343, 15 S Ct 273; Hopt v Utah, 110 US 574, 28 L Ed 262, 4 S Ct 202; Beckwith v Bean, 98 US 266, 25 L Ed 124; Brown v State, 135 Fla 30, 184 So 518; Coffee v State, 25 Fla 501, 6 So 493.

41. Wong Sun v United States, 371 US 471, 9 L Ed 2d 441, 83 S Ct 407; Opper v United States, 348 US 84, 99 L Ed 101, 75 S Ct 158, 45 ALR2d 1308; Warszower v United States, 312 US 342, 85 L Ed 876, 61 S Ct 603; Dennis v United States (CA10 Colo) 346 F2d 10, revd on other grounds 384 US 855, 16 L Ed 2d 973, 86 S Ct 1840; Smith v Texas (CA5 Tex) 329 F2d 498; Belvin v United States (CA5 Fla) 273 F2d 583; Cooley v State, 233 Ala 407, 171 So 725; Pate v State, 36 Ala App 688, 63 So 2d 223; State v Romo, 66 Ariz 174, 185 P2d 757; Pigg v State, 219 Ark 879, 245 SW2d 209; People v Cobb, 45 Cal 2d 158, 287 P2d 752; People v Corrales, 34 Cal 2d 426, 210 P2d 843; Martinez v People, 129 Colo 94, 267 P2d 654 (recognizing that a confession alone is not sufficient to establish the fact that a crime has been committed); Nelson v State (Sup) 50 Del 96, 123 A2d 859; Solar v United States (Mun Ct App Dist Col) 94 A2d 34, 35 ALR2d 1039; Frazier v State (Fla) 107 So 2d 16; Tucker v State, 64 Fla 518, 59 So 941; Bines v State, 118 Ga 320, 45 SE 376; Jefferies

In support of the rule stated, the Supreme Court of the United States has stated: "The general rule that an accused may not be convicted on his own uncorroborated confession has previously been recognized by this Court, . . . and has been consistently applied in the lower federal courts and in the overwhelming majority of state courts. . . . Its purpose is to prevent 'errors in convictions based upon untrue confessions alone,' . . . its foundation lies in a long history of judicial experience with confessions and in the realization that sound law enforcement requires police investigations which extend beyond the words of the accused. Confessions may be unreliable because they are coerced or induced, and although separate doctrines exclude involuntary confessions from consideration by the jury, . . . further caution is warranted because the accused may be unable to establish the involuntary nature of his

v State, 92 Ga App 483, 88 SE2d 713; State v Hale, 45 Hawaii 269, 367 P2d 81; People v Lueder, 3 Ill 2d 487, 121 NE2d 743; Brown v State, 239 Ind 184, 154 NE2d 720, cert den 361 US 936, 4 L Ed 2d 360, 80 S Ct 375; State v Saltzman, 241 Iowa 1373, 44 NW2d 24; State v Cardwell, 90 Kan 606, 135 P 597; State v Calloway, 196 La 496, 199 So 403; State v Morgan, 157 La 962, 103 So 278, 40 ALR 458; State v Jones, 150 Me 242, 108 A2d 261; Wood v State, 192 Md 643, 65 A2d 316; People v June, 294 Mich 681, 293 NW 906; Steward v State (Miss) 32 So 2d 791; State v McQuinn, 361 Mo 631, 235 SW2d 396; State v Smith, 65 Mont 458, 211 P 208; Vanderheiden v State, 156 Neb 735, 57 NW2d 761; Gallegos v State, 152 Neb 831, 43 NW2d 1, affd 342 US 55, 96 L Ed 86, 72 S Ct 141; Sefton v State, 72 Nev 106, 295 P2d 385, cert den 352 US 954, 1 L Ed 2d 244, 77 S Ct 329; State v Pickard, 104 NH 11, 177 A2d 401; State v Lucas, 30 NJ 37, 152 A2d 50; State v Carter, 58 NM 713, 275 P2d 847; State v Maranda, 94 Ohio St 364, 114 NE 1038; State v Scarberry, 114 Ohio App 85, 18 Ohio Ops 2d 394, 180 NE2d 631; Lankister v State (Okla Crim) 298 P2d 1088; State v Schleigh, 210 Or 155, 310 P2d 341; Commonwealth v Lettrich, 346 Pa 497, 31 A2d 155; State v Boswell, 73 RI 358, 56 A2d 196; State v Blocker, 205 SC 303, 31 SE2d 908; Witham v State, 191 Tenn 115, 232 SW2d 3; Carr v State, 158 Tex Crim 337, 255 SW2d 870; State v Ferry, 2 Utah 2d 371, 275 P2d 173; State v Goyet, 120 Vt 12, 132 A2d 623; Pepoon v Commonwealth, 192 Va 804, 66 SE2d 854; State v Marcy, 189 Wash 620, 66 P2d 846; State v Blackwell, 102 W Va 421, 135 SE 393; Konopisos v State, 26 Wyo 350, 185 P 355.

Annotations: Admissibility, in homicide prosecution, of deceased's clothing worn at time of killing. 68 ALR2d 903 at page 936.

Corroboration of extrajudicial confession or admission. 45 ALR2d 1316.

statements."[42] It has been held that the wisdom of the rule lies in the fact that no man should be convicted of a crime, the commission of which he confesses, unless the State shows, by other testimony, that the confessed crime was in fact committed by someone. The contrary position to this rule would authorize a return of conditions that existed in the days of the inquisition.[43]

The corroborative evidence must consist of facts or circumstances appearing in evidence which are independent of the confession and consistent therewith and which tend to confirm and strengthen the confession.[44] Because this rule impinges upon the province of the primary finder of facts, however, its application should be scrutinized lest the restrictions it imposes surpass the dangers which give rise to them.[45]

C. CORPUS DELICTI

§ 279. In general

The general rule is that in every criminal case the prosecution must prove the corpus delicti beyond a reasonable doubt,[46] or else the accused is entitled to an acquittal.[47]

Inasmuch as each case must depend on its own peculiar circumstances, no universal and invariable rule can be laid down as to the character and sufficiency of evidence neces-

42. Smith v United States, 348 US 147, 99 L Ed 192, 75 S Ct 194.

43. East v State, 146 Tex Crim 396, 175 SW2d 603.

44. People v Lueder, 3 Ill 2d 487, 121 NE2d 743; Bergen v People, 17 Ill 426; State v Guild, 10 NJL 163; People v Lytton, 257 NY 310, 178 NE 290, 79 ALR 503.

45. Smith v United States, 348 US 147, 99 L Ed 192, 75 S Ct 194.

46. Perovich v United States, 205 US 86, 51 L Ed 722, 27 S Ct 456; Sanders v State, 167 Ala 85, 52 So 417; Smith v State, 133 Ala 145, 31 So 806; People v Ives, 17 Cal 2d 459, 110 P2d 408; People v Theodore, 174 Cal App 2d 237, 344 P2d 393; Joe v State, 6 Fla 591; Territory v Duvauchelle, 28 Hawaii 350; People v Schryver, 42 NY 1; Commonwealth v Puglise, 276 Pa 235, 120 A 401; State v Campbell, 95 RI 370, 187 A2d 543, 6 ALR3d 499.

47. Sanders v State, 167 Ala 85, 52 So 417; Commonwealth v McKie, 67 Mass (1 Gray) 61; State v Brown, 103 SC 437, 88 SE 21.

sary to establish the corpus delicti, beyond saying that there must be proof, first, that a certain result has been produced, as that a man died, a building has been burned, or a piece of property is not in the owner's possession, and, second, that someone is criminally responsible for the result.[48]

Sufficient proof of both of these elements must be made.[49]

In proving the corpus delicti, the reasonable rule is that the law demands the best proof, and only the best proof, of the corpus delicti which, in the nature of the case, is attainable.[50] There is no one kind of evidence always to be demanded in proof of the corpus delicti, any more than of any other fact. It can seldom be proved by direct or positive testimony.[51] Accordingly, the generally prevailing rule is that direct and positive proof is not essential; all the elements of the corpus delicti may be proved by presumptive or circumstantial evidence.

§ 280. Effect of confession; corroboration

While the corpus delicti may not be established by the admissions or confessions of the defendant alone, it may be established by such admissions or confessions in connection with other facts and circumstances.[52] The grounds on which the rule requiring other proof of the corpus delicti rests are the hasty and unguarded character which confessions often have, the temptation which for one reason or another a person may have to say that which he thinks it most for his interest to say, whether true or false, the liability

48. Territory v Duvauchelle, 28 Hawaii 350; Brown v State, 239 Ind 184, 154 NE2d 720, cert den 361 US 936, 4 L Ed 2d 360, 80 S Ct 375; Joseph v State, 236 Ind 529, 141 NE2d 109, 69 ALR2d 824, cert dismd 359 US 117, 3 L Ed 673, 79 S Ct 720; State v Brown, 103 SC 437, 88 SE 21.

49. Sanders v State, 167 Ala 85, 52 So 417; People v King, 213 Cal 89, 1 P2d 15; State v Sullivan, 34 Idaho 68, 199 P 647, 17 ALR 902; State v Hill, 47 NJ 490, 221 A2d 725; State v Brown, 103 SC 437, 88 SE 21.

50. State v Cardwell, 90 Kan 606, 135 P 597; State v Simler, 350 Mo 646, 167 SW2d 376.

51. Willard v State, 27 Tex App 386, 11 SW 453.

52. State v Romo, 66 Ariz 174, 185 P2d 757.

which there is to misconstrue or report inaccurately what has been said, the danger of a conviction when no crime may have been committed, the difficulty of disproving what may be said, and the feeling that the rule best accords with the humanity of the criminal law and with the great degree of caution applied in receiving and weighing the evidence of confessions in other cases.[53]

A confession will be sufficient if there are such extensive corroborative circumstances as will, when taken in connection with the confession, establish the prisoner's guilt in the minds of the jury beyond a reasonable doubt.[54] Thus, the corpus delicti may be established by the confession and other evidence, considered together.[55] However, it is not necessary to prove the corpus delicti by evidence entirely independent and exclusive of the confession.[56]

D. IDENTIFICATION OF ACCUSED

§ 281. In general

Proof beyond a reasonable doubt of the identity of the

53. State v Saltzman, 241 Iowa 1373, 44 NW2d 24; Commonwealth v Killion, 194 Mass 153, 80 NE 222; State v Dena, 28 NM 479, 214 P 583; Mackey v State, 30 Okla Crim 31, 234 P 782; Boyle v State, 27 Okla Crim 196, 226 P 389.

54. Masse v United States (CA5 Fla) 210 F2d 418, cert den 347 US 962, 98 L Ed 1105, 74 S Ct 711; Vogt v United States (CA5 Tex) 156 F2d 308.

55. Smith v State (CA5 Tex) 329 F2d 498 (applying Texas law); Edgil v State, 36 Ala App 379, 56 So 2d 677; People v Williams, 151 Cal App 2d 173, 311 P2d 117, cert den 355 US 961, 2 L Ed 2d 535, 78 S Ct 547; Nelson v State (Sup) 50 Del 96, 123 A2d 859; Cross v State, 96 Fla 768, 119 So 380; Groover v State, 82 Fla 427, 90 So 473, 26 ALR 373; State v Yoshida, 44 Hawaii 352, 354 P2d 986; Allen v State, 230 Miss 740, 93 So 2d 844; Brower v State, 217 Miss 425, 64 So 2d 576; Sullivan v State, 216 Miss 809, 63 So 2d 212; State v Knapp, 70 Ohio St 380, 71 NE 705; State v Schleigh, 210 Or 155, 310 P2d 341; State v Bates, 76 SD 23, 71 NW2d 641; Brown v State (Tex Crim) 376 SW2d 577; Rodgers v State, 164 Tex Crim 375, 298 SW2d 827.

56. Masse v United States (CA5 Fla) 210 F2d 418, cert den 347 US 962, 98 L Ed 1105, 74 S Ct 711; People v Cullen, 37 Cal 2d 614, 234 P2d 1; Sullivan v State, 216 Miss 809, 63 So 2d 212; State v Cooper, 10 NJ 532, 92 A2d 786; State v Knapp, 70 Ohio St 380, 71 NE 705; State v Bates, 76 SD 23, 71 NW2d 641; Anderson v State, 34 Tex Crim 546, 31 SW 673; State v Blackwell, 102 W Va 421, 135 SE 393.

accused as the person who committed the crime is essential to a conviction.[57] The evidence, however, need not be positive and certain, but may be inferred from all the facts and circumstances in evidence.[58] Identification of the defendant may be established entirely by circumstantial evidence.[59] The defendant may be identified by proof of any peculiarity of size, appearance, voice, features, or clothing.[60]

§ 282. Fingerprints, palmprints and footprints

The weight to be given evidence of the correspondence of fingerprints and palmprints, where offered to prove the identity of the accused as the person committing a crime, is for the determination of the jury in the light of all the surrounding facts and circumstances.[61]

The weight of evidence of the correspondence of footprints found in connection with a crime, with the track, foot, or shoe of one accused of the crime, or with the track,

57. **Annotation:** Necessity and sufficiency of identification of accused as the person charged, to warrant extradition. 93 ALR2d 912 at page 919.

58. Butler v United States (CA8 ND) 317 F2d 249, 6 ALR3d 582, cert den 375 US 836, 11 L Ed 2d 65, 84 S Ct 67, cert den 375 US 838, 11 L Ed 2d 65, 84 S Ct 77; People v Brengard, 265 NY 100, 191 NE 850, 93 ALR 1465; Commonwealth v Boden, 399 Pa 298, 159 A2d 894, 88 ALR2d 223, cert den 364 US 846, 5 L Ed 2d 70, 81 S Ct 89.

Annotation: Necessity and sufficiency of identification of accused as the person charged, to warrant extradition. 93 ALR2d 912 at pages 926 and 936.

59. People v Barnum, 147 Cal App 2d 803, 305 P2d 986.

60. People v Van De Wouwer, 91 Cal App 2d 633, 205 P2d 693.

Annotations: Requiring suspect or defendant in criminal case to demonstrate voice for purposes of identification. 24 ALR3d 1261.

Identification of accused by his voice. 70 ALR2d 995 at page 1012.

61. Moon v State, 22 Ariz 418, 198 P 288, 16 ALR 362; People v Jennings, 252 Ill 534, 96 NE 1077; Mason v Commonwealth (Ky) 357 SW2d 667; Breeding v State, 220 Md 193, 151 A2d 743 (holding that testimony that a fingerprint had five characteristics similar to that of a murder victim was admissible, the objection of its sufficiency going to the weight to be given evidence rather than to its admissibility); State v Cerciello, 86 NJL 309, 90 A 1112; People v Roach, 215 NY 592, 101 NE 618; State v Tew, 234 NC 612, 68 SE2d 291; State v Helms, 218 NC 592, 12 SE2d 243; Rushing v State, 88 Okla Crim 82, 199 P2d 614; Jamison v State, 209 Tenn 426, 354 SW2d 252.

foot, or shoe of his horse, where offered to identify the accused as the guilty person, is dependent largely upon the circumstances of the particular case, and is of course to be determined by the jury.[62]

§ 283. Blood tests

In criminal cases in which the results of blood-grouping tests are introduced in evidence for the purpose of establishing identity—that is, to show that particular blood was the blood of a particular individual—the courts, although holding the evidence admissible, have uniformly ruled that such evidence is not conclusive on the question of identity, such evidence being, without more, by the very nature of the test, insufficient to establish identity.[63]

E. PROOF OF DEFENSES

§ 284. In general

The burden which rests on the defendant in a criminal prosecution falls short of that imposed upon the prosecution. The defendant has only to raise in the minds of the jury a reasonable doubt of his guilt, springing out of all the evidence in the case, and is entitled to an acquittal if any reasonable doubt exists upon that point.[64]

62. Richardson v State, 221 Ark 567, 254 SW2d 448; People v O'Leary, 22 Ill 2d 52, 174 NE2d 191, cert den 368 US 906, 7 L Ed 2d 100, 82 S Ct 187; State v Adams, 85 Kan 435, 116 P 608; State v Jeffries, 210 Mo 302, 109 SW 614; Ferrell v Commonwealth, 177 Va 861, 14 SE2d 293; State v Simons, 172 Wash 438, 20 P2d 844.

Annotations: Footprints as evidence. 35 ALR2d 856 at page 882.

Fingerprints, palm prints, or bare footprints as evidence. 28 ALR2d 1115 at page 1150.

63. State v Thomas, 78 Ariz 52, 275 P2d 408, ovrld on other grounds State v Pina, 94 Ariz 243, 383 P2d 167; State v Walters, 145 Conn 60, 138 A2d 786, app dismd and cert den 358 US 46, 3 L Ed 2d 45, 79 S Ct 70; State v Beard, 16 NJ 50, 106 A2d 265; Commonwealth v Statti, 166 Pa Super 577, 73 A2d 688.

Annotation: Blood grouping tests. 46 ALR2d 1000 at page 1036.

64. Asher v State, 201 Ind 353, 168 NE 456, 67 ALR 118.

Annotation: Entrapment to commit offense against obscenity laws. 77 ALR2d 792.

§ 285. Former jeopardy

Since a plea of former jeopardy sets up affirmative matter and is not a denial of any allegations of the indictment, the burden of proving this issue, from the start, is on the defendant, and if it is not proved by him, the issue must be answered in the negative. To sustain a plea of former jeopardy, the defendant must introduce sufficient evidence to affirmatively show that there was a former prosecution in the same state for the same offense; that some person was in jeopardy on the first prosecution; that the persons are identical in the two prosecutions; and that the particular offense, on the prosecution of which the jeopardy attached, was such an offense as to constitute a bar.[65]

§ 286. Alibi

The view has been taken that an alibi is the most perfect, physically conclusive evidence of the accused's innocence.[66] An alibi is a complete defense, and if the defendant introduces sufficient evidence so that the jury entertains a reasonable doubt as to whether the defendant was present at the time and place alleged in the indictment and established by the prosecution's evidence, it is their duty to acquit.[67]

Since the defense of an alibi may be so easily fabricated,

65. Grayson v State, 92 Ark 413, 123 SW 388; State v Ellsworth, 131 NC 773, 42 SE 699.

Annotation: Conviction from which appeal is pending as bar to another prosecution for same offense. 61 ALR2d 1224.

66. State v Danelly, 116 SC 113, 107 SE 149, 14 ALR 1420.

A detailed discussion of the substantive defense of alibi may be found in § 237, infra.

67. Falgout v United States (CA5 La) 279 F 513, 29 ALR 1115; Prince v State, 100 Ala 144, 14 So 409; People v Gormach, 302 Ill 332, 134 NE 756, 29 ALR 1120; Carlton v People, 150 Ill 181, 37 NE 244; French v State, 12 Ind 670; State v Wagner, 207 Iowa 224, 222 NW 407, 61 ALR 882; State v Ardoin, 49 La Ann 1145, 22 So 620; Pollard v State, 53 Miss 410; State v McClellan, 23 Mont 532, 59 P 924; Henry v State, 51 Neb 149, 70 NW 924; State v Minton, 234 NC 716, 68 SE2d 844, 31 ALR2d 682; Turner v Commonwealth, 86 Pa 54; State v Jackson, 36 SC 487, 15 SE 559; Legere v State, 111 Tenn 368, 77 SW 1059; Means v State, 10 Tex App 16.

it is necessarily viewed with considerable suspicion.[68] Further, owing to the ease with which persons may be mistaken in dates long after the occurrence of a particular event, the ease with which an alibi may be made, and the difficulty of proving the contrary, courts have not generally considered evidence of an alibi conclusive, such evidence is merely to be weighed by the jury.[69]

F. INSANITY

§ 287. In general

The term "insanity" is a legal rather than a medical one.[70] A condition recognized by the medical profession as mental illness does not have to be present in order for a court to find your client legally insane. Conversely, under some tests of legal insanity it is possible for a court to find that a person who suffers from a severe mental illness is legally sane.

In an insanity defense it is not enough for you to prove that your client is suffering from some form of mental illness. You must also demonstrate that the effect of his mental illness meets the test of legal insanity under the applicable standards of a particular jurisdiction.

You must familiarize yourself with both the dynamics of mental illness and the various legal rules set up to test insanity. You must know both legal principles and psychiatric theory. Psychiatric testimony in court may be ineffectual unless you direct and interpret such testimony in relation to the applicable legal theory.

Your client's mental state at various times will be important in formulating the defense. You and your expert

68. Russell v State, 115 Tex Crim 608, 28 SW2d 138; Bowman v State, 114 Tex Crim 68, 24 SW2d 407.

69. People v Connors, 253 Ill 266, 97 NE 643; Kelly v State, 239 Miss 683, 124 So 2d 840, 85 ALR2d 1199.

70. Annotations: Mental or emotional condition as diminishing responsibility for crime. 22 ALR3d 1228.

Release of one committed to institution as consequence of acquittal of crime on ground of insanity. 95 ALR2d 54 at page 108.

witnesses must answer these questions: Was he responsible when he allegedly committed the crime? Is he sufficiently sane to plead to the charge, to stand trial or to receive sentence? It may even be important, thereafter, to determine whether he is sufficiently sane to undergo punishment.

The weight and sufficiency of the evidence to establish insanity as a defense is exclusively for the jury.[71] Positive and direct testimony is not required to establish insanity as a defense, nor are specific acts of derangement necessary therefor.[72]

Whether or not your client was legally insane under the applicable test at the time he allegedly committed unlawful acts will be resolved on the basis of your expert's testimony. There are, however, certain proofs you may be able to offer which can help your expert (and/or the jury) to find that your client was legally insane.

Determine whether there is any history of mental illness, including prior treatments for mental disorder or mental disorders, among members of your client's immediate family. Proof of any such histories will support your defense. Further, proof that your client is unable or unwilling to admit a prior mental illness, or that he suffers from feelings of inadequacy (if you can establish the fact of such illness or deep-rooted feelings) are also indicative of mental disorders.

Proof that your client believed his acts were divinely commanded or inspired or that he has received direct messages from a deity will support the contention that he suffered from insane delusions. Some persons do not believe

71. Beasley v State, 50 Ala 149; Hornish v People, 142 Ill 620, 32 NE 677; Plake v State, 121 Ind 433, 23 NE 273; State v Scott, 49 La Ann 253, 21 So 271.

Annotations: Test of insanity in federal criminal trial. 1 ALR Fed 965.

Appealability of orders or rulings, prior to final judgment in criminal case, as to accused's mental competency. 16 ALR3d 714.

72. Rinkard v State, 157 Ind 534, 62 NE 14; State v Wright, 134 Mo 404, 35 SW 1145; State v Simms, 68 Mo 305.

they are committing an unlawful act when they act under the direction of a power higher than the law.

Inform your experts if you detect or can prove that your client experiences intense feelings and emotions which cause him agitation while he discusses the reasons for his acts. Your expert will also be guided if he is aware of any restlessness, irritability, or preoccupation on the part of your client when you attempt to discuss the facts of the case with him.

The experts and the trier of the facts should be made aware of any conduct by the defendant which indicates a mental defect which would prevent or mar his ability to distinguish right from wrong.

§ 288. Burden of proof

The presumption that the defendant in a criminal case is sane means that the burden of proof as to insanity rests upon the defendant, and he must establish insanity by a preponderance of the evidence.[73] Stated differently, the same evidence will establish the defense of insanity in a criminal case which would prove insanity in a civil case.[74]

The Federal rule is preferable. It provides that the government must establish by proof beyond a reasonable doubt the defendant's sanity, whether at trial, sentence, or execution. If there is any doubt about the burden of proof in a particular jurisdiction, contend that no person should

73. Parsons v State, 81 Ala 577, 2 So 854; State v Trout, 74 Iowa 545, 38 NW 405; Commonwealth v Spencer, 212 Mass 438, 99 NE 266; State v Speyer, 207 Mo 540, 106 SW 505; State v Hartley, 22 Nev 342, 40 P 372; Graves v State, 45 NJL 347; Long v State, 109 Ohio St 77, 141 NE 691; State v Ross, 92 Ohio App 29, 49 Ohio Ops 196, 62 Ohio L Abs 562, 108 NE2d 77, app dismd for want of debat q 158 Ohio St 248, 49 Ohio Ops 25, 108 NE2d 282; Coyle v Commonwealth, 100 Pa 573; State v Quigley, 26 RI 263, 58 A 905; State v Bundy, 24 SC 439; State v Brown, 36 Utah 46, 102 P 641; State v Clark, 34 Wash 485, 76 P 98.

74. People v McCann, 16 NY 58.

Annotation: Presumption of continuing insanity as applied to accused in criminal case. 27 ALR2d 121, at pages 145 and 155.

be made to stand trial if there is a reasonable doubt of his ability to make or assist in making a rational defense.[75]

It has been held that the federal procedural rule that once accused has placed insanity in issue, prosecution bears the burden of proving sanity beyond a reasonable doubt is not of constitutional dimension and, therefore, states are free to develop their own rules.[76]

§ 289. When to call for a psychiatric examination

Consider having your client undergo psychiatric evaluation at an early stage in the proceeding. Such an evaluation is necessary if he displays severe symptoms of mental illness which make communication with him difficult. Psychiatric evaluation is also called for if your client has a history of mental illness or if the nature of the crime or his demeanor point to possible psychiatric problems.[77]

Learn the nature of any of your client's psychiatric problems as early as possible. While these problems will not always warrant the assertion of an insanity defense or of a claim of present insanity, they will indicate whether you can believe your client or rely on his judgment.

In certain cases, the results of an evaluation may convince a prosecutor to agree to a dismissal of the charge or to accept a reduced plea in exchange for your client's agreement to voluntary civil commitment or to professional treatment of his problems.

If your client starts to undergo some form of therapy early in the case, he has the advantage, if convicted, of appearing before the sentencing judge as a man on the way to voluntary reform and rehabilitation. An opinion from

75. United States v Handy (CA9 Cal) 454 F2d 885, cert den 409 US 846, 34 L Ed 2d 86, 93 S Ct 49; State v Corley, 108 Ariz 240, 495 P2d 470; State v Myers, 94 Idaho 570, 494 P2d 574; People v Childs, 51 Ill 2d 247, 281 NE2d 631.

76. Nilsson v State (Tex Crim) 477 SW2d 592.

77. Annotation: Validity and construction of statutes providing for psychiatric examination of accused to determine mental condition. 32 ALR2d 434.

the therapist working with him to the effect that he is not dangerous or that imprisonment would interrupt his therapy can make the difference between a prison sentence and probation. Even if a prison term is imposed, the judge may be persuaded that a short sentence which allows early resumption of his therapy program is preferable to a long term.

§ 290. Know the law of the particular jurisdiction

You must be thoroughly familiar with the law regarding insanity in the jurisdiction in which the trial is to be held. In addition to your inability to effectively present your client's defense without such knowledge, it is necessary too, in order to be able to properly select a psychiatric expert and to indicate the nature of the legal problem to him.

§ 291. The M'Naghten rule

The most common and the most primitive rule applied to determine criminal responsibility for an act is the one set forth in the M'Naghten Case.[78] This rule provides that to establish a defense on the ground of insanity, it must be clearly proved that, at the time of the committing of the act, the party accused was laboring under such a defect of reason, from disease of the mind, as not to know the nature and quality of the act he was doing; or, if he did know it, that he did not know what he was doing wrong.

The rule, sometimes referred to as the "right-wrong test," concerns itself only with the defendant's ability to distinguish between "right" and "wrong" with reference to the particular crime, rather than in an abstract sense. If the defendant had the capacity to know his act was wrong at the time of his commission of the crime, he will be held fully responsible therefore, even if at that time he was mentally ill and unable to refrain from doing the act.

78. M'Naghten's Case, 10 Clark & F 200, 8 Eng Reprint 718.

Annotation: Modern status of M'Naghten "right-and-wrong" test of criminal responsibility. 45 ALR2d 1447.

Under the M'Naghten rule a person who commits a crime while laboring under an insane delusion as to the existing facts is judged as though the delusionary facts were real. For example, a defendant suffering from the delusion that his victim was stealing from him would not be excused for murdering the victim. The facts of his delusion, even if true, would not have excused the crime. If, however, he had been laboring under the delusion that he was the state executioner and that he had to execute the victim as part of his job, he would be excused for murder by reason of insanity.

In order for an insane delusion to exempt a defendant from responsibility, the delusion must be the result of a "disease" of the mind which rendered him incapable of reason toward the object of his delusion. An insane delusion is an unreasonable belief in the existence of facts and not merely a mistaken belief based on reasoning and reflection.

While the technical definition of insanity under the M'Naghten rule is unduly restrictive and is opposed to a modern psychiatric theory, it is usually broadly interpreted so as to permit the introduction of all psychiatric evidence as to the defendant's mental condition.

§ 292. The New Hampshire rule

New Hampshire was the first jurisdiction to reject the rigid and artificial legal rule established as the test for insanity.[79] It held that a person is not criminally responsible for his acts if they are "the offspring or product of mental disease." The rule was later amplified when the court held that an insanity defense raises the question of whether, when he committed an act, the defendant had the mental capacity to harbor a criminal intent and whether he did in fact harbor such an intent.[80] The court noted that:

79. State v Pike, 49 NH 399, ovrld on other grounds Hardy v Merrill, 56 NH 227.

80. State v Jones, 50 NH 369, 372, 373.

"Whether the defendant had a mental disease . . . seems to be as much a question of fact as whether he had a bodily disease; and whether the killing of his wife was the product of that disease, was also as clearly a matter of fact as whether thirst and a quickened pulse are a product of fever . . . The difficulty is intrinsic, and must be met from whatever direction it may be approached. Enough has already been said as to the use of symptoms, phases, and manifestations of the disease as legal tests of capacity to entertain, to be weighted by the jury upon the question whether the act was the offspring of insanity: if it was, a criminal intent did produce it, and it was crime."

The instructions as to insane impulses seem to be quite correct, and entirely within the same principle. If the defendant had an insane impulse to kill his wife, which he could not control, then mental disease produced the act. If he could have controlled it, then his will must have assented to the act, and it was not caused by disease, but by the concurrence of his will, and was therefore a crime.

§ 293. The Durham rule

The Durham rule has been highly praised by most legal writers who have analyzed it. It has not, however, been warmly greeted by most other courts which have since had occasion to reconsider the concept of legal insanity. Most state and federal courts, having considered the rule, have elected to reject it.

The enlightened New Hampshire rule did not make significant headway until the adoption of the "Durham rule."[81] In Durham, the court noted that the objection to the M'Naghten right-wrong test is that it rests upon particular symptoms and does not take sufficient account of psychic realities and scientific knowledge. The court also rejected the "irresistable impulse" test as an inadequate

81. Durham v United States, 94 App DC 228, 214 F2d 862, 45 ALR 2d 1430. The second reversal after the new trial is reported as Durham v United States, 99 App DC 132, 237 F2d 760.

one which fails to recognize mental illnesses which are marked by brooding and reflection. Instead, the court held that a person is not criminally responsible for his illegal acts if those acts are the product of mental disease or mental defect. The term "disease" is defined as a condition which cannot either improve or deteriorate and may be congenital, the result of injury, or the residual effect of a physical or mental disease.

The Durham rule shouldn't have any effect on the type of psychiatric examination to which defendants are subjected. Its effect will be felt in your in-court examination of the psychiatric experts. It will allow you much greater latitude in demonstrating the basic cause of your client's actions. You should, with the help of your expert psychiatric witnesses, establish that your client suffered from a mental disease or defect. Show that there was a causal connection between his mental abnormality and the unlawful act your client allegedly committed. As is the case in the New Hampshire and M'Naghten rules, the issue is one of fact for the jury.[82]

§ 294. The irresistible impulse test

Some states use the "irresistable impulse" test as a supplement to the M'Naghten right-wrong test. The theory of this test is that a person who knows that he is committing a legally wrong act should be excused from responsibility, if he lacks the freedom of will to resist the impulse to commit the unlawful act. If you rely upon this defense, remember that the excusable impulse must be induced by and be the product of mental disease affecting your client's volative, rather than cognitive powers. In theory, an act committed out of passion or overwhelming emotion but which is unconnected with a disease of the mind does not warrant an acquittal on the ground of insanity. Temporary or emotional insanity is therefore distinguishable from

82. Wion v United States (CA10 Colo) 325 F2d 420, cert den 377 US 946, 12 L Ed 2d 309, 84 S Ct 1354; Voss v United States (CA8 Mo) 259 F2d 699; Andersen v United States (CA9 Nev) 237 F2d 118.

irresistable impulse. Do not raise this defense unless your psychiatric experts are prepared to testify that the impulse was the causal result of some mental disease.

§ 295. Long term insanity or delirium tremens

If your client had suffered from a long term of insanity or delirium tremens at the time he committed an unlawful act, he will be exempted from responsibility under the same conditions as he would for insanity from any other cause. It is necessary for you to distinguish delirium tremens from voluntary drunkenness. While voluntary drunkenness will generally not furnish a complete defense (it may, however, reduce a defendant's degree of responsibility), delirium tremens is a remote, rather than immediate, result of voluntary drinking and can afford a complete defense if the other elements of the particular insanity defense are present.

§ 296. Mental disorder as a basis for reducing the degree of responsibility

Do not make the mistake of only considering insanity as a possible complete defense. Very often your client's mental unsoundness, while insufficient to warrant an acquittal, may be used to negate a finding of specific intent. If the crime charged requires proof of specific intent, your client's mental disorder can serve to diminish his responsibility or reduce the grade of the offense.

No person should be convicted of a crime if he lacks the requisite state of mind to commit that crime. The crime of murder, for example, usually cannot be committed in the first degree if the defendant's mental condition prevents premeditation. Similarly, if he could not form an intent to kill or formulate "malice aforethought" a defendant may only be found guilty of manslaughter rather than murder in the second degree.

If you raise the defense of diminished responsibility, your expert psychiatric witness will not be concerned with the

M'Naghten right-wrong test or the Durham rule. Instead, he should analyze your client's motive in order to render an opinion as to whether he had the requisite criminal intent when he allegedly committed the crime.

When you consider using this theory, remember that you can contend that a person acting from unconscious impulses produced by a mental illness cannot exert free will. Without free will there can be neither premeditation nor criminal intent.

You will not have negated the presence of malice or criminal intent simply by proving your client is mentally unsound or unstable. You must go further and show that the unsoundness actually interfered with his ability to entertain the state of mind necessary for harboring malice or criminal intent. You can attempt to prove that your client's acts were the result of unconscious fears, tensions, delusions, impulses, etc.

The prosecution may contend that any volitional act is the result of some conscious or unconscious motivation. However, few enlightened persons today seriously believe that an individual's every act is dictated by his free will and conscious choice. You should not experience difficulty in obtaining expert testimony to show that unconscious determined processes often dictate actions which only seem to be the effect of conscious rationalizations. It is not only Freudians who accept the fact that while most "normal" individuals exercise some degree of free choice, many of their actions are determined by unconscious forces which they themselves don't recognize. If this is true of a normal person, it is particularly true of people suffering from some form of mental unsoundness.

This theory shouldn't be carried too far. Any expert witness who maintains that a person's every act is determined by forces over which he has no control will be greeted by skepticism and demolished on cross-examination.

In some jurisdictions the mere commission of a particular unlawful act gives rise to the presumption that malice was present. If this type of crime is charged, your expert psychiatric testimony should clearly eliminate the possibility of malice. The witness should indicate that the defendant's act was prompted by unconscious drives or tension rather than by malice.

§ 297. Negating the presence of specific intent

Proof that your client has long suffered from mental disorientation or that he has been incapable of emotional adjustment to life situations are indicative of an inability to form a specific intent. Disturbances in his ability to reason abstractly and indications of the disintegration of his personality are also proofs of an inability to form a specific intent.

You can indicate your client's inability to form a specific intent by showing that he was not previously inclined toward acts of violence. You may be able to prove that the defendant is unable to distinguish between reality and fantasy, even though he has doubts about the reality of delusions. If such was the case, show that his behavior before the alleged commission of the unlawful act was not in keeping with his usual behavior; that he committed the act in a robot-like state; that he didn't resist arrest; admitted the commission of the crime willingly and expressed regret for any harm done.

Introduce proof of any abnormal conduct which fortifies the contention that your client's mental state made it impossible for him to formulate the requisite criminal intent.

§ 298. How mental condition affects the voluntariness of confessions

Statements made by criminal defendants are not admissible into evidence unless they are the product of a free will or of a rational intellect.[83] Statements which are not such products of the free will or rational intellect are involuntary as a matter of law.

Do not assume that statements are only rendered involuntary as a result of impermissible police pressure or police failure to confer the required warnings. Defendants often confess during a period of intense agitation or emotion when they are not in command of their faculties.

You can utilize expert testimony to establish the lack of free will in much the same way you would use it to establish reduced responsibility for a crime. You may establish that a defendant's low mentality caused him to confess under circumstances of police pressure which would not have affected someone of greater learning or mentality.[84] Certainly, a defendant's mental dullness is one of the factors to be taken into consideration in determining the voluntariness of his confession.

§ 299. Ability to plead or stand trial

No person who is presently insane may be made to plead to the indictment, stand trial, be sentenced, or be executed. The test commonly used to determine the defendant's ability to plead to the indictment or to stand trial is whether or not his mental disorder renders him incapable of making or assisting in a rational defense. If the trial court has any reasonable ground to believe that a defendant is mentally disordered or mentally incapable of making a rational defense, it must suspend the criminal proceeding and hold an inquiry on the matter. This inquiry may be held with or without a jury, depending on the statutes and rules of the court in the particular jurisdiction. If the defendant is found to be so disordered within the general rules stated above, the court will postpone the criminal

83. Rothblatt, HANDBOOK OF EVIDENCE FOR CRIMINAL TRIALS p 115.

84. Payne v Arkansas, 356 US 560, 2 L Ed 2d 975, 78 S Ct 844; Fikes v Alabama, 352 US 191, 1 L Ed 2d 246, 77 S Ct 281, reh den 352 US 1019, 1 L Ed 2d 561, 77 S Ct 553.

proceedings until he regains his sanity. In the interim, he will usually be confined to a mental hospital as an insane person.

The reasons for the rule are clear. A defendant would be denied the right to stand trial on the merits if he had to stand trial at a time when he was incapable of making an intelligent defense. In certain instances the defendant may be the only person in possession of knowledge which could prove his innocence. To compel him to stand trial at a time when he is incapable of communicating vital information to his attorney would violate due process.[85] It may be possible to validly argue that a defendant's rights are violated if he is incarcerated in a mental institution to await trial for a period longer than the maximum sentence which could have been imposed had he stood trial.

§ 300. Indicia of present mental incompetence

The primary indication of your client's inability to stand trial will usually be his inability to communicate with you about the crime. If he displays wild facial expressions, muteness, or an inability to understand what is happening to him, consider the possibility that he is presently incompetent. Incompetence may also be indicated by inappropriate smiling or giggling; slovenliness of dress; lack of personal cleanliness; incoherent, angry, or senseless remarks; threatening or obscene gestures or speech; constant twitching, etc.

If your client displays some of these symptoms and you feel he is presently insane you should, if he is financially able to do so, retain an expert psychiatrist to examine him and report to you. His findings can form the basis for a motion for a competency hearing. If your client can't afford to retain an expert, move for a competency hearing or for a psychiatric examination at the state's expense.

85. United States ex rel. Mazy v Ragen (CA7 Ill) 149 F2d 948, cert den 326 US 791, 90 L Ed 480, 66 S Ct 476; Youtsey v United States (CA6 Ky) 97 F 937; United States v Gundelfinger (DC Pa) 98 F Supp 630.

Be sure your motion sets forth good reason for belief in your client's present insanity. It should contain specifics to illustrate his incompetence, his inability to understand the proceedings and his place in them, and his inability to make a rational defense.

§ 301. Raising the issue

The issue of a defendant's competency to stand trial may generally be made any time at or after arraignment, either orally or by written motion. It usually can be made by the defense, the prosecutor, or by the court on its own motion, after observing the defendant's actions and conduct. The issue can even be raised over your objection. The defendant, however, may not be compelled to give evidence against himself at a hearing as to his present sanity.

In some states the question of a defendant's present capacity to stand trial is raised by a special plea.[86] In Massachusetts the problem of raising the issue has been largely eliminated by a requirement that all defendants charged with certain specified crimes must undergo routine mental examination prior to trial.[87] The result of the examination is filed with the court and is available to both the prosecution and defense.

In whatever form the issue is raised, try to make a showing sufficient to raise a reasonable doubt in the mind of the judge as to your client's present capacity to stand trial. Do not attempt to get a sanity hearing based on unsupported conclusory allegations. In some jurisdictions the trial judge is permitted to decide the method to determine the defendant's present capacity to stand trial. Other states require a jury trial, and still others require that the trial judge hear the issue himself.

Almost all jurisdictions provide for a preliminary psychi-

86. Ga Code (1933) § 27.1504; Orange v State, 77 Ga App 36, 47 SE2d 756; Md Anno Code (1951) Art 59 § 6; Wyo Comp Stat (1945) § 10-904.

87. Mass Anno State (1942) Ch 123 § 100A.

atric examination. In some states this is done through the use of impartial experts, while in others, the defendant is committed to a mental institution for testing and observation.

§ 302. Test of competency to stand trial

The test generally used to determine whether a defendant is sufficiently sane to stand trial is whether he has the capacity to understand the nature and object of the proceedings against him, his own condition with reference to them and whether he is capable of making or assisting in a rational defense.

Some jurisdictions employ an unfortunate rule regarding insanity at trial. They hold that the trial is only to be postponed if the defendant became insane after commission of the offense. In those jurisdictions persons who recently became insane cannot be made to stand trial, while persons having suffered mental deficiencies for a longer period of time are placed on trial.

The reasoning behind this rule apparently is that a person who suffered a mental illness at the time of his commission of a crime can raise the insanity defense at trial. This, however, begs the question, since the tests of responsibility for commission of an unlawful act and for ability to stand trial are quite different. A person may not be sufficiently rational to stand trial, yet still be legally responsible for his acts.

If your client is being tried in a jurisdiction that still follows this antiquated rule, consider arguing that the court is depriving him of due process of law. Your client may have defenses other than insanity—such as self-defense or justification—which he is incapable of communicating to you because of his mental condition. To force him to trial under these circumstances would be to deprive him of his right to a fair trial.

Some state statutes add mental deficiency or "feeble-mindedness" to insanity as ground for the postponement of pending criminal proceedings against accused persons.[88] Other states, such as Maryland and Massachusetts, have special procedures for handling "defective delinquents," while a large number of states have enacted special legislation dealing with "sexual psychopaths." A few states permit commitment where the person charged with a crime appears to be epileptic [89] or alcoholic.[90]

§ 303. The practical effect of a determination of insanity at the time of trial

The finding that your client is insane at the time of trial can be of great practical assistance to you at an eventual trial. Your client, if found presently insane, will probably be confined to a mental hospital. After he is pronounced sane and returned, you can argue at trial the improbability that your client developed the mental illness between the time of the commission of the crime and the time of the finding of insanity. Further, sympathy will develop for your client as a result of the time he spent incarcerated in a prison hospital without a determination of his guilt or innocence. The passage of time serves to diminish any emotional dislike for your client as the result of the nature of his alleged crime.

§ 304. Sanity at time of sentence or execution

A defendant may not be sentenced or executed if he is not then sane. The test of sanity at sentencing or execution is similar to the test at the time of trial. The accused must be able to understand the nature of the proceedings, and his sentence in relation to them.

As a practical matter, in order to prevent the imposition of sentence or an execution, you must be prepared to

88. NJ Rev Stat § 30; 4-82: Pa Stat (Purdon, perm ed) tit 50 § 51 (except on conviction of first degree murder): Va Code §§ 19-202, 53-88; Wis Stat § 357.13(1).

See also Kan Gen Stat § 62-1531: Tenn Code § 4519.

89. Md Anno Code (1951) Art 16 § 58.

90. NJ Rev Stat (1937) § 30:4-82.

establish that your client became insane after the trial. If you allege that he is suffering from long-term insanity, you will be hard put to explain your failure to raise the issue at trial. If the issue was raised at trial and your client was found sane, that ruling may be binding as to his then mental condition. You will therefore have to allege and show new mental disorder.

CHAPTER TEN

THE JURY

A. RIGHT TO A JURY TRIAL

§ 305. Nature and basis of right

The right to a jury trial in criminal cases is a basic fundamental to the American system of justice.[1] Moreover,

1. Duncan v Louisiana, 391 US 145, 20 L Ed 2d 491, 88 S Ct 1444, reh den 392 US 947, 20 L Ed 2d 1412, 88 S Ct 2270.

See also Rothweiler v Superior Court of Pima County, 100 Ariz 37, 410 P2d 479, 16 ALR3d 1362.

Wisdom and experience have demonstrated that constitutional guaranties of jury trials are necessary for the protection of persons accused of crime. Ex parte Milligan (US) 4 Wall 2, 18 L Ed 281.

Annotations: Right of accused in misdemeanor prosecution to change of venue on grounds of inability to secure fair trial and the like. 34 ALR3d 804.

Applicability, in proceedings under

the right to have a jury trial is a personal right which is not to be denied the accused against his will.[2]

Article III of the United States Constitution provides that the trial of all crimes, except in cases of impeachment, shall be by jury,[3] and the Sixth Amendment to the Constitution provides that in all criminal prosecutions the accused shall enjoy the right to a speedy trial by an impartial jury. Both the Third Article and the Sixth Amendment

statutes relating to sexual psychopaths, of constitutional provisions for the protection of a person accused of crime. 34 ALR3d 652.

Propriety of jurors asking questions in open court during course of trial. 31 ALR3d 872.

Right to trial by jury in criminal prosecution for driving while intoxicated or similar offense. 16 ALR3d 1373.

Taking and use of trial notes by jury. 14 ALR3d 831.

Right to jury trial in juvenile court delinquency proceedings. 100 ALR2d 1241.

Rule or statute requiring opposing party's consent to withdrawal of demand for jury trial. 90 ALR2d 1162.

Indoctrination by court of persons summoned for jury service. 89 ALR2d 197 at page 215.

Propriety of criminal trial of one under influence of drugs or intoxicants at time of trial. 83 ALR2d 1067.

Substitution of judge in criminal case. 83 ALR2d 1032.

Criminal trial of deaf, mute, or blind person. 80 ALR2d 1084.

Consolidated trial upon several indictments or informations against same accused, over his objection. 59 ALR2d 841 at page 846.

Right of accused to insist, over objection of prosecution or court, upon trial by court without a jury. 51 ALR2d 1346.

Exclusion of public during criminal trial. 48 ALR2d 1436.

Comment note—Beliefs regarding capital punishment as disqualifying juror in capital case—post-Witherspoon cases. 39 ALR3d 550.

Prejudicial effect of court's direction or caution to party-witness not to discuss case with anyone, including his counsel, during recess or the like. 46 ALR2d 517.

Mandamus or prohibition as remedy to enforce right to jury trial. 41 ALR2d 780.

Hostile sentiment or prejudice as ground for continuance of criminal trial. 39 ALR2d 1314.

Fingerprints, palm prints, or bare footprints as evidence. 28 ALR2d 1115 at page 1141.

Impaneling or selection of jury in accused's absence. 26 ALR2d 762 at pages 793 and 795.

Interrogation or poll of jurors, during criminal trial, as to whether they have read newspaper articles pertaining to alleged crime or the trial. 15 ALR2d 1152.

2. State v Ricks, 173 Kan 660, 250 P2d 773.

3. US Const Art 3 § 2.

relate to prosecutions that are strictly criminal in character.[4]

§ 306. Extent of right

The due process clause of the Fourteenth Amendment imposes upon the states the requirement of Article 3, § 2, of the Federal Constitution and of the Sixth Amendment that jury trials be available to criminal defendants.[5] Moreover, state legislature cannot, by a mere change of name or form, convert that which is in its nature a prosecution for a crime into a civil proceeding and thus deprive parties of their right to a trial by jury.[6]

§ 307. Nature of offense

The United States Supreme Court has declared that there is a category of petty crimes or offenses which is not subject to the Sixth Amendment jury trial provision nor to the Fourteenth Amendment jury trial requirement applicable to the states.[7] Hence, the constitutional guaranty of

4. United States v Regan, 232 US 37, 58 L Ed 494, 34 S Ct 213; Callan v Wilson, 127 US 540, 32 L Ed 223, 8 S Ct 1301.

The provisions of the Sixth Amendment, although occurring later, are not to be regarded as modifying or altering the original provision made in the Third Article. Brown v Epps, 91 Va 726, 21 SE 119.

5. Dyke v Taylor Implement Mfg. Co. 391 US 216, 20 L Ed 2d 538, 88 S Ct 1472.

The due process clause guarantees a right of jury trial in all state criminal cases which—were they to be tried in a federal court—would come within the Sixth Amendment's guaranty of trial by jury. Duncan v Louisiana, 391 US 145, 20 L Ed 2d 491, 88 S Ct 1444, reh den 392 US 947, 20 L Ed 2d 1412, 88 S Ct 2270, stating that in determining whether the due process clause of the Fourteenth Amendment guarantees the Sixth Amendment right to a trial by jury, it is of little relevance that the framers of the amendment did not intend its jury trial requirement to bind the states.

6. Ashley v Three Justices (Ashley v Wait) 228 Mass 63, 116 NE 961, 8 ALR 1463, error dismd 250 US 652, 63 L Ed 1190, 40 S Ct 53; Hedden v Hand, 90 NJ Eq 583, 107 A 285, 5 ALR 1463.

7. Duncan v Louisiana, 391 US 145, 20 L Ed 491, 88 S Ct 1444, reh den 392 US 947, 20 L Ed 2d 1412, 88 S Ct 2270.

See also the separate opinion in Cheff v Schnackenberg, 384 US 373, 16 L Ed 2d 629, 86 S Ct 1523, stating that the right of trial by jury in criminal cases secured by Article 3, § 2, clause 3, and by the Sixth Amend-

jury trial does not extend to petty crimes.[8]

Whether a particular offense is to be classed as a crime so as to require a jury trial, or as a petty offense triable summarily without a jury, depends primarily upon the nature of the offense.[9] The task of distinguishing a petty offense from a serious one is connected with the accused's right to have a jury trial fall upon the courts.[10] The penalty authorized for a particular crime is of major relevance in determining whether it is serious or not, and may in itself, if severe enough, subject the trial to the Federal Constitution's Sixth Amendment guaranty of a jury trial; the penalty authorized by the law of the locality may be taken as a gauge of its social and ethical judgments of the crime in question.[11]

ment of the Federal Constitution, does not extend to prosecutions for petty offenses.

8. Dyke v Taylor Implement Mfg. Co. 391 US 216, 20 L Ed 2d 538, 88 S Ct 1472.

Minor offenses were tried by magistrates and justices of the peace without a jury at common law and before the adoption of the state constitutions, and it is the general rule that the constitutional right to a jury trial does not apply to such cases. State v Hauser, 137 Neb 138, 288 NW 518.

9. District of Columbia v Colts, 282 US 63, 75 L Ed 177, 51 S Ct 52.

But compare Rothweiler v Superior Court of Pima County, 100 Ariz 37, 410 P2d 479, 16 ALR3d 1362, stating that the statutory offense of driving while under the influence of intoxicating liquor, which was not a common-law offense, is a serious, rather than petty, crime which is triable before a jury when properly demanded, since upon conviction the defendant is subject to imprisonment of 10 days to 6 months, a fine of $100 to $300, and suspension of his right to drive for a period not to exceed 90 days, or any combination of the three.

10. The boundaries of the petty offense category have always been ill-defined, if not ambulatory. The task to define these boundaries for the purpose of the constitutional right to trial by jury falls on the courts, which must either pass upon the validity of legislative attempts to identify those petty offenses which are exempt from jury trial, or where the legislature has not addressed itself to the problem, must themselves face the question in the first instance; in either case it is necessary to draw a line in the spectrum of crime, separating petty from serious infractions. Duncan v Louisiana, 391 US 145, 20 L Ed 2d 491, 88 S Ct 1444, reh den 392 US 947, 20 L Ed 2d 1412, 88 S Ct 2270.

11. In determining whether the length of the authorized prison term or the seriousness of other punishment is enough in itself to require a jury trial, the Supreme Court of the United States refers to objective criteria, chiefly the existing laws and practices in the nation; the critical factor is the length of the sentence autho-

As a rule, a jury trial cannot be constitutionally demanded in connection with a prosecution for violation of a municipal ordinance or in municipal or city courts that are minor courts.[12] This is particularly so if the proceeding is held not to be a criminal prosecution within the meaning of the constitutional guaranty of jury trial in criminal prosecutions,[13] and is not, and has no reference to, a violation of a criminal law of the state.[14]

The United States Supreme Court has held that prosecutions for criminal contempt are within the rule that the due process clause of the Fourteenth Amendment imposes upon the states the requirement of Article 3, § 2, of the Federal Constitution and of the Sixth Amendment that jury trials be available to criminal defendants.[15]

rized and not the length of the penalty actually imposed. Duncan v Louisiana, supra, pointing out that the United States Constitution does not require a jury trial with respect to crimes carrying possible penalties up to 6 months if they otherwise qualify as petty offenses, but a crime punishable by 2 years in prison is, based on past and contemporary standards in the United States, a serious crime and not a petty offense, and hence the defendant in such a case is entitled to a jury trial.

12. Re Davis, 28 Ariz 312, 236 P 715; State ex rel. Sellars v Parker, 87 Fla 181, 100 So 260; Hunt v Jacksonville, 34 Fla 504, 16 So 398; Loeb v Jennings, 133 Ga 796, 67 SE 101, affd 219 US 582, 55 L Ed 345, 31 S Ct 469; Floyd v Eatonton, 14 Ga 354; Re Moynihan, 332 Mo 1022, 62 SW2d 410, 91 ALR 74; State v Hauser, 137 Neb 138, 288 NW 518 (drunken driving in violation of city ordinance).

See also St. Paul v Robinson, 129 Minn 383, 152 NW 777, recognizing the rule where such a violation of a municipal ordinance is a petty offense.

13. Liberman v State, 26 Neb 464, 42 NW 419; Ogden v Madison, 111 Wis 413, 87 NW 568.

14. Natal v Louisiana, 139 US 621, 35 L Ed 288, 11 S Ct 636; Miller v Birmingham, 151 Ala 469, 44 So 388; Hunt v Jacksonville, 34 Fla 504, 16 So 398; Pearson v Wimbish, 124 Ga 701, 52 SE 751; Re Kinsel, 64 Kan 1, 67 P 634; State v Fourcade, 45 La Ann 717, 13 So 187; St. Paul v Robinson, 129 Minn 383, 152 NW 777 (ordinance providing for prosecution of persons using streetcar tickets not issued directly to them); Liberman v State, 26 Neb 464, 42 NW 419; State v Trenton, 51 NJL 498, 18 A 116; Anderson v O'Donnell, 29 SC 355, 7 SE 523; Ogden v Madison, 111 Wis 413, 87 NW 568.

15. Dyke v Taylor Implement Mfg. Co. 391 US 216, 20 L Ed 2d 538, 88 S Ct 1472.

See also Bloom v Illinois, 391 US 194, 20 L Ed 2d 522, 88 S Ct 1477 recognizing the rule to be true at least with respect to serious, as distinguished from petty, criminal contempts.

§ 308. Impanelment of jury

Ordinarily a party or an accused has no vested right to any particular juror or jurors; all that he can insist on is an impartial jury of the requisite number in his own case and, at the most, a substantial compliance with the statutes governing the selecting and summoning of jurors.[16] As a result, the accused cannot insist upon the attendance of all the veniremen directed to be summoned.[17]

A party or an accused is not entitled, in the absence of statute, to any particular number of the jury panel at the beginning of a trial.[18] Thus he cannot demand the presence of the maximum number of jurors provided for by statute to be drawn or summoned.[19]

While an accused's presence is not always necessary at the ordering of matters purely preliminary to the trial, he is entitled to be present during the trial, and the trial commences when the impaneling of the jury begins.[20] Pursuant to this rule, the record of a felony case should show the presence of the accused during the impaneling of the jury.[21] However, there is authority to the effect that the

16. Quillen v State (Sup) 49 Del 163, 112 A2d 848; State v Sturdivant, 31 NJ 165, 155 A2d 771, cert den 362 US 956, 4 L Ed 2d 873, 80 S Ct 873, wherein the 14th juror on a panel was chosen from among persons produced by an undersheriff who telephoned several large commercial companies to send employees to the courthouse to serve as jurors.

17. Young v State, 149 Ala 16, 43 So 100; State v Hoozer, 26 La Ann 599.

18. Blankenship v State, 10 Okla Crim 551, 139 P 840.

19. Blankenship v State, supra.

It is proper to proceed without absent veniremen for whom attachments have been issued. State v Rountree, 32 La Ann 1144 (murder).

20. Hopt v Utah, 110 US 574, 28 L Ed 262, 4 S Ct 202; Echert v United States (CA8 Neb) 188 F2d 336, 26 ALR2d 752; Commonwealth v Ventura, 294 Mass 113, 1 NE2d 30.

21. Lewis v United States, 146 US 370, 36 L Ed 1011, 13 S Ct 136; Brown v State, 24 Ark 620; Dougherty v Commonwealth, 69 Pa 286; French v State, 85 Wis 400, 55 NW 566, ovrld on other grounds Boehm v State, 190 Wis 609, 209 NW 730.

accused may waive his right to be present during the impaneling of the jury.[22]

§ 309. Effect of conviction in violation of right

If the accused's right to a jury trial is violated, a conviction obtained without the jury is invalid for any purpose.[23] In fact, so imperative is the right of a defendant charged with crime to a jury trial that if denied it, he is not required to show that he was injured by reason of the deprivation, and without making any such showing, he is entitled to have his conviction set aside.[24]

On the other hand, defects and irregularities in the selection and impanelment of a jury may or may not be prejudicial to such a degree as to constitute a deprivation of the right to jury trial and thereby to call for a reversal of a conviction.[25] The appellate court will indulge any proper presumption in favor of the proceedings summoning and impaneling a jury, and will not reverse for irregularities where no injury is shown, unless the objection is made before the jury is sworn, as required by statute.[26]

22. Kuzminski v Waser, 374 Ill 428, 29 NE2d 594.

23. Callan v Wilson, 127 US 540, 32 L Ed 223, 8 S Ct 1301; Windsor v McVeigh, 93 US 274, 23 L Ed 914; Re McQuown, 19 Okla 347, 91 P 689.

24. People v Hartman, 103 Cal 242, 37 P 153.

25. Gulf, C. & S. F. R. Co. v Shane, 157 US 348, 39 L Ed 727, 15 S Ct 641 (if it deprives a party of a substantial right, it is prejudicial); Kinsey v State, 49 Ariz 201, 65 P2d 1141, 125 ALR 3; People v Searcey, 121 Cal 1, 53 P 359; People v Ebanks, 117 Cal 652, 49 P 1049; People v Chrisoulas, 367 Ill 85, 10 NE2d 382, 112 ALR 990; Harrison v State, 231 Ind 147, 106 NE2d 912, 32 ALR2d 875; Broadway Mfg. Co. v Leavenworth Terminal R. & Bridge Co. 81 Kan 616, 106 P 1034; Viita v Dolan, 132 Minn 128, 155 NW 1077; Thomas v State, 117 Miss 532, 78 So 147 (accused absented himself during examination of part of jurors); State v Rouner, 333 Mo 1236, 64 SW2d 916, 92 ALR 1099; State v Rodriguez, 23 NM 156, 167 P 426; Queenan v Territory, 11 Okla 261, 71 P 218, affd 190 US 548, 47 L Ed 1175, 23 S Ct 762 (mere irregularities not prejudicial); Harjo v United States, 1 Okla Crim 590, 98 P 1021.

The defendant in a criminal case has no cause of complaint and can take no exception for such irregularities in selecting and impaneling the grand jury by which he was indicted as do not prejudice him. Agnew v United States, 165 US 36, 41 L Ed 624, 17 S Ct 235; State v Rouner, 333 Mo 1236, 64 SW2d 916, 92 ALR 1099.

26. Karnes v Commonwealth, 125 Va 758, 99 SE 562, 4 ALR 1509; State v Barnes, 54 Wash 493, 103 P 792.

B. WAIVER OR RELINQUISHMENT OF RIGHT TO JURY TRIAL

§ 310. In general

The pronounced trend in the decisions, particularly the later cases, is in favor of the rule which permits an accused, regardless of the character of the offense with which he is charged, whether a misdemeanor or a felony, to waive his right to jury trial.[27] The United States Supreme Court, after an extensive review and analysis of the authorities on the question, has ruled that the effect of the federal constitutional provisions in respect of trial by jury is not to establish a tribunal as a part of the frame of government, but only to guarantee to the accused the right to a trial by jury, and that while the provision of Article 3, § 3, of the Constitution, confers a right upon the accused which cannot be withheld from him, he may at his election waive or forgo that right.[28] Along these lines, there are numerous decisions by state courts upholding the constitutionality of positive legislative enactments to the effect that

27. Munsell v People, 122 Colo 420, 222 P2d 615; Journigan v State, 223 Md 405, 164 A2d 896, 83 ALR2d 1026, cert den 365 US 853, 5 L Ed 2d 817, 81 S Ct 818; Commonwealth v Rowe, 257 Mass 172, 153 NE 537, 48 ALR 762 (holding that the right can be waived, but that a court without a jury is without jurisdiction of a criminal case); State v Hernandez, 46 NM 134, 123 P2d 387; Ex parte Kortgaard, 66 ND 555, 267 SW 438, 105 ALR 1107; Marfield v Cincinnati, D. & T. Traction Co. 111 Ohio St 139, 144 NE 689, 40 ALR 357, 363 (dictum); State v Harvey, 117 Or 466, 242 P 440; Commonwealth v Petrillo, 340 Pa 33, 16 A2d 50.

The right of trial by jury in criminal cases is a personal right which may be waived. People v Bradley, 7 Ill 2d 619, 131 NE2d 538, 56 ALR2d 832.

A defendant in a criminal case may waive his right to a trial by jury insofar as he is personally concerned. State v Ricks, 173 Kan 660, 250 P2d 773, holding, however, that the defendant does not have a right to compel the court to try his case without the assistance of a jury.

28. See Adams v United States, 317 US 269, 87 L Ed 268, 63 S Ct 236, 143 ALR 435, reh den 317 US 713, 87 L Ed 568, wherein the United States Supreme Court seems to have resolved all doubt, as regards the Federal Constitution, upon the question by holding that one charged with the commission of a crime, whose education qualifies him to make a free and intelligent choice, may, with the considered approval of the court, though without the benefit of advice of counsel, waive his constitutional right to a jury trial.

one charged with crime has the right to waive trial by jury and elect to be tried by the court, and these decisions also sustain the validity of such proceedings.[29] On the other hand, conceding that the accused, even in the absence of counsel, may, by a plea of guilty, waive his right to a jury trial, the view is generally taken that such a waiver must rest upon an adequate preliminary statement of the court delineating the rights of the accused and the consequences of the proposed plea or waive, with the implication, at least tacit, that the accused should reasonably comprehend his position and appreciate the possible effects of his choice.[30] The procedure for waiver differs in the various jurisdictions.

§ 311. Factors mitigating against waiver

The presence of a jury greatly increases the possibility of reversible error in terms of the hearing by them of objectionable matter which would be deemed not to have affected a trial judge sitting as the trier of the fact. Additionally, the very process of jury selection can contain the seeds of ultimate reversal whether through improper prosecutorial remarks or because of prejudicial publicity,[31] systematic exclusion of a particular racial or ethnic group,[32] prejudicial remarks by court officers, or other circumstances which may be prejudicial to your client.[33]

§ 312. Factors indicating waiver as advantageous

Among the other considerations are the identity and

29. Hallinger v Davis, 146 US 314, 36 L Ed 986, 13 S Ct 105 (the defendant pleaded guilty to murder, and the state statute in such case allowed the court to "proceed by examination of witnesses to determine the degree of the crime and give sentence accordingly"); State v Worden, 46 Conn 349; Re Dawson, 20 Idaho 178, 117 P 696; State v Berg, 237 Iowa 356, 21 NW2d 777; Re Staff, 63 Wis 285, 23 NW 587.

30. People v Terry, 366 Ill 520, 9 NE2d 322; Mullen v State, 28 Okla Crim 218, 230 P 285.

31. Irvin v Dowd, 366 US 717, 6 L Ed 2d 751, 81 S Ct 1639.

32. Whitus v Georgia, 385 US 545, 17 L Ed 2d 599, 87 S Ct 643, conformed to 223 Ga 127, 153 SE2d 446.

33. Parker v Gladden, 385 US 363, 17 L Ed 2d 420, 87 S Ct 468.

predilection of the judges who would preside at the jury or nonjury trial, the nature of the crime and of the evidence, which would be excluded in a jury trial but which a judge sitting as the trier of the facts might hear, whether a particular judge might be inclined to be lenient at sentence because the defendant spared the bother and expense of a jury trial, etc.

The final decision whether to waive the jury should be left to your client. If he insists upon a jury trial against your wishes, accede to his request. If you decide that his best interests would be served by a waiver of a trial by jury, give your client a detailed analysis of your reasoning. However, even as you attempt to convince him of the desirability of following your advice, assure him that if he insists upon a jury trial, you will nevertheless endeavor to represent him vigorously and to the best of your ability.

§ 313. Seriousness of offense as factor

Some states take the view in connection with a waiver of a jury trial that there is no basis for a distinction with respect to whether the offense in question is a felony or a misdemeanor.[34] In fact, lately there has been a noticeable trend in the more recent cases to recognize the right of an accused to waive the right to jury trial with respect to felonies, and to deny that there is any reasonable basis for holding that such a waiver may be effective with respect to misdemeanor cases and not with respect to felony cases.[35] "We are unable," says the United States Supreme Court, "to find in the decisions any convincing ground for holding that a waiver is effective in misdemeanor cases but not

34. Re Dawson, 20 Idaho 178, 117 P 696; Re Staff, 63 Wis 285, 23 NW 587.

35. Munsell v People, 122 Colo 420, 222 P2d 615; People v Spegal, 5 Ill 2d 211, 125 NE2d 468, 51 ALR2d 1337 (murder case); People ex rel. Swanson v Fisher, 340 Ill 250, 172 NE 722, ovrlg Harris v People, 128 Ill 585, 21 NE 563; Journigan v State, 223 Md 405, 164 A2d 896, 83 ALR2d 1026, cert den 365 US 853, 5 L Ed 2d 817, 81 S Ct 818; State v Hernandez, 46 NM 134, 123 P2d 387, ovrlg Territory v Ortiz, 8 NM 154, 42 P 87; Ex parte Kortgaard, 66 ND 555, 267 NW 438, 105 ALR 1107; State v Harvey, 117 Or 466, 242 P 440; Commonwealth v Petrillo, 340 Pa 33, 16 A2d 50.

effective in the case of felonies."[36] But at least in capital cases and prosecutions for murder, it has been held that the accused cannot waive trial by a jury of 12 competent jurors.[37]

§ 314. Acquiescence and approval of prosecution and court

In some jurisdictions and cases, the rule is that the defendant cannot waive a jury trial without the acquiescence of the prosecutor and the Judge. Under this view, before any waiver of the right of one charged with crime to trial by jury can become effective, the consent of government counsel and the sanction of the court must be had, in addition to the express and intelligent consent of the defendant.[38] In fact, some courts have said that even if there has been a waiver of a jury trial by the parties, the court may disregard it and require the issues to be submitted to a jury.[39]

Whether a jury waiver should be approved by the court is a matter resting in its discretion.[40] Furthermore, it is

36. Patton v United States, 281 US 276, 74 L Ed 854, 50 S Ct 253, 70 ALR 263, disapproved on other grounds Williams v Florida, 399 US 78, 26 L Ed 2d 446, 90 S Ct 1893, Williams v Florida, decided by the United States Supreme Court on June 22, 1970, contains a good discussion on the nature of the right to a jury trial and traces the history and development of the jury from the early times when it performed a different "inquisitory" function.

37. The accused is competent to waive any irregularity or right, constitutional or statutory, except, in a capital case, the right of trial by a jury of 12 men, and that extends to waiver of the right of trial by jury of 12 men competent to act as jurors. Oborn v State, 143 Wis 249, 126 NW 737.

One who pleads "not guilty" to an accusation of murder is entitled to be tried by a jury of 12 men, which right he cannot waive even by consenting to proceed with 11 in the jury box when one is found mentally unfit. State v Rogers, 162 NC 656, 78 SE 293.

38. State v Mead (Ind) 4 Blackf 309; State v Kaufman, 51 Iowa 578, 2 NW 275.

39. Jones v State, 155 Fla 558, 20 So 2d 901; Wittenberg v Onsgard, 78 Minn 342, 81 NW 14; Jayne v Kane, 140 Va 27, 124 SE 247.

40. United States v Holt (CA2 NY) 333 F2d 455, cert den 380 US 942, 13 L Ed 2d 961, 85 S Ct 1020.

Whether a jury waiver should be approved by the court is a matter

said that the duty of the trial court in that regard is not to be discharged as a mere matter of rote, but with sound and advised discretion, with an eye to avoid unreasonable or undue departures from the mode of trial or from any of the essential elements thereof, and with a caution increasing in degree as the offenses dealt with increase in gravity.[41]

The Federal Rules of Criminal Procedure declare that cases required to be tried by jury shall be so tried unless the defendant waives a jury trial in writing with the approval of the court and the consent of the government.[42] This Rule is inapplicable in cases such as those involving petty offenses, in which neither the Constitution nor any federal statute requires a jury trial.[43] The Rule is also inapplicable where the accused pleads guilty, since a plea of guilty leaves no issue of fact to be submitted to a jury.[44]

§ 315. What constitutes waiver

Insofar as there may be a waiver of the right to jury trial with respect to a criminal case, failure to demand a jury trial may under certain circumstances constitute such a waiver.[45] Where, however, a statute provides that such a

resting in its discretion. Mason v United States (CA10 Utah) 250 F2d 704.

41. State v Ricks, 173 Kan 660, 250 P2d 773 (holding that a defendant's waiver of trial by jury in a felony case does not compel the court to try the case without a jury over the objection of the state).

42. Rule 23(a), Fed Rules of Crim Proc.

See Singer v United States, 380 US 24, 13 L Ed 2d 630, 85 S Ct 783, holding the Federal Rule to be valid.

43. United States v Au Young (DC Hawaii) 142 F Supp 666.

44. Lipscomb v United States (CA8 Mo) 226 F2d 812, cert den 350 US 971, 100 L Ed 843, 76 S Ct 445, reh den 350 US 1003, 100 L Ed 866, 76 S Ct 550, ovrld on other grounds Bistram v United States (CA8 ND) 237 F2d 243, as stated in Lipscomb v United States (CA8 Mo) 298 F2d 9, cert den 369 US 853, 8 L Ed 2d 12, 82 S Ct 941, reh den 369 US 891, 8 L Ed 2d 291, 82 S Ct 1163.

45. State v Mills, 39 NJL 587; People v Cook (NY) 45 Hun 34; State v Packenham, 40 Wash 403, 82 P 597.

The accused cannot object to the lack of a jury trial on the hearing by the court of a plea in bar setting up the statute of limitations in a prosecution for robbery, where no objection was made by him at the time. United States v Nimerick (CA2 Vt) 118 F2d 464, 152 ALR 620, cert den 313 US 592, 85 L Ed 1546, 61 S Ct 1117.

waiver must clearly and affirmatively appear upon the record, waiver cannot be assumed or implied from the silence of the accused or his mere failure to demand a jury trial.[46]

In some criminal trials, a jury waiver is required by statute or procedural rules to be in writing and in such a case, a waiver without a writing is ineffective and void.[47]

§ 316. Withdrawal of waiver

Whether a person who is accused of crime who has regularly waived a jury trial will be permitted to withdraw the waiver and have his case tried before a jury is ordinarily within the discretion of the trial court.[48] Usually, if an accused's application for withdrawal of waiver is made in due season so as not to substantially delay or impede the cause of justice, the trial court should allow the waiver to be withdrawn.[49]

Whether a motion for the withdrawal of a waiver of trial by jury made prior to the actual commencement of the trial of the case is timely depends primarily upon the facts and circumstances of the individual case. Where there is no showing that granting the motion would unduly delay the trial or would otherwise impede justice, such a motion was held to be timely.[50] But a motion for withdrawal of a jury trial waiver will be denied if an inordinate delay will

46. Simmons v State, 75 Ohio St 346, 79 NE 555.

47. Hatchett v Government of Guam (CA9 Guam) 212 F2d 767, cert dismd 348 US 801, 99 L Ed 633, 75 S Ct 17 (under Rule 23(a) of the Federal Rules of Criminal Procedure).

48. People v Melton, 125 Cal App 2d Supp 901, 271 P2d 962, 46 ALR2d 914; State v Kavanaugh, 203 La 1, 13 So 2d 366; Newton v State, 211 Miss 644, 52 So 2d 488.

See, however, State v Bannock, 53 Minn 419, 55 NW 558, where it was held that a waiver of trial by jury, voluntarily made, may not be withdrawn.

49. People v Melton, 125 Cal App 2d Supp 901, 271 P2d 962, 46 ALR2d 914; Butler v State, 97 Ga 404, 23 SE 822.

50. People v Melton, 125 Cal App 2d Supp 901, 271 P2d 962, 46 ALR2d 914.

result.[51] In any event, motion for withdrawal of waiver made after the commencement of the trial is not timely and should not be allowed.[52]

§ 317. Waiver of full number of jurors

The trend of the recent authorities is in favor of the view that the constitutional right of an accused to a trial of the charge against him by a jury of 12 persons is a right which the accused may waive, even in a felony.[53] There would seem to be no default if the waiver of a full jury is had with the consent of the state counsel and the sanction of the court.[54] A statute providing for waiver by the accused of a full jury of 12 with respect to certain offenses, including low grades of felonies, was held to be constitutional.[55]

Ordinarily an accused's voluntary consent in open court, either personally or through his counsel, and either orally

51. People v Colton, 92 Cal App 2d 704, 207 P2d 890; State v Rankin, 102 Conn 46, 127 A 916.

52. Commonwealth v Rowe, 257 Mass 172, 153 NE 537, 48 ALR 762 (after presentation of state's evidence); State v Frohner, 150 Ohio St 53, 37 Ohio Ops 406, 80 NE2d 868 (after sentence on plea of guilty).

53. Kirk v State, 247 Ala 43, 22 So 2d 431; People ex rel. Swanson v Fisher, 340 Ill 250, 172 NE 722, ovrlg Harris v People, 128 Ill 585, 21 NE 563; State v Kaufman, 51 Iowa 578, 2 NW 275 (provision that the right of trial by jury shall remain inviolate); Ex parte Kortgaard, 66 ND 555, 267 NW 438, 105 ALR 1107 (provision that the right of trial by jury shall be secured to all and remain inviolate); Ex parte Hollingsworth, 46 Okla Crim 353, 287 P 840 (where Constitution, in addition to preserving right to jury trial, provides for waiver of jury as to all issues joined in any court); Commonwealth ex rel. Ross v Egan, 281 Pa 251, 126 A 488 (holding that there can be waiver, at least as to lesser felonies like larceny); State v Lane, 40 Wash 2d 734, 246 P2d 474 (holding that in a burglary prosecution where one juror became ill and the accused consented to proceed with 11 jurors, the right to be tried by 12 jurors was effectively waived).

Waiver of full jury. Standards Relating to Trial by Jury, American Bar Association Project on Minimum Standards for Criminal Justice, Tentative Draft, May, 1968 p 40.

54. Ex parte Kortgaard, 66 ND 555, 267 NW 438, 105 ALR 1107; State v Lane, 40 Wash 2d 734, 246 P2d 474 (holding that a defendant is not constitutionally prevented from waiving trial by a jury of 12 and submitting to trial by a jury of 11 when the twelfth juror fell ill, and ovrlg State v Ellis, 22 Wash 129, 60 P 136).

55. Lavery v Commonwealth, 101 Pa 560.

or in the form of a written stipulation, to submit to trial before a jury of fewer than 12 members, constitutes an effective waiver of his right to trial before a full jury.[56] Moreover, a defendant's participation without objection in a trial before a jury of fewer than 12 members constitutes a waiver of a full jury.[57] On the other hand, the mere participation in a trial with less than a full jury upon objecting to the proceeding does not constitute a waiver.[58]

It has been held that a defendant in a capital case if he goes to trial before a jury cannot waive his right to be tried by 12 jurors and consent that he be tried by a fewer number.[59] Such distinction as to capital cases has been assigned to the principle that in capital cases, in favorem vitae, the prisoner can waive nothing.[60]

The Federal Rules of Criminal Procedure state that juries must consist of 12, but at any time before verdict the parties may stipulate in writing with the approval of the court that the jury may consist of any number less than 12.[61] Under the provisions of the Federal Rules of Criminal Procedure permitting a trial by less than 12 jurors upon stipulation of the parties in writing with the approval of the court, it has been held that technical imperfection in the form of the stipulation is not decisive, the determinative question being whether under basic constitutional principles the waiver was intelligently made with the accused's consent.[62] Notwithstanding the express language

56. People v Scudieri, 363 Ill 84, 1 NE2d 225; State v Ellard, 95 NH 217, 60 A2d 461, cert den 335 US 904, 93 L Ed 438, 69 S Ct 400; State v Lane, 40 Wash 2d 734, 246 P2d 474.

57. Phipps v Commonwealth, 205 Ky 832, 266 SW 651; Re Wilkins, 7 Okla Crim 422, 115 P 1118.

58. Simmons v State, 88 Ga 272, 14 SE 613.

59. Commonwealth v Petrillo, 340 Pa 33, 16 A2d 50.

60. Re Staff, 63 Wis 285, 23 NW 587, noting various cases to such effect, but confining its holding to the decision that the legislature can provide for a waiver of jury trial as to felonies.

61. Rule 23(b), Fed Rules of Crim Proc.

62. Horne v United States (CA5 Ga) 264 F2d 40, cert den 360 US 934, 3 L Ed 2d 1549, 79 S Ct 1460.

of the rule, a writing has been held not to be an essential prerequisite of a waiver.[63]

C. VOIR DIRE EXAMINATION

§ 318. In general

The accused, the prosecution and the court itself are usually granted the right to examine prospective jurors on their voir dire in order to enable them to select a jury composed of men and women qualified and competent to judge and determine the facts in issue without bias, prejudice, or partiality.[64] The juror is examined on his voir dire, which means in other words, on his oath to speak the truth.[65] The examination of a prospective juror is for the purpose of obtaining a fair and impartial jury, each member of which has a mind free and clear of all interest, bias,

63. Rogers v United States (CA7 Ill) 319 F2d 5, cert den 375 US 989, 11 L Ed 2d 475, 84 S Ct 524; Horne v United States (CA5 Ga) 264 F2d 40, cert den 360 US 934, 3 L Ed 2d 1549, 79 S Ct 1460.

64. Murphy v Lindahl, 24 Ill App 2d 461, 165 NE2d 340, 82 ALR2d 1410; Kujawa v Baltimore Transit Co, 224 Md 195, 167 A2d 96, 89 ALR2d 1166; Dowd-Feder, Inc. v Truesdell, 130 Ohio St 530, 5 Ohio Ops 179, 200 NE 762.

By statute, any party to a jury case has an absolute right to examine prospective jurors on the voir dire. State v Higgs, 143 Conn 138, 120 A2d 152, 54 ALR2d 1199.

Full knowledge of all relevant and material matters that might bear on possible disqualification of a juror is essential to a fair and intelligent exercise of the right of counsel to challenge either for cause or peremptorily. Marvins Credit, Inc. v Steward (Mun Ct App Dist Col) 133 A2d 473.

Annotations: Right of defense counsel to compel prosecuting attorney to disclose information as to prospective jurors. 78 ALR2d 309.

Right of counsel in criminal case personally to conduct the voir dire examination of prospective jurors. 73 ALR2d 1187.

65. Ryder v State, 100 Ga 528, 28 SE 246; State v Duvall, 135 La 710, 65 So 904, error dismd 239 US 626, 60 L Ed 474, 36 S Ct 162; Lohman v People, 1 NY 379.

Practice Aids: Selecting the jury, see 5 Am Jur Trials 143, Selecting the Jury—Plaintiff's View; 5 Am Jur Trials 247, 261, Selecting the Jury—Defense View.

Voir Dire Examination. Standards Relating to Trial by Jury, American Bar Association Project on Minimum Standards for Criminal Justice, Tentative Draft May, 1968 p 63.

or prejudice that might prevent the finding of the true and just verdict.[66]

Under the Federal Rules of Criminal Procedure, the court may permit the defendant or his attorney and the attorney for the government to conduct the examination of prospective jurors, or may itself conduct the examination. If the court conducts the examination itself, the defendant or his attorney and the attorney for the government may supplement the examination by such further inquiry as it deems proper, or the court shall itself submit to the prospective jurors such additional questions by the parties or their attorneys as it deems proper.[67]

Under the pervading principle of criminal law, guaranteed by constitutional provision or secured by statute, that nothing shall be done except in the presence of the accused, he is entitled to be present during the examination of prospective jurors on their voir dire.[68]

You will be given a list containing the names of the panel of prospective jurors, usually when the jurors are brought into the courtroom. In most jurisdictions the list will also specify the occupations and addresses of the prospective jurors.

If you have decided to challenge the entire panel for cause, do so before they are brought into the courtroom. If your challenge is based on an event which takes place in the courtroom during the *voir-dire* examination, such as highly improper remarks by the prosecutor, make your motion out of the hearing of the prospective jurors. An

66. Lauderdale v State, 233 Ark 96, 343 SW2d 422.

The reasons for a voir dire examination of jurors are twofold, namely, to ascertain whether a cause for challenge exists, and to ascertain whether it is wise and expedient to exercise the right of peremptory challenge given to parties by the law. Johnston v State, 239 Ind 77, 155 NE2d 129.

The information elicited in examining prospective jurors on voir dire serves the dual purpose of permitting the court to determine whether a venireman is qualified to act as a juror, and of aiding each party in the exercise of his rights to peremptory challenges. State v Higgs, 143 Conn 138, 120 A2d 152, 54 ALR2d 1199.

67. Rule 24(a), Fed Rules of Crim Proc.

68. Practice Aids: See 21 Am Jur 2d, Criminal Law § 292.

easily understood bias will arise against you on the part of the prospective jurors if they believe that you think it impossible for them to decide the case fairly.

§ 319. Preparation of questions

Unless you are highly experienced, prepare your questions in advance. Besides preventing your overlooking important matters, this will free your mind for evaluating the jurors.

In those jurisdictions, such as the Federal courts, where the court questions the jury, you will be able to note quickly the questions on your list asked by the court and later submit the additional questions omitted by the judge.

§ 320. Compel the prosecutor to disclose his witnesses

Ask the prosecutor to disclose all the witnesses that will testify against the defendant. You want to question the jury as to whether or not they are acquainted with them.

If the prosecutor refuses, address the jury as follows: "Since the prosecutor refuses to disclose whom his witnesses will be, I cannot ask you if you know them. But if it turns out that you are acquainted with one or any of them, do I have your promise that you will forget any feeling of friendship, and consider his testimony as you would that of a total stranger? I know this is a difficult request, but it is important that I have your solemn assurance of it." The prosecutor's unfairness will be quite apparent to the jury.

§ 321. General Techniques of Interrogation

Impress the jurors with your sincerity and fairness. Project yourself into the mind of each of them. Would you react favorably to a person who did not demonstrate complete fairness? If you, as defense counsel, do not appear sincere and fair from the very start, the jury may never trust you. Address the jurors during the *voir-dire* as though you have confidence in their ability to decide the case fairly on the basis of all of the evidence presented while giving the defendant the benefit of all of the presumptions to which he is entitled. Do not, however, make the mistake of doing this through excessive flattery or cajolery. The most effective and subtle form of flattery is to express genuine interest in each juror and in his occupation and particular interests or abilities.

§ 322. Phrasing of questions

Question the jury in a friendly tone. Use "thank you" and "please" liberally. Nobody likes to be addressed discourteously.

Learn to phrase delicate questions diplomatically. For example, in examining a woman, do not ask "Are you married?" If she is not, her answer may cause her embarrassment. Ask, instead, "Is it Miss or Mrs. Jones?"

§ 323. Avoid complex language

In conducting your voir dire examination, speak simply. Start your examination with a clear statement of the nature of the case. You should state in general terms what your defenses are. You are attempting to prepare issues such as reasonable doubt, circumstantial evidence, burden of proof, corroboration of testimony, and the like, in a manner comprehensible to the lay mind. This can be done only with a minimum of legal terminology and a maximum of simple language.

§ 324. Develop rapport early

During the selection process you are able to chat with each juror individually. This will be your only occasion to address him as a person rather than merely a member of a unit. It is at this stage of the case that you must achieve rapport between yourself and the jury. Make them like you.

§ 325. Never embarrass a prospective juror

Never ask a juror a question which could embarrass or humiliate him. If you make the mistake of embarrassing a juror, apologize immediately. While such an apology may negate the possibility of residual anger against you on the part of other jurors, do not permit the offended juror to remain on the panel.

§ 326. Objections to improper questions or statements of law during voir dire

Be quick to object to any incorrect statement of law made by the prosecutor. Indicate why it is incorrect and caution him to leave statements of law to the court unless he is prepared to state the law accurately. Where the prosecutor objects to your stating the law correctly or otherwise, urge upon the court that you are trying to determine whether any implied bias exists in the minds of the jurors against either the defendant or the issues of law in the case.

Have a copy of your Requests to Charge with authoritative cases noted as you state the law to the prospective jurors. If the prosecutor objects to one of your questions as being an improper statement of the law, you will have supporting authority at your fingertips. This will demonstrate your competence to the judge and jury, and will tend to discredit the prosecutor.

Object to questions asked by the court if you consider them prejudicial. Be careful not to antagonize the Judge. Limit your objections to questions that you deem seriously prejudicial.

If the prosecution makes any statements of law to the grand jury, you are entitled to amplify them. While the explanation of law is generally one of the court's functions, you are permitted to explain legal propositions to which the prosecutor has opened the door. For example, if the prosecutor refers to the grand jury's indictment you should explain, preferably in the form of questions beginning with the phrase "Are you aware that", that the indictment is merely an accusation, that the grand jury meets in secret closed sessions, that the defendant is often not aware of the proceeding, that he is not represented before the grand jury by counsel or otherwise, and that no witnesses are called on his behalf.

§ 327. Prepare jurors for trial objections

The following explanation may be apt: "You understand that courts of law have certain rules of procedure, the same as rules of parliamentary procedure at meetings. And if either the prosecutor or myself object during the trial, it is because we think that the other is trying to introduce evidence that is not proper according to the rules."

§ 328. Disclose unfavorable aspects of defense during examination

One of the most devastating blows to any defense is the "surprise" that the prosecutor may suddenly spring on the jury. However, you can minimize such damage by preparing the jury at the very beginning for the harmful evidence against the accused.

Of course, you cannot anticipate every move the prosecution will make. Still, there are certain definite bits of damaging evidence that you should be aware of beforehand.

Take, for example, the defendant with a criminal record. If you decide that the defendant must testify, you know that his record will be brought out on cross-examination. Knowing the prejudicial effect that a criminal record has on a jury, you must reduce the potential effects of such disclosure by unfolding the defendant's record on the voir-dire. At the same time, tell them that the law does not consider his record in determining the facts of the case or the guilt of the accused.

You might state it this way: "The defendant will take the stand and testify in his own behalf. He has a criminal record. His Honor will charge you that you may consider his record only in deciding how much belief you are to give to his testimony as a witness. You will be charged not to consider his criminal record in determining the facts of this case. Now, Mr. Smith, do you promise that if you are selected you will determine the facts in this case and only the facts, and that you will follow His Honor's instructions that the defendant's past criminal record has nothing whatsoever to do with those facts?"

You should use the voir-dire examination to inform the prospective jurors of the defendant's constitutional right not to testify. If you do not plan to have your client take the stand, make sure that each juror understands his right not to testify and will not draw any unfavorable inferences from his failure to take the stand. It is sometimes helpful to dwell upon a defendant's rights in this regard even if you intend to put your client on the stand. The jury is likely to be impressed with a defendant who elects to testify when they are aware of his right to decline to testify.

§ 329. Scope of examination

Reasonable latitude should be given parties in the voir-dire examination of jurors to gain knowledge as to their mental attitudes toward the issues to be tried, for the purpose of aiding them in striking jurors if they are not successful in challenging them for cause.[69] The prosecution and the accused should be given the right to inquire freely about the interest, direct or indirect, of the proposed juror,

69. Atlanta Joint Terminals v Knight, 98 Ga App 482, 106 SE2d 417, 79 ALR2d 539; Mainville v State, 173 Wis 12, 179 NW 764; Chybowski v Bucyrus Co., 127 Wis 332, 106 NW 833.

A wide latitude is allowed counsel in examining jurors on their voir dire. State v Higgs, 143 Conn 138, 120 A2d 152, 54 ALR2d 1199; State v Grillo, 16 NJ 103, 106 A2d 294.

that may affect his final decision.[70] However, an examination of jurors on voir dire should generally be restricted to questions which are pertinent and proper for testing the capacity and competency of the juror.[71]

The scope of counsel's questions, on voir dire inquiry should be governed by a wise and liberal discretion of the court.[72] The trial Judge's discretion controlling the scope of your examination is not absolute. He may be guilty of error if he restricts your inquiries into matters which might be the basis of a challenge for cause. The appellate courts have found error and reversed convictions where the record disclosed a clear abuse of discretion which prejudiced the rights of the defendant. Therefore, always have the *voir dire* examination recorded by the court reporter. In exercising its discretion as to the extent to which the parties may go in examining prospective jurors on the voir dire, the court should grant such latitude as is reasonably necessary to fairly accomplish the purposes of the voir dire, and particularly with reference to the defendant in a criminal case. If there is any likelihood that some prejudice is in the juror's mind which will even subconsciously affect his decision, the party who may be adversely affected should be permitted questions designed to uncover that prejudice; otherwise, the constitutional right of trial by an impartial jury might well be impaired.[73]

Sometimes local jurisprudence may limit the examina-

70. Vindicator Consol. Gold Min. Co. v Firstbrook, 36 Colo 498, 86 P 313; Quay v Duluth, S. S. & A. R. Co., 153 Mich 567, 116 NW 1101; Smith v Eames, 4 Ill 76; Otsego Lake Twp. v Kirsten, 72 Mich 1, 40 NW 26; State v Huffman, 86 Ohio St 229, 99 NE 295; Scribner v State, 3 Okla Crim 601, 108 P 422; State v Chapman, 1 SD 414, 47 NW 411; State v Marfaudille, 48 Wash 117, 92 P 939.

71. Lauderdale v State, 233 Ark 96, 343 SW2d 422 (stating that to ask a venireman on voir dire whether he was a segregationist or an integrationist would have no bearing on his fairness as a juror to sit in the trial of a case being tried for dynamiting a building).

72. It is discretionary with the trial judge whether any questions shall be asked jurors on their examination beyond those prescribed by statute. Commonwealth v Phelps, 209 Mass 396, 95 NE 868.

73. State v Higgs, 143 Conn 138, 120 A2d 152, 54 ALR2d 1199.

tion of a proposed juror in a criminal case to statutory questions respecting his competency.[74]

§ 330. Questions for individual jurors

The following pattern questions should be used as a guide in preparing your own voir dire examination of each juror. Of course, this list is not rigid and inflexible. If a juror answers a particular question in an unsatisfactory manner, you may have to pursue the line of inquiry further than the list indicates. Be prepared for such responses.

Note that many of the questions are really requests to charge, stated in interrogatory form. Thus, in fact, you should first prepare your affirmative requests to charge and then recast them in the form of questions. That way, your authority for your requests to charge can be used as authority to support your voir dire questions if they should be objected to by the prosecutor.

The jury will thus hear the important principles of your case, stated in the voir dire, repeated by you in your opening statement and summation, and then stated by the Judge in his charge. Consequently, these principles will be firmly implanted in the minds of the jurors.

Let us take an assault case as an example. While the prosecutor is questioning, you should note the names of the jurors, their occupations (the husband's occupation if the juror is a married woman). You then approach the first juror, and begin:

1. "Mr. Jones, you live at 200 Central Avenue. Have you ever served as a juror on a criminal case?"

2. (If he answers "no"): "Have you ever served as a juror

74. Monday v State, 32 Ga 672.

The voir dire examination is not usually confined strictly to the questions formulated in the statute, but may be varied and elaborated as the circumstances require, so as to obtain a fair and impartial jury whose minds are free and clear from all interest, bias, or prejudice that might prevent their finding a just and true verdict. Pinder v State, 27 Fla 370, 8 So 837.

on a civil case?" (If he answers "yes," then explain the important distinction between criminal and civil cases).

3. (If he has answered "yes" to Question 1): "Did you ever serve as a juror on a case where the charge was assault?"

4. "Was the charge felonious assault?"

5. "How many cases have you served where the charge was assault?"

6. "Was an agreement as to a verdict reached in each case?"

7. (If he has served as juror on a case of felonious assault): "Having served as a juror on a case where the charge was felonious assault, do you know what the term felonious assault means?" (If he answers "no" as to this term, be prepared to explain it. If you are going to urge the plea of self-defense, discuss the elements of self-defense. If your case is based upon no proof of a crime, ask about the meaning of "corpus delecti." If your basis for defense is to be the inadequacy of the circumstantial evidence, discuss the rigid rules applied to circumstantial evidence. In other words, *mold your questions to the defense you will urge.)*

8. "You know, of course, that the fact that a person was injured must be proved by direct evidence. Do you understand what is meant by the term direct evidence? That is, facts testified to by persons who saw what they are testifying about?"

9. "You realize, of course, that the indictment in this case is no evidence of any kind? That it is merely a piece of paper used to bring the defendant into court, the same as a complaint in a civil case?"

10. "Of course, you know a man is presumed innocent until he is proven guilty beyond a reasonable doubt?"

11. "You also realize, of course, that you must give the defendant the benefit of this presumption of innocence without any mental reservations whatsoever? And that you

are to consider this presumption of innocence as actual proof of innocence until it is overcome by proof of guilt beyond a reasonable doubt. Now do I have your promise that you will give the defendant the full benefit of that presumption of innocence?"

12. "Do you understand that all the elements of the crime charged must be proven beyond a reasonable doubt, and that if one element is not proven, would you then vote not-guilty?"

13. "If the prosecution fails to prove the guilt of the accused with that degree of moral certainty that amounts to proof beyond a reasonable doubt, would you then vote non-guilty?"

14. "You understand, do you not, that the burden of proving the defendant guilty beyond a reasonable doubt rests with the prosecution, and that the accused need not introduce any evidence whatsoever?"

15. "Knowing that, would you require the accused at any time to satisfy you as to his innocence?"

16. (If you have decided that the accused will not testify): "And knowing that, you realize that the defendant is not bound to explain his side of the case since the burden of proof does, in fact, rest with the prosecutor. So that you would not consider the accused's failure to testify as an indication of his guilt, would you?"

17. "Knowing the charge against the accused, John X., could you give him the same fair trial that you would give him if he were charged with a lesser crime?"

18. "Do you know anything about the facts of this case other than what you have heard in court today?"

19. "Have you read about this case in the newspapers or heard about it over the radio or television?" (At this point, if the juror answers "yes," you should proceed carefully. Even if the juror admits to an opinion of guilt derived from the newspapers, the court will permit him to remain on

the jury, if he declares under oath that he could nonetheless act impartially and fairly. It becomes your job to show the court that he has such an opinion of guilt that it will require evidence to remove it. You must draw out this admission without appearing as if you are out to get the juror, since many prospective jurors will dodge answering in order to stay on the jury.)

20. "What newspapers have you read?"

21. (Nonchalantly): "I suppose you have formed some opinion as to the guilt or innocence of the accused, or about the merits of this case from what you read in the newspapers?"

22. (If he answers "yes," then nonchalantly say): "I suppose it would require evidence to remove or change your opinion?" (If he answers "yes," challenge him for reason.)

23. (If he answered "no" to any of the questions concerning prior opinion gleaned from newspapers): "Knowing what you know about this case and any opinion you have formed about it, would you be satisfied to be tried by a jury having your frame of mind?"

24. "Would you set aside any opinion you may now have and judge this case solely on the evidence introduced during the trial and the instructions of law given to you by the court?"

25. "Do you realize that the court will instruct you as to the law, but that you are the sole and exclusive judge(s) of the facts?"

26. "Would you judge this case solely on the evidence before you, and not allow the fear of later criticism affect your verdict?"

27. "Would you give the accused the benefit of your individual judgment in arriving at a verdict in this case?"

28. "Now, if you came to the conclusion that the prosecution had not proven the guilt of the accused beyond a

reasonable doubt, and you found that a majority of the jurors believed the defendant was guilty, would you change your verdict only because you were in the minority?"

29. "Would the fact that you were in the minority influence your vote at all?"

30. "If the widow of the deceased were to testify, would her appearance so upset or influence you that you could not give the accused a fair trial?"

31. "You understand, of course, that an impartial trial by an unbiased jury is a constitutional guarantee no matter what the charges are against the defendant?"

32. "Do you realize that you are bound to reach a verdict solely on the evidence introduced during the trial?"

33. "If from your experiences you believe or have the feeling that certain facts exist, but these facts have not been proven by satisfactory evidence, would you discard your beliefs or feeling and decide this case only on the evidence or lack of evidence?"

34. "Do you understand that the comments of the prosecutor are not evidence in this case?"

35. "In deciding whether or not you are going to believe a witness, would you consider the witness's conduct on the stand, his opportunity and ability to observe, his bias or prejudice, and the probability or improbability of his story?"

36. (If there will be accomplice testimony against the defendant): "Do you understand what is meant by the term *'accomplice'?"* (Be prepared to explain it if the answer is "no.") (See Requests to Charge).

37. "Do you understand that the testimony of an accomplice is considered to be testimony from a tainted source and must be scrutinized by you with great care and caution?"

38. (In a jurisdiction where corroboration of accomplice

testimony is required): "His Honor will instruct you that in order for you to convict the defendant, the testimony of the accomplice must be supported by other evidence that connects the defendant to the crime, and extends to every material fact necessary to establish the crime. His Honor will also instruct that this supporting testimony must come from a believable and unimpeached source. Now, do you promise to follow these instructions?"

39. (If there are child witnesses against the defendant): "In judging the credibility of a child witness, would you take into account his age, intelligence, ability to perceive and observe, realizing that the life or liberty of the accused is at stake? Would you further consider carefully the child's extreme imagination, tendency to mix fact with fiction, and his great susceptibility to suggestions?"

40. (If there may be an identification witness): "In weighing the identification of the defendant, will you consider the witness's capacity for memory, for observation, his familiarity with the defendant and any bias or prejudice he may have toward the accused?"

41. "Will you also consider the amount of time that the witness had to observe the defendant?"

42. "Do you recognize from your daily experiences the frailty of mental observation?"

43. "During the experiences of your personal life, have you ever mistakenly confused a stranger for a person whom you knew well?"

44. "Do you agree that the identity of the defendant as the person who committed the crime must be shown with such certainty as to eliminate any possibility of error?"

45. (If the prosecution's case is based on circumstantial evidence): "Do you know that circumstantial evidence is like a chain which must bind the defendant to the crime, and that that chain is only as strong as its weakest link?"

46. "Do you agree that every element of a circumstantial

evidence case must be totally inconsistent with innocence; consistent with and pointing to guilt, and that if the evidence does not point directly to guilt, you must render a verdict of not guilty? Will you faithfully apply that rule of law?"

47. If the defendant will testify and has a criminal record, see § 328, supra.

48. "Will you consider and judge the defendant's testimony by the same rules and standards you would use in judging the testimony of any other witness in this case?"

49. (If the defendant is a black): "Have you had any dealings or experiences with black persons that might make it difficult for you to sit in impartial judgment on this case?"

50. "Will the fact that the defendant is a black (or Puerto Rican, etc.) affect in any way your judgment in this case?"

51. "Do you promise to consider only the facts and evidence in this case, and to completely disregard the defendant's race, creed and color?"

52. (If the defendant or any of your witnesses will testify through an interpreter or in poor English): See above matter relating to this situation.

53. (If your defense will be self-defense): "Do you believe that a person is justified in killing another human being if he believes that he is in actual danger of being seriously injured or killed by his attacker?"

54. "Do you have any feeling against a person who uses a knife or a gun to protect himself or his family?"

55. "His Honor will instruct you that a person has a right to use a knife or a gun in self-defense under certain circumstances. Do you promise to heed that information?"

56. "Do you appreciate and understand that the question

you will eventually have to decide in this case is whether the defendant acted in proper self-defense?"

57. "Do you further understand that the burden will be upon the prosecution to prove beyond a reasonable doubt that the accused did not act in self-defense?"

58. "You realize, of course, that if a reasonable doubt exists in your mind as to whether or not the defendant was justified in acting in self-defense, then you must resolve that doubt in favor of the defendant, and render a verdict of not-guilty."

59. (If your defense will be intoxication): "Are you a member of any organization which is trying to combat the sale, distribution or use of intoxicating beverages?"

60. "It may develop from the evidence that the defendant was intoxicated at the time he committed the crime charged. His Honor will instruct you that it is for you to determine the extent of the defendant's intoxication, and whether his intoxication was such as to prevent him from forming the intent necessary to constitute the crime. His Honor will further charge you that should you find the defendant was too intoxicated to form that intent you must render a verdict of not-guilty. Now, do you promise to heed that instruction?"

61. (If your defense will be insanity): "Are you aware that the law does not hold a person responsible for his act, if he was insane at the time he committed the crime?"

62. "Do you agree with that proposition of law?"

63. "His Honor will instruct you that should you find the defendant, when he committed the crime, was acting under such a defect of reason as not to know the nature and quality of his act, he is legally insane and must be acquitted."

64. "Now, do you agree that if the accused was insane, or so insane as not to know the nature and quality of his act

or not to know that what he was doing was wrong, he must be acquitted?"

65. "If you find that the defendant was legally insane when he committed the crime, do you promise to follow the court's instruction and render a verdict of not-guilty?"

66. "Are you related to anyone on the District Attorney's staff?"

67. "Are you related to any police or law enforcement officers?"

68. (If the answer is yes): "Have you ever discussed with him whether he believes that persons charged with crimes are probably guilty?"

69. (If the answer is yes): "Do you believe that the defendant in this case is probably guilty?"

70. "Have you ever been a witness for the prosecution in a criminal case?"

71. "Have you ever been the victim of a crime?"

72. (If the answer is yes): "Please relate the circumstances of the crime to us."

73. "If, when you are considering the evidence in the jury room, you have two theories, one of which is consistent with my client's guilt and the other consistent with his innocence, do I have your promise that you will adopt the theory consistent with innocence and vote for acquittal?"

74. "Do you agree that you are enforcing the law just as vigorously by voting for acquittal if there is a reasonable doubt as to guilt as you do by voting for conviction when there is no such doubt?"

D. METHODS AND FACTORS INVOLVED IN SELECTING AND CHALLENGING JURORS

§ 331. In general

When you select a particular juror, keep in mind the

nature of your case as well as the character and background of the defendant and witnesses. For the most part, the type of juror you would select if you were representing a plaintiff in a civil negligence case is the type you want in defending a criminal case.

In reality, the limited number of peremptory challenges available render it impossible for you to select the most desirable possible jury. Your ability to seat desirable jurors is also limited by the available pool of jurors. Your function will simply be to eliminate the most undesirable jurors from the panel.

§ 332. Jury selection chart

In his excellent CYCLOPEDIA OF TRIAL PRACTICE, Sydney C. Schweitzer, Esq. of the New York Bar suggests that counsel at the outset of his case make a chart with various important characteristics and factors of consequence to counsel in evaluating the prospective jurors. The chart should reflect counsel's then idea as to the challenging of each individual juror thereon and provide defense counsel with a workable basis for the evaluation of a jury panel.

§ 333. Challenges for cause and to the array

The allowance of challenges for cause has always been deemed essential to the fairness of trial by jury.[75]

The right of the prosecution and of the accused to challenge a prospective juror for cause stand on the same ground, one being as sacred as the other.[76]

A challenge to the array or panel may be made and sustained in a criminal case for such a prejudicial defect or

75. Lewis v United States, 146 US 370, 36 L Ed 1011, 13 S Ct 136.

Annotation: Professional or business relations between proposed juror and attorney as ground for challenge for cause. 72 ALR2d 673.

76. McFadden v Commonwealth, 23 Pa 12.

irregularity in the selection and summoning of the jurors as affects the integrity of the entire panel. Such a challenge relates to the entire array and not only to the individual persons on it.[77] A challenge to the array goes to the form and manner of making up the whole panel, and relates to the legality of drawing, selecting, or impaneling the array.[78]

§ 334. Peremptory challenges

A peremptory challenge is an arbitrary and capricious species of challenge to a certain number of jurors without showing any cause.[79] The right to make peremptory challenges in a criminal case is a valuable and substantial right,[80] and it is not essential to such a challenge that any bias or prejudice on the part of a juror be shown.[81]

A peremptory challenge is not exercised in the selection of jurors, but in their rejection.[82] A peremptory challenge enables the party to say who shall not try him, but not to say who shall be the particular jurors to try him.[83]

Peremptory challenges can be exercised as a matter of right only to the extent allowed by statute, and must be taken subject to the legislative limitations placed upon the manner of their exercise.[84]

77. Challenge to the Array. Standards Relating to Trial by Jury, American Bar Association Project on Minimum Standards for Criminal Justice, Tentative Draft May, 1968 p 61.

78. United States v Gordon (CA7 Ill) 253 F2d 177.

79. Peremptory challenges. Standards Relating to Trial by Jury, American Bar Association Project on Minimum Standards for Criminal Justice, Tentative Draft May, 1968 p 70.

80. State v Supinski (Mo App) 378 SW2d 602; State v Jackson, 43 NJ 148, 203 A2d 1, 11 ALR3d 841, cert den 379 US 982, 13 L Ed 2d 572, 85 S Ct 690.

81. State v Thompson, 68 Ariz 386, 206 P2d 1037.

82. State v Ward, 246 La 766, 167 So 2d 359, cert den 380 US 972, 14 L Ed 2d 268, 85 S Ct 1329; State v Supinski (Mo App) 378 SW2d 602.

83. State v Persinger, 62 Wash 2d 362, 382 P2d 497, app dismd and cert den 376 US 187, 11 L Ed 2d 603, 84 S Ct 638.

84. Anderson v State, 81 Nev 477, 406 P2d 532.

As a rule, peremptory challenges are allowed in all criminal cases other than those in justices' courts.[85]

By virtue of the Federal Act of 1840,[86] the federal courts were enabled to adopt the laws and usages of the states with respect to the challenging of jurors, whether peremptorily or for cause,[87] and now by rule in criminal cases,[88] the number of peremptory challenges in federal cases is prescribed.

The right to exercise peremptory challenges is a right which may be waived,[89] and generally speaking, where fair opportunity has been given, but the right to challenge peremptorily has not been exercised, it will be deemed to have been waived.[90]

§ 335. Number of peremptory challenges

The number of allowable peremptory challenges is subject to the discretion of the legislature, and varies from jurisdiction to jurisdiction. The power of the legislature, in this respect, is limited only by the necessity of having an impartial jury.[91] The tendency of legislation is to allow both the accused and the prosecution the same number of peremptory challenges, although some statutes allow the prosecution only half or a certain other proportion of such challenges to which the accused is entitled.[92]

85. Reed v Peacock, 123 Mich 244, 82 NW 53.

86. US Rev Stat § 800.

87. Sawyer v United States, 202 US 150, 50 L Ed 972, 26 S Ct 575; United States v Shackleford (US) 18 How 588, 15 L Ed 495.

88. Rule 24(b), (c), Fed Rules of Crim Proc.

89. State v Thompson, 68 Ariz 386, 206 P2d 1037; State v Supinski (Mo App) 378 SW2d 602; Nash v State, 110 Neb 712, 194 NW 869.

90. State v Thompson, 68 Ariz 386, 206 P2d 1037; McDonald v State, 172 Ind 393, 88 NE 673; Johnson v State, 88 Neb 565, 130 NW 282.

91. Hayes v Missouri, 120 US 68, 30 L Ed 578, 7 S Ct 350 (holding that the number of peremptory challenges may be varied for different communities); State v Rector, 166 SC 335, 164 SE 865; State v De Weese, 51 Utah 515, 172 P 290.

92. Hayes v Missouri, 120 US 68, 30 L Ed 578, 7 S Ct 350; United States v Shackleford (US) 18 How 588, 15 L Ed 495; United States v Marchant (US) 12 Wheat 480, 6 L Ed 700; Sealy v

In many jurisdictions, the number of peremptory challenges allowed is determined by the nature and degree of the offense as defined by the statute,[93] and on the basis of the offense as a felony[94] or misdemeanor,[95] or on the basis of the penalty as it may be governed by the character of the offense and the sentence passed upon the accused.[96]

By the terms of the Federal Rules of Criminal Procedure, if the offense charged is punishable by death, each side is entitled to 20 peremptory challenges.[97] If the offense charged is punishable by imprisonment for more than one year, the government is entitled to 6 peremptory challenges and the defendant or defendants jointly to 10 peremptory challenges.[98] If the offense charged is punishable by imprisonment for not more than one year or by fine or both, each side is entitled to 3 peremptory challenges.[99] Under the Federal Rules of Criminal Procedure, each side is entitled to 1 peremptory challenge, in addition to those otherwise allowed by law, if 1 or 2 alternate jurors are to be impaneled, and 2 peremptory challenges if 3 or 4 alternate jurors are to be impaneled.[1] As is the case under the Federal Rules of Civil Procedure, the additional peremptory challenges may be used against an alternate juror only, and the other peremptory challenges allowed by law may not be used against an alternate juror.[2]

Any error by the court in limiting the number of pe-

State, 1 Ga 213; People v McQuade, 110 NY 284, 18 NE 156.

93. People v Minchella, 268 Mich 123, 255 NW 735, 93 ALR 805, cert den 293 US 619, 79 L Ed 707, 55 S Ct 217, 345, cert den 294 US 717, 79 L Ed 1250, 55 S Ct 547.

94. Harrison v United States, 163 US 140, 41 L Ed 104, 16 S Ct 961; Sealy v State, 1 Ga 213; Harris v United States, 4 Okla Crim 317, 111 P 982.

95. Reagan v United States, 157 US 301, 39 L Ed 709, 15 S Ct 610.

96. Freeman v People (NY) 4 Denio 9.

97. Rule 24(b), Fed Rules of Crim Proc.

98. Rule 24(b), Fed Rules of Crim Proc.

99. Rule 24(b), Fed Rules of Crim Proc.

1. Rule 24(c), Fed Rules of Crim Proc.

2. Rule 24(c), Fed Rules of Crim Proc.

remptory challenges to jurors is not prejudicial where those allowed were not exhausted.[3]

In criminal cases the right to challenge is usually given to each party separately because the judgment may be widely different even though the defendants are tried jointly.[4] Thus, apart from statutory provisions to the contrary, when two or more persons are put on trial jointly for crime, they are each entitled to the full number of peremptory challenges allowed by law.[5]

The number of peremptory challenges allowable to the prosecution in a criminal case involving joint defendants is dependent upon the terms of the applicable statute. Sometimes that number is specifically provided for in the statute,[6] and in other instances it is made determinable by some formula involving reference to the number to be allowed the defendants.[7]

The Federal Rules of Criminal Procedure permit the trial court to exercise its discretion in determining whether additional peremptory challenges should be granted multiple defendants.[8]

§ 336. Physical characteristics

Physical characteristics are particularly important to the lawyer defending a case in the Federal courts where selection of jurors is made without personal interrogation, and only after the Judge has asked all the questions. Generally

3. Meridian City Lines v Baker, 206 Miss 58, 39 So 2d 541, 8 ALR2d 854.

4. Kunk v Howell, 40 Tenn App 183, 289 SW2d 874, 73 ALR2d 1304.

5. United States v Marchant (US) 12 Wheat 480, 6 L Ed 700; Hawkins v State, 9 Ala 137; People v Caruso, 170 Mich 137, 135 NW 968.

A waiver of a defendant's full right in this respect cannot be implied from the mere fact that he, or any of his codefendants, failed to require a separate trial. People v Caruso, supra.

6. People v Pilbro, 85 Cal App 789, 260 P 303; Carroll v State, 139 Fla 233, 190 So 437.

7. Butler v State, 92 Ga 601, 19 SE 51; Spies v People, 122 Ill 1, 12 NE 865, 17 NE 898, error dismd 123 US 131, 31 L Ed 80, 8 S Ct 22.

8. Rule 24(b), Fed Rules of Crim Proc.

speaking, the heavy, roundfaced, jovial-looking person is the most desirable. The undesirable juror is quite often the slight, underweight and delicate type. His features are sharp and fragile, with that lean "Cassius" look. The athletic-looking juror is hard to categorize. Usually he is hard to convince; but once convinced he will usually go all the way for you. Of course, these generalizations and those that follow should be discarded if the questions you submit to the court or ask of the jurors yourself uncover actual bias or prejudice.

Other things that belie a prospective juror's prejudices are sex, age, marital status, and ethnic or racial background. Common sense combined with some appreciation of how the mind works will go a long way in helping you understand prospective jurors.

§ 337. Occupations and skills

You want jurors whose minds can be molded. To that end, you do not want persons incapable of understanding the salient facts of your defense; nor do you desire persons of superior intelligence whose preconceived ideas will be difficult to dislodge. This latter type is also particularly dangerous because they will usually dominate the other jurors.

Generally, retired police officers, military men and their wives are undesirable. They have adhered to a strict line of conduct throughout their lives. They believe if a man is arrested, he is probably guilty. However, where the defendant is a veteran, it may be desirable to keep a veteran on the jury. He will be sympathetic, particularly if the defendant has a good war record.

Salesmen, actors, artists and writers are highly desirable. They have enjoyed wide and varied experiences, have witnessed the good and bad in people and are prone to forgive an indiscretion in another. They tend to accept life more readily and are not easily shocked by a crime. They will require more evidence of defendant's guilt before they will convict.

Bankers, bank employees, members of management, and low-salaried white-collar workers are generally undesirable. They have been trained either to take or give orders, are forced to toe the line, and usually expect others to do the same.[9]

If your defense entails the calling of expert witnesses, make sure that none of the jurors can claim any expertise in that field. This also holds true for areas to be covered by the prosecution's expert witnesses. A juror who possesses such expert knowledge is likely to dominate the rest of the jury. In such an instance, you will, in effect, be trying your case before a one-man jury, thereby reducing your chances of gaining a split in the jury.

§ 338. Previous jury service

All other things being equal, new jurors are desired over experienced jurors. The principles of reasonable doubt and presumption of innocence will be received more readily by a new juror. Similarly, an emotional summation should have greater impact.

§ 339. Prejudice against crime or against the use of certain defenses

A prejudice in favor of the enforcement of the law does not constitute disqualification for jury duty.[10] Every good citizen should be prejudiced against crime, and if this were to be regarded as a prejudice against the person being tried, no jury could ever be obtained to try anyone accused of crime.[11]

A juror generally is not disqualified from sitting on a

9. **Annotation:** Exclusion of attorneys from jury list in criminal cases. 32 ALR2d 890.

10. United States v Noelke (CC NY) 1 F 426.

11. United States v Borger (CC NY) 7 F 193.

jury trying a person accused of a particular crime by the fact that he has a prejudice against such a crime[12] if the prejudice is not such as to influence his verdict.[13]

The question of whether a proposed juror in a criminal case is prejudiced against or favorably inclined toward any particular defense is not a test of his qualifications for jury duty.[14] The test is whether he is able to consider the facts of the case impartially, render a verdict according to the evidence, and abide by the instructions of the court on the law applicable to the particular defense.[15]

§ 340. Prejudice or scruple in favor of, or against, certain forms of punishment

A person who is opposed to or has conscientious scruples against capital or other particular forms of punishment is not in a condition impartially to hear and examine the evidence in a prosecution for a crime for which such punishment may be imposed. He does not stand indifferent between the prisoner and the state,[16] and when on the voir dire examination of a prospective juror it develops that he has such conscientious scruples, the state may challenge

12. Corley v State, 162 Ark 178, 257 SW 750; Spies v People, 122 Ill 1, 12 NE 865, 17 NE 898, error dismd 123 US 131, 31 L Ed 80, 8 S Ct 22; Garlitz v State, 71 Md 293, 18 A 39; Higgins v Minaghan, 78 Wis 602, 47 NW 941.

An admission by a prospective juror that he had a prejudice against hit-and-run drivers did not disqualify him from serving as a juror in a prosecution for failing to stop after an accident, where the juror said that he could give the defendant a fair trial and that as far as he knew, the defendant was innocent. State v Marcus, 240 Iowa 116, 34 NW2d 179.

13. State v McClain, 256 Iowa 175, 125 NW2d 764, 4 ALR3d 134; State v Marcus, 240 Iowa 116, 34 NW2d 179.

In a prosecution for homicide caused by a spring gun the jurors may be asked on their voir dire examination whether or not the fact of setting a spring gun would create in their minds such prejudice or bias that they could not sit as fair and impartial jurors in the case. State v Marfaudille, 48 Wash 117, 92 P 939.

14. Gammons v State, 85 Miss 103, 37 So 609.

Practice Aids: Proof of prejudice against defenses of certain types, see 2 Am Jur Proof of Facts 495, Bias or Prejudice, Proof 1.

15. State v Dean, 65 SD 433, 274 NW 817, 112 ALR 527.

16. Logan v United States, 144 US 263, 36 L Ed 429, 12 S Ct 617; State v Owen, 73 Idaho 394, 253 P2d 203.

him for cause,[17] and the court may excuse him.[18] However, a prospective juror cannot be expected to say in advance of trial whether he would in fact vote for the death penalty in the case before him; the most that can be demanded of a venireman in this regard is that he be willing to consider all of the penalties provided by law, and that he not be irrevocably committed, before the trial has begun, to vote against the penalty of death regardless of the facts and circumstances that might emerge in the course of the proceedings.[19]

Where the death penalty may be imposed, a prosecutor has the right to ascertain the views of prospective jurors on capital punishment, so that he can intelligently exercise his challenges against jurors whose consciences would preclude them from imposing the death penalty.[20] As a general rule, the right to challenge a juror in a capital case on the ground of his opposition to capital punishment is confined to the prosecution, by whom it may be waived, and is not extended to the defendant.[21] However, since in all cases of

17. Sawyer v United States, 202 US 150, 50 L Ed 972, 26 S Ct 575; Logan v United States, 144 US 263, 36 L Ed 429, 12 S Ct 617; Demato v People, 49 Colo 147, 111 P 703; Monday v State, 32 Ga 672; Corens v State, 185 Md 561, 45 A2d 340; Williams v State, 32 Miss 389; Johnson v State, 88 Neb 565, 130 NW 282; Pumphrey v State, 84 Neb 636, 122 NW 19; Commonwealth v Bentley, 287 Pa 539, 135 A 310; Commonwealth v Minney, 216 Pa 149, 65 A 31; Hyde v State, 16 Tex 445.

18. Veney v State, 251 Md 182, 246 A2d 568, cert den 394 US 948, 22 L Ed 2d 482, 89 S Ct 1284.

In a prosecution for murder, scruples of a prospective juror against capital punishment constitute ground for excusing him for cause, even though by statute the jury is empowered, upon a finding of guilt of murder in the first degree, to eliminate capital punishment as a penalty otherwise mandatorily required. United States v Puff (CA2 NY) 211 F2d 171, 48 ALR2d 540, cert den 347 US 963, 98 L Ed 1106, 74 S Ct 713, reh den 347 US 1022, 98 L Ed 1142, 74 S Ct 876, 348 US 853, 99 L Ed 672, 75 S Ct 20.

19. Witherspoon v Illinois, 391 US 510, 20 L Ed 2d 776, 88 S Ct 1770, reh den 393 US 898, 21 L Ed 2d 186, 89 S Ct 67, holding that a prospective juror who has conscientious scruples against the death penalty is not qualified to sit as a juror where the charge is murder in the first degree.

See also Corens v State, 185 Md 561, 45 A2d 340; Williams v State, 32 Miss 389.

20. People v King, 240 Cal App 2d 389, 49 Cal Rptr 562, 21 ALR3d 706, cert den 385 US 923, 17 L Ed 2d 146, 87 S Ct 236.

21. State v Hicks, 319 Mo 28, 3

this character it is the duty of the court to see that an impartial jury is impaneled and that it is composed of men above all exception, circumstances may arise where it is proper for the court to set aside the juror on its own motion.[22]

As to the time when the right to challenge for this cause is exercisable, it has been held that a juror may be discharged after he is sworn, and before evidence is given, where it is discovered that he is opposed to capital punishment.[23]

§ 341. Preconceived opinions about the case

A juror who has formed a preconceived opinion of the case ordinarily cannot be impartial.[24] Recognizing this fact, the modern rule is that the formation of an opinion disqualifies a juror, and it is not necessary in order to disqualify him that he shall have expressed or declared such opinion before being called as a juror in the case.[25]

Usually, however, to disqualify one as a juror, the opinion he has formed must relate to the material issues and facts in the case.[26] A prospective juror who states that he has formed an opinion as to the guilt of the accused may be examined fully as to the extent of the opinion formed.[27]

SW2d 230; Long v State, 187 Tenn 139, 213 SW2d 37.

22. Williams v State, 32 Miss 389.

23. State v Diskin, 34 La Ann 919; Lewis v State, 17 Miss (9 Smedes & M) 115; People v Damon (NY) 13 Wend 351; People v Wilson (NY) 3 Park Crim 199.

24. State v Chapman, 1 SD 414, 47 NW 411.

Practice Aids: Proof of preconceived opinions, see 2 Am Jur Proof of Facts 495, Bias or Prejudice, Proof 1.

25. Irvin v Dowd, 366 US 717, 6 L Ed 2d 751, 81 S Ct 1639; Leick v People, 136 Colo 535, 322 P2d 674, cert den 357 US 922, 2 L Ed 2d 1366, 78 S Ct 1363; Nomaque v People (Ill) Breese 109 (Beecher's ed 145), ovrld on other grounds People ex rel. Merrill v Hazard, 361 Ill 60, 63, 196 NE 827; French v Smith, 4 Vt 363.

26. State v Pearce, 87 Kan 457, 124 P 814; Kujawa v Baltimore Transit Co. 224 Md 195, 167 A2d 96, 89 ALR2d 1166; State v Thorne, 41 Utah 414, 126 P 286.

27. Scribner v State, 3 Okla Crim 601, 108 P 422.

A juror may be questioned as to the strength of an impression to which he has previously testified and as to

§ 342. Exposure of juror to pretrial publicity

The mere fact that a juror has seen or heard pretrial publicity is not necessarily a ground for disqualification, and a juror will not be held disqualified if he satisfies the court that he can and will be impartial despite his having been exposed to pretrial publicity.[28] The true doctrine is that if the juror's conceptions are not fixed and settled, nor warped by prejudice, but only such as would naturally spring from public rumor or newspaper report, and his mind is open to the impressions that it may receive at the trial, and he may be convinced according to the law and the testimony of the trial, he is not an incompetent juror.[29]

whether he is able to render a verdict according to the evidence in spite of such impression. Lohman v People, 1 NY 379.

28. Thiede v Utah Territory, 159 US 510, 40 L Ed 237, 16 S Ct 62; Hopt v Utah, 120 US 430, 30 L Ed 708, 7 S Ct 614; State v Giudice, 170 Iowa 731, 153 NW 336; State v Brady, 100 Iowa 191, 69 NW 290; Garlitz v State, 71 Md 293, 18 A 39; State v Rodriguez, 23 NM 156, 167 P 426; State v Fujita, 20 ND 555, 129 NW 360; State v Cunningham, 173 Or 25, 144 P2d 303; State v Thorne, 41 Utah 414, 126 P 286; Mainville v State, 173 Wis 12, 179 NW 764.

29. Singer v State (Fla) 109 So 2d 7.

CHAPTER ELEVEN

OPENING STATEMENT TO THE JURY

A. INTRODUCTION

§ 343. General purposes

The opening statement is a crucial part of a criminal

trial, since it creates a first impression in the minds of the judge and the jury which may be hard, if not impossible, to dispel at a later time. Ordinarily, the prosecutor has the advantage of making the first opening address to the jury, and for this reason the defendant must be prepared with a strong and persuasive statement of his own to dislodge any unfavorable ideas the prosecutor may have placed in the minds of the judge or jury. These first impressions, unless controverted on the spot by defense counsel's opening, may well become the standard by which the entire proof and evidence in the case will be later weighed and considered by the jury. It is a rare case indeed, where a defendant may feel that it is to his advantage not to speak at this crucial point of the case.

If you have been skillful in your voir-dire examination, you have given the jury a taste of the case and its issues. Your opening statement should now go beyond that taste and really wet their appetite. It should create an interest in your defense. Remember that the prosecutor in most jurisdictions *must* make an opening statement. If he has done a competent job, he has impressed the jury with the defendant's guilt. It is only natural then, having heard but one side of the story, that they should be inclined to believing the defendant's guilt. Your job, therefore, becomes clear. You must nullify the prosecution's opening advantage.

But do not stop there. Proceed to change the jury's opinion. You accomplish this by bringing their attention to the facts of the case that call for an acquittal. You create an atmosphere lighter than the blackness painted by the prosecutor.

If permitted by the law of the particular jurisdiction, move for a directed verdict of acquittal if the prosecution fails to make out all of the elements of the crimes charged in his opening statement. In this regard, you can prepare a list of the elements of the crimes charged in advance of trial. You can check off these various elements during the prosecutor's opening to see whether he had included all of the necessary elements.

The defense attorney who presents a sound and favorable opening address will win the interest of the jury and insure himself favorable consideration of his contentions and the theory of the defense. He will also leave the jury with a friendly feeling and an identification with the cause of the accused. Also, a successful opening statement will have created a skeleton or framework in the minds of the jury which they can use to keep a clear picture of the proof as it unfolds.

It is important to note at this point that many of the guide-lines and principles involved in counsel's concluding argument or address are applicable as well to his opening. For this reason it might be well to scan the material in this work presented under the chapter discussing summation.[1]

§ 344. Delayed opening

In some jurisdictions, defense counsel is permitted to reserve his opening statement until the conclusion of the prosecution's case.[2] This is not usually the best policy. As a general rule you will do best to take the sting out of the prosecutor's opening statement at once.

You can consider a delayed opening if you are certain that you will be calling witnesses on behalf of your client, and the prosecution's case is likely to be short and you are not certain of the prosecution's theory. If the first two of these elements are present, the third might impel you to defer opening so as not to commit yourself to a particular defense theory which might prove inapplicable.

The problem of whether to delay your defense opening can sometimes be handled nicely when there are co-defend-

1. §§ 444 et seq., infra.

2. **Annotation:** Time as of which defense counsel in criminal case may make opening statement. 93 ALR2d 951.

ants in the case represented by different attorneys. In such cases you can try to reach agreement with the other defense attorney for one of you to open immediately after the prosecutor, with the other reserving his opening until the close of the prosecution's case. Such an arrangement, of course, is contingent upon the approval of the trial judge. Such permission will generally not be granted if each of the defendants is represented by the same attorney. Of course, you should never waive the opening altogether under any circumstances.

§ 345. Exclude all prosecution witnesses

The prosecutor's opening statement will usually set forth the testimony of his witnesses. If the prosecutor's witnesses are present it will serve as a last-minute refresher lecture for them. Often he will ask them to listen very carefully to his opening. Also, during *your* opening statement, the prosecution witnesses will hear your defense and can prepare for your cross-examination. Therefore, you should request that the court exclude all witnesses from the courtroom before the prosecutor starts his opening address. The prosecution witnesses will thus be unable to hear one another's testimony, and possibly crucial inconsistencies are very likely to develop.

§ 346. Length of opening

Defense counsel's opening statement should be short enough to hold the interest of the jury, while at the same time long enough to give a clear cut picture of the defense's case.

Defense's opening statement should be timed so that it remains an entity unto itself, but does not detract from the central effect of the defense case and over-all presentation. Obviously, the precise length of an opening must depend upon the circumstances of each case, the complexity of the crime of which the defendant is accused, as well as the particular circumstances and also the exigencies of the moment as observed by defense counsel in the instant case.

§ 347. Waiver

Many attorneys believe that where they are in doubt as to the course of their defense, or where they have a "secret defense," it is best to waive the opening statement. They may be mistaken.

You need not give a full opening statement if you have such doubts. However, it is dangerous to waive it entirely. The prosecutor has favorably impressed the jurors with his opening. If you decline to answer him, you are leaving his remarks unchallenged.

Instead of waiving the opening statement when you are in doubt about what to say, you should open with a superficial statement that tells practically nothing about your defense, but still removes the wounds of the prosecutor's remarks.

B. STRUCTURE AND CONTENT

§ 348. Emphasize the issues and your defense

Face the issues squarely. Explain the facts to the jury and what your defense will be. Emphasize, in simple language, of course, the legal theory underlying your defense. Show them how your evidence will support this defense. In this way the jury will understand why certain evidence is being introduced, and will listen to your case patiently. They will also withhold judgment until your defense is presented *in toto.*

In an assault case, for example, when the prosecutor proves that the defendant shot or stabbed the complainant, the jury may conclude that the defendant is guilty. They will not reach this conclusion if you have previously explained that every person has the right to use reasonable force in self-defense. They will know that the true issue is whether or not the defendant *had the right* to shoot or stab the complainant.

If the charge is forgery or larceny, point out that the issue is intent. Emphasize that the crime of forgery or larceny depends on more than the physical acts of the defendant. The accused did sign the check, but did so innocently; the accused did take the property, but he did it without any criminal intent. Alert the jury to the defense of lack-of-intent. They will then view the evidence with the proper perspective.

Make the jury well aware that there are two sides to every story. Show how your defense is contrary to the version of the facts given by the prosecutor. Then, during the testimony of the prosecution witnesses, the jury will not be prone to jump to hasty conclusions. They will reserve their opinions until they have heard your side. Remember, it is far easier to mold an open mind than to change one that has already formed an opinion.

§ 349. Prosecutor's reference to matters which he does not later attempt to prove

As a practical matter, an attorney who is prosecuting may be excused for stating facts which he expects and believes he will prove, but which later cannot be shown because they are irrelevant or, for some good reason unknown to him at the time, cannot be established later.[3] Accordingly, either in response to an objection duly made or on its own motion, the trial court may admonish the prosecuting attorney as to his opening statement or instruct the jury to disregard any remarks made therein not

3. State v Williams, 28 Nev 395, 82 P 353.

Ordinarily, error may not be predicated upon the opening statement of a prosecuting attorney to the jury although, for some reason, he later fails to introduce evidence to support some of the narrative related in the opening statement, unless such unsupported portions were made in bad faith and were manifestly prejudicial. Hilyard v State, 90 Okla Crim 435, 214 P2d 953, 28 ALR2d 961.

later supported by the evidence. Where this is done, it is usually held that the harmful effect of the opening statement, if any, has been cured.[4]

As a general rule, courts recognize the fact that proof frequently fails to come up to expectations, and so the tendency is to permit a prosecuting attorney a reasonable latitude in stating to the jury the facts proposed to be shown. And where no substantial prejudice results, and there is nothing to show that the prosecuting attorney acted in bad faith, the appellate court will usually refuse to reverse or to remand for a new trial because of a reference by the prosecuting attorney to matters which he subsequently made no attempt to prove.[5]

§ 350. Object to prosecutor's improper statements

Object to any improper remarks made by the prosecutor in his opening address. If he discusses the law, hold him to accurate statements. Do not hesitate to object if he refers to improper, incompetent evidence designed to inflame or beguile the jury. If necessary, have the court admonish the prosecutor against making any further improper statements.[6]

§ 351. Disclose weaknesses in your defense

An essential function of the opening statement is the

4. People v Wolcott, 137 Cal App 355, 30 P2d 601; People v Davis, 26 Cal App 647, 147 P 1184; Sterling v State, 89 Ga 807, 15 SE 743; State v Welsh, 138 Kan 379, 26 P2d 592; Clark v Commonwealth (Ky) 243 SW2d 52; People v Swift, 172 Mich 473, 138 NW 662; State v Levy, 262 Mo 181, 170 SW 1114; State v Geiger, 129 NJL 13, 28 A2d 57, affd 129 NJL 518, 30 A2d 406; People v De Simone, 181 App Div 840, 168 NYS 976, affd 225 NY 261, 121 NE 761; Crawford v State, 105 Tex Crim 281, 288 SW 213.

5. Handley v State, 214 Ala 172, 106 So 692; Rutledge v State, 41 Ariz 48, 15 P2d 255; Bridges v State, 176 Ark 756, 4 SW2d 12; People v Berryman, 6 Cal 2d 331, 57 P2d 136; People v Gordon, 71 Cal App 2d 606, 163 P2d 110; State v Thompson, 241 Iowa 16, 39 NW2d 637; Commonwealth v Tucker, 189 Mass 457, 76 NE 127; Makley v State, 49 Ohio App 359, 3 Ohio Ops 250, 17 Ohio L Abs 305, 197 NE 339, error dismd 128 Ohio St 571, 192 NE 738; Commonwealth v Henderson, 242 Pa 372, 89 A 567; State v Layne, 196 Wash 198, 82 P2d 553.

6. **Annotation:** Prejudicial effect of prosecuting attorney's remarks, in opening statement to jury, that another defendant has been convicted or has pleaded guilty. 48 ALR2d 1004.

anticipation of the strong points to be presented by the prosecutor, and conversely, the weaknesses of the defense case.

It is always desirable in planning one's trial strategy to anticipate disclosures by the prosecution of highly unfavorable and damaging evidence against the accused. Defense attorney should always carefully consider in advance whether to disclose such weaknesses in his own opening address in an effort to lessen its effect and dispel the devastating impact such evidence may have upon the jury if it is first advanced by the prosecution.

No matter how damaging the evidence against the accused is, expose it. You can be sure that the prosecutor will! If he explodes it on an unsuspecting jury during the presentation of his case, you might be unable to undo the harm. Besides, the evidence sounds a lot less damaging if it comes from you. The jury will feel that it cannot be too bad if the defendant's own attorney tells us about it.

Bring out the weaknesses in your own case and try to explain them away. If you cannot offer an explanation, argue that even with these unfavorable factors, the accused is still entitled to their verdict of not-guilty. You minimize the prosecution's case while highlighting the facts favorable to your defense.

§ 352. Spotlight complainant's quirks

During your opening statement, call attention to any neurotic or psychotic traits you have observed in the complainant during the preliminary hearing. Tell the jury to watch the complainant carefully as he testifies. Tell them that if they are alert they will notice certain peculiarities, how he hesitates before he answers, how he perspires, how his hands shake, how his answers will probably betray a persecution complex. When the complainant takes the stand, the jury will be looking for these quirks. They will follow and understand the purpose of your cross-examination. And when the quirks appear, you will have little trouble destroying the complainant's credibility.

§ 353. How to conclude your opening address

In concluding his opening address, defense counsel should ask the jurors to keep their minds open until all of the evidence has been presented by the prosecution, and by the defense. Defense counsel may well remind the jury of any instruction it may already have received from the court on this point. Counsel may also ask the jury to withhold making any definite decision until they have been instructed by the court on the law of the case.

Counsel should ask the jury not to be unduly swayed on the basis of who talked first to them or who presents the first proofs to them. The opening statement should be finally concluded with counsel indicating by words, acts, and general attitude, his total reliance and belief in the fairness and intelligent evaluation by the jury.

C. MANNER AND STRATEGY OF DELIVERY

§ 354. In general

The manner of delivery and the tone of one's opening address must, in the final analysis, depend upon the style of the attorney rendering the statement of the case. Above all he must be himself, and must not affect an assumed or artificial mannerism. As a general rule, in most cases and with most juries, oratory or bombast, with a loud aggressive approach should be avoided. At the same time, defense counsel's delivery should be positive, and without confusion, uncertainty, or any hesitancy on his part. He should know his case thoroughly and should present his statements with as little reference as possible to notes or memoranda.

When addressing the jury in your opening statement, remember that you are not making a speech to a group of strangers. Rather, you should speak as though you were talking informally to a group of friends. Look directly at the jury and talk directly to them. Do not turn attention to the judge, the prosecutor, or the spectators.

Try to keep your voice interesting. Do not speak in a singsong or monotone. You can avoid this type of boring delivery by practicing with a tape recorder. Effective use of the voice can greatly heighten the effectiveness of your presentation to the jury.

Your statement of the case should create goodwill for the accused. It should create interest in the defense you will urge, and arouse sympathy for the plight of the accused. You must display sincerity and earnestness. Do not make it appear as if the defendant is just another client paying you a fee. The jury will instantly get the feeling that you don't really believe in his innocence, but are only going through the motions. Instead, give the jury the impression that you and the defendant are one. The jurors should identify you with the accused. When they retire to deliberate, they should be uncertain as to who uttered the words used in your opening statement and summation—yourself, the witnesses or the defendant.

Your delivery must be convincing. To make certain of this, try your opening statement out on your relatives or layman friends before going into court. Informally explain the case to them as you plan to explain it to the jury. If your listeners understand your case and seem interested and sympathetic, then your opening statement is ready for the jury. But if your audience is not receptive, the opening statement probably needs more work.

You want the jury to believe what you say. Speak informally to them. Your tone should be conversational and lively. Short, snappy sentences, vivid descriptions—these are your tools.

Use the opening only to set forth those facts which you intend to prove or disprove. Save any argument for summation. While prolixity is desirable, do not give the jurors the impression that you are simply "going through the motions." Your opening statement should be calculated to give the jury the impression that you believe in the case.

The opening statement should be delivered with the same force, impact, and emotion as the summation if you decide to use more than a cursory opening statement.

§ 355. Use simple language

In delivering the opening address to the jury, use simple language. All technical, unfamiliar terms should be explained in everyday language. Do not tell the jury that the prosecution's case rests on "circumstantial evidence," without explaining what circumstantial evidence is. Do not say that there is a lack of "proximate cause" and leave it at that. The jury will not understand. For example, in a homicide case, explain that the prosecution must prove that the acts of the accused caused the death of the victim.

Your use of simple language will enable the jury to follow much easier the testimony, the points of your defense, and the development of your case. If the facts are not made clear at the outset, then during the trial the jurors will feel the same way you do when you enter a theatre in the middle of a movie. Before you can figure out the plot, much of the important dialogue will have escaped you.

If laymen have to ask you for clarification after listening to your proposed opening, you will know that it requires more work in order to achieve the desired state of clarity.

CROSS-EXAMINATION

§ 374. Controlling the witness' answers
§ 375. Attacking story piece-by-piece
§ 376. Accent improbabilities and contradictions
§ 377. Test the witness' memory and faculties
§ 378. When and how to use silence
§ 379. Previewing your defense
§ 380. Demand production of memoranda used by witness
§ 381. Handling witness' contradiction of document
§ 382. How to handle an interfering judge
§ 383. When and how to stop

E. ATTACKING PARTICULAR TESTIMONY

§ 384. Identification
§ 385. Intoxication
§ 386. Testimony as to confession of defendant

F. CROSS-EXAMINING DIFFERENT TYPES OF WITNESSES

§ 387. The very old and the very young
§ 388. Females
§ 389. Prosecutrix in sex crime
§ 390. Police Officers and officials
§ 391. Expert witnesses
§ 392. The pathologist
§ 393. Rehearsed witness
§ 394. Honest witness
§ 395. Biased witness
§ 396. Witness with criminal record
§ 397. Stool pigeon and accomplice
§ 398. False or lying witness
§ 399. Evasive witness
§ 400. Positive witness
§ 401. Stubborn witness
§ 402. Contrary or unruly witness
§ 403. Stupid or illiterate witness
§ 404. Weak, unsure witness
§ 405. Conceited, flippant, or blustering witness
§ 406. Witness who avoided pre-trial interrogation

A. INTRODUCTION

§ 356. General objectives

Cross-examination is a most vital part of your defense. In many cases it is your *only* defense.[1]

In mastering the techniques of cross-examination you must be familiar with its objectives. Generally your objectives are: (1) to discredit the direct examination and testimony of the witness, and (2) to bring out something in favor of the defendant.

You can accomplish the first objective in a number of ways: (1) by showing that the witness is incompetent to testify as to the events he claims to have observed; (2) by showing that the passing of time and suggestions of others have colored or exaggerated his recollection of facts; (3) by indicating contradictions in his testimony; (4) by inducing him to admit his uncertainty as to statements he made directly; (5) by exposing his bias or prejudice; or (6) by impeaching his character. These and other methods of discrediting direct testimony will be discussed in the sections that follow.

§ 357. When to cross examine; extent of examination

If the witness has not hurt you, leave him alone. Do not

1. **Annotations:** Propriety of cross-examining witness as to illicit relations with defendant in criminal case. 25 ALR3d 537.

Right of defendant in criminal case to inspection of statement of prosecution's witness for purposes of cross-examination or impeachment. 7 ALR3d 181.

Impeachment of accused as witness by use of involuntary or not properly qualified confession. 89 ALR2d 478.

Court's own witnesses (other than expert) in criminal prosecution. 67 ALR2d 538 at page 551.

Preventing or limiting cross-examination of prosecution's witness as to his motive for testifying. 62 ALR2d 610.

Cross-examination of character witness for accused with reference to particular acts or crimes. 47 ALR2d 1258.

Right of accused in homicide case to cross-examine prosecution's witness as to latter's pending or contemplated civil action against accused arising out of same transaction. 41 ALR2d 1205.

Cross-examination of witness in criminal case as to whether, and with whom, he has discussed facts of case. 35 ALR2d 1045.

cross-examine. Cross-examination of a harmless witness can only open the door to unfavorable testimony that the prosecutor inadvertently overlooked or could not legally introduce. The only exception arises where you are aware of additional facts that the witness has knowledge of but did not mention during his direct examination. However, even in such a case, proceed with caution. If you are unable to draw out these facts dismiss him with contempt. Do not go back over his harmless testimony.

You might ask yourself the following questions: Did the witness testify to anything against the defendant? Did his testimony injure the defendant? Did the witness make a favorable impression upon the jury against the defendant? If the answers to these questions are negative, do not risk cross-examining him.

Do not attempt to clear up a rambling story that obviously confused the jury. A rambling story will generally be dismissed by the jury as unreliable.

On the other hand, cross-examine the witness who has damaged the defendant. If you fail to do this, the prosecutor will probably argue that key testimony went unimpeached. You need not cross-examine, however, if you are certain that your own case will irrefutably discredit his testimony. Even then it might be desirable to question the witness if only to nail him down on the point or points you intend to contradict.

If the bulk of a witness' testimony has been truthful and accurate, cross-examination directed at such portions of the testimony will merely serve to bolster it. In such cases you must attack only the weak portions of the testimony. Your aim should be to discredit the doubtful or untrue portions of the testimony. If you can accomplish this, you will create doubt in the minds of the jurors as to the truthfulness of the remainder of the witness' testimony. However, during the cross-examination, you must constantly bear in mind the elements of the offense and the total state of the prosecutor's proof on those elements, so that you do not assist the prosecution by supplying any missing links in its case.

B. CONFRONTATION OF WITNESSES

§ 358. In general

It is fundamental that both the defendant and the jury should be confronted with the witnesses under oath and have the benefit of their sworn testimony in chief and under cross-examination.[2]

The right of the accused to be confronted by his accusers before the tribunal which pronounces upon the facts[3] protects him against the peril of conviction by means of ex parte testimony or affidavits given in his absence or when he had no right to cross-examine.[4]

The right of a person on trial for a crime to be confronted with witnesses against him is secured or guaranteed by the Sixth Amendment to the Federal Constitution and by the constitutions of all except a small number of the states. Moreover, it is now established that the confrontation provision of the Sixth Amendment is obligatory on the states by reason of the Fourteenth Amendment of the United States Constitution.[5]

2. People v Crump, 5 Ill 2d 251, 125 NE2d 615, 52 ALR2d 834.

Annotations: Accused's right to, and prosecution's privilege against, disclosure of identity of informer. 76 ALR2d 262.

Validity and construction of statutes providing for psychiatric examination of accused to determine mental condition. 32 ALR2d 434 at page 452.

3. There is a detailed discussion of the accused's right of confrontation in business and white collar criminal trials in Bailey and Rothblatt, DEFENDING BUSINESS AND WHITE COLLAR CRIMES §§ 174 et seq.

4. State v Mannion, 19 Utah 505, 57 P 542.

5. The right of cross-examination secured by the confrontation clause of the Sixth Amendment is made applicable to the states by the Fourteenth Amendment. Roberts v Russell, 392 US 293, 20 L Ed 2d 1100, 88 S Ct 1921, reh den 393 US 899, 21 L Ed 2d 191, 89 S Ct 73.

Bailey and Rothblatt, DEFENDING BUSINESS AND WHITE COLLAR CRIMES § 175.

§ 359. Nature and purpose of right of confrontation

An accused's right to confront witnesses against him is basically a trial right, and includes both the opportunity to cross-examine and the occasion for the jury to weigh the demeanor of the witness.[6]

The main and essential purpose is to secure the opportunity of cross-examination.[7] Thus, the constitutional right of one accused of crime to be confronted with witnesses contemplates that they shall be examined in his presence and be subject to cross-examination by him.[8] In other words, the right of cross-examination is an integral part of the right of confrontation.[9]

The secondary advantage of confrontation is that the accused has an opportunity, not only of testing the recollection and sifting the conscience of the witness, but of compelling him to stand face-to-face with the jury in order that they may look at him and judge by his demeanor upon the stand and the manner in which he gives his testimony whether he is worthy of belief.[10]

§ 360. Waiver

The right to be confronted by witnesses is a personal privilege which a defendant may waive.[11] Moreover, in

6. Barber v Page, 390 US 719, 20 L Ed 2d 255, 88 S Ct 1318.

7. Douglas v Alabama, 380 US 415, 13 L Ed 2d 934, 85 S Ct 1074; Pointer v Texas, 380 US 400, 13 L Ed 2d 923, 85 S Ct 1065; Brown v United States (CA6 Mich) 234 F2d 140, affd 356 US 148, 2 L Ed 2d 589, 78 S Ct 622, 72 ALR2d 818, reh den 356 US 948, 2 L Ed 2d 822, 78 S Ct 776; Smith v State, 200 Ark 1152, 143 SW2d 190; People v Valdez, 82 Cal App 2d 744, 187 P2d 74, cert den 338 US 835, 94 L Ed 510, 70 S Ct 42; Harris v Commonwealth (Ky) 315 SW2d 630; Garcia v State, 151 Tex Crim 593, 210 SW2d 574.

8. Ralph v State, 124 Ga 81, 52 SE 298.

9. People v Smith, 38 Ill 2d 13, 230 NE2d 188.

10. Mattox v United States, 156 US 237, 39 L Ed 409, 15 S Ct 337, quoted with approval in Douglas v Alabama, 380 US 415, 13 L Ed 2d 934, 85 S Ct 1074.

11. Diaz v United States, 223 US 442, 56 L Ed 500, 32 S Ct 250; Re Baird, 150 Cal App 2d 561, 310 P2d 454, 68 ALR2d 628; State v Logan, 344 Mo 351, 126 SW2d 256, 122 ALR 417; State v Vanella, 40 Mont 326, 106 P 364; Garcia v State, 151 Tex Crim 593, 210 SW2d 574.

some jurisdictions, where an accused is represented by counsel, his counsel may, in the presence and on behalf of the accused, make an effective waiver of the privilege of confrontation.[12] In other jurisdictions, however, it is the rule that the right cannot be waived except by a defendant in person.[13]

The waiver may be by express consent, by failure to assert the right in time, or by conduct inconsistent with a purpose to insist on it.[14]

Where a defendant expressly consents that secondary evidence of the testimony of a witness may be used against him on the trial, he waives his right of confrontation by such witness.[15] Thus, the right is waived where the accused consents to the prosecution's reading into evidence the testimony of an absent witness given in some prior proceeding,[16] or the deposition of an absent witness,[17] or where

12. Cruzado v Puerto Rico (CA1 Puerto Rico) 210 F2d 789; Rosenbaum v State, 33 Ala 354; State v Ganaway, 243 Iowa 1316, 55 NW2d 325; State v Williford, 111 Mo App 668, 86 SW 570; State v Rouse, 138 SC 98, 135 SE 641.

13. State v Rouse, 138 SC 98, 135 SE 641; Bell v State, 2 Tex App 215.

The right of an accused person to confront the witnesses against him is too important a right for the court to permit it to be waived by implication, by counsel, or by anything short of an express waiver by the prisoner, even if that is to be permitted. Dutton v State, 123 Md. 373, 91 A 417.

The privilege of being present in person, so as to confront one's accusers on trial for a criminal offense, may, in felonies other than capital, be waived by the defendant himself, but not by his counsel; in misdemeanors such waiver may be made through counsel with the consent of the court. Harriet Cotton Mills v Local Union, Textile Workers Union, 251 NC 218, 111 SE2d 457, 79 ALR2d 646, cert den 362 US 941, 4 L Ed 2d 770, 80 S Ct 806.

14. Cruzado v Puerto Rico (CA1 Puerto Rico) 210 F2d 789; Bonar v Commonwealth, 180 Ky 338, 202 SW 676; Harriet Cotton Mills v Local Union, Textile Workers Union, 251 NC 218, 111 SE2d 457, 79 ALR2d 646, cert den 362 US 941, 4 L Ed 2d 770, 80 S Ct 806; State v Rouse, 138 SC 98, 135 SE 641; Field v State, 155 Tex Crim 137, 232 SW2d 717.

15. Diaz v United States, 223 US 442, 56 L Ed 500, 32 S Ct 250; State v Fooks, 65 Iowa 452, 21 NW 773; Bonar v Commonwealth, 180 Ky 338, 202 SW 676; United States v Sacramento, 2 Mont 239.

16. Diaz v United States, 223 US 442, 56 L Ed 500, 32 S Ct 250; Cruzado v Puerto Rico (CA1 Puerto Rico) 210 F2d 789 (right can be waived in this manner by counsel on behalf of the accused); Bonar v Commonwealth, 180 Ky 338, 202 SW 676.

17. Diaz v United States, 223 US

the accused stipulates to a statement of what a witness would testify if present.[18] Thus stipulation for presentation of the people's case upon a transcript of the preliminary hearing waived the defendant's right of confrontation.[19]

C. PREPARATION FOR EXAMINATION

§ 361. In general

Your preparation must be complete. You should be as familiar with the material covered by your examination as you are with the witnesses who are testifying. Only in this way will you be able to take advantage of inaccuracies and contradictions.

§ 362. Know the witnesses

Ascertain the names and addresses of all possible witnesses who may testify at the trial. Learn as much about these witnesses as time permits. Try to obtain information about their private lives, particularly any unfavorable background material. Investigate and search for anything that would give rise to prejudice against the defendant. Investigate court records and subpoena police files for any prior criminal record. Obtain every possible documentary record that the witness ever signed or swore to—marriage licenses, divorce papers, tax returns, etc. Look into any other records, such as birth, school, motor vehicle and possible probation reports (many are subject to subpoena). Get the transcript of every bit of testimony that he ever gave under oath.

§ 363. Outline the preliminary hearing

The preliminary hearing is particularly important. You

442, 56 L Ed 500, 32 S Ct 250; Bonar v Commonwealth, 180 Ky 338, 202 SW 676; State v Vanella, 40 Mont 326, 106 P 364.

18. Diaz v United States, 223 US 442, 56 L Ed 500, 32 S Ct 250; Bonar v Commonwealth, 180 Ky 338, 202 SW 676; State v Wagner, 78 Mo 644.

19. People v Wallin, 34 Cal 2d 777, 215 P2d 1.

should have a detailed outline of the testimony of every witness who testified at the preliminary hearing. Determine what portions of these testimonies are harmful and what portions will be helpful. You can thus prepare a list of worthwhile questions.

While the witness testifies at the trial, note carefully any conflicts between his present testimony and that given at the preliminary hearing. Capitalize on these conflicts. This is the most effective way of discrediting his entire testimony. This should be comparatively easy if your outline of his testimony at the preliminary hearing was carefully prepared.

§ 364. Interview witnesses before the trial

You have the right to interview any prosecution witness whom you know will testify. No witness belongs entirely to the prosecution. Take advantage of this right. Learn exactly what he claims to have seen or heard. Obviously, this will aid you in preparing for his cross-examination.

If a witness refuses to be interviewed or is otherwise uncooperative, you can bring this out when you question him. His failure to allow himself to be interviewed should put him in an unfavorable light. The jury will instantly become suspicious of his motives. Does he have something to hide? Why should he refuse to talk to anyone if he is telling the truth?

§ 365. Concentrate during direct examination

Aside from some note taking, do not allow anything to divert your attention from the witness during his direct examination. Try to get inside the witness. Observe his mannerism, his expression, and his reaction. When you rise to cross-examine, you should feel as though you know the witness.

When a key prosecution witness is testifying, tell your client to write any suggestions he has for you rather than telling them to you so that he does not interrupt your concentration.

The intensity of the cross-examiner's concentration during the witness' direct testimony is often the hallmark of the great trial attorney.

§ 366. Check-list of subjects to cover

Here is a list of important points that you should have with you when you start cross-examination of a witness. Before you finish, review these points to see whether you have covered all of them.

1. *Bias or prejudice.*
2. *Motive for exaggeration or distortion.*
3. *Previous conflicts with law.*
4. *Memory.*
5. *Faculties.*
6. *Opportunities for observation.*
7. *Testimony at preliminary hearing.*
8. *Prior statements to prosecutor or police.*
9. *Memoranda used.*

D. TECHNIQUES FOR CONDUCTING CROSS-EXAMINATION

§ 367. In general

Inexperienced attorneys often make the mistake of conducting cross-examination while seated at or standing near the counsel table in order to be close to their notes. It is better to be near the witness, however, not only to enable you to better see and understand the witness, but to impress the witness with the fact of cross-examination. The greater tension will assist you in breaking down prosecution witnesses.

It has been said that when you know what you are after you should act as though you don't know. Conversely, on those rare occasions when you have to tread on untried ground, ask your questions as though you know exactly what you're doing. This can be accomplished by casually referring to the one or two facts of which you are certain in order to convince him that you know of the entire matter.

§ 368. Be fair, courteous, and humble

Avoid brow-beating and ridiculing the witness. Remember, most jurors consider the witness to be at a disadvantage during cross-examination. They are quick to sympathize with a witness who is being handled unfairly. If, on the other hand, you are fair and considerate, and the *witness* becomes offensive, the jury's sympathy will shift to you. Then if you tear into him, the jury will enjoy it almost as much as you.

A fair and courteous manner serves another purpose. It lulls a witness into a false sense of security. He begins to feel more sure of himself and less afraid of you. Once his defenses are down, his answers become more spontaneous. Without thinking, he will yield the information you are searching for. Before he knows what has happened, he will have put his foot in his mouth.

In certain cases it is advisable to deliberately begin your cross-examination in a halting, unsure manner. This manner can be used to lower the guard of a witness from whom you desire to elicit information which he is not prepared to reveal. A fumbling start can lull the witness into a false initial sense of security.

If you have decided to thoroughly impeach the witness, do it in a way that will not offend the jury. Make the jury feel that you have no other alternative but to destroy the witness, however distasteful the task may be to you. If the witness has given highly damaging testimony, it should not be too hard to convince the jury that your only course is an all-out attack. But once you have begun, do not pull any punches. Be dramatic in your destruction. Otherwise the effect will be lost.

§ 369. Ask clear and simple questions

A longwinded, unintelligible question gives the witness an opportunity to ask to have the question repeated. Then, while you are rephrasing the question, he has time to formulate his answer. But if he insists upon having simple, clear questions repeated, the jury will be quick to see through his game. He will discredit himself.

§ 370. Keep the jury's interest

Nothing can destroy the effectiveness of your cross-examination like boredom. If the jury becomes bored with your questions, they will miss the significance of the responses. Where you anticipate a long, drawn-out series of questions, try to relieve the boredom by introducing variety into your queries—variety both in tone and mood. Humor will effectively stimulate interest. It might also become necessary to violate the rule of calm, unemotional questioning, simply to forestall boredom.

§ 371. Evaluate the witness

Each witness is a distinct problem. No one person thinks like another. What a person sees is influenced by his background, his experience, his temperament, his faculties, his intelligence, and many other factors. You must evaluate each of these factors, as well as what you desire your examination to cover, and then proceed with your questions. Your questions must be phrased to suit the person being examined. Failure to follow this rule usually results in an aimless and insignificant examination.

Study the witness's manner and demeanor while he is testifying on direct. Study his face and physique. Apply those principles already discussed as to judging character by physical appearance.

When you are uncertain as to whether a witness is personally against you, ask a few trifling and harmless questions. His reaction to them will indicate his attitude. If it becomes evident that he is neutral or possibly anti-prosecution, then your examination can be adjusted to fit this attitude. If, on the other hand, you begin by questioning such a witness sharply, you might turn him against the defendant.

Your study of the case should have revealed the key issues. You know what the controversial points are; where the disputes exist; what your strong points are; what portions of the prosecution's case can be contradicted; where the prosecution's case is weak. Challenge the witness on these key issues. Anchor his answers. Nail down these points so that no doubt remains as to what he said, so that he cannot change his position. It is much easier to hit a stationary target.

§ 372. Exploring the unknown

With very few exceptions, always know answers to questions asked. Never ask a question unless you know what the answer will be, and that it cannot hurt you. This principle is fundamental. Do not ask a question merely in the hope of getting a favorable answer. The reply might be disastrous.

Very often the prosecutor will deliberately limit the scope of his questions. He hopes that you will fill in the gaps with your own. It is far more effective from his standpoint for you to get hit with unfavorable testimony than for him to introduce it on direct. Or it may be that the evidence would not be admissible on direct. He sits back and waits for you to open the door. Your questions then inadvertently uncover this evidence and permit him to admit it on redirect examination.

Do not fall into this prosecution trap. Do not probe blindly behind the questions asked on direct, especially if the witness is a shrewd type, such as a detective or an expert.

Never pose a question merely because your client asks you to do so. If you consider the question inadvisable, do not ask it. Otherwise, you might try to phrase it in a manner that will assuage your client without risking a damaging reply. But this is dangerous. Later explain to your client the reasons for not using his question.

§ 373. Direct your questions toward an objective

Direct your questions toward an objective. Each of your questions should yield an answer which is part of a sequence. At the end of that sequence lies your objective. Direct your questions toward that objective.

Each answer strengthens the answer that preceded. Step by step the witness gets more deeply involved. If he attempts to change his position, refer back to each and every answer he previously gave. His attempted change will thus serve to completely impeach him. When you have reached your objective, close that part of your examination.

Do not tip your hand as to desired responses. Prosecution witnesses naturally tend to be partisan. They desire to aid the side they represent. If you advertise the purpose behind your questions, it will probably be thwarted. The witness will attempt to alter his answers to dodge the responses you desire. You will receive a "no" if your voice or manner indicates that you seek a "yes." It is therefore important to conceal your purpose from the witness. Do not let him know just what your objective is.

The exception to this rule arises where you desire to trap the witness. This technique will be discussed later in this chapter.

When an opening presents itself, proceed directly to your objective. Look for a weak spot while the witness is testifying. When you find it, do not beat around the bush.

Immediately begin to probe in that area. Do not let him regain his composure.

If you are aware of a weak spot before beginning your examination, such as some ground of prejudice against the accused or some reason for the witness to color his testimony, proceed directly to that point. Do not waste time with insignificant questions. The jury may miss the importance of this weak spot if you obscure it with collateral matters.

§ 374. Controlling the witness' answers

Insist on answers that are responsive to your questions. You must remain master of the situation. Your examination should revolve around a line of reasoning which is fixed and dominated by you. Induce the witness to supply the facts you want. Insist upon the witness fairly answering your questions. If he is dodging them with indirect or qualified answers, press him for a direct response. Keep after him until he realizes he cannot evade you any longer. If it becomes necessary, ask the court to admonish the witness to answer your questions.

Press for definite and specific answers until his evasiveness becomes clear to the jury. The jury will then easily conclude that his testimony is worthless.

§ 375. Attacking story piece-by-piece

It is often effective to whittle away a witness' story piece-by-piece. You might not always have that one explosive question which blows the witness's story sky-high. However, a gradual destruction can be just as effective.

Take the story of the witness, given on direct examination, and put it in a different light. Ask the witness whether it really happened the way he described it. Maybe it could have occurred *this* way. Maybe the remark he overheard was actually an innocent remark. Maybe he heard it entirely out of context. Maybe what he saw was distorted by his position or by the light.

Go back over his story. Hit those material matters where he was weakest on direct examination, those matters about which he was hesitant, confused or unable to discuss positively. Knock out a piece here and a piece there. Keep digging until the foundation of his story is no more. Then, when his disintegration is complete and apparent, end your examination.

You trap a witness by leading him from one question to another. Start with an accepted and undisputed fact. Proceed from this fact through a series of questions to the conclusion which you wish to establish. Act as if you know little about the subject matter of your questions. The witness must be kept in ignorance of the trap you are setting. Keep each question closely related to the preceding one. Try to have them flow like a story. The attention of the witness should be kept constantly upon the accepted and harmless details. His suspicions must not be aroused. Continue leading him into your trap until he gives the crucial answer. If you have done your job well, he will not realize the significance of that final answer, and when he does become aware it will be too late.

§ 376. Accent improbabilities and contradictions

Bring out improbabilities in the witness' testimony. Try to show that the testimony of the witness is completely inconsistent with the experience and knowledge of the average juror. Show that the witness' testimony is improbable. You have been effective if your cross-examination leads the juror to the conclusion that the story told by the witness offends common sense. You can best accomplish this by ending your examination with a flat statement by the witness of a fact, or facts, which are contrary to the juror's sense of probability.

Try to elicit contradictions. You have previously requested that the court exclude all of the prosecution witnesses from the courtroom. This enables you to question each witness without his having heard the testimony of the previous witness. You have carefully anchored the testimony of each witness as to time, places, persons present, statements made, and other important details. Appropriate interrogation should lead to contradictions from subsequent witnesses on these anchored details. If one witness claims the incident took place in one way and you cause another witness to testify that it happened another way, the prosecution's case is obviously weakened.

When a witness contradicts a statement he has made previously, you have him in a very disadvantageous position. Press your advantage all the way. Ask him the following questions: "Which statement is true—your testimony today or the statement you made previously? Did you forget about the testimony you gave previously, or this letter that you wrote before you testified today? Did you tell the prosecutor about it? Were you trying to deceive or mislead him? What was your aim in telling this story when you had told another story previously?"

It is a good idea to press this advantage right at the beginning, even if the contradiction is not of a major fact. It immediately weakens any favorable impression made by the witness' direct examination. You have scored a point right at the onset. The witness is now afraid of you. He is wary of your trapping him again. You will be able to elicit more truthful answers from him. Perhaps you can take him back to his original story and have him tone it down somewhat, or even repudiate parts of it.

Only attack a contradictory statement which is relevant and material to an important point. That is, the statement should either refer to an issue in the prosecution or demonstrate the prejudice of the witness. Argue, however, that other inconsistent points can demonstrate the unreliability of the witness as a reporter of the events in question.

When you attempt to lay a foundation for impeachment testimony by asking a prosecution witness whether he has ever made any contrary statements, the witness will often claim not to remember if he did so or say something like, "I don't think so, but maybe I did." Take the position that any response short of a direct admission of the inconsistent statement entitles you to impeach the witness.

You may impeach a witness by proving he made a prior unsworn oral statement as well as by proving prior written statements or sworn testimony. Similarly, the witness' failure to mention important facts in his prior statements can furnish an inconsistency upon which to fashion an impeachment.

§ 377. Test the witness' memory and faculties

Test the witness' memory. The testimony of any witness becomes incredible if he remembers a particular detail but forgets other material details. Test his memory on these equally important peripheral details or occurrences. If he fails to remember them, suggest that those he failed to remember were conveniently forgotten because they might be beneficial to the defendant; or suggest to the jury that such a "convenient" memory is worthless.

Besides the use of prior statements, you can also impeach prosecution witnesses by demonstrating that they were not able to clearly observe or discern the events in question. To do this you may, for example, prove that the witness was a narcotics addict, that he was intoxicated at the time in question, that he was unable to see clearly without eyeglasses, or that he could not hear without the use of a hearing aid.

It is improbable that a man with poor eyesight could correctly observe an occurrence. Therefore, you might test the vision of such a witness. You can do this by casually asking the witness how he was dressed when he observed the crime. If he says nothing about having worn glasses, ask whether he had been wearing glasses. If he answers in the affirmative, inquire as to the kind of glasses he was wearing. You might ask him to produce them. If he answers that he was not wearing glasses at the time, ask whether he owns a pair of glasses. If he does, again inquire into the kind of glasses he wears and ask him to produce them. Ask about his eyesight without glasses.

You might question a witness who has testified to an overheard conversation as to his hearing ability. Inadequate hearing can be detected by dropping your voice during the course of your examination to see if the witness can hear you.

§ 378. When and how to use silence

Some witnesses are vulnerable to a "silent treatment." The one who has been lying or telling half-truths will be nervous and uneasy on the stand. As you begin, look at him sternly in silence for a few moments until the courtroom becomes tense. Then shoot a question at him that will throw him off balance. Follow this with other disconcerting questions.

This technique should be successful with the ignorant, timid, or inexperienced witness. Do not attempt it on the intelligent or experienced witness.

The witness who delays in answering your questions, or looks embarrassed, is also a good subject for the silent treatment. While you are waiting for his answer, say to him, "Take all the time you need." Look at your watch and keep urging him to take his time. Then, if he continues to hesitate a great deal, release him with a "Never mind, that's all." Dismiss him with disgust.

§ 379. Previewing your defense

Where you are presenting an affirmative defense—such as self-defense, insanity or intoxication—it is at times appropriate to put to the witness some questions that will acquaint the jury with that defense. This technique is particularly recommended where the witness has made statements contradictory to the defendant's version of what occurred. However, this technique should not be employed where your defense is alibi or some other secret defense, because it will enable the prosecutor to adjust his case to meet your defense. You might lose the important element of surprise.

Put your preview questions in a form that gives the witness an opportunity to either deny, modify, or agree with the defendant's forthcoming evidence.

§ 380. Demand production of memoranda used by witness

If the witness used any memoranda to refresh his memory, demand that he produce them for your inspection. This technique is very important in cross-examining a policeman or detective.

If he denies having spoken to anybody about the case, as many witnesses will do without thinking, he will have effectively discredited himself. Everybody knows each witness is spoken to by the prosecutor or police before he testifies, so no juror will believe his denial. The jury might indeed suspect that perhaps the entire story is a fabrication.

Phrase your questions to each of the witnesses so that their answers will sound identical. This will point up the coaching and preparation by the prosecutor.

§ 381. Handling witness' contradiction of document

When a witness has contradicted a written document, do not hit him with it immediately. He might claim that his oral statement was a slip of the tongue. Go over his contradictory statement again. You might say: "Mr. Jones, as I have it, you testified on direct examination as follows: (Read what he said). Is that what you said on direct examination? Is that correct?" The witness will usually answer "Yes." Continue by asking, "Do you have doubts about it? because I don't want to make a mistake. If you have any changes or qualifications, would you please make them now?" When he answers "No," you have pinned him down to the point where he can no longer retreat. *Now* you hit him with the document that he contradicted. Take your time in reaching your climax—but when you strike, strike fiercely.

§ 382. How to handle an interfering judge

Very often a judge who is biased in favor of the prosecution will interrupt your cross-examination with questions while you are in the process of effectively destroying the witness. The judge's questions will break your train of thought and, at the same time, attempt to rehabilitate the witness. In most such instances, the effectiveness of your interrogation will be lost.

The best way to try to stop this interference is to say to the Judge (in a respectful manner): "Your Honor, I intend to cover those points. Will Your Honor permit me to develop them in my own way?" This should politely put the Judge in his place. However, if he continues to interfere, persist in advising him that you intend to cover all of the points he is making, and you respectfully would prefer that he permit you to conduct your cross-examination in your own way.

Be emphatic. Assert your rights firmly—though tactfully—at the very beginning and you should gain the respect of the court. But cower before the court, and this type judge will ride roughshod over you.

§ 383. When and how to stop

The knowledge of when to stop cross-examination is one of the most difficult things for novices to learn.

When you have scored your point, stop. Stop when you have gained a victory. You have made your point; be content to leave it alone. Pass on to another subject. Do not continue to press the witness on that particular point. If you do, he may correct or modify his testimony, and you will lose the advantage you gained.

If you have managed to discredit the witness in some manner, do not blindly plunge ahead like a wild animal who, having smelled blood, is out to make the final kill. Too often the witness in such circumstances will give an answer which seriously jeopardizes the entire defense.

E. ATTACKING PARTICULAR TESTIMONY

§ 384. Identification

In many instances the entire case against the accused will rest upon the testimony of the identification witness. You have prepared the jury when you selected them and, in your opening statement, re-emphasized that identification testimony is completely untrustworthy. The accused's fate depends upon your ability to destroy the witness.

This witness is probably the most hostile of all prosecution witnesses; he will probably impress the jury as being sincere and honest. Always expect that he will positively identify the accused.

The courtroom identification of the defendant should be demonstrated as worthless. Point out that the witness was already prepared to pick out the defendant because the latter was seated at the counsel table, so the defendant was obviously seen at the counsel table even before the witness took the stand. He saw the defendant there when the trial began. He saw the defendant there when he entered the courtroom before he took the witness stand. It is only natural that he will pick out the defendant as the person who allegedly committed the crime.

Point out conflicts in the testimony of different prosecution witnesses. Pin down the witness as to time, circumstances and opportunity he had to observe the person who committed the crime. Bring out, if possible, conflicts and discrepancies in the testimonies of all witnesses who were present. Each witness will probably disagree substantially on the first description they gave of the culprit—the clothing worn, facial characteristics, height, size, color of hair, etc.

After having a witness pinned down as to the description

he gave to the police, ask him if he gave information about the voice, color of hair, the height, size and shape of the face, complexion, physique, jaws, nose, forehead, color of the eyes, description of the clothing or anything else. Be sure to pin him down completely on the description. "Was there anything else you said with respect to the description of this person?" Then you might conclude as follows. "Well, that particular description you gave me may fit the general description of any number of people. Isn't that correct?"

Demonstrate the witness' poor memory. Ask the witness what persons have interrogated him since the case started. He will usually refer to detectives, police, assistant prosecutors and various others. Then ask him to give a description of each person who interrogated him. You might ask him to describe what clothes the district attorney wore at their last meeting—his tie, the color of his suit or anything else. You might have an office associate sit briefly in the courtroom next to you and then walk out of the courtroom shortly before you proceed to interrogate the witness on matters of memory. Then, during the course of your interrogation, have the witness describe in detail what your office associate looked like, pinning him down to specific details. Finally, if the witness says he didn't observe these things, end this line of interrogation.

Complainants who were not familiar with the defendant prior to the commission of the crime are vulnerable to effective cross-examination. Your questioning should concentrate on the impediments to proper identification which were present at the time the crime was committed. You should elicit the facts of poor lighting conditions, the speed with which the crime was committed, the witness' opportunity to observe the culprit, and the witness' state of mind at the time in question. If the witness is completely confident of his identification and refuses to recognize the possibility that he may be in error, you are afforded the opportunity of later arguing that he is a person who is willing to let an innocent man be convicted rather than to question his own ability to perceive events.

Inquire whether or not any photographs were shown to the witness, and when they were shown. Then develop it that the image of the photograph became impressed on his mind, and in identifying the accused in person, he had in mind the image of the accused on the photograph. Thus, this was not an independent identification of the accused, but an identification influenced by the photograph.

If there was no lineup and only the defendant was present, emphasize this. Show that the defendant was actually selected by the police to be identified. You should argue that any identification made of your client without a line-up or any identification made from a photograph at which he was not represented by counsel is violative of his rights under the due process clause.[20]

Develop specifically the discussion that the police and/or detectives had with the witness the day he was taken to the stationhouse to make his first identification of the defendant. Inquire as to whether or not a lineup was held at the stationhouse. Ask the witness if he knows what a lineup is. If the witness does not give a proper description of a lineup, then you describe it to him as follows: "Men are put up in a line. The victim looks over the line and tries to pick out the guilty party."

Have the witness relate exactly what took place from the moment he arrived at the stationhouse until he finally identified the defendant. Emphasize those factors which the police had dwelt upon that caused him to make his identification.

Point up, as follows, the unfairness of not having a lineup: "Did you say to the detectives or to the district attorney, before you identified or picked out the defendant at the stationhouse, that they should put the suspect in a line or with a group to see if you could pick him out of the line or group of persons?"

20. Gilbert v California, 388 US 263, 18 L Ed 2d 1178, 87 S Ct 1951; People v Ballot, 20 NY2d 600, 286 NYS2d 1, 233 NE2d 103.

You can effectively end your cross-examination as follows: "So you looked at this defendant and he was the only one there. Is that correct?" You will thus climax the inference that no one else could possibly have been identified because the defendant was there alone.

If there was a lineup, try to demonstrate that the persons in the lineup were not of the same height, age, general appearance and racial backgrounds as the accused. Show that the defendant was not permitted to select his own position in the line. Point out that there was no tape or stenographic recording taken of questions, answers, and statements of all persons who participated in the lineup.

Of course, the defendant is now entitled to have counsel present at lineup.[21] Further, if you establish that an identification made by a witness, even if not violative of his right to counsel or right against self-incrimination, was made under circumstances so unfair as to amount to a violation of due process. There must be a hearing to determine whether the witness would have been able to make an in-court identification without the improper circumstances.

You should, on cross-examination, inquire into the matter of statements made to the witness by police officers prior to the identification. Such conversations with police officers are often suggestive in themselves. For example, the witness may have been told, "We picked up a fellow who we think committed this crime. We had a tussle with him then he tried to escape. As a result, he is still walking with a slight limp." Such questions should be asked only with great caution. They should not be asked at all if the answer might suggest that your client was also being held on other charges. In such circumstances, consider requesting a voir dire examination of the witness out of the hearing of the jury.

Try to show that the witness testified to details not from his memory of the event but rather to what newspapers, TV and radio reported had taken place. Ask the witness if

21. United States v Wade, 388 US 218, 18 L Ed 2d 1149, 87 S Ct 1926.

he follows TV and radio, and inquire as to what newspapers he reads. Then develop it that he naturally would have read and/or heard the events and details of the particular crime through these media. You might also ask if he has discussed the case with any members of his family; if so, inquire if any members of his family had learned the details of the crime through the newspapers, TV or radio. Finally, conclude by asking if the description he gave was what he actually remembered; or was it based on what he remembered having read in the papers, heard on TV or radio, or what he heard from his wife or members of his family who had furnished the details from the same sources.

If the witness has close friends or relatives in the police department, pursue a line of inquiry showing that he had discussed the case with that particular friend or relative. Try to show that this friend or relative would have aided and advised him in making a positive identification of the defendant.

If possible, show that the identification was induced by passion and prejudice injected by the police. Show that detectives might have provoked and aroused the passions and prejudice of the witness in order to insure the identification of the accused. This situation is particularly probable where there was a homicide. It is very easy for the police to induce a witness to identify the defendant as the culprit by saying very unfavorable things about the defendant, by trying to evoke deep emotion or feeling against the cold-blooded manner in which the victim was killed.

The witness usually believes that the police have inside information—informers who have shown conclusively that the defendant is the person who committed the crime. The police might even tell the witness that the defendant has confessed. They might say that the conspirator who participated with the defendant in the commission of the crime has confessed. So when the witness finally arrives at the stationhouse to make his identification, he has been set up to select the defendant as the person who committed the crime. In view of this, the following cross-examination is suggested:

> Q: "After the crime took place, you reported the matter to the police. Is that not a fact?"
>
> Q: "You conferred with Detective Jones from time to time with respect to this robbery. Did you not?"
>
> Q: "On the day you made your identification, were you advised by Detective Jones to come down to the stationhouse?"
>
> Q: "They said that they had the fellow who held you up. Isn't that a fact?"
>
> Q: "So when you went to the police station you knew that Detective Jones wanted you to identify somebody that he had arrested. Isn't that so?"

Your questions should fit the facts. This line of interrogation should suggest that the victim went down to the stationhouse expecting to see the man who had robbed him. He assumed that the detectives had picked out the correct man. His decision to identify the defendant was already influenced by the police, so if the police were wrong, his identification was equally wrong.

§ 385. Intoxication

In a case where intoxication is the issue or constitutes the crime charged, as in a charge of driving while intoxicated, ascertain whether or not the witness had ever seen the accused before the day in question. If the answer is negative the witness cannot truthfully state what the normal appearance and mannerisms of the defendant are. His opinion that the defendant was intoxicated is invalid. Go further and inquire into the witness's familiarity with the various medical symptoms and physical conditions that may cause an appearance similar to that of intoxication—bloodshot eyes, slurred speech, staggering walk, etc.

If the witness testifies that he was present while the defendant was drinking, ask him if he did any drinking himself. Ask him how many drinks the defendant had. Ask whether he personally approves of drinking in public. Ask whether he belongs to or favors any organization which advocates the suppression of the liquor traffic. This line of questioning might bring out prejudice in the witness against the defendant's alleged intoxication.

§ 386. Testimony as to confession of defendant

The witness who testifies to a confession made by the defendant should be thoroughly questioned about the circumstances surrounding the confession. Who was present? Was the accused represented by counsel before, during or after the time the confession was taken? How long was he questioned? Was he allowed to sleep? Was he given food? Was he allowed to make any phone calls? Was force used by any person present? Were promises of immunity made by any person present? Were there any promises of leniency? Did anybody make a false statement to the accused in order to induce the confession? Did the accused know he was giving a statement that would later be used against him? Did he make a voluntary narrative statement or was the statement in a question and answer form? If the latter, were all questions and answers taken down by the stenographer? Was the accused's memory clear at the time? Was he given an opportunity to read the statement and correct any errors? Was the statement in his own words or did they use their language for his?

Any witness should, of course, be questioned to make certain that your client was properly advised of his rights. Inquire carefully into the circumstances under which the warnings were given. Try to establish that any waiver of rights by your client was not done intelligently and with full understanding.

The issue as to whether your client was entitled to a warning may, in certain cases, depend upon whether he was undergoing "custodial interrogation." In such cases, your cross-examination should be aimed at establishing that at the time of the questioning your client was not free to depart and that he believed himself to be in police custody.

F. CROSS EXAMINING DIFFERENT TYPES OF WITNESSES

§ 387. The very old and the very young

Juries instinctively sympathize with the child witness. Therefore, your cross-examination must be gentle, never harsh or domineering. The jury will resent such "unfair" tactics even if you succeed in discrediting the child's testimony.

Where the prosecutor offers the testimony of a child without a voir dire examination, object to the testimony of the child. Insist upon a voir dire and cross-examine the child thoroughly as to his qualifications. Pay particular attention to whether or not the child understands the meaning of an oath. Ascertain whether or not anybody has explained the meaning of it to him. Ask whether or not he knows what it is to lie. Object, under any circumstances, to the child being sworn.

Child witnesses will almost invariably have been coached by their parents or the prosecution to state that they are aware of the difference between the truth and a lie. It is, however, often useful to ask a child if he knows the difference between a lie and a fib or between a lie and a white lie. The answer may well indicate the child's belief that it is not wrong to speak untruthfully in certain circumstances.

Testimony is easily implanted in the minds of children by interested persons.[22] Their parents, the complainant, or the prosecutor will constantly rehearse them. The child, especially the intelligent one, will carefully memorize his story. The story will come out perfectly on direct examination. You can expose this memorization by having the child

22. People v Oyola, 6 NY2d 259, 189 NYS2d 203, 160 NE2d 494.

meticulously and rapidly repeat his testimony. As he speaks rapidly, the memorized portions of his testimony will stand out from those that were not memorized. He may be using words that are not natural for his age and speaking vocabulary.

Another technique is to start your cross-examination with unimportant matters, allowing the child to gain confidence. Ask him about his school, his teachers, his friends. Then, slowly begin to probe him on matters that he does not expect. Continue by going over his testimony given on direct. Again, the rehearsed portions should stand out from the answers he gave the unexpected questions.

Children are extremely imaginative. Their stories can be pure fiction or part fact and part fiction.[23] If the child has let his imagination run away with him, encourage him to exaggerate. Gently lead him further and further until his story reaches the point of ridiculousness.

Handle older persons very tenderly. Do not show them up or make fun of them. Be polite; just smile if they make a silly remark. Dismiss them courteously.

§ 388. Females

Jurors may become annoyed with counsel who markedly alters his manner when examining girls or women. Your demeanor should remain constant throughout the trial. Do not act in a condescending manner to female witnesses and avoid becoming overly solicitous of their feelings. Conversely, if a female witness becomes highly emotional in an attempt to appeal to the jury, remain unmoved. She may become angry and upset, and thereby more susceptible to penetrating cross-examination by your stoic rejection of her emotional outbursts.

An intelligent woman will very often be evasive. She will avoid making a direct answer to a damaging question.

23. People v Oyola, supra.

Keep after her until you get a direct answer—but always be the gentleman.

§ 389. Prosecutrix in sex crime

Try to treat the prosecutrix in a sex crime as you would any other woman witness. However, expect her to be more emotional.

The complainant in a rape case will sometimes turn out to be a person caught in a compromising situation who is trying to brazen her way out of it, or she may be a rejected woman seeking revenge, often upon any male and not necessarily upon the one who rejected her. In such cases, develop the facts which led up to the supposed rape. Try to show the lack of force through the complainant's voluntary relationship with your client. Stress any opportunities which the complainant might have had for escape, resistance, or outcry. The careful development of these elements may well convince the jury that your client, rather than the complainant, is the "wronged" party.

If the gravamen of the crime is forcible sexual intercourse, develop in your cross-examination that there were no signs of bleeding or laceration; that there were no physical indications of force having been applied; that there was no physical evidence of the act, such as stains, semen, torn clothing, missing buttons, signs of struggle, or any similar signs that would corroborate a forcible sex crime.[24] Ascertain when the alleged attack was reported to the police; was it right after the attack or did she delay going to the police? Did she reveal the attack to others? Develop any other facts that might indicate the attack was an afterthought on her part.

§ 390. Police officers and officials

It is advisable to prepare yourself for the cross-examination of police witnesses by becoming familiar with the basic

24. People v Oyola, 6 NY2d 259, 189 NYS2d 203, 160 NE2d 494.

principles of criminal investigation. You should be able to obtain training manuals from your local police academy. There is also a wide range of literature by experts in police science with regard to the proper methods of investigating various crimes.

These witnesses will normally try to determine the motive behind your questions before they answer. Keep your questions disconnected. Use the jump-around technique. Put your questions rapidly so he cannot keep up with you. If you can keep him in the dark as to the motives and reasons for your questions, he may succumb more easily.

Police officers are generally careless as to the form and manner in which they noted statements made to them. Generally they add a great deal to their testimony besides what they have noted. Dwell at length upon their failure to write down the statements the defendant is alleged to have made. Carefully examine any notations they did make. Question them about any testimony that is not found in their notes.

Generally, follow this negative approach throughout your cross-examination. In other words, point up what they *failed* to do or see, not what they claimed they did or saw.

Do not cross-examine police witnesses in such a way as might reveal your client's prior criminal record. So, for example, avoid asking a police officer why his attention centered upon your client.

Proper cross-examination of a police officer requires a close familiarity with the many departmental forms that are required to be filed in addition to the police blotter. If you carefully examine all of these available forms, you will more often than not discover discrepancies which can be put to good use during cross-examination. Juries are often impressed with the argument that the inadequacy or indifference revealed in the reports is also true of the manner in which the entire investigation was conducted.

§ 391. Expert witness

The inexperienced trial attorney will generally find himself overmatched when cross-examining an expert who is a courtroom veteran. In any event, the attack on the expert should be one of indirection. Try to keep your true objective hidden. For example, if you want to impeach the witness through the use of textbooks, get him to agree to the author's qualifications before asking him about the book. A direct attack on his testimony will rarely yield dividends to the defense. If you can discredit even a part of an expert's testimony, you will generally have done well.

A direct attack upon an expert is called for when his testimony deviates from what is considered customary and usual in his particular field. Do not attempt a direct attack on an expert witness unless you yourself are in command of the particular field. The direct attack can attempt to demonstrate, for example, that scientific tests performed by the witness failed to meet professional standards or that his investigation omitted some vital element. This type of cross-examination can set the groundwork for later testimony by your expert witness which will demonstrate the unreliability of the methods used by the expert.

The collateral attack on the witness can be used to demonstrate his bias for the prosecution, his pecuniary interest, or the amount of time he spends in court as a witness.

When cross-examining an expert witness, never ask broad questions which will allow him to expand upon his remarks made on direct testimony. Such answers will reinforce his previous testimony. Your questions should be sharp and direct. Never allow the expert to turn his answer into a lecture or discourse. The asking of direct questions which call for "yes" or "no" answers is also the best method with which to deal with the evasive expert witness. If such a witness continues to volunteer unrequested information, request the judge to caution him not to volunteer testimony. Also, request that the jury be instructed to disregard such volunteered testimony.

Never cross-examine an expert on his field unless you are thoroughly familiar with the subject matter of his testimony. Prepare your cross-examination with the aid of your own expert. Have the prosecution expert clearly explain any technical terms used in his direct testimony that might be helpful to the accused.

Ask him precisely what he knew about the case before he started his study of the subject in question. A truthful reply will indicate he knew a great deal before. Consequently, you can show that the result he arrived at was due in part to information he received from persons other than those who testified. The answer to the prosecutor's hypothetical question will thus be shown to be the result of evidence, outside of the evidence given under oath, supplied by the prosecution and others. This might lead to invalidating his answer to the hypothetical question.

Because of the risks inherent in cross-examining an expert, you should not take on one whose testimony supports only a minor technical aspect of the prosecution's case. At best, unless you are fully prepared to attempt to demolish the witness, you should ask only a few questions which you have designed to demonstrate the narrowness of the testimony.

In cross-examining an expert who was a major prosecution witness, consider the possibility of limiting your attack to an area in which you are sure of yourself. If you can discredit the witness in any particular, you will later be able to argue to the jury that the expert's lack of ability in this area is indicative of the general unworthiness of his entire testimony.

It is essential for you to obtain, in advance of trial, copies of any reports made by the witness so that you will have the opportunity to discuss and dissect them with your own expert. One of the most effective methods of cross-examination is then to confront the prosecution's expert with the published contradictory statements of someone who the witness agrees is also expert in the field. If the witness refuses to recognize others in the field as experts, he will show himself to be egotistically opinionated and intellectually arrogant. If, on the other hand, he recognizes the expertise of others, he will be hard put to explain the contradictions. In explaining contradictions he may assist your defense by admitting the existence of a reasonable difference of opinion. He may attempt a complicated technical explanation which the jury cannot follow, or he may dogmatically insist that he is correct, thereby indicating the narrowness of his views.

It is frequently rewarding to ask the witness whether he has read a particular recent article in a technical journal in his field of expertise. A doctor may be asked whether he read a particular article in a medical journal which has some relevance to the subject matter of his testimony. It is most unlikely that he will have read it. (Your expert witnesses or independent research can lead you to such articles.) When he admits that he hasn't read it, indicate that you thought as much. This will help establish you in the minds of the jurors as one who is knowledgeable in the particular field.

If the prosecution's expert witness is familiar with your witness, get him to admit the qualifications of your expert. The jury will be more impressed with your expert if a prosecution witness has described him as a recognized authority in his field.

One effective method of cross-examination is to inquire about the expert's compensation, if he is not on the public payroll. Such examination should leave the jury with the impression that the expert may be coloring his testimony in order to earn a fee. Ascertain how many times the expert has testified for the prosecution. If possible, demonstrate that he is a so-called "professional witness" paid by the prosecutor. The danger of this type of cross-examination is that the prosecutor is likely to retaliate with similar cross-examination of your expert witnesses. The method, therefore, is best used when you will not be calling expert witnesses to testify on behalf of the defense.

§ 392. The pathologist

One of the most important areas in the cross-examination of the prosecution expert who conducted the autopsy in a homicide prosecution is related to the establishment of the time of death. Science has yet to produce a method capable of exactitude in this regard.

If this is an issue, always ascertain the method used by the witness to arrive at an estimated time. If the witness states that he used a rectal thermometer and based his estimate on the corpse's temperature, question him about the various factors which affect the rate at which bodies cool. A text on pathology will provide you with information concerning such matters as the effect of the temperature of the place where the body was found and the amount of clothing or covering around the body. If you can show, on cross-examination, the failure of the witness to consider these factors, his opinion as to the time of death will be of little value. Also inquire about other methods of estimating the time of death.

Sometimes, post-mortem staining or lividity is used to establish the time of death. This method rests upon the tendency of a body which is in a fixed position for a length of time to develop a gravitational staining caused by the percolation of blood through the tissue toward the lowest point. The lower part of the body will be a brighter red or bluish color, and the color can be matched with a chart to estimate how long the body has remained in that position.

Another method of ascertaining time of death is based on the degree of rigor mortis (rigidity of muscles occurring after death).

The time of onset of rigor mortis after death and its duration vary according to the activity and general condition of the muscles before death. Therefore, it is of basic importance to know if the victim was struggling when death occurred. If he was, the action of the sympathetic nervous system in increasing the blood supply to the muscles will have significantly affected the time of the onset of rigor mortis.

If the time of the deceased's last meal is known, analysis of the stomach contents can be used in determining the time of death.

Familiarize yourself with the various tests and their inaccuracies and question the witness to obtain an admission that more accurate knowledge about the circumstances surrounding the death or a more sophisticated autopsy could well have produced a more precise estimate of the time of death. Questioning of this kind will give the jury the impression that, were it not for the carelessness of the autopsy, the time of death could have been exactly ascertained and your client might not have been charged with criminal responsibility for it.[25]

Remember that no known method for ascertaining the time of death is infallible.

§ 393. Rehearsed witness

You are sometimes able to discredit the direct testimony of a witness by showing that it was carefully prepared under the guidance of the prosecutor. Ask the witness, who has he talked to about the case? Where did the conversation take place? Who was present at this conversation? How many of such conversations took place?

An honest answer to these questions will indicate that his testimony, as well as that of the other prosecution witnesses, was rehearsed by the prosecutor or police. Instead of an honest recollection of what occurred, his story will appear prefabricated and unworthy of the jurors' belief.

§ 394. Honest witness

Do not cross-examine an honest witness on the details of

25. **Practice Aids:** 2 Am Jur Proof of Facts 261, AUTOPSY.

the story he told on direct examination; he will only repeat and reemphasize them. Instead, question him on collateral matters. Test his memory, his ability to judge distances, his opportunity for observation, and similar matters. Point out any errors or mistakes in judgment or observation, or his natural bias in distorting facts in favor of the prosecution. If you can catch him in some inaccuracy, you have scored enough.

Be friendly towards the honest witness. He may respond in friendliness and cooperation to you.

§ 395. Biased witness

The biased witness is vindictive. He will do his utmost to hurt the defendant if you give him a chance. He can be relied upon to give an answer contrary to the one you want. You can spot the biased witness. He will lay particular stress on the parts of his testimony that he believes to be most damaging. He will display satisfaction when he scores a damaging blow. It will show in his manner and in his face.

You can take advantage of his desire to hurt the defendant. He can often be led into giving a favorable answer for the accused. For example, if you want him to say that it was light when the incident took place, ask him if it was not a fact that it was dark when the incident took place. He is apt to say, "No, it was light." Such tactics are justified by the nature of the witness.

Where the defendant is faced with more than one biased witness, question each of them about his conferences with the others and with the prosecutor. Bring out the number of such conferences. Show that each one rehearsed and carefully tailored his own story to that of the others—all under the guidance of the prosecutor and/or the police. The jury will naturally take a dim view of testimony prepared in such a manner.

Probe behind the personal ill feeling and animosity the

witness bears against the defendant. If the defendant was able to explain the reasons for the witness's hostility, or if your investigation revealed the reasons, bare each of these reasons to the jury. Otherwise, try to determine his motive for testifying as he did. Try to demonstrate the presence of bias and prejudice as well as any other reasons for his frame of mind.

§ 396. Witness with criminal record

A typical method of impeachment is by proof of the witness' former convictions. Some states regulate this form of impeachment by statute, limiting it to proof of the conviction of a felony or of an "infamous" crime. Most states, however, permit such impeachment by proof of any conviction. You can never seek to impeach by proof of arrests and accusations. The proof of a prior conviction, if denied by the witness, is generally had by subpoenaing the Clerk of Court of the conviction along with the records.

Do not be satisfied with merely establishing that the witness has been convicted of a crime. Go into the circumstances of that crime, particularly if it was a felony. If he is a despicable character, handle him in such a way as to make the jury despise him. Do not inhibit him. Let his true personality come out. Let him describe his criminal acts. If he minimizes these acts, then *you* place them in their proper perspective.

§ 397. Stool pigeon and accomplice

Develop the circumstances around the defendant's implication by the stool pigeon or accomplice. What did he say concerning the defendant's participation in the case when he first spoke to the prosecutor or police? Did he claim his own innocence or did he admit his guilt at the beginning? At what point did he change his story to implicate the defendant? What happened in between these two stories? Did he make any other statements to persons other than the prosecutor? Did he speak to any police officers? Are any of his statements contradictory? Pin him down to the dates, places and stories that were given.

If the accomplice was not indicted for his part in the crime, bring this out to the jury. Show that he had been given immunity in return for implicating the defendant. Show that he is saving his own skin by turning on the defendant. Show that he had to implicate someone or *he* would be the defendant on trial.

On the other hand, if you can show that—based on an examination of their backgrounds—the accomplice and the defendant were *not* more than passing friends, then it is improbable that they committed the crime together.

§ 398. False or lying witness

In the case of vital eye-witnesses, you may try to establish the witness' general bad reputation in his community for honesty, integrity, and truthfulness. If you decide to use character impeachment testimony, it is important to obtain character witnesses whose positions in the community command respect.

There are four rules to be observed when cross-examining an untruthful witness: (1) Adopt a superior attitude; (2) Allow the witness to testify freely; (3) Question him on collateral matters; (4) Use the jump-around technique.

You must convince the witness that he will be exposed to the jury as a liar unless he admits the truth. Make him feel you are on to his game, that you know what portions of his testimony are untruthful. If you convince him of your potential ability to expose his lies, he will lose his confidence. Once you have instilled in him the fear of being detected, your task of destroying him becomes easier. Even if you are unable to completely expose his lies, his nervousness brought on by the fear of exposure will leave him vulnerable to attack on summation.

Let the witness testify freely. Encourage him to exaggerate. Do not object to irrelevant or hearsay testimony that he might be giving. Give him the impression that his exaggerations are damaging the defendant. He will be induced to push his imagination still further. Then, when it becomes apparent even to him that his story is absurd, ask him to retract and repudiate his earlier testimony.

A witness who has committed perjury in the past should be forced to admit this to the jury. Describe the circumstances of the perjury in detail. Ask him whether the oath meant anything to him at that trial. Suggest that it is equally meaningless to him at this trial.

§ 399. Evasive witness

When you encounter an evasive witness, demand that this witness give you a clear and direct answer. Keep after him. After an unresponsive answer, you might have the court reporter read the question to him again. Then say, "Did you hear the question? Do you understand the question? Then, why don't you answer it? Please tell the jury why you refuse to answer that question."

Hit this witness with rapid-fire questions. If you continue to get "I don't remember" replies or other evasive responses, ask the Judge to instruct him to answer your questions directly and responsively. Such instruction will impress the jury with the evasive tactics of the witness. It will place him in an uncomfortable position. This will usually force him to respond truthfully.

If the witness continues his evasiveness after being admonished by the court, dismiss him summarily. But before you dismiss him, deliver a final blow. Ask whether he understood the last question. If he answers yes, say: "Perhaps you prefer not to answer it?" If he again answers yes, say: "Very well, Mr. Witness, step down. I have no further questions." One last remark may be fitting: "By the way, do you know what today's date is? Thank you, Mr. Witness, for that last answer at least. Please step down."

§ 400. Positive witness

Sometimes you will encounter a witness who refuses to make any statement in other than positive terms. If you cannot induce this witness to qualify his answers, encourage him to make positive statements concerning matters about which nothing can be positive, or else try to induce contradictory statements.

§ 401. Stubborn witness

The stubborn witness may be one of two types. He may hold back the facts. Such a witness is always hostile and afraid of you. Ask him few questions. Just draw out what you need and leave him alone.

A stubborn witness may also qualify as a "bulldog" type. This type takes a position and refuses to retreat. Your job is to make his position appear ridiculous.

§ 402. Contrary or unruly witness

The contrary witness (as well as the stubborn or unruly one) will often harbor deep hostility toward your client. You should be able, without excessive questioning, to turn the witness' hostility toward your client against you. If you can accomplish this, the hostility and bias will be on the surface for the jury to see. This can be an effective method of impeaching credibility.

Do not quarrel with an unruly and insulting witness. Appeal to the court to warn him to behave. This should dramatize the tactics of the witness to the jury.

§ 403. Stupid or illiterate witness

Do not brow-beat the stupid witness. The jury will resent such tactics. Instead, be gentle and help him along. He may become your friend and offer you some favorable testimony. If he persists in remaining hostile, question him on collateral matters. His limited intelligence will usually prevent his giving the appropriate answers. Once he lapses into total confusion, his testimony will be worthless.

§ 404. Weak, unsure witness

There is a certain type of witness who is never sure of himself. If hard-pressed, he will change his testimony. Be friendly with him, but be firm. If you gain his confidence, he will usually volunteer the testimony you are seeking. If, on the other hand, you alienate him with harsh treatment, he will go into a shell and become uncooperative.

§ 405. Conceited, flippant, or blustering witness

A conceited witness sometimes acts as if he knows everything. He believes he has an impressive and convincing answer to any question you can ask. Encourage his egotistical attitude. Let him think you are very much impressed with his intelligence. Meanwhile, try to lead him unobtrusively into a trap. Keep your real purpose hidden at all times. Once you have him trapped, attack him fiercely.

The flippant or smart-aleck witness destroys himself. His manner antagonizes the jurors. Be patient with him. Do not lose your temper. Give him enough rope and he will hang himself. If he becomes particularly obnoxious, have the court admonish him to answer your questions.

The blusterer will exaggerate the simplest facts as well as the most important ones. You can point up his exaggeration by goading him. Lead him into ridiculous exaggerations.

§ 406. Witness who avoided pre-trial interrogation

The witness who earlier refused to talk to you or your representative can be handled in the following manner: Call to his attention the occasion when you or your representative attempted to speak to him. Ask whether or not it was true that he refused to answer any questions: "Why did you refuse to tell your story? Did the police or prosecutor advise you that it was wrong to tell the truth? Is that why you refused to talk to us? If that isn't the reason, were you afraid you would testify differently when you got into court? Are you angry at the defendant or are you a friend of the complainant?"

One word of caution with regard to this line of questioning. Use it only on a witness who appears to have something to hide and one whom you have well under control (e.g. the evasive witness, the biased witness, the false or lying witness). If you use such questions indiscriminately, you may receive some surprising answers.

CHAPTER THIRTEEN

OBJECTIONS AND MOTIONS

A. OBJECTIONS TO EVIDENCE

§ 407. When to object

Your function at the trial is that of an advocate. You are not there as a Professor of Law grading an examination paper. Do not object merely because a question is improper. Object only when either the answer or the form of the question is improper *and* will result in harm to your client's cause. Continued objections for no apparent reason may give the jury the impression that you are afraid of the truth. However, do not allow the fear of the jury's possible adverse reaction prevent you from objecting to improper and damaging questions or answers.

§ 408. Timing of objections

Object to improper questions as soon as they are asked. Do not give the witness time to answer them. If the witness has begun to answer, request him to stop. If the question has been fully answered, repeat your objection and request the Judge to strike the answer and to caution the jury to disregard the answer. If the answer was a highly improper one, couple your objection with a motion for a mistrial.

The first time that a witness answers a question before there has been a ruling on your objection, ask the judge to caution him not to answer until there has been a ruling. Repeat this request each time the witness blurts out an answer. While such admonitions will not have a great effect on an overeager witness, they will serve to point up his impetuosity to the jury and thereby help to discredit him.

§ 409. Anticipate objectionable matter

You will often be able, during the course of a trial, to see that the prosecutor is heading in a direction which will lead to a line of improper questions. If you can see this approaching, request permission to approach the bench for a conference. Explain your fears to the Judge, and ask the prosecutor whether he intends to pursue the particular line of questioning. If he indicates that such is his intention, note your objection and request a ruling. If the Judge declines to rule at such an early stage, request that the evidence be developed initially out of the hearing of the jury so that he can rule upon it without the danger of undue prejudice. Make sure that any such conference at the bench is transcribed so as to preserve your objections for appeal.

§ 410. Form of objection

The rules vary from state to state as to the form in which objections must be taken to preserve them for appeal. Some states require that you except to any overruling of an objection in order for you to preserve that objection. In other states, the objection is itself sufficient to preserve claims of error. However, some states, such as New York, which no longer require exceptions to be taken during the trial, still require exceptions in order to preserve objections to the Court's instructions to the jury or to its failure to instruct it in a certain manner.

If exceptions are not required in order to preserve your claims of error, do not take them. The trial judge is likely to get annoyed at the taking of the objection and to regard it as a form of exhibitionism.

§ 411. Keep objections specific

An objection to an improper question should pinpoint the precise nature of your objection. Avoid general objections such as, "I object on the ground the question is improper." Point out the nature of the impropriety. For example, "Your honor, the question calls for a hearsay answer. It does not fall within the exceptions which allow admissions as there is no proof that my client knew that his statement was against his interest at the time he made it."

The usual rule is that an appellate court will not find error in the overruling of a general objection unless there was no theory upon which the evidence could have been received. On the other hand, specific objections must be reviewed on their merits. Hence, if you make a general objection which is overruled, follow it with a specific objection. Include every ground you can think of which renders the question objectionable.

§ 412. Obtain a ruling

Trial judges will often seek to avoid a direct ruling on

your objections. Your function in such an instance is to pin them down. If you object to a line of questions and the Judge says something like, "Well, we'll give him another few minutes on this line before we break it off," insist on a ruling. Ask the Judge directly whether your objection has been sustained or overruled. At other times prosecutor's evidence will be admitted "subject to connection." If this occurs, it will be necessary to again object and seek a ruling at the close of the prosecution's case if the evidence was not properly connected.

The prosecutor will often question a witness along a particular line which you believe inadmissible. For example, a series of questions may be asked about a transaction, and you may believe each answer is based upon hearsay. Object to each question. If the trial judge expresses annoyance at your continued interruptions, indicate that your only desire is to achieve a fair trial for your client. Ask the court whether you can have a continuing objection to the entire line of questions.

§ 413. Make a record

It is essential that you "make a record" during the trial of the case. That is, you must make certain that the transcript reflects your objection to all improper questions and proceedings and that these objections are made in a manner which will "preserve" them for the appeal.

B. MOTIONS

§ 414. Motions for a mistrial or the withdrawal of a juror

Motions for a mistrial or for the withdrawal of a juror (either may be proper in the particular jurisdiction) should be made whenever prejudice or harm of an unremediable nature occurs. The appropriate motion should be made as soon as the particular error takes place. Failure to move promptly may be deemed a waiver of your right to make the motion.

Tactical reasons may occasionally impel you not to seek a mistrial. If the trial is going well and you believe that the prejudice was so obvious that it will necessarily result in a reversal, you may well be advised not to seek a mistrial. You must also bear in mind that your motion for a mistrial will probably result in a waiver of your right to claim double jeopardy.

Motions for mistrial can also be based upon such diverse and miscellaneous grounds as improper conduct of jurors (such as visiting the scene of the crime without Court approval), prejudicial newspaper publicity (newspapers sometimes print the contents of suppressed confessions during the course of a trial), improper remarks to the jury by court officers or officials, variance between the proof and the indictment or bill of particulars, illness of a defendant or defense witness, etc. In any case in which the prosecutor, or the court, *sua sponte,* seeks a mistrial, take the position that you do not actively oppose it but insist that your client may not again be placed in jeopardy for the same offense.[1]

1. **Annotation:** Absence of convicted defendant during hearing or argument of motion for new trial or in arrest of judgment. 69 ALR2d 835.

CHAPTER FOURTEEN

PRESENTATION OF THE DEFENSE

E. CONDUCTING THE DIRECT EXAMINATION

F. REDIRECT EXAMINATION

A. WHEN NOT TO PRESENT A DEFENSE

§ 415. In general

The prosecution has rested its case. You have thoroughly cross-examined the prosecution's witnesses. You now must decide whether or not to put in a defense, and whether to call defense witnesses or possibly the accused.

If the prosecution has put in a poor case and there is an excellent chance that the jury may completely ignore and disregard the flimsy evidence presented, you should rest and rely upon this lack of evidence. Argue that the prosecution has failed to meet its burden of proof and has not established the guilt of the accused beyond a reasonable doubt.

B. SUBSTANTIVE DEFENSES

§ 416. In general

The law sanctions many defenses in order that persons

charged with a crime may not be unjustly convicted or prosecuted a second time for the same act.[1] It is the right of an accused and his counsel to utilize any and all defenses in his behalf,[2] and an accused may present as many defenses as he has or thinks he has.[3]

An affirmative defense is one that admits the doing of the act charged, but seeks to justify, excuse, or mitigate it,[4] or, as in former jeopardy, to invoke a bar arising out of facts dehors the record.

§ 417. Character and reputation; custom and usage

Good character or reputation of the accused is not a defense as a matter of law, but is a fact for consideration of the jury in connection with other facts.[5]

A custom or usage prevailing in a community or neighborhood cannot be set up as a defense to a prosecution for crime, even though such custom or usage may have been

1. Commonwealth v Hargreaves, 50 Pa D & C 641.

2. Tschuor v Meck, 72 Ariz 200, 232 P2d 848.

3. People v De Rosa, 378 Ill 557, 39 NE2d 1.

As to insanity as a substantive defense, see Bailey and Rothblatt, WHITE COLLAR CRIMES §§ 123–132.

As to defenses, other than insanity, tending to negative criminal state of mind or moral responsibility, see Bailey and Rothblatt, WHITE COLLAR CRIMES §§ 105–122.

Annotation: Modern status of the rules as to voluntary intoxication as defense to criminal charge. 8 ALR3d 1236.

Practice Aids: 13 Am Jur Trials 465, Defending Minor Felony Cases.

As to proving insanity, see §§ 287–304, supra.

4. Halko v State (Sup) 54 Del 180, 175 A2d 42.

Annotation: Free exercise of religion as defense to prosecution for narcotic or psychedelic drug offense. 35 ALR3d 939.

5. Hermansky v United States (CA8 Neb) 7 F2d 458; Springfield v State, 96 Ala 81, 11 So 250; State v McGuire, 84 Conn 470, 80 A 761; Greer v State, 159 Ga 85, 125 SE 52; People v Munday, 280 Ill 32, 117 NE 286; Dorsey v State, 179 Ind 531, 100 NE 369; State v Hillman, 203 Iowa 1008, 213 NW 603; State v Demaree (Mo) 362 SW2d 500, 17 ALR3d 312; Heartsill v State (Okla Crim) 341 P2d 625; State v Totten, 72 Vt 73, 47 A 105; Cupps v State, 120 Wis 504, 97 NW 210, same result reached on reh 120 Wis 532, 98 NW 546.

for a long time acquiesced in by the community in which it prevails.[6]

§ 418. Alibi

In terms of being a defense in criminal law, the term "alibi" indicates that line of proof by which an accused undertakes to show that because he was not at the scene of the crime at the time of its commission,[7] having been at another place at the time,[8] he could not have committed the crime. In other words, by an alibi the accused attempts to prove that he was at a place so distant that his participation in the crime was impossible.[9]

An alibi is a complete defense by itself, and is neither helped nor hurt by other defenses.[10] An alibi is the most perfect, physically conclusive evidence of the accused's innocence.[11] An alibi precludes the possibility of guilt.[12]

In some jurisdictions there are statutes which require the accused to give notice to the prosecution of his inten-

6. Ullrich v State, 186 Md 353, 46 A2d 637, 165 ALR 1107, wherein it was held that a custom by undertakers to conduct at their homes funerals of persons whose bodies they have prepared for burial at their business establishments does not justify an undertaker in doing so where he thereby violates a zoning ordinance excluding undertaking establishments from residential districts.

7. Tomlinson v United States, 68 App DC 106, 93 F2d 652, 114 ALR 1315, cert den 303 US 642, 82 L Ed 1102, 58 S Ct 645, cert den 303 US 646, 82 L Ed 1107, 58 S Ct 645; Singh v State, 35 Ariz 432, 280 P 672, 67 ALR 129; State v Hubbard, 351 Mo 143, 171 SW2d 701; State v Steen, 185 NC 768, 117 SE 793; State v Payne, 104 Ohio App 410, 5 Ohio Ops 2d 87, 77 Ohio L Abs 558, 149 NE2d 583; State v Poole, 161 Or 481, 90 P2d 472; Commonwealth v Russell, 149 Pa Super 326, 27 A2d 494.

8. State v Wagner, 207 Iowa 224, 222 NW 407, 61 ALR 882; Huckett v State, 121 Neb 364, 237 NW 159; Commonwealth v McQueen, 178 Pa Super 38, 112 A2d 820; Windham v State, 162 Tex Crim 580, 288 SW2d 73.

9. People v Thomas, 393 Ill 573, 67 NE2d 192; State v Baker, 246 Iowa 215, 66 NW2d 303; State v Ovitt, 126 Vt 320, 229 A2d 237.

For the matter of proving the defense of alibi, see § 286, supra.

10. People v Doody, 343 Ill 194, 175 NE 436.

11. State v Danelly, 116 SC 113, 107 SE 149, 14 ALR 1420.

12. Basoff v State, 208 Md 643, 119 A2d 917.

tion to rely on alibi as a defense.[13] Some statutes require notice as to the place at which the defendant claims to have been when the crime was committed and the witnesses on whose testimony he will rely in establishing his defense.[14]

§ 419. Wrongdoing or negligence of victim

The doctrine of particeps criminis has no place in the administration of criminal law.[15] Thus it is no defense that the victim of a crime may also be guilty of wrongdoing.[16]

Contributory negligence is not available as a defense in a criminal prosecution, and cannot purge an act otherwise constituting a public offense of its criminal character.[17]

§ 420. Entrapment

The defense of entrapment was not known at common law, and is not recognized in some states.[18] Although it is

13. People v Wudarski, 253 Mich 83, 234 NW 157, 95 ALR 782; State v Thayer, 124 Ohio St 1, 176 NE 656, 75 ALR 48; State v Kopacka, 261 Wis 70, 51 NW2d 495, 30 ALR2d 476.

14. Annotation: Validity and construction of statute requiring defendant in criminal case to disclose matter as to alibi defense. 45 ALR3d 958.

15. State v Mellenberger, 163 Or 233, 95 P2d 709, 128 ALR 1506.

16. State v Posey, 88 SC 313, 70 SE 612.

17. Broxton v State, 27 Ala App 298, 171 So 390; People v Tracy, 199 Cal App 2d 163, 18 Cal Rptr 487; State v McKinstry, 2 Conn Cir 42, 193 A2d 905; State v Taylor, 67 Idaho 313, 177 P2d 468; State v Plasphol, 239 Ind 324, 157 NE2d 579; State v Custer, 129 Kan 381. 282 P 1071, 67 ALR 909; Thiede v State, 106 Neb 48, 182 NW 570, 15 ALR 237; State v Phelps, 242 NC 540, 89 SE2d 132; State v Hanahan, 111 SC 58, 96 SE 667; Keller v State, 155 Tenn 633, 299 SW 803, 59 ALR 685; Fox v State, 145 Tex Crim 71, 165 SW2d 733; Maxon v State, 177 Wis 379, 187 NW 753, 21 ALR 1484.

One who is guilty of criminal negligence is not relieved from criminal responsibility by the contributory negligence of the person injured or killed. Cain v State, 55 Ga App 376, 190 SE 371.

18. People ex rel. Klein v Schacher (Mag Ct) 47 NYS2d 371; Warden v State, 214 Tenn 398, 381 SW2d 247, 6 ALR3d 513.

See also United States ex rel. Hall v Illinois (CA7 Ill) 329 F2d 354, cert den 379 US 891, 13 L Ed 2d 94, 85 S Ct 164 (wherein the court said that there is some question whether Tennessee and New York have recognized the doctrine of entrapment).

The defense of entrapment has

firmly recognized in the federal courts,[19] the doctrine there does not extend to acts of inducement by a private citizen who is not an officer of the law. But when a state officer has induced a person otherwise innocent to commit a crime in order to punish him therefor, the United States cannot take over the task of punishment by prosecuting for the federal offense without allowing the defense of entrapment, the same as if the inducement had been by a federal officer.[20]

Although in every arrest there is a certain amount of entrapment in order to outwit the persons who are violating the law or who are about to violate the law, it is not the deception that is forbidden. The type of entrapment the law forbids is the inducing of another to violate the law.[21]

§ 421. Statutes of limitation

In criminal cases the common-law rule was that there was no limitation of time within which offenses might be prosecuted.[22] Thus, unless a period of limitation is fixed by statute for a particular offense,[23] or unless there exist unusual circumstances which bring high prejudice or other

been now recognized in New York by virtue of the Revised New York Penal Law enacted in 1965 and effective in 1967.

19. Sherman v United States, 356 US 369, 2 L Ed 2d 848, 78 S Ct 819 (sale of narcotics).

20. Henderson v United States (CA5 Fla) 237 F2d 169, 61 ALR2d 666.

21. Hill v United States (CA5 Miss) 328 F2d 988, cert den 379 US 851, 13 L Ed 2d 54, 85 S Ct 94; Butler v United States (CA4 Md) 191 F2d 433 (sale of narcotics).

22. United States v Fraidin (DC Md) 63 F Supp 271; Bush v International Alliance, Theatrical Stage E. & M. P. M. O. 55 Cal App 2d 357, 130 P2d 788; State v McCloud (Fla) 67 So 2d 242; Synnott v State, 38 Okla Crim 281, 260 P 517.

23. Dean v State, 240 Ala 8, 197 So 53 (arson); People v Dougherty, 266 Ill 420, 107 NE 695 (forgery); State v Mallett, 125 NC 718, 34 SE 651, affd 181 US 589, 45 L Ed 1015, 21 S Ct 730 (conspiracy to cheat and defraud); State v Gregory, 191 SC 212, 4 SE2d 1 (embezzlement).

Limitations are for the legislature. United States v Ganaposki (DC Pa) 72 F Supp 982; People ex rel. Reibman v Warden of County Jail, 242 App Div 282, 275 NYS 59; Bennett v District Court of Tulsa County, 81 Okla Crim 351, 162 P2d 561 (not for courts).

equitable considerations into play, a prosecution for the offense is not barred by lapse of time.[24]

Statutes of limitation on criminal prosecutions[25] must be liberally construed in favor of the accused,[26] and exceptions from the benefits of such statutes are to be construed narrowly and strictly against the state.[27]

Generally, the statute of limitations begins to run from the time of the commission of an offense,[28] or when the crime is complete,[29] and not from the date the crime is discovered.[30]

§ 422. Double jeopardy

The Federal Constitution and most state constitutions generally provide that no person shall for the same offense be twice put in jeopardy.[31] The double jeopardy provision of

24. Weems v State, 210 Miss 824, 50 So 2d 398.

25. State v Morey, 103 NH 529, 176 A2d 328; State v Brown, 22 NJ 405, 126 A2d 161.

26. United States v Mendoza (DC Cal) 122 F Supp 367; Mead v State (Fla) 101 So 2d 373; People v Ross, 325 Ill 417, 156 NE 303; State v Colvin, 284 Mo 195, 223 SW 585; Jacox v State, 154 Neb 416, 48 NW2d 390; State v Morey, 103 NH 529, 176 A2d 328; People v Guariglia, 187 Misc 843, 65 NYS2d 96, affd 272 App Div 784, 69 NYS2d 759; Synnott v State, 38 Okla Crim 281, 260 P 517.

27. State v Brown, 22 NJ 405, 126 A2d 161; State v Patriarca, 71 RI 151, 43 A2d 54, 160 ALR 387.

28. Sautter v Contractors' State License Board, 124 Cal App 2d 149, 268 P2d 139; State v Bithorn (Mo) 278 SW 685 (obtaining money by false pretenses).

29. Pendergast v United States, 317 US 412, 87 L Ed 368, 63 S Ct 268 (criminal contempt).

30. Sautter v Contractors' State License Board, 124 Cal App 2d 149, 268 P2d 139; State v Weiler (Mo) 338 SW2d 878 (false pretenses).

31. United States v Benz, 282 US 304, 75 L Ed 354, 51 S Ct 113; Kepner v United States, 195 US 100, 49 L Ed 114, 24 S Ct 797; Martin v State, 163 Ark 103, 259 SW 6, 33 ALR 133; State ex rel. Williams v Grayson (Fla) 90 So 2d 710, 63 ALR2d 777; Harris v State, 193 Ga 109, 17 SE2d 573, 147 ALR 980; Pivak v State, 202 Ind 417, 175 NE 278, 74 ALR 406; Commonwealth v McCan, 277 Mass 199, 178 NE 633, 78 ALR 1208; State v Fredlund, 200 Minn 44, 273 NW 353, 113 ALR 215; State v Shimman, 122 Ohio St 522, 172 NE 367, 73 ALR 1502; State v Brooks, 215 Wis 134, 254 NW 374, 94 ALR 401.

Annotation: Modern status of doctrine of res judicata in criminal cases. 9 ALR3d 203.

the United States Constitution applies only to proceedings in federal tribunals.[32]

The constitutional provisions against double jeopardy protect an accused not only against the peril of a second punishment,[33] but also against being tried again for the same offense.[34]

The legislature cannot deprive citizens of a constitutional protection against double jeopardy,[35] but the protection may be waived.[36]

It has been held that jeopardy attaches in a criminal case where a defendant is placed on trial: (1) on a valid indictment or information, (2) before a court of competent jurisdiction, (3) after arraignment, (4) after plea, and (5) when a competent jury has been impaneled and sworn to make true deliverance in the case.[37]

C. PREPARING YOUR DEFENSE

§ 423. In general

We will assume, for the purposes of the remainder of this Chapter that you must present a defense and call witnesses; that you have no choice. Your defense, for example, is alibi and the prosecution has proved a substantial case to go to the jury establishing the identity of your accused

32. Brock v North Carolina, 344 US 424, 97 L Ed 456, 73 S Ct 349.

33. Rupert v State, 9 Okla Crim 226, 131 P 713.

34. Stroud v United States, 251 US 15, 64 L Ed 103, 40 S Ct 50, reh den 251 US 380, 64 L Ed 317, 40 S Ct 176; Davidson v People, 64 Colo 281, 170 P 962; State v Duvall, 135 La 710, 65 So 904, error dismd 239 US 626, 60 L Ed 474, 36 S Ct 162; State v Labato, 7 NJ 137, 80 A2d 617; State v Watson, 209 NC 229, 183 SE 286; State v Brunn, 22 Wash 2d 120, 154 P2d 826, 157 ALR 1049.

35. United States v Aurandt, 15 NM 292, 107 P 1064; Ex parte Bornee, 76 W Va 360, 85 SE 529.

36. State ex rel. Lopez v Killigrew, 202 Ind 397, 174 NE 808, 74 ALR 631; State v Gillis, 73 SC 318, 53 SE 487.

37. State v Birckhead, 256 NC 494, 124 SE2d 838, 6 ALR3d 888.

The meaning of double jeopardy. 74 Harvard L Rev 3.

at the scene of the crime. You must prove that he was not present, and thus establish his innocence.

You cannot establish his innocence unless your case has been thoroughly and carefully prepared. You must have the entire story from the defendant and from your witnesses. You need a detailed list of the chronological sequence of the facts. The time, every date, must be checked and rechecked with your client and witnesses. Only then can you be completely satisfied that there are no inconsistencies between the accused's story and the story of the witnesses. You are to be fully aware of any possible discrepancies or defects in the story of the accused and his witnesses.

You must also study carefully the transcripts or notes of the testimony of the prosecution's witnesses at the preliminary hearing, as well as at the trial. You will then be fully prepared to meet the essential issues. You will be in a position to point up the improbabilities in the story of their witness, and highlight the truthfulness in the story of the defendant and your own witnesses.

§ 424. Order of proof

The most important consideration in planning your order of proof is that of logical presentation. Generally, present the most favorable or sympathetic aspects of your defense first. This gives the jury incentive to pay closer attention to the evidence that will follow.

Start off with a witness whose testimony you are convinced cannot possibly be shaken by the cross-examination of the prosecutor. It does not matter how important his testimony is for the case. It is only important that he will make a very favorable impression. You can be certain that the prosecutor will vigorously cross-examine your first witness at great length. If your witness leaves the stand unshaken, you have made a good start in impressing the jury. The likelihood is that the prosecutor will then relent and not attempt as vigorous a cross-examination on the witnesses that follow. If it is possible that your first witness be an important one whose testimony is most material, so much the better.

The accused should testify last. The reason is obvious. All witnesses have been excluded from the courtroom in most cases, but the defendant must be there throughout the trial. He is in the very favorable position of listening to the testimony of all the witnesses, and is able to give testimony with a distinct advantage over others, having heard the testimony and cross-examination of all who preceded him.

The one exception to this rule occurs when expert testimony is to be predicated upon the defendant's testimony. In such cases it is more logical and orderly to have the expert's testimony follow that of the defendant. If the expert testifies before the underlying facts are introduced, he will merely confuse the jury. His testimony may also be objectionable as lacking the proper foundation. However, there is rarely, if ever, reason to have your client testify in advance of some other fact witnesses.

§ 425. Should the defendant testify?

It goes without saying that in the usual circumstance your client has the absolute right not to testify regardless of whether any other affirmative evidence is presented on his behalf. On the other hand, as a practical matter, there are many elements to be considered before deciding whether or not you should place your client on the stand and subject him to cross-examination by the prosecutor.

Notwithstanding the rule that no inference can be drawn from a defendant's failure to testify and the presence of an instruction to that effect, most jurors will think that a defendant who does not take the stand has something to hide. Conversely, his testimony may convey the image of honesty, particularly if you stressed to the jurors on the voir dire that the defendant does not have to testify. In this respect it is probably advisable to have your client testify even if he has nothing to add to what is already in the case beyond his own protestations of innocence.

One of the reasons for not putting a defendant on the stand is the fact that he will be impeached through the showing of prior convictions. If you decide to have your client testify, bring out the prior record. Do not leave it for cross-examination.

You must determine whether or not the defendant will be able to withstand vigorous cross-examination (in this regard you must analyze the methods and ability of the particular prosecutor) and whether he will come across to the jury as likeable and sympathetic or obnoxious and distasteful.

The final major consideration is whether or not the defendant is likely to be impeached by the use of prior statements or evidence which the prosecution is only permitted to use on rebuttal and not in its direct case. If a prosecutor believes that a defendant will testify, he may withhold the use of a second confession. This is done in the hope that if the defendant can manage to explain away the confession in evidence he will be demolished by later proof of a second confession which reinforces the first. Also, in certain limited areas, evidence which has been suppressed or excluded may be used to impeach a defendant's credibility.

In the final analysis, the decision whether or not to take the stand rests with the defendant. If you conclude that he should not testify, inform him of the reasons for your decision and argue strongly against his decision. If he persists, you should consider stating for the record, out of the hearing of the jury, the fact that the defendant is proceeding against your advice. On the other hand, some reluctant defendants cannot be convinced to testify under any circumstances.

§ 426. Use of an accomplice as your witness

Persons alleged to have been accomplices of your client

can be most effective witnesses. Your direct examination of them should stress the fact that they were not coerced to testify for your client and that they have no reason not to tell the truth.

§ 427. Character witnesses

The introduction of character witnesses by the defense is the only method by which your client's character may be put in issue. If you decide to use proof of this nature, you will generally be limited to proof of the defendant's reputation in the community with regard to those character traits involved in the crime. Hence, in an assault prosecution you might attempt to prove his reputation for peacefulness. In an embezzlement or perjury prosecution, on the other hand, his honesty might be the pertinent trait.

In qualifying your character witnesses, establish that they know the defendant, that they have discussed him with others in the community (or at work, a vacation, resort, etc.) and are aware of his reputation in the community with regard to a particular character trait. Inform the jury during the voir dire that evidence of the defendant's good character can create a reasonable doubt where otherwise none would exist. You are also entitled to have the jury instructed to that effect.

D. PREPARING YOUR WITNESSES

§ 428. Orienting your witness

In order to avoid any possible embarrassing statements by your witness when he testifies, you must prepare him so he does not falter on the witness stand. His evidence must be presented in the most convincing manner. Go over his testimony with him before he goes to the witness stand.

Tell him the exact order in which you intend to deal with the various subjects of his testimony. Also explain any language or terminology that may come up which may be difficult for him to understand.

Make certain that the witness knows not to answer questions which he does not understand and that he does not volunteer information. However, remember that a witness' credibility will be sorely affected if he demonstrates complete recall during his direct testimony but is unable to remember any further details on cross-examination.

Explain to him what hearsay evidence is, and that he cannot give the conclusions or describe the opinions or feelings of other people. Point out that he cannot say, "The complainant got angry." Tell him it is far more effective—and it is certainly the only legally admissible way of describing the complainant's anger—for him to describe what actually happened: that the complainant banged his fist and said, "I don't have to stand for this kind of miserable abuse!" If the complainant used foul language, have the defendant repeat the specific foul language. Explain to him that he is thus telling the facts far more vividly and in a way that is legally permissible.

§ 429. Prepare witness for cross-examination

It is most important for you to prepare your witnesses for prosecutor's cross-examination.

The defendant *must* therefore be subjected in advance to a thorough cross-examination by you. You have an idea of what the prosecutor is going to ask. If you do not, you are not prepared for the trial. Say to him, "Look, I am now the prosecutor. I am going to cross-examine you. Almost certainly, though, the real prosecutor will do a more effective job on you, because he knows more." Then, show him how easily he can be led into traps.

§ 430. Attitude and conduct

It is not sufficient to merely prepare your witnesses for the questions which will be asked of them on direct and cross-examination. Their decorum must be such as will create no antagonism towards them on the part of the jury.

Jurors will automatically distrust witnesses who seem rude and discourteous.

Advise your witnesses to dress properly, to look at the attorney rather than the jury when answering questions, and not to act in a hostile or haughty manner.

Caution your witnesses to remain calm and unruffled throughout. They must avoid being sarcastic or belligerent, even in the face of provocation.

§ 431. Manner of answering

Where your witness or client is testifying to disputed facts, have him testify in a positive, somewhat emotional voice. His words and manner should pinpoint the dispute. It must be vigorous and definite. When testifying to any circumstances or facts which might be unfavorable, have your client or witness do it fairly and candidly. It is much easier to face these unfavorable factors on direct examination than under the sarcastic and grueling interrogation of the prosecutor. Further, the witness will be able to handle the prosecutor's cross-examination much more effectively if, on direct examination, he presented these unfavorable factors in a candid and honest manner.

E. CONDUCTING THE DIRECT EXAMINATION

§ 432. In general

The advance preparation for direct and cross-examination is almost as important for you as it is for your witnesses. Simplify your questions to ensure that they are not so complex as to confuse the jury. Start the question with "who," "when," "what," "where." Do not use the word "subsequent"; use the word "later." If possible, use illustrations and exhibits to simplify the testimony. Whenever you can, avoid compound questions.

Always examine your proposed questions with a view toward their admissibility. Too many inexperienced trial lawyers discover that their well-prepared questions are improper and become too confused to ask proper questions which would elicit the proper response.

§ 433. Develop a foundation

Do not begin your examination by asking the witness what he saw or heard. Lay the proper groundwork for your decisive evidence. Make clear the exact time and date when the crime is alleged to have taken place. Have the witness locate and describe all of the persons who were present, as well as all of the important objects and pieces of evidence. If the incident took place outdoors, have him describe the weather and physical conditions of the atmosphere. Ask the witness how far away he was from the fight; when did he first observe what was going on; what were the weather conditions; was it light or dark; what attracted his attention to what took place? Then interrogate concerning every factor, however unimportant, that would serve to impress upon the jury his truthfulness and his ability to observe what took place.

If these preliminaries are fully covered, the witness will be able to tell his story in a straight, clear manner, perhaps re-emphasizing the details and factors previously described. There should be no interruption by him or yourself to interject any details that were omitted. The story, as it must unfold, will be natural, clear, and effective.

§ 434. Substance of accused's testimony

The jury is interested in the accused and wants to know everything about him: where he works and how long he has worked at his present position, the kind of work he does, whether he is married or single, the number of children he has, and all other information concerning his family background. These preliminary questions also serve to reduce his nervousness and permit your client to testify easily about the decisive matters.

If your client has a criminal record, including a conviction or a number of convictions, it will sound much better if he tells about it himself in the direct examination. This takes the sting out of it and prevents the prosecutor from bringing it out—it sounds much worse coming from his mouth on cross-examination. Such an open approach also gives you the opportunity to excuse or explain it in the most satisfactory way.

The fact of your client's prior criminal record should have been brought out by you both in the voir dire and in your opening statement if you had decided that he would testify.

On the voir dire, it should have been done in the form of questions. You should also have extracted a promise from the jurors that they would not allow their determination of the defendant's guilt or innocence to be affected by his prior record. You should remind them of this promise during the summation.

When your client takes the stand, go through his conviction record by asking him whether he had been convicted of the particular crime on a certain date. He should answer in the affirmative without hesitation or equivocation. Do not ask him to explain the circumstances surrounding the conviction.

Of course, if your client is a person of good character, have his testimony of good character precede him. The jury will be more favorably impressed with the defendant after listening to his character references. They will be inclined to listen to him more favorably and with greater respect for his truthfulness.

§ 435. Use demonstrative techniques

Have your witness demonstrate exactly what took place. If there was a fight, have him show where the defendant received the blows. Have him describe it exactly and point to the parts of the body involved. Suggest that he use yourself or a court officer to illustrate what parts of the body were struck. If the complainant used a knife and made a stabbing motion with it, have the witness demonstrate it similarly. If the complainant made a threatening gesture with a gun or any other object, have a demonstration of the manner in which this gesture was made clearly exhibited to the jury.

§ 436. Do not repeat answers of witness

Repetition of the answers of your witness will only annoy the court, cause objections by the prosecutor, and make it appear to the jury as if his testimony is unsatisfactory. If any important portion is slurred over by the witness, restate the question in a different form so that the important portion is repeated without its being obvious.

§ 437. Use of leading questions

A leading question is one which either suggests the answer or assumes facts which have not been proved.

As a general rule, you should avoid leading questions. These will only draw objections from the prosecutor. Use questions that are not leading but have some slight form of suggestion. For example: "State whether or not there was any exchange of words between you and the complainant." Then follow it up with: "State, if anything, what he said to you and what you said to him."

As a general proposition, you are not permitted to ask leading questions of your witnesses during their direct testimony. You may, however, resort to leading questions on direct examination when a witness' memory is exhausted, in eliciting preliminary matter, in questioning witnesses with certain disabilities such as age or lack of intelligence, and most importantly, when questioning hostile witnesses.

A witness may be hostile even if he has no interest adverse to that of your client. The hostility may emanate from any cause, including the sheer whimsey of the witness. Decisions of trial judges as to whether to characterize a witness as hostile are seldom interfered with on appeal.

You must therefore make the strongest possible showing when seeking a characterization of hostility. One of the other benefits of a declaration of hostility is that it allows you to impeach the witness by proof of prior inconsistent statements. If you are surprised by a witness who recants prior favorable statements made to you, explain the circumstances to the court out of hearing of the jury, and seek permission to impeach through the use of his prior statements.

§ 438. Offer of proof

If an objection to your questions is sustained, make an offer of proof. If you do not make an offer of proof after the prosecutor's objections to your questions are sustained, there is very little you can do on appeal to protect the record.

Ask that the court permit you to make an offer of proof outside the presence of the jury. You might do it as follows: "I would like to make an offer of proof as follows: That the defendant, at the time the crime was committed, said certain things which were in the hearing of the complainant, and that the complainant answered those questions and by answering to these questions, showed he understood fully what the defendant had said."

Another manner of offering proof is as follows: "I offer to prove by Joe Jones, a witness now in court, that (here you state the evidence the witness is prepared to give). This proof is offered for the purpose of establishing (here you state the purpose of the evidence)." Remember your offer of proof must state facts specifically and with certainty.

F. REDIRECT EXAMINATION

§ 439. Nature and purpose

The successful redirect examination is that which explains and neutralizes the apparent contradictions, admissions, or apparently false statements developed by the prosecutor on his cross-examination.

In order to conduct a successful redirect examination, if one becomes necessary, you must concentrate as strongly during the cross-examination of your witnesses as you do during the direct examination of prosecution witnesses.

§ 440. Scope and extent

The general rule is that redirect examination is limited to those matters touched upon on cross-examination which you would have been unable to properly develop on direct examination.

If incompetent testimony is admitted during the cross-examination, you can continue to pursue the particular line of inquiry on redirect examination. If the prosecutor objects, argue that he opened the door to the particular line of questions and that your client will be prejudiced if you cannot fully explore the area.

While the scope of redirect examination is limited, the Court may, in its discretion, permit you to expand your redirect examination beyond the scope of cross-examination. As a tactical matter, do not count in advance upon the exercise of such discretion in your favor. If the prosecutor was permitted to inquire into new matters on cross-examination, use that fact in contending that you should be given the same courtesy on redirect.

§ 441. Rehabilitation of witness

It frequently happens that a cross-examining prosecutor has distorted the testimony of one or more defense witnesses. Happily, it is usually not too difficult to restore the witness' testimony on redirect examination. A skilful and dexterous cross-examiner may force a witness to answer out of context, or restrict the witness to "yes" and "no" answers in situations where the answer becomes misleading. It will frequently happen that a witness admits confusion or uncertainty when he is cross-examined on a certain point. In such an instance the defense counsel may settle the matter and eliminate the confusion or uncertainty in his redirect examination, keeping in mind that the prosecutor will have still another crack at the witness in this regard.

A truly effective cross-examination may well have caused your witness to lose his composure. If such is the case, restore his confidence at the outset of the redirect examination. Conduct the redirect examination in a soothing tone of voice. Your initial questions should be direct and uncomplicated. These initial questions should be calculated to allow the witness to regain his composure rather than to rehabilitate him.

The rehabilitation process should pick up at the point at which your witness was first apparently impeached by the prosecutor. At that point his testimony should be reconstructed and clarified so as to once again become acceptable to the jury.

One of the basic tools used in rehabilitation is that of refreshing a witness' recollection. This is of great help when your witness has become confused during cross-examination with regard to names, dates, or events. It is permissible to rehabilitate your witness by rebutting the effect of matters which were brought out during cross-examination. If, therefore, the cross-examination casts doubt on your witness' ability to remember events properly, you may attempt, on redirect, to establish that he has a good memory. Similarly, you can rehabilitate by showing that in fact your witness had good vision, a good sense of distance, keen hearing, a good sense of smell, etc.

Defense counsel may use redirect examination to refresh the recollection of a witness, and to correct a mistake brought out upon cross-examination upon such matters as time, place, identity, and the like. Defense counsel should always attempt to reconcile or explain inconsistencies of this nature, unless the point is trivial and without effect upon the principal issue or the credibility of the witness, or unless he feels he will do more harm than good by pursuing the matter.

In using memoranda or documents to refresh the recollection of the witness, defense counsel will do well to remember that the writings will be examined by the prosecution and used in recross-examination. Accordingly, defense counsel may do well to avoid the use of any material which may contain damaging matter or which may disclose information otherwise unknown to the prosecution.

Do not have your witness explain or clarify testimony on which he was not impeached. In so doing you will merely expand the possible scope of the prosecutor's recross-examination. The remaining favorable portions of your witness' testimony which were not affected by the cross-examination should be stressed in your summation rather than on redirect.

§ 422. Semantic errors

It frequently happens that the prosecutor on cross-examination will attempt to discredit a defense witness by exaggerating semantic differences or errors in the testimony and blow them up out of all proportion. If the error indeed occurred, but is of no consequence, you will be able to show that it was a natural mistake, or at least minimize the damage in the minds of the jury. In redirect examination it is often possible for an astute defense counsel to turn such errors, keeping in mind that he is dealing with a lay jury, to his own advantage. Sometimes you may re-establish the witness' testimony by pointing out that the seeming inconsistencies were merely a matter of semantics and definition, and you may clarify the same on redirect. Otherwise, you may show that the inconsistency is minor, or that the disagreement is relatively miniscule and of no consequence.

Counsel can develop the nature of the semantic problem in such a fashion as to discredit the prosecutor for taking advantage of it, and to swing the sympathy of the lay jury to the well-meaning witness.

§ 443. Waiver

Counsel should remember that if the previous examination of a witness by both sides has been lengthy, the jury may be bored, or even irritated, when counsel rises to question the same witness upon the same subject matter for redirect examination. If this is the case, counsel might better waive his redirect examination, or if he does not wish to do so at least preface his remarks with a statement to eliminate such a prejudice, conscious or unconscious, from the minds of the jury.

If your witness' testimony has been left substantially intact, it is probably best not to conduct a redirect examination. Such an examination always gives the prosecutor the opportunity to conduct a recross examination. Such a reexamination is always potentially destructive. If, however, a material part of your witness' testimony has not withstood cross-examination, or if the witness has been impeached to such a degree that you think the jury is likely to disbelieve or disregard his testimony, a redirect examination is in order.

CHAPTER FIFTEEN

NATURE AND PURPOSE OF SUMMATION

E. MANNER OF DELIVERY

F. PERSONALIZE AND HUMANIZE THE DEFENDANT

A. INTRODUCTION

§ 444. In general

Summation is the finishing touch, your final opportunity to convince the jury of your client's innocence. A well-presented case can be lost by a listless summation. A spirited, effective summation can change a lost cause into an acquittal. You must make the most of this opportunity—your case might well depend upon it. The opportunities that are presented and the means of taking advantage of them will be explained in the pages that follow.

In a number of jurisdictions, a denial of final argument has been treated as a violation of due process. It will come as no surprise if the United States Supreme Court one day rules that such a denial of argument is a denial of the right to effective counsel under the Sixth Amendment. This Amendment now applies to the several states.[1]

1. Escobedo v Illinois, 378 US 478, 12 L Ed 2d 977, 84 S Ct 1758; Gideon v Wainwright, 372 US 335, 9 L Ed 2d 799, 83 S Ct 792, 93 ALR2d 733.

A New York attorney has stated, in commenting on the importance of summation: "Close cases are won or lost by the summation. It is in the summation, of all places, that a man must keep his eye on the spinal column of his case and not keep running off on the ribs. It is in the summation, of all places, that a man should sink himself into his case and get the case instead of himself into the jury box or up to the bench. It is in the summation, of all places, that a man should feel and make the court or jury feel, not that his client is fortunate in having him as a lawyer, but that he is fortunate in having his client's case."[2]

§ 445. Crystallization of evidence

The average case brings out much triviality. You must separate the trivial from the meaningful. The average juror is untrained in legal evidence and is unable, without assistance, to appreciate the importance of much of the testimony as it relates to the issues. You must fit all the pieces of evidence and testimony together so that they form a complete, understandable picture for the jury to see.

§ 446. Highlight confusing and conflicting evidence

Successful cross-examination may have brought out inconsistencies in the prosecution's case. The significance of these inconsistencies may be overlooked by the jury—or they may have overlooked the inconsistencies themselves. You must make sure this does not happen. Each inconsistency must be spotlighted and explained.

Your summation should recall the events of the trial. Each contradiction, each confusing and impeaching matter is spotlighted and explained. The strong points of your case are driven home. When you have finished, each important bit of evidence should stand out in bold relief. The jury will

2. Address by Emory R. Buckner before the Association of the Bar of New York City, January 31, 1929, which appears in Advocacy; Soonavala and Tripathi, Its Principles and Practice (Bombay, 1953) p 525.

be prepared for your final emotional appeal to their sense of justice.

B. BASIC OBJECTIVES

§ 447. In general

When you are preparing and delivering your summation, bear these five summation objectives in mind: (1) To win the friendship of the jury for both the defendant and yourself; (2) To explain clearly the law that entitles the defendant to a verdict of not-guilty; (3) To clearly state the facts that require the jury to acquit the defendant; (4) To secure the jury's belief in your case by supporting it with the evidence in the record; (5) To arouse the juror's sympathies toward the defendant.

C. ADVANCE PREPARATION

§ 448. In general

Preparation for your final argument should begin long before the case goes to trial. It begins when you interview the defendant and his witnesses, and continues when you conduct the preliminary hearing. Think constantly about the theory of your defense, plus the explanation of the unfavorable evidence. Plan how to place the important facts before the jury in the most effective manner.

Make an outline, which you can revise, modify, and change, before the trial even begins.

§ 449. Take notes during trial

During the trial you must remain alert to evidence that can be used in your final argument. While the prosecution witnesses are testifying on direct examination, make notations of points you intend to use. Also note weak spots you have brought out on cross-examination.

Before delivering your summation, run through your notes of the trial and underline with a colored pencil those points you will raise to the jury. Then list those points and have them in front of you when you argue to the jury. You do not have to worry about forgetting words since you have not memorized any speech. You cannot lose your place. A glance at your list and each item will suggest what thought to discuss and what thought should follow. Your words will flow more naturally, spontaneously and effectively.

§ 450. Obtain minutes before summation

If your fee arrangements with your client permit, purchase the minutes of the trial before your final argument. Examine them for appropriate statements. Use them in your summation as follows: "The prosecution's witnesses virtually concede that they have not proven their case beyond a reasonable doubt. I shall quote from the testimony of the prosecution's witnesses, not my witnesses or the defendant." Then, point by point, turn quickly to the exact words used by the prosecutor's witnesses, which support your defense.

If the trial is a lengthy one, you must review the transcript each evening as it is made available to you. As you review and analyze the testimony, expand your trial notes by indexing and cross-indexing all pertinent testimony. You will then be able to prepare the final draft of your summation from your notes rather than from the transcript. This daily endeavor will avoid the necessity of reaching and reviewing volumes of testimony on the evening before you begin your summation.

Always examine the transcript with an eye towards the prosecutor's opening statement. It is most effective to demonstrate to the jury, point by point, those items which the prosecutor stated he would prove, but which he failed to prove.

§ 451. Outline your argument

When your thoughts are formulated, you are ready to prepare an outline of your final argument. Do not rely on your ability to speak "off the cuff." This is a foolhardy stunt that could prove disastrous to your client. By the same token, do not write out your entire summation. An outline that consists of major headings is sufficient. Attempt to memorize only effective phrases and short paragraphs on vital matters.

If you feel it necessary to write out your final argument, do not take it with you when you go before the jury. You will be tempted to read from it. This will detract from its simplicity and sincerity. It might tend to put the jurors to sleep.

The outline you prepare before trial is not final. It should contain space for you to make additions during the trial. It is a good idea to prepare the outline of your summation at the same time that you prepare the outline of your opening statement. The promises made in your opening statement will then be finalized and reemphasized in your closing argument.

§ 452. Arrange a logical presentation

One of your basic objectives is to present the evidence in a clear, cohesive fashion. You have a product to sell: the defendant's innocence or the failure of the prosecution to prove a case against the defendant beyond a reasonable doubt. Hammer away on each favorable aspect of your case until you have made your sale. Emphasize every fact, and add them one by one to your conclusion.

D. TIME ALLOWED FOR SUMMATION

§ 453. In general

In criminal prosecutions the time allowed counsel for argument is ordinarily within the sound discretion of the trial court.[3] Denial of argument by counsel to the jury or

3. Butler v United States (CA8 ND) 317 F2d 249, 6 ALR3d 582, cert den 375 US 836, 11 L Ed 2d 65, 84 S Ct 67, cert den 375 US 838, 11 L Ed 2d 65, 84 S Ct 77; Decker v State, 113 Ohio St 512, 150 NE 74, 42 ALR 1151.

Annotations: Propriety of court's

court is considered sufficient to entitle the accused to a new trial,[4] except, perhaps, where the evidence against the accused is so strong that a verdict of guilty must have been rendered at all events,[5] or where there is no prejudicial error.[6]

There is authority for the view that in a criminal prosecution the constitutional guaranty that a person accused of crime shall have the right to be heard by counsel prohibits a trial court from predetermining the time in which counsel may argue the case before the jury,[7] precluded from stopping the argument when it is manifest that the discussion is complete and the subject exhausted.[8]

§ 454. Effect of constitutional provision, statute, or rule of court

The right to be heard by counsel is usually grounded in

limitation of time allowed counsel for summation or argument in criminal trial. 6 ALR3d 604.

Right of accused to additional argument on matters covered by amended or additional instructions. 15 ALR2d 490.

4. State v Mayo, 42 Wash 540, 85 P 251.

5. Hunt v State, 49 Ga 255.

6. A refusal by the trial court to permit any argument has been held not of itself a sufficient ground for reversal. People v Don Carlos, 47 Cal App 2d Supp 863, 117 P2d 748, wherein the court stated that when the argument of counsel is directed to the court without a jury, the court is in a better position than counsel to decide when it is sufficiently informed and ready to rule upon the matter, and is clothed with sufficient authority to order the argument at an end. However, the authority of this case on this point may be weakened by the statement of the court that if it should be considered error not to have permitted the defendant's counsel to argue further, the error was one not resulting in a miscarriage of justice and so was not ground for reversal.

7. Williams v State, 60 Ga 267; Hunt v State, 49 Ga 255. In State v Campbell, 14 NC App 596, 188 SE2d 558, defendant was convicted on three separate indictments of felonious possessions of LSD. At trial the Court limited defense counsel's jury argument to thirty minutes. The Court of Appeals of North Carolina awarded defendant a new trial. The Court held that limiting of defense counsel's jury argument to thirty minutes was prejudicial error. There was no indication of waiver and North Carolina law allowed more time for final argument.

8. Williams v State, 60 Ga 367.

an applicable statute or constitution, and the constitutional right to be heard is specifically recognized as a qualifying factor limiting the court's discretion.[9] Likewise, a statutory provision limiting counsel to a given period of time for argument in certain types of prosecutions deprives the court of discretionary power to limit such an argument to less than the statutory period.[10]

Where a rule of court fixes the time for argument by counsel, with authority in the court to grant extensions, it has been held that prima facie the time so fixed is sufficient, and that the discretion of the judge in refusing additional time to counsel is not abused, where it does not appear that the issues are so complicated, or the evidence so voluminous, as to make the case exceptional.[11] Where a rule of court prescribed a minimum time for argument, it has been held that a limitation to a shorter time was error.[12] Where a rule of court fixed both a minimum and a maximum period to be allowed for argument, it was held in

9. Jackson v State, 239 Ala 38, 193 So 417; Crawford v State, 112 Ala 1, 21 So 214; Peagler v State, 110 Ala 11, 20 So 363; Yeldell v State, 100 Ala 26, 14 So 570.

10. Kittles v State, 74 Ga App 383, 39 SE2d 766, reversing a conviction for voluntary manslaughter where the trial court, following the conclusion of the evidence and a request by counsel for 2 hours for argument, imposed a limitation of 1 hour. The court held that a statutory provision limiting argument in capital felony cases to 2 hours gave counsel 2 hours as a matter of right, and that the trial court had no power in its discretion to limit such argument to less than 2 hours. The court further held that the error was not cured by the fact that counsel actually consumed only 35 minutes in argument and when the trial court reminded him that he had time left, he stated that he did not wish to argue the case further. The court stated that the colloquy did not amount to a withdrawal of the former erroneous ruling by the trial court or to a waiver by counsel of his right to 2 hours of argument.

11. In Cook v State, 22 Ga App 770, 97 SE 264, a prosecution for blackmail, the case not being exceptional as to issues or evidence, the court said that it could not hold as a matter of law that the judge of the trial court had abused his discretion in refusing to grant counsel for the accused an extension of time in which to argue the case.

12. People v Smith, 363 Mich 157, 108 NW2d 751, a prosecution for assault and battery, holding that it was error for the trial court to limit counsel to 20 minutes, where a rule of court provided that either counsel could have at least one-half hour if he desired.

one case that the trial court had no authority to limit counsel to less than the maximum time fixed by the rules, so long as counsel acted in good faith.[13]

§ 455. Agreement of parties

Where attorneys for the state and for the defendant agree in advance upon limiting the argument to a given time, the courts have generally held counsel to their agreement.[14]

In some cases, time limitations have been upheld on the ground that counsel requested the time allotted him or consented to the limitation.[15]

13. People v Labadie, 66 Mich 702, 33 NW 806.

14. In Matthews v State, 243 Miss 568, 139 So 2d 386, a prosecution for murder resulting in a conviction of manslaughter, in which the trial judge allowed unlimited time for argument until the attorneys for the state and for the defendant advised the trial judge that they had agreed upon limiting the argument to 15 minutes, the court held that the defendant could not be heard to argue on appeal that his attorney was not permitted to argue more than 15 minutes.

In State v McGregor (Iowa) 266 NW 22, a prosecution for operating a motor vehicle while intoxicated, in which the state waived its opening argument, and by agreement of counsel the defendant was given 20 minutes to present his case to the jury and the state 20 minutes to reply thereto, it was held that the defendant was properly refused permission to make a closing argument to answer the argument of the state, since the arguments had been completed as per the agreement of counsel.

In Moorehead v United States (CA5 Miss) 270 F 210, cert dismd 257 US 643, 66 L Ed 412, 42 S Ct 52, a prosecution for conspiracy to steal goods and chattels in which the defense counsel were limited, with their advance approval to one hour argument, it was held that there was no abuse of discretion where it appeared that it was nearly 12 o'clock at night when the case went to the jury, and the counsel in the case had agreed to conclude the case that night, counsel for the defense stating that they preferred to do so.

15. In People v Prewett, 40 Cal App 416, 180 P 844, a limitation of 1½ hours on the defense argument in a murder prosecution was sustained where defense counsel, on being asked by the court, said that he would only require 1½ hours and was then told that that was all the time he would be allowed.

In People v Murphy, 17 Cal App 2d 575, 62 P2d 592, a prosecution for selling stock without a license, it was held that the trial court did not err in limiting the arguments to the jury by respective counsel to 1¼ hours, where the attorney for the defendants consented to that limitation and it did not appear that the defendants were prejudiced thereby.

In State v Stidham (Mo) 258 SW2d

§ 456. Appellate Interference

It is generally agreed by the great weight of authority that the matter of limiting the time of argument by counsel is within the sound discretion of the trial court. Appellate courts generally state that they will interfere only where such discretion has been abused. The exercise of the court's discretion will not be interfered with by an appellate tribunal in the absence of a clear showing of its abuse to the prejudice of the substantial rights of the complaining party.[16] Otherwise, the appellate courts tend not to substitute their judgment for that of the trial judge who is familiar with the details of the case.

§ 457. Determination and propriety of time limitations

The courts cannot cut down arbitrarily the time to a certain limit in all cases. They must exercise proper discretion, granting longer or shorter time, as the intricacy, mass of matter, nature of the offense or cause of action, and the means or circumstances on which the defense may rest, may seem to require.[17] No precise rule can be laid down as

620, ovrld on other grounds State v Tyarks (Mo) 433 SW2d 568, where the record showed that counsel asked for 30 minutes for argument and was given that period, his assignment of the limitation of time as error was treated as wholly without merit.

16. Butler v United States (CA8 ND) 317 F2d 249, 6 ALR3d 582, cert den 375 US 836, 11 L Ed 2d 65, 84 S Ct 67, cert den 375 US 838, 11 L Ed 2d 65, 84 S Ct 77.

17. In State v Hewett, 103 Wash 52, 173 P 726, cert den 249 US 611, 63 L Ed 801, 39 S Ct 386, in which counsel were limited in their argument to the jury to a period of 3 hours, it was held that the matter of the allotment of time for argument rested within the discretion of the trial court, since the trial judge was familiar with the issues to be argued and all the minutiae of the case, upon which he could determine the time that should be consumed in properly presenting the issues to the jury.

In United States v Kay (CA2 NY) 101 F2d 270, cert den 306 US 660, 83 L Ed 1056, 59 S Ct 789, a prosecution for false pretenses in which it was assigned as error that the court had unduly restricted counsel's time in summation, it was stated, in finding no error, that there were always matters to be disposed of by the trial court in the course of a trial by the exercise of a sound discretion, and that the limitation of time for argument was a matter of this character.

In Jackson v State, 239 Ala 30, 193 So 417, it was held that the trial court must be accorded a presumption that its discretion has not been abused.

In Cox v State, 21 Ga App 238, 94

to the time limit to which the trial court may properly restrict the argument of counsel, since what might be a reasonable limitation in one case would unquestionably be unreasonable in another. Whether the discretion of the court has been properly exercised depends entirely upon the circumstances of each case, the number of witnesses examined, the volume and character of the evidence, the time consumed in the trial of the case, as well as any other matters which properly have a bearing upon the time necessary to present the case fully to the jury.[18]

SE 47, it was held that the discretion exercised by the trial court in refusing an extension of time would not be held to have been abused unless such abuse was manifest.

Annotation: Propriety of court's limitation of time allowed counsel for summation or argument in criminal trial. 6 ALR3d 604.

18. State v Hoyt, 47 Conn 518; State v Page, 21 Mo 257.

See also Teague v Commonwealth, 172 Ky 665, 189 SW 908.

The limitations upon the argument of counsel in the following cases have been held to be reasonable: Yeldell v State, 100 Ala 26, 14 So 570 (twenty-five minutes on a trial for assault with intent to murder, where the facts were few and simple, with but a slight conflict, and only a few witnesses were examined, the evidence all being set out in two and a half pages of transcript); State v Hoyt, 47 Conn 518 (four hours on a trial for murder, there being no claim at the trial that the time was insufficient, and it appearing that counsel did not occupy the full time but fell short twenty-five minutes); Lucas v Commonwealth, 149 Ky 495, 149 SW 861 (thirty minutes on a charge of murder); State v Page, 21 Mo 257 (fifteen minutes in a prosecution for trespassing on school lands); State v Collins, 70 NC 241 (one and one-half hours for a charge of murder); Seattle v Erickson, 55 Wash 675, 104 P 1128 (fifteen minutes in a prosecution for violation of an ordinance prohibiting the possession of watered milk with intent to sell the same for human food); State v Shores, 31 W Va 491, 7 SE 413 (four hours for a charge of burglary).

The limitations placed upon the argument of counsel have been held unreasonable in the following cases: Hunt v State, 49 Ga 255 (forty minutes in a prosecution for assault with intent to murder, where the evidence was conflicting as to whether the stabbing was done in self-defense); White v People, 90 Ill 117 (five minutes on a trial for larceny where nine witnesses were examined); Dille v State, 34 Ohio St 617 (thirty minutes on a trial for burglary and larceny where the accused was defended by two counsel, eleven witnesses were examined, and the evidence, which occupied a half day in its delivery, was circumstantial and conflicting); State v Rogoway, 45 Or 611, 81 P 234 (one hour on a trial for arson, where three days were required to try the case, twenty-one witnesses were examined, whose testimony filled one hundred sixty pages of transcript, and much of the evidence was circumstantial and conflicting); State v Mayo, 42 Wash 540, 85 P 251 (one hour and one half on a prosecution for murder, where the trial

The time given must be reasonable and of such length as not to impair the right of argument or to deny a full and complete defense.[19] Thus, the limitation in a criminal prosecution must not be such as to deprive the accused of the right to make his defense to the jury and to be heard by his counsel on the whole case.[20]

§ 458. Procedural conditions for contesting ruling

Numerous cases hold that in order to justify a subsequent reversal of judgment on the ground that a time limitation on argument was too severe, the record must show that the appellant not only excepted to the order limiting the time and then consumed the time allotted

consumed more than four days, over twenty witnesses were examined, whose testimony made a typewritten volume of more than five hundred pages, and the preliminary examination of the jury disclosed that there existed in the public mind a considerable prejudice against the accused).

Allowing the prosecuting attorney fifteen minutes for his closing argument after counsel for defense had taken twenty-five minutes for his argument, although each side had been granted but fifteen minutes, is not an abuse of discretion. State v Silvey (Mo) 296 SW 128.

Where the issues raised on the trial of an action are not complicated, and the testimony is neither voluminous nor conflicting except upon one or two points, it is not an abuse of discretion for a trial court to limit the time allowed for oral argument before the jury to forty-five minutes for each side. Christiansen v William Graver Tank Works, 223 Ill 142, 79 NE 97; Braeunig v Russell, 170 Ohio St 444, 11 Ohio Ops 2d 200, 166 NE2d 240, 3 ALR3d 1334.

It has been held that, in a prosecution for mail fraud against a corporation and 30 individual defendants under a 33-count indictment, the trial having lasted approximately 4 months, the trial court does not abuse its discretion in limiting the time for summation arguments by the attorneys representing the defendants to periods ranging from 1 hour and 15 minutes to 2½ hours, depending on the number of defendants represented by the attorney, where the trial court carefully evaluated the time requirements from its vantage point, discussed the various possibilities of time allocation with the trial attorneys, obtained approval of a time allocation schedule from the majority of them, and then allowed the defense a total of 3 full court days for summation. Butler v United States (CA8 ND) 317 F2d 249, 6 ALR3d 582, cert den 375 US 836, 11 L Ed 2d 65, 84 S Ct 67, cert den 375 US 838, 11 L Ed 2d 65, 84 S Ct 77.

19. State v Rogoway, 45 Or 601, 78 P 987, mod on reh on other grounds 45 Or 611, 81 P 234.

20. White v People, 90 Ill 117; Dille v State, 34 Ohio St 617; Seattle v Erickson, 55 Wash 675, 104 P 1128; State v Mayo, 42 Wash 540, 85 P 251.

him, but that he also requested more time, giving reasons for such request.[21] In the following cases it was held or recognized that before error will be found because of improper limitation of the time for argument, the party complaining must have consumed such time as was allotted him, or the record must show that such was the case.[22]

Where a rule of court requires that a request for additional time be made prior to the argument of the case, it has been held that a request made after the argument has begun may be refused even in a capital case.[23]

E. MANNER OF DELIVERY

§ 459. In general

The jury's belief that you believe what you are saying is the key to an effective summation. A clear and sincere

21. Crawford v State, 112 Ala 1, 21 So 214; Morrison v State (Ark) 297 SW 830; People v Phillips, 120 Cal App 644, 8 P2d 228; People v Rice, 90 Cal App 590, 266 P 295; Bloodworth v State, 161 Ga 332, 131 SE 80 (statute); Robinson v State, 158 Ga 47, 122 SE 886; Lindsay v State, 138 Ga 818, 76 SE 369 (rule of court); Clarke v State, 89 Ga 768, 15 SE 699 (statute); Hand v State, 88 Ga App 775, 77 SE2d 746 (statute); Redman v State, 28 Ind 205; Williams v Commonwealth, 82 Ky 640; State v Townzell (Mo) 286 SW2d 785; Williams v State, 14 Okla Crim 100, 167 P 763; King v State, 67 Tex Crim 63, 148 SW 324; Sanderson v Commonwealth, 200 Va 51, 103 SE2d 800.

22. Barnard v United States (CA9 Or) 342 F2d 309, cert den 382 US 948, 15 L Ed 2d 356, 86 S Ct 403, 404, reh den 382 US 1002, 15 L Ed 2d 491, 492, 86 S Ct 567, 568; Crawford v State, 112 Ala 1, 21 So 214; Robinson v State, 158 Ga 47, 122 SE 886; Wright v United States, 4 Indian Terr 116, 69 SW 819; McLeod v State, 130 Miss 83, 92 So 828; Dixon v State, 46 Neb 298, 64 NW 961; Fisher v State, 54 Okla Crim 109, 16 P2d 267; Hampton v State, 50 Okla Crim 2, 295 P 398; Williams v State, 14 Okla Crim 100, 167 P 763; Perez v State, 125 Tex Crim 575, 69 SW2d 420; Collier v State, 108 Tex Crim 339, 1 SW2d 295; Blonk v State, 93 Tex Crim 638, 248 SW 375; Holmes v State, 68 Tex Crim 17, 150 SW 926; King v State, 67 Tex Crim 63, 148 SW 324; Taylor v State (Tex Crim) 42 SW 285; Huntly v State (Tex Crim) 34 SW 923; State v Patchen, 37 Wash 24, 79 P 479.

23. Lindsay v State, 138 Ga 818, 76 SE 369, a prosecution for murder, wherein it was held that a refusal to grant additional time for argument was upheld in part because the accused had not applied to the trial court for additional time before the argument of the case began, as required by the rules of the court.

delivery is the one most likely to convince a jury that the attorney believes in what he is saying.

During your examination you should never lose contact with the eyes of the jurors. The continued contact between their eyes and yours will produce a rapport which will greatly assist you in your task of persuasion.

§ 460. The proper position

Do not pace up and down in front of the jury box. Stand in one place. The pacer only succeeds in distracting the jurors. His speech is not directed to the jury, but rather to the spectators and the courthouse walls. This will not benefit his client.

Stand about four feet in front of the jury box. Position yourself in the center where you can see the entire jury at a glance. Always look directly at the jurors. This way they are fully aware of you, and you are fully aware of them. If you think a particular juror, because of his special background, will understand a telling point, face him squarely when you make that point.

§ 461. Use of oratory

Attempts to overwhelm and confuse the court with an oratory of empty words will only win for counsel the disdain he deserves.

Your attitude should be friendly, conversational, and direct. Have it appear as if this is a friendly conversation with the jury to convince them, by reason and logic, of the justice of your cause. Your statements should still be forceful, but your voice should only be raised when you reach an important point.

Oratory in itself is not to be disparaged, however. It is only when the oratory is strained that its use is to be decried. If picturesque speech flows naturally from counsel's enthusiasm for his case, it will be persuasive and its use will be valuable in the oral summation.

In sum, when you have finished your argument, the jury should feel that you have presented a good case rather than delivered a masterful speech.

§ 462. Gestures

Do not be unduly concerned about your manners or gestures during the summation. Any gesture which flows naturally will not hurt you. It is not difficult for the average laymen to detect a feigned gesture or emotion by the lawyer. And you should generally refrain from using gestures except to make an important point. Your continuous use of gestures can have the effect of shifting the jury's attention from your words to your actions.

§ 463. Be colorful

Start your summation with a dramatic opening sentence which will stimulate the jury immediately. For example, if the defendant is married and has a family, use these facts to advantage. Place his family in front of the courtroom in view of the jury and in line with the defendant. This will also help counteract the presence of the complainant's or decedent's family.

Color may also be supplied by an occasional illustration or anecdote. Your illustrations should be simple, homey ones. Never overuse illustrations to the point of appearing flippant.

§ 464. Be frank and sincere

Use candor and sincerity throughout the trial, particularly in summation. If the jury believes you are not dealing fairly with the facts, they will discount most of what you say. You must demonstrate your fairness. They must be convinced that you are reciting the evidence accurately, without any exaggeration or partisan interpretation. Then they will be more easily convinced that the conclusions you draw from the evidence are correct.

Do not be afraid to appear nervous. It is far better than appearing cocky. As long as your nervousness is genuine and sincere, the jury will sympathize with and favor you.

Always remember that you are not on display for your proficiency in English. You are there to plead the defendant's cause. If you honestly believe in the justice of your defense, your thoughts and words will flow naturally.

§ 465. Speak simply but vividly

Candor and sincerity march hand in hand with simplicity. You cannot have one without the other.

Simplicity is likewise indispensable to clarity. And the importance of clarity cannot be overstated.

Simplicity comes from the use of everyday language, words that the juror knows and uses—slang if necessary. If a particular prosecution witness was impeached on cross-examination, the jury will understand when you say, "The bottom dropped out of the prosecution's case." Such language is forceful and drives your point home. If testimony borders on the unbelievable, you might say to the jury, "Does this witness think you parked your brains and common sense in the parking lot—with your car—when you came into this court?"

Avoid the use of legalisms. Do not try to impress the jury with your learning and erudition. You want them to understand you, not to esteem you. If technical terms were used by expert witnesses, do not repeat those terms without first defining them for the jury in everyday language.

Speak vividly. You can attain this simply by your choice of language. Certain words form pictures in the minds of the listeners. For example, a word like "brainwashing" is a good term to describe a confession you claim was coerced from the defendant. "Stool pigeon" can be effectively pinned on an accomplice or informer. These are words full of emotion, imagery and special appeal—words around which a winning argument can be formed.

§ 466. Keeping your cool

An attorney who loses his temper thereby loses his capacity to represent his client in the best possible manner. It is not suggested that counsel should not, for cause, exhibit temper—only that he must remain in full control of his capacities.

Sarcasm is ordinarily inappropriate. If it is resorted to, it must be adroitly and sparingly used to be effective. Use of ridicule in argument is hazardous, and counsel must employ it with great care. Carlyle sensed this when he stated, "Sarcasm is the language of the devil; for which reason I have long since as good as renounced it."[24]

It is vital that counsel show full respect to the court during summation. At times, counsel's enthusiasm for his case or his disagreement with a judge's position may seem to justify remarks that are not entirely respectful. The attorney who cannot avoid voicing his momentary irritations with the court is simply not temperamentally suited to be a trial lawyer. Respect for the court does not require servility, however.

Counsel should also avoid familiarity with the trial judge, so that there will be no hint of partiality during the proceedings.

§ 467. Pacing your summation

It is desirable to pace the speed of your delivery during the course of the summation. You should cover uninvolved or unimportant material at a faster pace than your discussion of complicated material. Make sure that the jury understands the key points of your argument. Do not rush through them.

One determinant of the pace you set should be your estimate of the jury's intelligence. The voir-dire examination should have given you a good idea of their ability. You

24. As quoted in Catveras and Edwards, New Dict of Thoughts (rev ed), Doubleday & Co. (New York, 1961) p 30.

can make your delivery at a somewhat faster pace with an intelligent jury so as to avoid boring them.

F. PERSONALIZE AND HUMANIZE THE DEFENDANT

§ 468. Describe accused's family and occupational background

The best way to personalize and humanize is to show the defendant in his environment. If there are any favorable circumstances at all surrounding the crime, do not fail to include them in your argument. You might point out how hard the accused worked to support his family before he turned to crime and describe his present family and job situation.

§ 469. Minimize undesirable characteristics

The fact that the defendant's character is not desirable should not deter you from humanizing him. There is good in the worst of us. Find that good and display it to the jury.

I do not mean that you should whitewash the defendant. Face up to his defects. At the same time call upon the jury to disregard everything not connected to the crime with which he is charged.

"You were not called upon to sit in judgment on the past criminal record of the defendant, or the kind of life he is living. You were called upon to decide whether or not he is guilty of the crime charged in the indictment, and nothing more. This is not Russia or a totalitarian country where people are condemned just because of what they are, or the ideas they hold.

"In an American Court of Justice, we lay aside all of our prejudices and try a man on the basis of evidence alone. We lean over backwards not to be unfair to a man or to bear down on him because of his background; we don't permit a verdict based upon prejudice. If any suggestion is made to implant prejudice because of his background, occupation or any other factor, this is unAmerican, this is undemocratic, and should be rejected completely."[25]

§ 470. Minimize significance of criminal record

If you had decided before the trial that you would put the defendant on the stand, when selecting the jury you should have told them of the defendant's record. At that time you explained (or should have) that his record should be considered as bearing on his credibility only—that a criminal record is no evidence of guilt. You must now expand upon this in your final argument. Point out that the defendant voluntarily exposed his criminal record by testifying in his own defense; otherwise the jury never would have known of his past crimes. Tell the jurors the court will instruct them that they are to disregard previous convictions except when evaluating the defendant's credibility, the same as they would with any other witness. You might also point out that the Goddess of Justice holding the scales wears a blindfold and metes out justice not knowing who is being judged. Each person who comes before her is clothed with the presumption of innocence. Justice requires proof of guilt beyond a reasonable doubt before she tips the scales against a defendant. Whether the accused has or has not a criminal record, his justice must be meted out fairly.

If the defendant's criminal record is old, then you might use these brushes with the law to your advantage. Point out his honest effort to live down his past; make clear as well the good reputation he has recently established. The jury will look at the defendant's rehabilitation with favor. They may sympathize with his personal plight.

25. These illustrations are based on actual final arguments delivered by many of the outstanding lawyers acknowledged in the preface. However, we suggest that you do not use them verbatim, but that you paraphrase and adapt them to your particular style and form of summation so that they blend naturally into the scheme of your closing argument.

§ 471. Emphasize defendant's rights

If the defendant's past and present record is bad, do not gloss over it. The prosecutor will certainly emphasize it.

Again you should lay great stress on the impartiality of the law. Argue that fact and not prejudice should govern the verdict. Here is one way to argue it: "I appeal to your intelligence in determining this issue. I don't want sympathy. Sympathy cannot bring back the life of the victim. Neither will prejudice. Do not make that mistake. The accused is entitled to the same consideration at your hands that you would give to an upstanding resident of your community.

"The law does not discriminate; the law is impartial. In measuring the conduct of the defendant, you cannot use a yardstick different from the one you would use if you were measuring the conduct of an intimate friend, a relative or a next-door neighbor.

"Your duty is a solemn one; it calls into play the highest degrees of citizenship and courage. Because there was a homicide it doesn't follow that the law has to have a victim. The accused must be proven guilty to a moral certainty and to the satisfaction of each and every one of you beyond a reasonable doubt before you can convict him."

§ 472. Stress defendant's good character

Evidence of the defendant's good character always forms a vital part of your defense. Therefore, it makes common sense to highlight such evidence in your summation. This is another place in your summation when an emotional argument is effective. If the defendant is being accused by a stool pigeon or accomplice, your appeal to the jury might be as follows: "What is the use of working and sweating and toiling? What is the use of being a good husband and of taking care of your wife and children? What is the use of being honest in your business and of trying to live decently for others? What is the use, I say, if your whole life can be destroyed by a word from the mouth of a confessed felon?

Where an accomplice or stool pigeon is not in the picture, your appeal should be a little more restrained: "What is the accused's reputation? What has he done in life before he came to trial in this court? If you find that he is a man of good character, that his reputation is unblemished, that he has never been in any trouble before and people speak well of him, that he has been an honest, law-abiding citizen, you have a right to assume that he is not the person who would commit this kind of crime, and that his testimony is worthy of belief. Such a good reputation is enough to create a reasonable doubt where otherwise a reasonable doubt might not exist. With such a doubt your verdict must then be not-guilty."

CHAPTER SIXTEEN

SUMMATION: ACHIEVING YOUR OBJECTIVES

E. EXPLAIN THE LAW

F. NEUTRALIZE UNFAVORABLE FACTORS

G. EMPHASIZE PROSECUTION'S WEAK POINTS

H. DISCREDIT UNFAVORABLE WITNESSES

I. ATTACKING IDENTIFICATION TESTIMONY

J. ATTACKING CONFESSION

K. EMPHASIZE STRONG POINTS

L. MINIMIZE WEAK POINTS

M. ESTABLISH DEFENSES

N. TECHNIQUE

O. CONTENT

A. BEGINNING YOUR SUMMATION

§ 473. In general

In criminal actions, it is usually held that since the prosecution has the burden of proof, it also has the right to open and close.[1] In some jurisdictions, if the accused presents no evidence, he has a statutory right to open and close.[2]

In Florida, the accused is entitled to make the closing argument if he offers no evidence other than his own testimony.[3]

Peculiarly, the prosecution is allowed to retain the right to open and close even in cases where the accused admits his crime but offers an affirmative defense, such as double jeopardy. Sanity hearings are an exception, and the accused is allowed to open and close.[4]

§ 474. Strategy and technique

It is frequently useful to begin summation with a concise statement explaining why counsel's client should prevail.[5] Your statement of the facts should be logical and unemotional. The same goes for any statements of law. Your recital of the facts and law should be fair, but from the

1. United States v El Rancho Adolphus Products, Inc. (DC Pa) 140 F Supp 645, affd United States v Hohensee (CA3) 243 F2d 367, cert den 353 US 976, 1 L Ed 2d 1136, 77 S Ct 1058, reh den 354 US 927, 1 L Ed 2d 1441, 77 S Ct 1376.

2. Hart v State, 88 Ga App 334, 76 SE2d 561; State v Raper, 203 NC 489, 166 SE 314; State v Garlington, 90 SC 138, 72 SE 564.

3. Green v State (Fla) 80 So 2d 676; Hall v State, 119 Fla 38, 160 So 511.

4. People v Carmen, 43 Cal 2d 342, 273 P2d 521; Toussaint v State, 92 Tex Crim 374, 244 SW 514.

5. Bayer and Balicer, Cross Examination and Summation (2d ed) p 237.

In the words of attorney Frederick Bernays Wiener:

"You have got to lodge effectively in the court's mind in the first two minutes what the case involves so that the judges' interest and understanding can be seized and held. You have got to give your secret away at the outset, because an oral argument is not a 'whodunit.' You want to tell them the secret right in the first paragraph, and not simply in the last chapter." Weiner, Curable Faults in Oral Argument. 7 SC LQ 573.

most favorable standpoint to the defendant. Save your emotion for later in the argument, after the jury is convinced of the fairness of your discussion of the facts.

After a concise statement of the facts, counsel should state the secondary points supporting his position. During the balance of the argument, he should present an analysis of each specific point.

To take a different approach, counsel may introduce his summation with a relevant anecdote or an apt quotation. Or he may begin by praising his own client, or referring to an obvious act of malice by the opposing counsel. Another possible opening might be a comment on a notable incident that occurred during the trial, such as a striking admission by the opposite side, or its failure to counter one of the telling points advanced by counsel. Whatever the opening thrust, it will be more digestible if it is confined to a single point and succinctly presented.

B. CONTENT OF THE INTRODUCTION

§ 475. Discuss responsibilities of jurors

Your introductory statement to the jury should emphasize the grave responsibility they assumed and the solemn promises they made when they were selected. You might begin: "Ladies and Gentlemen of the Jury. When you were selected and sworn as jurors in this case, each of you promised that you would give the accused the same fair and careful consideration, the same benefit of the presumption of innocence and reasonable doubt that you would expect at the hands of twelve of your fellow citizens. I know you mean to keep that promise."

Prejudice is a disease that cannot be entirely eliminated. It can work both for and/or against the defendant. It can convict the defendant with the criminal record; the defendant charged with a reprehensible crime; the black defendant. It can acquit the defendant charged with a crime sanctioned by the "unwritten law."

You can try to eliminate or combat prejudice as follows:

"You and I—all of us—whether we know it or not, acquire impressions throughout our lives. Everything we do and see leaves an impression, sometimes subconscious, but nevertheless an impression.

"We read from day to day about robberies, holdups, gunmen, killings. Of course, this information we acquire, whether we read it, see it on television or listen to it on the radio, has left some subconscious impressions that we cannot throw off. These impressions are brought into the jury box.

"An actor in the theater would call these impressions of ours 'atmosphere.' It is here now. It's here in this building. It pervades the courtroom; it pervades the jury box. It has impressed each one of us in some way whether we are aware of it or not.

"We all approach certain cases from certain angles with certain impressions, or you might say with certain leanings or prejudices. Let me give an example: Suppose a 19-year old boy were here, charged with the crime of statutory rape—that is, having a voluntary act of sexual intercourse with a girl under 18 years of age. Let us say she was 17½. Well, the minute you heard a case of that kind with a law so strict, there is no doubt the defendant would start off with a break, is there? You would be favorably disposed toward him. However, when you hear of murder, a holdup or a robbery—crimes of that kind—instead of being for the defendant, you are for the prosecution. I don't say that happens willingly. But subconsciously, whether you want it or not, there isn't a presumption of innocence at all; there is, in fact, a presumption of guilt.

"Let's take another example. You are walking along the street and suddenly you see a crowd. You see a policeman run up and catch a man by the sleeve and start to lead him away. You know nothing about the circumstances, but in your eyes that man looks like a criminal. Isn't that the way the human mind functions? However, no matter what you think, that man is innocent until he has been proven guilty according to the rules of law. That's what His Honor will tell you; that's the law, and that's what should be applied.

"I know that you will judge this case without any ill-will or prejudice toward the accused. I know you will judge this case on the believable evidence presented in this courtroom, and upon nothing else."

§ 476. Discuss the presumption of innocence

Most acquittals are not based on the belief that the defendant is innocent, but rather upon a reasonable doubt of the proof of his guilt. Therefore, it is most important that your introductory remarks be based upon (1) the fact that the defendant is presumed to be innocent; (2) that the burden throughout the trial rests upon the prosecution to prove the defendant guilty beyond a reasonable doubt; and (3) that the prosecution has neither overcome the presumption nor satisfied the burden of proof.

But it is not enough merely to state these rules. Explain them. Talk about their origin and their relation to our democratic system of American justice. Their importance should be emphasized and re-emphasized. Remind the jury that the presumption of innocence and the rule of reasonable doubt have been developed throughout decades of judicial experience. They are not merely for the protection of the defendant, but for the protection of everyone. Refer to the presumption of innocence as legal evidence, not simply a rule.

The following is an approach which has been used with some success in arguing a defendant's presumption of innocence:

"What is an indictment? An indictment is a complaint; it's a piece of paper that brings the defendant into court. It's like a summons in a civil case. The summons in the civil case brings the defendant into court for his trial; the indictment in a criminal case brings the accused into court.

Just because a man is sued does not make him liable. By the same token, just because a man is indicted does not make him guilty. The civil lawyer must prove that his client, the plaintiff, is right. Also, the plaintiff, the prosecutor in this case must prove that he has a case. When you are in a civil court suing for money, there is no presumption favoring the plaintiff's being right, nor is there a presumption favoring the defendant's being right.

"In a criminal case, however, it is a different matter. The law in the criminal case says every defendant is presumed to be innocent. That is a presumption of fact. But realize that the State with all of its power, resources and moral persuasion is the plaintiff and is fighting against one lonely defendant!

"For example, take an ordinary baseball game. Both teams start from scratch—that would be like a civil case. No runs, no hits, everything is equal before the pitchers start. In a criminal case, however, the law gives the team—the defendant—one run to start off with. That one run I would call the presumption of innocence. It is the job of the other side, the prosecution, to overcome that one run lead and bat in an extra run to win the game or case."

§ 477. Discuss reasonable doubt

Be sure that each member of the jury knows the vital difference between the rule of preponderance of evidence in a civil case and reasonable doubt in a criminal case. Emphasize this, whether or not the jurors have had previous criminal case experience. Take nothing for granted.

Here is a way to illustrate reasonable doubt:

"What is a reasonable doubt? There is a path that leads to the detention pen, and men are taken from the detention pen to the City Prison. From the City Prison there is a van that goes to the banks of the Hudson to a place called Sing Sing Prison. There they have a section they call the Deathhouse. In the back of the Deathhouse is a square white-painted chamber. There sits a grim instrument of death with straps and electrodes. In murder trials, on occasions, they take the convicted defendant down from this courthouse into that deathhouse, along that last mile to what they call 'the little green door.' There they strap him in and throw the switch, and they burn him until he's dead, slice him open, and take out his heart, and then ship the mass of burned flesh back to the family. Then the State says, 'We're finished.'

"That's the pathway. In the middle of that pathway our law has planted a big tree called 'reasonable doubt.' It blocks that pathway completely. The laws says that before you can send any man down that road to his death you have to remove that tree from the pathway. Not a single branch must remain in that road. Now, bearing in mind what I have said to you—that every defendant is presumed innocent—the natural question is, has the prosecution proven its case beyond a reasonable doubt? Has the prosecution removed the tree of reasonable doubt from the pathway that leads to the electric chair in Sing Sing?" (Now begin to discuss the facts.)

C. MAIN ARGUMENT IN SUMMATION

§ 478. In general

You might begin this phase of your summation by saying simply: "Let us examine the evidence upon which you are asked to find beyond a reasonable doubt that Joe Jones is guilty of this serious crime."

Your examination of the evidence comes next. It should be divided as follows: (1) The destruction of the prosecution's case, and (2) the marshalling of the evidence on behalf of the defendant. In the first part, you expose the inherent improbability of the prosecution's testimony. You attack the credibility of their witnesses. You search out inconsistencies and contradictions and parade them in front of the jury. You find and assail the weakest point in the prosecutor's case.

In the second part of your argument, you assemble the facts which support your defense. You explain away any weaknesses in your own case, such as contradictory statements made by the defendant to the police, flight of the defendant, etc.

In a difficult case, you might open your argument by placing your defense before the jury. When describing your defense, never use the expressions, "theory of the defense" or "theory of the defendant." Your defense is not a "theory"—it is a "fact"! Speak of the "theory of the prosecution" instead.

D. STRATEGY AND TECHNIQUES

§ 479. Present facts in manner most favorable to defendant

Summarize briefly the prosecution's version of what took place. Play down that version. Make the prosecution's case appear incredible and unworthy of belief. However, do it in a dignified manner. Point out each and every loophole in his theory. If necessary, use your fingers to illustrate each different theory the prosecution has advanced, and then show improbability.

Your discussion of the defendant's version should be fair. Do not abuse the imagination of your jury. Persuade the jury not by exaggeration, but by a logical presentation of the facts. Arrange the facts in one way and one result may follow; arrange them in another way and you may reach the opposite result. Your manner in stating the facts will also help. Lend your own personality to the case.

When presenting the facts as they benefit the defendant, deal first with those that are incontroverted. Draw possible favorable inferences from these facts. Then pass to the controverted facts. Show how they are consistent with the defendant's innocence as well as consistent with the incontroverted facts.

§ 480. Focus the jury's attention on the true issue

It is often a good tactic to focus the jury's attention upon a single issue if your defense has narrowed down to that one issue. This can be done by presenting a series of issues and telling the jury which one of them is the "real" issue they are to decide.

This approach should not be used if you relied upon a shotgun defense at trial.

§ 481. Anticipate and counter prosecutor's arguments

Explain every unfavorable fact to the jury. Otherwise the prosecution will emphasize these facts in summation and they will stand out unanswered. You must, therefore, anticipate the prosecutor's argument. This is not as difficult as it might sound. You know the testimony he elicited on direct examination. You are aware of the line of cross-examination he pursued. You should know what he considers his strongest evidence.

Suggest to the jury that this is what you assume the prosecutor will urge. Then proceed to answer these arguments as best you can. Remember, if you do not answer them in your final argument, you will never again have the opportunity to do so.

Even in the few jurisdictions where the prosecutor sums up first, you should still anticipate his arguments when you prepare the outline of your final statement. If you rely on notes taken during the prosecutor's summation, you may conceivably overlook a point that seemed unimportant at the time the prosecutor said it, and whose importance would have been recognized had you calmly reviewed the case in the leisure of your office or home.

§ 482. Posing questions for prosecutor to answer

Where you sum up first, and have an excitable and inexperienced prosecutor opposing you, it may be a good tactic to throw questions at him. Tell the jury that you have certain specific questions the prosecutor must answer. Set forth these questions in simple clear language. If the prosecutor is unable to answer them properly, and the jury is left dissatisfied, your case will be won. If the questions are properly selected, he might have to skip back and forth through his prepared material to answer you. He might, consequently, have no logical order in his summation. It will prevent him from delivering an intelligent, forceful and clear final argument. He may spend more time in answering you than in developing his own arguments. He may become so involved in the factual matters you have thrown at him that he will fail to stress the stronger parts of his case.

§ 483. Stress the duties and responsibilities of jurors

You can usually determine whether the Judge has taken a friendly, hostile or neutral view of your case. You can sense the kind of charge he will give. In most jurisdictions the Judge may comment on the evidence, including the right to point out particularly relevant and pertinent bits of evidence. He may assist the jury in marshalling the evidence. In some jurisdictions the Judge may even entertain a view of the facts and express this view to the jury. The jury then may adopt or reject this view.

You have the absolute right to attempt to counteract what you believe might be an unfavorable charge. You do this by stressing to the jury that they alone are the final judges of the facts and the importance of their role.

§ 484. Reject speculation and suspicion

In his summation, counsel must be aware that the jury may be inclined to speculate or be unduly suspicious of his client, the accused. He may counteract such suspicion or speculation as follows:

"In an American court of justice where we practice democracy and democratic justice, we do not convict the accused on suspicion. Some people will say, 'Where there's smoke there's fire. I guess he must be guilty.' We don't try cases on hunches. If we did, we would not need a jury; we could sit home and try the case in the newspapers, or with some fellow in the cigar store or the local bar. That's not trying the case according to law, according to the evidence. In a democratic American Court of Justice we try our cases on sound, reliable, decent evidence and on nothing else.

"If you agree to speculate, to guess, to surmise as to the innocence or guilt of anybody, you are violating your oath as a juror in this democratic court of justice. If you are going to adopt the theory of 'Where there is smoke there is fire,' then you will be violating your duty and betraying our trust in democratic justice.

"There may be some evidence, but that is not sufficient, and the law says that insufficient evidence is not evidence. If there is literally no evidence or the evidence is insufficient, then you have only one duty and that is to vote not-guilty.

In a murder trial it might be effective to add: "Murder is a capital crime. Any jury that takes the life of a man by its verdict, without complete evidence of guilt; any juror who closes his mind to the evidence or to the law—as it was instructed him by the Judge—because of passion or prejudice, and who pronounces a death sentence on another human being—that juror is as guilty of murder as the person who snuffed out the life of the deceased in this case."

"There is no middle course. The prosecution either establishes its case beyond all reasonable doubt or else it fails completely. There is no room for 'maybe' or 'probably,' or even 'almost certainly.' Unless you can honestly say, 'Yes he did it,' without qualification, without reserve, the verdict must be not-guilty."

§ 485. Lead jury to conclusions

Your conclusions may be presented to the jury in one of two ways: (1) by stating the facts and conclusions which you draw from the facts; (2) by stating the facts and asking the jury what conclusions they would draw from them.

Try to use each method during different parts of your argument, but never attempt to force your conclusions on the jury. Lead them to the desired conclusion. Develop your thought to the point where a juror is able to grasp it himself and form the conclusion you desire. Your explanation must go far enough to ensure that the point you are making is not overlooked. But do not destroy the technique of your getting the juror to reason for himself. A conclusion that is reached by the juror is a conclusion that is firmly implanted in his mind.

An occasional illustration is effective when you want to drive an important point home. If one of the jurors is a plumber, or an electrician, an illustration dealing with his occupation will most effectively demonstrate a point. Look directly at the particular juror when giving such an illustration. Not only will this procedure flatter him, but that point will be vividly impressed upon his mind. Use as many of these types of illustrations as possible.

§ 486. Tie the facts to your defense

You have discussed the facts. You have explained your defense. Now you must tie them together. Show how the physical facts bear out your defense. Point out the witnesses who have given testimony consistent with your defense, as well as the witnesses or exhibits that corroborate that particular testimony. Be certain to highlight cross-examination that brought out testimony favorable to your defense.

§ 487. Minimize the prosecutor's histrionics

Where you feel that the prosecutor has presented an emotion-filled case with little evidence but lots of atmosphere, then you might address the jury as follows: "We have here a drama being staged by the prosecutor. You, the jury, are the audience. You've seen mystery plays where hands come out from dark windows and clutch the throat of the heroine and there are green lights cutting the darkness on stage. The audience shrieks and quivers and you and I have to look around at the exit signs to make sure we're in a theater instead of a graveyard or a morgue. What would happen if the lights suddenly illuminated the stage? You would see the clutching hands are nothing more than stuffed gloves at the end of a stick propelled by a stagehand.

"The case presented by the prosecutor is all atmosphere. I am turning the light on for you to show you that all of the prosecution's 'clutching hands' are just stuffed gloves. The prosecutor is throwing the green spotlight on the situation to give you a little atmosphere—that's all, just atmosphere. I am trying to turn on the light to show how artificial, unreal and empty the prosecution's case is. His entire case is empty, with absolutely no evidence of guilt."

E. EXPLAIN THE LAW

§ 488. In general

The law of your case must be stated clearly, simply, and interestingly. Your simple language will greatly assist the jury in understanding the usual legal mumbo-jumbo in many of the charges of the court. Psychologically, when the jurors hear the court give an instruction you have discussed, it makes them feel that you have played fair with them throughout the trial. In a way, the court's charge then becomes a second summation in your favor.

§ 489. Explain your defense

Do not rely on the judge's charge to clear up anything you leave unexplained. On the contrary, your explanation will enable the jury to understand what the judge will be talking about.

Explaining your defense is only a part of your job. The jury must not only know the nature of your defense, but must also sympathize with it. To that end you must point out the reason and justice for your defense. Show the jury why the law allows the defense you are urging.

This is especially important in cases where your defense admits the commission of the act, but claims self-defense, insanity, intoxication or any similar affirmative defense.

§ 490. Circumstantial evidence

The following is presented as a typical way to handle the matter of circumstantial evidence:

"Circumstantial evidence, in order to be convincing and complete, must form one continuous chain of events with no links absent. If one link is missing, the case fails entirely. Are all the links in the circumstantial-evidence chain here? (Demonstrate this by using a chain of paper clips. Hold it in your hands.) Ladies and Gentlemen of the jury, let us regard these clips as links in the chain of circumstantial evidence necessary to convict the accused. First, I will put them down and then I will connect them. You have as a fact that a piece of blue overcoat material similar to the accused's blue overcoat was found at the scene of the robbery. We will call that the first link. Then there is evidence that the accused left his house wearing a blue overcoat similar to the material found near the scene of the crime. We will call that a link. Then we have the fact that the accused returned home that night at 7:30 P.M. but did not have his blue overcoat with him, but instead was wearing a gray topcoat. This is one more clip. I now join these three links into a small chain and put them to one side.

(Pick up the fourth clip) "We have the fact that the accused told his mistress not to tell anyone he possessed a blue overcoat and to say further, if questioned, that he had arrived home at about 5:30 P.M. and not 7:30 P.M. That represents another link. Then we have the fact that the accused left his blue overcoat at his aunt's house overnight and took it away the next morning. This is still another link. Then we have the further fact that the victim was wounded about 6:30 P.M. and the gun was found about 50 feet from where the shooting took place and in the direction of the aunt's house, where the accused left his blue overcoat. That is still another link. I now join these links together. We have two chains of three links each. We have this section on one side which establishes that the accused did own a blue overcoat. Then we have this section (pointing to the other links) which indicates the possibility—not the certainty, but only the possibility—that the accused might have been at the scene of the robbery at 6:30 P.M. when the victim was shot. But where is the link that joins these two sets of circumstances into a chain of guilt?

"What could that missing link be? It could be proof that the material found at the scene of the crime did actually originate from the defendant's coat; that the defendant was observed at the scene of the robbery at or about the time it took place; evidence that the accused had a motive to rob the complainant; or a statement by the accused admitting some participation in the shooting of the victim. But there is no evidence of any such character in the whole case.

"We must have that missing link. (Hold up the left section in one hand, the right section in the other, and hold them apart and keep drawing them farther and farther apart.) Ladies and Gentlemen of the Jury, the more you consider, the more these parts separate. Without that missing link, the defendant is an innocent man. Indeed, he must be and is entitled to an acquittal."

§ 491. Conspiracy

A discussion of conspiracy may take the following form:

"If an unlawful conspiracy is formed and a man commits an act in pursuance of it, then every person who belonged to that unlawful conspiracy is guilty of the act. If you should conspire to kill somebody and all but one of you should go home while the remaining person commits the deed, you would all be guilty. But if you conspire to do something which is lawful, something which you have the right to do, and if some member in carrying out the lawful design does an unlawful act, then the rest of you are not guilty of the unlawful act. It does not require very much sense of legal knowledge to understand that. This is human natural justice. Do you think the law is foolish and brutal enough to say that every man is responsible for that act? The answer is obvious."

§ 492. Accomplice testimony

The weight and sufficiency of the testimony of an accomplice and the need for corroboration may be set forth in summation in the following manner:

"The law says that an accomplice's testimony must be supported by independent evidence. The law itself does not trust an accomplice in a crime even if he were actually a man of previous good character. His testimony must be corroborated by evidence tending to connect the defendant, not with the accomplice, but with the committing of the crime. If there is no connecting evidence there is no case. Evidence that he may be guilty of some crime, evidence of flight, evidence that he might have gone away to flee some crime is not corroborating evidence. Evidence must be corroborating and point unerringly in the direction of the commission of the crime charged in this indictment. The corroboration must be independent evidence to connect him with this crime, and this corroboration must be proven beyond every reasonable doubt.

"What is the corroboration here? That the man could not be found by the police? That about the time the crime was committed, he disappeared? Well, has it been proven beyond every reasonable doubt that an innocent construction cannot be put on that disappearance?

"Leave out the so-called disappearance of the defendant and there is no case. Knock down one foundation, the entire building falls. The corroborating evidence also must stand by itself and connect the defendant with the commission of the crime regardless of the accomplice's testimony."

F. NEUTRALIZE UNFAVORABLE FACTORS

§ 493. Counteract unfavorable publicity

Counsel in summation should implore the jury to eliminate any possible prejudice against your client engendered by newspaper, radio, television or other publicity. Sometimes this may be done as follows:

"We are in an American court of law and justice. We try our cases in a legal democratic manner. We do not try our cases by lynch mobs. We do not try our cases by what is said in the newspapers, the *Daily News,* or any other newspaper. We try our cases in courts of law, under the rules of law; we are not interested in what Joe Doakes on the street corner thinks, nor even what your wife may think. We're interested only in the evidence as it came from the witness stand and the law as the Judge will tell it to you.

"If someone by any chance should discuss this case with you and find fault with your judgment, you simply tell him that he did not listen to the evidence; we tried the case on the evidence. We didn't try it on what some newspaper reporter picked out here and put in the newspaper. We tried the case on the evidence.

"We don't try cases on passion. We don't try cases on prejudice. We try our cases on the evidence."

§ 494. Counteract physical appearances, or ethnic considerations

In delivering his summation, counsel should always be sure to caution the jury against prejudice arising from the defendant's appearance or from his ethnic background or race. The following may be a guide in this respect:

"We don't try a man and convict him simply because he's Puerto Rican, black, Italian, Jewish, Irish or anything else. Nor do we try cases on the face of the man. Somebody may say that fellow looks tough, or his face looks evil. All of us agree, and I'm sure we have had the experience that the man who looks the toughest is sometimes the softest and the gentlest. We don't try our cases . . . (at this point you inject any other possible prejudicial factor in the background of the defendant). Ladies and gentlemen, we are here in an American court and the defendant is to be tried under a system of American justice. Whatever he may be, he is going to get the same kind of justice you would want if you were placed in the same unfortunate predicament as he is, or if someone near and dear to you were in such a predicament."

§ 495. Counteract prejudice against type of crime

Where the defendant is charged with a particularly atrocious crime, it is necessary to caution the jury as follows:

"Ladies and gentlemen, in your examination before you were selected as jurors, I asked whether you could put aside feelings of prejudice, passion, revulsion and pity, and decide this case on the evidence. Each of you swore that you would do that; that any prior reading of newspapers or opinions you might have heard expressed would not influence you in any way. You made that pledge. I am going to ask you now to carry out that pledge.

"This was a foul and atrocious crime and I realize that this was a very difficult case for any juror to try. The dominant thought of passion and prejudice might prevent even clear-thinking men from giving the calm, careful consideration that is required to the evidence. I know that you will give it calm, clear, careful thinking and consideration; prejudice, passion and revulsion will have no place in your deliberations. Evidence or lack of evidence alone will decide your verdict."

§ 496. Counteract damaging evidence

When you explain the adverse facts to the jury, do not hedge. Be ready to enter into a full and frank discussion of these facts. You must at least attempt to explain them away, otherwise your case will be lost. You offer a reasonable explanation for all the harmful and difficult evidence.

A damaging fact may sometimes be explained by having it considered in relation to all the facts and circumstances of the case. Argue to the jury that this fact taken by itself appears damaging, but when placed alongside the other evidence it is really harmless. If you contend that the prosecution witness was mistaken or testified falsely, say so.

Even if your explanations are not too strong, the jury will respect your candor and will listen more intently when you in turn attack the weaknesses of the prosecution's case.

Sometimes what appears to be a damaging fact upon examination proves to be helpful. For example: where an incriminating bit of documentary evidence was written by the defendant in pencil, you might argue that if the defendant was guilty, why did he make the notation in pencil and then leave it alone? Why did he not erase it? You would continue by saying: "The very fact that he permits the notation to remain is the best proof that he was not ashamed of it, and that fact points to his innocence. If he wanted to conceal the fact, he could have easily erased it."

After you have referred to both the unfavorable interpretation the prosecution is urging and the favorable one you have urged, you might address the jury as follows:

"Which is right? If you are in any doubt, you must resolve that doubt in favor of the accused. This is the rule under our system of law. This is the rule under the principles of our democratic government."

Some attorneys try to avoid the issue, confess, or bluster the court into confusion. This is less desirable.

G. EMPHASIZE PROSECUTION'S WEAK POINTS

§ 497. In general

If there is a weak spot in the prosecution's case, it should be stressed to the fullest. Remember, you are trying to establish a reasonable doubt in the minds of the jurors; not prove the innocence of the accused. The exposure of some weakness in the prosecutor's case may provide that doubt.

It is tactically effective to attack a prosecution witness or witnesses. It takes the pressure and spotlight off the defendant.

Highlight any discrepancies in the testimony of the prosecution's witnesses. For example, where a witness has testified one way at the preliminary hearing, or has given one statement to the police and testified differently at the trial, make the most of it. Even if the contradiction is of a relatively small point, it should be exploited. By pointing out the contradiction you might cause the jury to discount his entire testimony.

§ 498. Accent failure of prosecution's proof

If the prosecutor failed to prove any of the statements made in his opening address, make the most of it. You should have made careful notes of the points he made in his opening statement. Now call to the jury's attention all of these points that he failed to prove.

There might have been essential elements of the crime that the prosecutor could not prove. List all of the factors that the prosecutor should have been able to prove if the defendant were guilty. If there was no evidence to establish these factors, argue its absence to the jury.

Motive is a good example. If the charge is robbery and there is no evidence that the defendant was in need of money, argue that the prosecutor has shown no motive. You thus establish the improbability of your client's having committed the crime.

If the prosecutor had the power to call certain witnesses but did not, you should ask the jury to assume that that witness would have been unfavorable to the prosecution's case. This is highly effective. Here is one way to put it:

"I specifically call to your attention the fact that the prosecutor failed to call a witness who was present at the time this incident took place. Why wasn't he called? What explanation was given for his failure to be called? You have a right to assume that this witness was not called because, if he testified, he would have given a truthful version of what occurred, or a version contrary to the stories of the other prosecution witnesses."

§ 499. Highlight favorable evidence elicited on cross-examination

Favorable evidence obtained on cross-examination is probably more valuable than the testimony of your own witnesses. The jury might be wary of the carefully prepared defense witness who testifies favorably for the accused. But they cannot be wary of the prosecution witness who reluctantly gives testimony favorable to the defendant. Anything that this witness says for your side can be argued as beyond question.

Another reason for highlighting favorable cross-examination is to show the unfairness of the case against the defendant. Argue that it was up to the prosecution to present the entire picture. Instead, you had to coax the prosecution witness to reveal the whole truth. Such an argument is particularly effective where the witness was hostile and succumbed reluctantly to your interrogation.

However, on some occasions a prosecution witness unconsciously will give favorable testimony for the accused. The statement might not seem significant to the witness, but in your summation you take that "unimportant" answer or that "little detail" and show how it fits into the defendant's version of what occurred. Emphasize that even the testimony of the prosecution witness is consistent with your defense.

§ 500. How to attack a "perfect case"

Where the prosecutor's case seems airtight, attack it for its perfection and strength. Argue that the case is entirely improbable because of its very perfection. "It has been built up too strongly. It is impossible for everybody to give a perfect account of what took place unless they lied or were thoroughly rehearsed and coached. People just do not see things in an identical way when their positions and chances for observation vary. The case is a frame-up."

H. DISCREDIT UNFAVORABLE WITNESSES

§ 501. Pit witness' conduct against his testimony

Pick out any acts of the witness that are inconsistent with the testimony he has given. Ask the jury why a man would act that way if he were telling the truth. Rely on the old bromide, "Actions speak louder than words." Argue that his actions showed he was lying. Ask them to reject his entire testimony.

§ 502. Analyze witness' character; attack witness' motive

You may sometimes discredit a witness by analyzing his character. The witness whose character is questionable is a witness who is not to be trusted. If the character of a key prosecution witness is tarnished, parade it before the jury. Ask them whether they would trust such a man in their ordinary business dealings. Follow this up by asking them not to trust his testimony in this case. You might argue that a man who cannot be trusted in the business world should certainly not be trusted where a man's liberty is at stake. The more disreputable the witness's character, the more emotional should be your plea to the jury. Here are some examples:

"Isn't the character of a star witness the most important consideration for any jury? Isn't his character, aside from his being an accomplice, enough to create a reasonable doubt in this case? Would he be the type of fellow you would believe in your business dealings? Would you take any action in your private affairs on his statement? Look at the man's reputation; look at his upbringing. Don't you have to be extra careful about anything he says because of what he is? Isn't there a reasonable doubt, at least, as to this man's character? Because if there is a reasonable doubt as to his character, there is absolutely no case."

Here is a more emotional example:

"If a vicious criminal, when caught with the blood dripping from his fingers, turns and says, 'He told me to do it,' should twelve jurors accept that criminal's word and take the defendant's liberty? Would that not be a terrible miscarriage of justice? Where and what are our teachings, our instincts, our religious beliefs? Have we learned nothing from the past, that we should even dream of giving countenance to a monster like that?"

Your summation should highlight any personal spite or animosity that exists between the witness and the defendant. If the witness stands to gain financially from the defendant's conviction, stress this in your summation. If the witness has saved his own skin by accusing the defendant, by all means show this up to the jury. Here is an example of the latter:

"What is the motive of this stool pigeon? He can't put the blame on someone who is dead, or has disappeared, or is not around. He's got to deliver a live fish to the police. He has got to hook some fellow and testify against him. The prosecutor might ask you, why should the stool pigeon pick the accused? Why, because he knew that the accused would make a good victim in the minds of the authorities, the police. He knew he could sell the accused more quickly than he could any other person. He could probably prove something. . . I can't fully delve into this mysterious character's mind and try to understand it.

"Suffice it to say that this character is the type of individual who has no conscience. He would do anything to save his own skin. If the accused came into this devil's mind because he might have some grudge against the accused; the accused naturally was the man he would name as the person who helped him in this crime. Did this character want to satisfy the police and the prosecutor? Of course he did. He knew that his life and his liberty were in the hands of the prosecutor and the police; and self-preservation, of course, is the first law of nature."

§ 503. Discuss fallibility of prosecution witnesses

You can attack the memory and observations of the reputable, disinterested witness. You do not necessarily need to attack his memory in particular. Instead, point out the tricks that a person's memory can play. Refer to the willingness of the average citizen to aid the police. Show how this willingness can become an enthusiam which distorts the memory of the witness. He wants to aid the police, so his memory remembers things that never really happened. Suggest that two witnesses may perceive two different events.

However, if your cross-examination revealed that the witness's attention was directed at something else when the incident occurred, then urge that his preoccupation renders his testimony worthless. If the witness was at work or was talking to another, argue that he could not have accurately observed what he testified to. You might reason that if a person can be mistaken in his observations even when he is not preoccupied, then how can his observations be accepted when his attention was directed elsewhere.

§ 504. Recall unfavorable demeanor or appearance of prosecution witness

You may gain an advantage in summation by recalling a

disreputable witness to the jury visually. Rather than referring to a disreputable witness by name, use a descriptive term. Refer to him as "that fellow with the shifting eyes," or "the fellow who swaggered," or the "egotistical one."

Such terms serve two purposes. First, they recall the witness to the jury, visually. The jury will remember the characteristic you described. Secondly, if the jury agrees with your description of him, you need not go too deeply into the nature of his testimony to discredit him.

Often you can discredit a witness by describing his demeanor on the stand. The witness's conduct on the stand is a factor in evaluating his credibility. Were his answers evasive? Was his attitude hostile? Did his answers sound as if they were memorized? Was he too calm and collected? If so, drive it home to the jury.

§ 505. Accomplice testimony

It will usually be to your advantage on summation to indicate the untrustworthiness of an accomplice's testimony. Be certain to emphasize that the law looks with suspicion upon accomplice testimony. Explain that the law realizes a person caught redhanded in a crime might try to buy immunity or a lighter sentence by shifting the blame to another. Stress that the law views the evidence of an accomplice as evidence from a "corrupt source."

If the accomplice gave very effective testimony as to the manner in which the crime was committed, point out: "Of course, the accomplice gave good clear testimony as to the crime. Why shouldn't he? He's the one who committed it! He knows all about it. The lie is the part that drags in the defendant. All the accomplice had to do was weave the lie that the defendant helped him or that the defendant told him to do it into an otherwise truthful story."

§ 506. Exploitation of falsehood

Take full advantage on summation of the maxim *"Falsus*

In Uno, Falsus In Omnibus." Where you have established that a witness has testified falsely on a material point, you have a right to ask the jury to disregard his entire testimony. Advise them that they have the power to disregard everything the witness said.

After you have referred to their power, urge them to exercise it in this case. Here is how you might present this argument:

"Suppose some man came into your place of business and said 'I want to buy some merchandise on time, with sixty days' credit.' And he gives you a financial statement. You look him up and find out that he has lied in his statement. Now, what are you going to do about it? Are you going to ship him the goods? Are you going to trust him with your property?

"Of course you would never give this man credit. You would say: 'Get out of here, you liar. I wouldn't trust you with a cent of my merchandise. You proved yourself to be a liar. I wouldn't believe anything you said to me!'

"What has happened *here?* Are you going to trust *this* liar with something more important than mere merchandise—with a man's liberty? Are you going to take away the accused's liberty on the word of a liar? Isn't this lie sufficient to create a reasonable doubt? Isn't it something you can point to with common sense and reason when you say to your fellow jurors, 'I cannot vote guilty in this case. Here is a man who came into court and deliberately lied in my presence. How could I take his word for anything?' Isn't this a good enough reason for doubt?"

§ 507. How to discredit an infant witness

Emphasize to the jury that children often confuse fact with fantasy. They tell tall stories because it pleases them to be the center of attention. It gives them a feeling of strength and importance. Fantasy, therefore, satisfies a child's emotional need for attention. It also presents an easy way of avoiding unpleasant reality. Instead of the difficult task of facing up to reality, they fall back on fantasy.

Fantasy is often subconscious. One step beyond it is the intentional lie. Most lies come from the child's fear of telling the truth. He is afraid that the truth will anger or disappoint his parents. A lie may be told in order to maintain the child's status with his friends. Make the jury aware of these recognized psychological principles.

A young girl, at times, is the most unreliable and probably the most dangerous witness. This is particularly true in cases which revolve around her, as, for example, sex crimes. The alleged actions of the defendant toward her become highly exaggerated. An insult becomes a terrible attack. A foolish quip becomes an attempted seduction. Point out to the jury that the law in most cases does not trust the testimony of a female victim in a sex crime. The law requires that her testimony be corroborated by credible evidence.

§ 508. How to discredit the expert witness

If an expert testified for the prosecution, point out that experts can be bought by the dozen. Explain that the expert comes to a conclusion depending on which side he is, and then he finds reasons to support his conclusion. Attack him on the basis of any absurd conclusion he arrived at. Exploit any weaknesses in his reasoning that were uncovered during cross-examination. Talk about the fees he has received, as well as his past experiences in testifying as an "expert" for the prosecution.

I. ATTACKING IDENTIFICATION TESTIMONY

§ 509. In general

In most cases the commission of the crime is clearly established and the sole issue remaining is to determine whether or not your client committed it. His identification may have been established by his confession or admission, or by fingerprints, footprints, handwriting or other circumstantial evidence. But in most cases, his identification rests upon the testimony of a witness who states that he saw the defendant commit the crime.

You must impress upon the jury that the law considers untrustworthy any evidence as to the identity of the accused. It does not matter how credible or sincere the testimony of the victim may be, other facts must support the identification. A verdict of guilty based upon identification testimony alone can very well result in the conviction of an innocent person.

What happens very often? A police officer phones the victim and tells him to come down to the police station. "We've got your man," the police officer says. When the victim comes down to the police station and sees the suspect there, he automatically thinks the police know that he is the culprit. The victim says, "Yes, that's the man who did it." He will testify without question at the trial that the accused is the person who committed the crime. Of course, identification under these circumstances is absolutely invalid.

§ 510. Questioning quality of witness's identification

Courtroom identification is often worthless. Argue that where a witness identifies the defendant in the courtroom, this identification is of no value. The witness saw the defendant seated at the counsel table when the trial began, he saw the defendant seated there when he entered the courtroom and before he took the witness stand. It is therefore logical to assume that he will pick out the defendant as the one who allegedly committed the crime.

Point up any conflict in the testimony of different prosecution witnesses. Prosecution's witnesses may disagree substantially in their description of the criminal—his facial characteristics, his height, size, clothing worn may differ substantially with each witness. If this is a fact, make the most of it in your argument to the jury.

Illustrate flaws in the description given to the police at the time of the arrest. If the description of the culprit given to police at the time of the arrest, as to height, color of hair, color of eyes, description of clothing, etc. is not too specific, argue to the jury that this description is vague and general and could fit almost anyone.

Argue that once a victim makes the statement that the accused is the man who committed the offense, it is, at best, opinion evidence only. It must be supported by facts to have any weight or validity. If the victim described the culprit as "a young person with a thin mustache," argue there was no description given of other physical characteristics such as the voice, height, size, shape of face, complexion, physique, jaw, nose, forehead, carriage, color of eyes, hair or anything else. The victim's positive statement, "That is him," cannot withstand the test of reasonable doubt and moral certainty under these circumstances.

§ 511. Discredit induced identification

Any identification that was induced by suggestion or by any other means—directly or indirectly, in good faith or otherwise—should be rejected as worthless. Argue that the police should be completely objective and scrupulously careful when the victim is brought in to pick out the culprit.

Remind the jury that the use of photographs impairs the value of identification. If a photograph of the accused was shown to the victim, the validity of his identification is considerably, if not completely, destroyed. Once a person has seen a photograph, the image of the photograph is impressed upon his mind. When he comes to identify the accused, he has in mind the face in the photograph rather than the face of the person who committed the offense. Thus, the use of the photograph does not enable the victim to form an independent judgment in making his identification of the man who committed the offense. If you were confronted with a case involving an in-court identification which was based, in whole or in part, upon an identification based upon a photograph, you should have moved for a hearing to determine whether there was an independent basis for the in-court identification. Whether or not you received such a hearing, you can argue that it is clear from the circumstances of the case that the witness could not have made the identification without the aid of the suggestion emanating from the display of the photograph or likeness.

Discredit an identification that was induced by newspapers, TV, radio, friends and relatives. If the victim or witness had read accounts of the culprit in the newspapers or had formed a description of him from information they had gathered from newspapers or other media, point out that the identification was not based upon independent recollection of the culprit, but rather suggestions induced by the papers, friends, and relatives, radio, TV, etc.

Discredit an identification that was induced by passion and prejudice injected in the case by police. Argue that when a homicide has taken place or where the crime has been particularly vicious, it is very easy for the police to say unfavorable things—prejudicial and emotional things which could cause any victim or so-called eye witness to identify the accused. This is often done by some unscrupulous police officers in order to ensure that the witness will make an identification where the police desire him to make one. Argue that the victim or witness was made to believe the police had inside information plus informers and stool pigeons who conclusively established that the defendant was the person responsible for the crime. The police might even have suggested that the defendant confessed.

When the witness came to the police station to make his alleged identification, he had been prepared and completely primed to select the defendant as the person who committed the crime. Argue to the jury that this was not an honest, true and proper identification for which any man's liberty should be taken away. Rather it was one induced by the police. If the police's identification and information were wrong, the entire identification is invalid simply because it was not an honest recollection of the victim or witness.

§ 512. The lineup

Discredit an identification made without a lineup. If there was no lineup and only the defendant was present, emphasize this. Point out that the defendant was the only one to be identified so that, in effect, the defendant was selected to be identified by the police. Point out what discussion the detectives had with the victim before he was brought to the station house in order to prepare him to identify the defendant.[6]

The Supreme Court has recognized that the assistance of counsel at a lineup is indispensible to protect a defendant's right to a fair trial with meaningful cross-examination.[7] This means that it is improper to hold a lineup in the absence of counsel or in the absence of an effective waiver of the right.

If you or your representative were present at the lineup you can argue, based upon the evidence in the case, that the defendant was not placed among persons of the same or similar age, height, appearance, or station in life, or that he was not permitted to select his own place in line. You may also be able to argue that the police exerted either subtle or direct pressure to have the witness identify someone in the line.

If the defendant was unrepresented at the lineup, there should be a hearing to determine whether there was an independent basis for the courtroom identification. Even if a Judge finds that there is such a basis, you may contest the issue before the jury.

Argue further that the victim and other witnesses conferred with each other before making the selection, and that they had the assistance of photographs or descriptions

6. § 367, supra.

7. United States v Wade, 388 US 218, 18 L Ed 2d 1149, 87 S Ct 1926.

from the police and other persons before they made their selection.

§ 513. Illustrating to the jury the uncertainty of identification

The following is suggested as a method of illustrating to the jury the uncertainty inherent in identification.

"How many times have you seen a person you thought you knew well? You said, 'Hello,' but when he turned around you realized he was not the man you thought. It was someone else who looked just like him. Let us suppose that you were the unfortunate fellow picked out by the victim as one of the persons who committed the crime, because you looked like the man the victim had in mind. Would you want to be convicted on the quality of such testimony? Would you think it just to convict anybody on this type of testimony?

"You must go into the jury room and ask yourself, 'Can I, with clear conscience and under oath, realizing the serious responsibility given to me, say to myself that I am satisfied beyond the reasonable doubt that the witness picked out and identified the right man when he picked out the accused?' The answer must be 'no.' The answer is 'there is grave doubt'; my verdict must be not-guilty."

J. ATTACKING CONFESSION

§ 514. In general

A confession is valueless if it is not supported by other clear evidence of guilt. In many jurisdictions, a confession is required by law to be corroborated by evidence tending to connect the defendant to the crime. Evidence that the crime was committed is not sufficient corroboration.

Point this out to the jury. Argue that the law, therefore, deems confessions to be unreliable evidence.

Refer to the pressures that a person is under when he is

being questioned by the police. Even though the police may not have used coercive methods to get the confession, point out that the mere presence of jailhouse walls is a form of mental coercion. The suspect is all alone with no person nearby to comfort him. He has no attorney to tell him that he need not speak at all. He is frightened. All he wants is to be left alone. Under these circumstances it is quite possible he will say things that are not true.

Explain that a confession cannot be accepted unless the jury fully understands all of the circumstances surrounding it. The jury must consider the defendant's motives. Are there other persons the defendant might be trying to protect? Was the defendant able to relate all of the facts surrounding the crime or only part of them? If the crime involved stolen property, was he able to account for all of the property or just some of it, or none of it? The answer to these questions will determine the reliability of the confession.

However, even if the answers are unfavorable to your case, the question of the police methods in obtaining the confession still remains. If coercion was applied or immunity was promised, the confession is involuntary and worthless.

§ 515. Distinguish between an admission and denial

The jury might consider an accusatory statement made in the presence of the defendant to be evidence of the defendant's guilt. Explain that this statement, if denied by the defendant, is no evidence.

§ 516. Analyze the defendant's interrogation

The prosecution will attempt to show that the police, when questioning the defendant, were only interested in justice and were not attempting to get a confession at the expense of truth. You must demonstrate otherwise to the jury.

Paint a vivid picture of a frightened and lonely person

being interrogated by expert inquisitors whose only purpose is to obtain a confession.

Show that the police were already convinced of the defendant's guilt before they began their questioning. If you can characterize the proceedings as an inquisition, the jury's sympathies will flow to the besieged defendant. The unfairness behind the questioning will diminish the value of the answers.

§ 517. Emphasize effects of coercion

Where it fits the situation, counsel should illustrate to the jury the coercive methods of the police. The following is an example in this regard.

"The defendant was taken and held in custody without a charge and without a crime. He was guarded and watched, and then he was browbeaten, bullied, and finally promised all the things in the world to save his life. Is this a fair way to question a man in the station house for such a long period of time without rest? When he starts to give an explanation, they don't let him talk. Would you want to be questioned that way? Is that the kind of statement you're going to use as a basis for a verdict? Is that fair? Is that honorable?

"This confession is the record of a group of conspirators who took an American citizen and outraged his liberty, who trampled on the Constitution that was made to protect him, and then committed the darkest and deepest perjury in this court of justice to cover up their deeds.

"There is a regular routine in the extraction of the confession: a little pressure, a little promise, a little suggestion. Here you have this person sitting in the station house with detectives buzzing in the corner. They say 'You don't have to involve yourself too much; all you have to say is the other guy did it. You didn't do all of it, you just helped him.' That's the way they work behind the scenes. Of course, all you see is the finished product. You don't see the sweat, threats, and everything else that went into it.

Now it is my job to show you what happened behind the scenes. It is my job to sort out the evidence and pick it to pieces, and show you what really happened: why the accused said what he did. What happens in some police stations in those back rooms could not be adequately described. If five or six or ten of those bullying detectives were working over you, you too would tell them that the moon was blue or green."

§ 518. Discredit an involuntary confession

Counsel should in every possible instance vividly describe and remind the jury of the worthlessness of an involuntary confession. He may do so as follows:

"So the law is wise when it says a confession cannot be accepted unless it is made voluntarily and freely. If the confessor is moved by fear or influenced by hope, then it is the fear that is speaking, it is the hope that arises above his courage. It is the accused, overcome by fear one moment, raised by hope another moment. Such a confession cannot count but must be completely rejected.

"The honor of this great country is meant to protect the liberty and life of its citizens from despots, malefactors and persecutors. It is infinitely more important to this great State and Country to know whether this confession was honestly obtained, than to know if any man was murdered, whosoever that man might be.

"The American system of justice seeks to alleviate condemnation of men based upon coerced false confessions. Condemnations of this sort often occur in Communist and totalitarian regimes." Assert the improbability of the waiver of the right to counsel.

You might argue that the defendant was mentally or physically coerced into making a confession regardless of the warnings. Ask the jury how they would react if they were forced to sign a statement without advice of counsel which has been denied them. Ask if they would think it proper to be held to that statement.

K. EMPHASIZE STRONG POINTS

§ 519. Illustrate the injustice of questioning defendant without the presence of his attorney

The police will have testified that the defendant was advised of his rights prior to the interrogation. In attacking the voluntariness of the confession (which you should do even if it was held voluntary after an exclusionary hearing) assert either that the requisite warnings were not given, that they were given but not understood, or that even if given and understood, the police nevertheless continued with a coercive investigation.

§ 520. Point out quality and integrity of your witnesses

The previous chapters were devoted to the specific task of destroying the prosecution's case. The next phase of your summation is the enhancement of your own case.

The natural place to start enhancing your case is with your witnesses. Refer to the testimony of any unimpeached witness which corroborated the defendant's testimony. When recalling this witness's testimony, refer to him by name. If he was alert or intelligent in appearance, indicate that his powers of observation were undoubtedly accurate. However, if he was slow or dullwitted, admit that, too. Point out that that is his nature and any other kind of performance would have been fabricated and untruthful. In fact, if the prosecutor was unable to shake him, you should take advantage of his slowness. Point out that a slow, dull-witted person who was not telling the truth would have quickly cracked under the skillful cross-examination of the prosecutor. The fact that he instead stuck to his story indicates his truthfulness.

If your witnesses were humble persons of small means, you might say: "Unfortunately the incident did not occur in the presence of distinguished witnesses such as doctors, public officials or judges, but instead occurred in the presence of simple, ordinary people. Yet, when you really think about it, the ordinary person might be a more reliable witness. Sometimes humble persons have better powers of observation than the intellectual. And there is also the possibility that the intellectual might in reality infer what really happened rather than relate what he truly observed. The simple fellow whose mind is not so weighed down is likely to catch things that are unusual. He will describe what actually took place."

If one of your witnesses, or the defendant, was rough and uncivil on the witness stand, praise him for his straightforwardness. Say that he was being himself and not attempting to ingratiate himself with the jury. He had something to say and said it in the only way he knew how. Urge the jury to judge what was said and not the manner in which it was said.

If a disinterested witness had testified for the defendant, make the most of him. Ask the jury why he would come forth to testify if he was not telling the truth. He had no axe to grind, nor was there money in it for him. He testified because he wanted the truth to be heard.

§ 521. Emphasize extenuating circumstances

If you have an affirmative defense which is based upon the defendant's actions under stress, urge the jury to judge his conduct by the forces and circumstances that existed at the time the act was committed. For example, if the defendant killed an innocent person he thought was a prowler, ask the jury to put themselves in the defendant's place. Argue that sitting in the calm, unemotional atmosphere of the courtroom, they might think that a reasonable person would ascertain who he was shooting. However, a person does not think calmly and unemotionally when he believes his life or property are at stake. He acts to protect himself, his family and his property. Urge the jury to ask themselves what they would have done *under those circumstances,* and not what they think the defendant should have done.

L. MINIMIZE WEAK POINTS

§ 522. Explain failure to call witnesses for defense

If you have rested on the prosecution's case, the jury may think you did not present a defense because you believed the case was hopeless. They might even question your belief in the defendant's innocence. Either of such thoughts on the part of the jury would prove disastrous. Therefore, it is best to explain your motives as follows to the jury:

"I have put in no defense in this case. I did not call any witnesses. Let me tell you why. My role is similar to a doctor's. When you are sick, you go to a doctor. He will examine you and may say: 'I have examined you and looked at the X-rays. There is nothing wrong with you, just a little gas pain. No operation is necessary.'

"A doctor and lawyer are on the same footing. I have examined this case. I have listened to the evidence. I have looked at it with the X-ray eyes of a lawyer who has had experience, and I have decided that the accused, my patient, is not suffering from anything. I'm not recommending any operations. I'm not bringing in a horde of witnesses, a lot of gadgets and operating tools. That's my diagnosis; my decision is 'The defendant rests.'"

§ 523. Explain failure of defendant to testify

If you did not place the defendant on the witness stand, you must decide whether or not to mention this in summation. You might say nothing at all. On the other hand, you might stress the defendant's right to remain silent and add that in your judgment you did not think it necessary for him to testify.

Your decision is made easier if the prosecution offered in evidence any statements of the defendant in which he protested his innocence. In such a case you can explain to the jury that there was no need for the defendant to testify. He gave his explanation when the police first questioned him. Therefore, there is no need to add further testimony to what the defendant has already said.

However, even if no statement of the defendant was introduced into evidence, it may be well to discuss your failure to place the defendant on the stand. The danger of the jury's drawing a bad inference requires you to impress them with the rights of the defendant. Here is one way to treat it:

"I must remind you that any juror who goes into the jury room and says that, because the accused did not take the stand he is guilty, that juror is guilty of contempt of this court. That juror is violating the laws of this State and of the Constitution of our great land; he would be trying a man not on laws, but on prejudice. The judge will charge you that the fact that I did not put the accused on the stand does not give any juror the right, either secretly or outspokenly in a jury room, to say that the accused must be guilty. You promised me you would not have any feelings against the defendant if he did not testify, and I judged to keep him off the stand. Our forefathers wrote into the Constitution that every man is presumed to be innocent and every man is entitled to a trial by jury—and no man is compelled to be a witness either for or against himself."

§ 524. Explain contradictions of defendant

Any contradictory statements made by the defendant to the police must be explained. If possible, try and show that the two statements do not really conflict. Show that each was true at the time it was said, but subsequent circumstances have made them appear contradictory.

If the contradictions cannot be explained away in this manner, then argue that any person under stress and strain would have said things he did not mean. You might argue it this way:

"The defendant was in the hands of the police and the prosecutor. The defendant told the story as best he could remember it at the time. As is always the case, some things he said were not true.

"The prosecutor read that statement in evidence, parts of which seem to be in conflict. You will find such conflicting statements in all cases. When men are being sweated without help, and are groping around blindly in the hands of bully cops, without the aid of anyone to protect their rights, you cannot expect a clear, logical narration. This defendant's rights have been violated from beginning to end!"

§ 525. Explain defendant's flight

You should always explain and minimize the effects of any attempt by the defendant to flee or escape. This may be done as follows:

"Suppose there *was* flight. Flight is no direct evidence of guilt. The man accused runs away; that is circumstantial evidence of guilt. Now, where circumstantial evidence is capable of two constructions—an innocent as well as a guilty one—the jury is bound under oath to apply only the innocent construction to that circumstantial evidence.

"Suppose the accused didn't want to get mixed up in a murder case, is that any evidence of guilt? Let us assume that this man had committed some *other* crime from which he ran away that week? Is that impossible? Does that evidence of flight show beyond a reasonable doubt that he ran away because of this particular crime that he was guilty of? Not at all. Certainly not beyond a reasonable doubt."

M. ESTABLISH DEFENSES

§ 526. Alibi

If your alibi witnesses consist of members of the defendant's family, the prosecution will understandably try to minimize their testimony. He will infer that a wife or parent will say almost anything to protect her loved one. Counter with this remark:

"Ladies and gentlemen, I can't help it if the accused was a law abiding citizen and was home in bed at three o'clock in the morning when the crime was committed. Naturally, the only person who could prove that he was there was his wife. If any one of us was charged with having committed a crime at three o'clock in the morning, who else could we produce to testify to our whereabouts at that hour but some member of our family?"

If you were able to present no alibi at all, you might say to the jury:

"Some of you may ask why we did not produce an alibi. How can we produce an alibi for what happened such a long time ago? I might have trotted in a fake alibi for this defendant. But are you going to punish him because I haven't tried to fool you or give you perjury? Are you going to hold that against me and the accused? How do I know where I was eight, nine months ago on August 6th, 1959? How can I tell? What alibi can I produce here that you wouldn't laugh at? What defense could I put in here except a denial that the accused was there."

§ 527. Temporary insanity

The following statements should serve to illustrate how to establish on summation the defense of temporary insanity.

(a) "What was the cause of what the accused did? He lost sleep, he lost courage, he lost hope, he was completely distraught. All of this load was on his shoulders. Our institutions are filled with men and women who had less cause for insanity than he did. Everyone knows the mind is at best very difficult to understand. It does one thing with one person and another thing with another. You can well imagine what happened to the mind of the accused. Do you think he is responsible or has been, ever since that terrible night?

"Is it not fair to assume that all of his troubles and burdens caused his mind to snap? Would you take a chance on your own mind under similar circumstances? I don't know about you, but most persons would have done just what the accused did, the thing for which you are being asked to send him to the electric chair."

(b) "Decent law-abiding citizens, even people with deeply religious convictions, become killers under unusual circumstances. Usually it is natural for us to show restraint in dealing with our fellow men. However, under circumstances where great emotion is involved something happens to snap this restraint, something we cannot control. A man who is normal in every way will suddenly find himself on trial for murder. Circumstances over which he has no control force him to kill, yet society in its ignorance treats such a man exactly as it treats a professional murderer, one who kills for profit."

§ 528. Self defense

Here is an example of a typical summation statement establishing the defense of self defense.

"Let me suggest to you that a person has a right to shoot and kill in the defense of his home and family—not when these vital things are in danger, but when he *thinks* they are in danger. The court will tell you that the accused has the right to decide upon appearances, and if he did, even though mistaken, he is not guilty. You are twelve persons sitting here months after the incident occurred, listening to the evidence, truthful and otherwise, to determine whether the defendant acted too hastily.

"No person need wait to see just how far an aggressor will go before he takes a life. The first instinct of a human being is to save his own life or the life of a loved one. He hasn't time to gamble. When he thinks it is time to save his life or the life of a loved one he has the right to act. Every man's home is a castle which even the government may not enter. Every man has the right to kill to defend himself, his family, his home or others.

"You must prove that the defendant premeditated, that he deliberated. You must prove the intent to kill; you've got to prove that this accused did not have the right to kill. You must prove it by evidence, not mere guesswork, not by how he seemed to act afterwards, or any other unfavorable factors that have developed against the accused. You must prove the point that the shooting was wrongful—that's the law. Where has the prosecution proven that the defendant had no right to shoot?"

N. TECHNIQUE

§ 529. In general

Just as the introduction to the summation should be brief, so too should the conclusion or recapitulation. If the argument has been meaningfully presented, it should not be necessary to rehash the points counsel has already made. At this point counsel should assert his most important premises concisely in a few sentences. Be concise and eloquent.

The jurors have been subjected to many distractions. Their untrained minds are not apt to retain an important proposition of fact or law for too long a time. To be fully effective, your salient arguments must be firmly implanted in their minds when they begin their deliberation.

O. CONTENT

§ 530. In general

Drive your important points home by repetition. The more vital the thought, the more often you should repeat it —but the repetition must be subtle. This is especially so in a long, involved case.

§ 531. Stress lack of proof of guilt beyond a reasonable doubt

Your entire summation is based upon one premise: the failure of the prosecutor to establish the guilt of the defendant beyond a reasonable doubt. Your argument has been pointed toward raising that doubt in the minds of the jurors. Therefore, your summation must finish on that note.

For example:

"And now I end as I began, by asking each of you—in view of the perplexities and difficulties which surround this case, and in view of the many contrary things and opinions presented to you—if you can, with satisfied judgment and safe conscience, say that this man is guilty? If your duty compels you to destroy this man, you must do it. But you *must not,* unless all the facts and weight of the case drive you irresistibly to the conclusion that the defendant is guilty; that you are convinced of his guilt to a moral certainty beyond a reasonable doubt."

§ 532. Stress the injustice of convicting the defendant on testimony of a scoundrel.

You have previously indicated to the jury that an accomplice's testimony must be corroborated. You have also attacked his credibility upon the ground that he is untrustworthy and trying to save his own skin at the expense of the accused. Now, in your concluding remarks you must stress the injustice of a conviction based upon the testimony of an unworthy character.

Here is an example:

"Could any of you in your consciences and minds convict a human being on the testimony and character of this kind of witness, with his record, his performance on the stand? I would not want it on my conscience, when I went home after this court proceeding was over and lay down on my pillow to sleep at night, that I convicted another person on the testimony of such a scoundrel. Could I look my children squarely in the eye and say to them, 'I have deprived a man of his liberty on decent, reliable, trustworthy evidence; on the evidence of a man that I trust'? No, I could not.

"Could you, with all due conscience, say to yourselves that you are prepared to take the liberty and reputation of the accused on such testimony? Would you award a civil judgment, take money out of a man's pocket, on the testimony of a character like this, regardless of what his story is? This scoundrel would lie for anything; he would lie to save his life; he would lie to save his liberty. Isn't that sufficient to create a reasonable doubt in any juror's mind?"

§ 533. Explain defendant's disadvantage if prosecutor speaks last

Where the prosecutor speaks last you are at a great disadvantage. He may raise points capable of being rebutted, but you must remain silent. Explain this disadvantage to the jurors. Point out that you cannot answer all of the arguments he will make. You can only guess at the arguments he will present, and attempt to answer them before he speaks. Then, ask them to give careful consideration to any unanswered argument he may advance. Tell the jury you are relying upon them to analyze his arguments and conclusions to see that they are consistent with the evidence. Tell them that you are sure they will reject those that are inconsistent.

Here is a way of explaining your disadvantages to the jury:

"Under the laws of our State, the prosecutor has the last word. When my voice is silenced, the prosecutor will speak. I know his great ability; I know the appeal he will make to this jury; I know the suspicious circumstances that will be woven into the appeal by a very skillful tongue and a very skillful brain.

"I must sit still and listen to it without any chance to reply. I can only ask you to weigh with care every word that is spoken. I will ask you to answer when I cannot speak, and to search out the facts and circumstances which justify an answer. I can only ask you to remember that you are to explain every fact and circumstance in this case consistent with this man's innocence."

§ 534. Apologize for your own shortcomings or overzealousness

During the course of a heated trial, you may have said or done something that offended one or more of the jurors. Your personal mannerisms might have unconsciously been offensive to a particular juror. Whatever the cause, you must do your best to smooth any ruffled feelings.

There is also the possibility that, despite careful preparation, you may have overlooked an important piece of evidence in your summation. Your peroration should admit this possibility and ask the jurors to treat it the same as the evidence you stressed.

You might address the jury in the following way:

"If I seemed to exceed the proper limits, I implore you to forgive me. For after all, I have had great anxiety for the accused. Ladies and gentlemen, his liberty is at stake. The witnesses for the prosecution have far less to lose at my hands than the accused at your hands. This burden that has been lying heavily on my shoulders will pass very soon to you. I must leave nothing to chance. If there is anything that I omit to say, and I am sure there will be plenty, I beg you not to pass it over. Think of those arguments and thoughts which have come up in the trial and which occur to you; give them the same weight, even more weight, than if they had been presented by this humble lawyer for the accused. You have heard the evidence. I am sure that in your discussions your memory will be refreshed as to the important and significant parts of the testimony that I failed to refer to."

§ 535. Re-emphasize great duty and responsibility of jurors

The following is presented as a means of re-emphasizing the heavy burden of duty and responsibility on the jury, collectively and individually.

"This case is now drawing to a close. We have had some hard tasks to perform. Your task, though, is the hardest of all. I have done everything I can to help you in that task. I have tried to deal fairly and fully with every relevant point. I have presented the case for the defendant with all of the energy at my command.

"Now the responsibility passes to you alone and to you individually, and no heavier burden could be placed on human shoulders. The liberty of a man is in your charge. Find your verdict on the evidence and the facts; find it without regard to suspicions or fears. Keep out emotion and prejudice of any kind. Act so that in years to come when you look back upon this trial, you can see a spirit of justice and think that what you did in this case was done honestly and sincerely. You can have peace of mind in the conclusion that you have rendered justice by finding a reasonable doubt and acquitting the defendant."

"For the sake of your consciences, I ask and plead with you again that you give this case your most serious consideration. This case is of great interest to you today. Tomorrow it may be of little interest, and in a couple of months it may be forgotten. The prosecutor may forget about this case; likewise the Judge, and maybe even I. But if by any stretch of the imagination you decide this case against this accused, he must live with your decision for the rest of his life."

§ 536. Implore each juror to think individually

Impress upon each juror the importance of his thinking as an individual even though he may be outnumbered:

"We picked you twelve men and women to be our judges.

We asked a number of the prospective jurors not to sit. We wanted to have you. You are people of different ages, backgrounds, nationalities, occupations, and professions. It is the combined experience of all of you that will be brought to bear on the issues involved in this serious case. But each of you has his own duty to the accused. Each of you, separately and individually, must be satisfied to the point of moral certainty before you conclude and concur in his conviction. Each of you, separately and individually, is bound in conscience to give him the benefit of any honest doubt you feel. If there is a strong-minded juror among you, he has no right to put pressure upon others with the intent of compelling them to agree with him. To be a party to any compromise would be to do violence to the solemn oath you took when you were chosen to be the judges of the facts in this case. No one likes disagreement, but it is your sworn duty to disagree with your fellow jurors if you, as an individual, cannot share that feeling of moral certainty, that feeling of total satisfaction that you must have before you can be a party to the conviction of this man who is accused of this crime."

§ 537. Describe prospective fate of defendant if convicted

Although most jurisdictions do not permit you to discuss punishment, you can reinforce the jurors' feeling of responsibility by describing the consequences of a conviction.

The following statement should meet these requirements: "If you are satisfied of the accused's guilt to a moral certainty and beyond a reasonable doubt, it would be improper of you to acquit him simply because you might feel that he is likely to go to jail for a considerable period of years. But in considering the care with which you should appraise the evidence, bear in mind what the consequences of a mistaken verdict of guilty might be: long years in the grim, bare solitude of a prison cell. What a terrible fate for a man not guilty of the crime charged. What bitter thoughts would torture his mind and the minds of his friends and relatives as he considers the irreparable wrong you would then have done him."

CHAPTER SEVENTEEN

INFLAMMATORY AND PREJUDICIAL REMARKS OF THE PROSECUTOR

C. CALLING ATTENTION TO DEFENDANT'S FAILURE TO TESTIFY

A. INTRODUCTION

§ 538. In general

It has been said that "the role of the prosecuting attorney is a difficult one in many respects, and his argument to the jury is a particularly difficult problem in discrimination. He must pursue his duty as a diligent prosecutor without transgressing his responsibility as an officer of the state, and, above all, he must refrain from unduly oppressing or burdening the accused with the vast resources or dominating position of the state government. In particular, he must at all times bear in mind that defendant is innocent until proved guilty, and, while it is his duty to forcefully present all material facts from which the judge or jury may conclude that defendant is guilty, he must, nevertheless, refrain from pre-condemning the accused on the authority of the government he represents."[1]

1. State v Gulbrandsen, 238 Minn 508, 57 NW2d 419.

§ 539. Do not open the door for prejudicial remarks

Prosecutors will often attempt to justify prejudicial remarks on the ground that you opened the door for them during your defense summation. Avoid such a possible argument by basing all of your remarks on summation upon the evidence in the case and upon the inferences which can fairly be drawn therefrom. Based upon the suggestions set forth in the preceding chapters, you should be able to deliver an effective summation without going outside the record.

§ 540. Have summations recorded

Have the prosecutor's summation recorded. Even where counsel may have failed to object, a remark may be deemed so highly prejudicial as to deny the defendant a fair trial. In such cases, appellate courts have reversed convictions even in the absence of objections and exceptions. However, if the summation is not recorded, these errors and grounds for reversal are lost.

§ 541. Objections by defense counsel

Be sure to register your objection to any prejudicial or inflammatory remark made by the prosecutor in his closing argument. If you fail to object, you will be precluded from raising that point as error on appeal.

Object to the prosecutor's prejudicial remarks immediately. First, apologize for the interruption. Then, state your objection, using the exact language of the prosecutor, and the grounds upon which you deem the remarks objectionable.

If the Judge objects to your interruption of the prosecutor's argument or appears annoyed at your objections, simply ask the Judge for permission to reserve your objections and exceptions to the prosecutor's remarks until the conclusion of prosecutor's summation. Then, make notation of all his prejudicial remarks. When he concludes his address, proceed to state your objections and exceptions in the same form as above.

Where the remarks appear to be clearly inflammatory, do not hesitate to interrupt.

If the prosecutor's remarks contain overt or subtle appeals to passion or prejudice, you will not want your objection and exception to highlight them. It will often be sufficient to merely note a general objection in as simple a manner as possible. If the objection is sustained, you will not have called any great amount of attention to the prosecutor's remark. If, for any reason, such a simple objection will not or does not suffice, request a conference at the bench. State your objection out of the hearing of the jury, but make certain that it is recorded.

B. WHAT CONSTITUTES PREJUDICIAL OR INFLAMMATORY REMARKS

§ 542. Comments upon duties and responsibilities of jury; references to public opinion

Unless calculated to inflame the minds of the jurors, a prosecuting attorney's appeal to the jury's civic responsibilities as law-abiding citizens is not misconduct, and he may make remarks illustrating the evil consequences which might result from their failure to perform their duty.[2]

Unless calculated to inflame the minds of the jurors, a prosecuting attorney's appeal to their civic responsibilities

2. Henwood v People, 57 Colo 544, 143 P 373; State v Pointer, 106 Or 589, 213 P 621.

Argument of counsel that if men like the accused could go out and wreck homes and shoot men in the back, and shoot into a crowd, and then be turned loose, there would be no safety in the community for law-abiding citizens, and there would be no necessity for courts and juries unless examples were made of cold-blooded murder, was justified in a prosecution for homicide where the accused was charged with the murder of an innocent bystander while attempting to kill another. Henwood v People, 57 Colo 544, 143 P 373.

Warning the jury of the necessity of doing its duty to keep the country from running red with blood does not transgress the bounds of legitimate argument or go beyond the scope of reasonable comment. House v State, 94 Miss 107, 48 So 3.

as law-abiding citizens is not misconduct.[3] But while a prosecuting attorney may warn the jury to perform their duty, he may not indulge in argument calculated to arouse in them fears of public disapproval, or of being recreant in their duty, and which on that account tends to coerce them into a verdict of conviction.[4]

It is improper, in the argument of state's counsel in a criminal prosecution, to urge a conviction on the ground of public opinion, because the people desire it or want the defendant "put away," or expect a conviction.[5] References to the probability that an acquittal of the defendant will encourage mob violence are universally condemned.[6]

Coercion of the jury by admonitions against compromising upon a verdict carrying a lesser penalty than that incident to the offense or degree of offense of which the

3. Henderson v United States (CA6 Tenn) 218 F2d 14, 50 ALR2d 754, cert den 349 US 920, 99 L Ed 1253, 75 S Ct 660, reh den 349 US 969, 99 L Ed 1290, 75 S Ct 879.

4. People v Fleming, 166 Cal 357, 136 P 291; State v Blackman, 108 La 121, 32 So 334; State v Miller, 263 Mo 326, 172 SW 385; State v Pointer, 106 Or 589, 213 P 621; Weatherford v State, 31 Tex Crim 530, 21 SW 251.

A charge by a prosecuting attorney that the defendant was so conscious of guilt that he had stacked the jury in order to defeat justice is improper, since jurors disposed to be lenient might surrender their conviction of right under an apprehension of being the juror denounced by the prosecuting attorney. Weatherford v State, supra.

To state that a verdict other than that sought by the prosecuting attorney will subject the jury to scorn or contempt is improper. Goff v Commonwealth, 241 Ky 428, 44 SW2d 306; State v Blackman, 108 La 121, 32 So 334; People v Fielding, 158 NY 542, 53 NE 497.

5. Pennington v State, 171 Tex Crim 130, 345 SW2d 527, 85 ALR2d 1130.

Annotation: Prejudicial effect of prosecuting attorney's argument to jury that people of city, county, or community want or expect a conviction. 85 ALR2d 1132.

6. Hemphill v State, 72 Tex Crim 638, 165 SW 462; Smith v State, 44 Tex Crim 137, 68 SW 995.

Statements by the prosecuting attorney in a rape case that unless the jury assessed the death penalty the people would take the law into their own hands in the future; that "if you turn the defendant loose, you cannot blame the people for taking the law into their own hands;" and that "it would be much worse than convicting an innocent man to turn this defendant loose and then in a week or two for him to rape one of your wives, sisters, or daughters" are improper. Hemphill v State, 72 Tex Crim 638, 165 SW 462.

defendant is shown to have been guilty is not proper, although only in a very few cases have the courts held that argument of this nature is sufficient ground for disturbing the conviction, especially where the jury has been cautioned against being influenced by such language.[7]

§ 543. Appeal to juror's interest as taxpayer

In various prosecutions where the offense charged was directly detrimental to the public interest, such as a breach of duty by a public officer, argument for the prosecution dwelling on this fact, and telling the jurors that the offense was directed against their immediate interest as taxpayers, has, in several cases, been held to be so improper as to constitute prejudicial error requiring a reversal of the conviction.[8] Argument for the prosecution referring to the expense of carrying on the case against the defendant, or the expense of law enforcement generally, has been held so prejudicial as to require reversal.[9] However, while such argument is admittedly improper, it constitutes reversible error only where, under all the circumstances, it appears to have generated prejudice actually affecting the verdict, and where the court is convinced from all the evidence

7. State v Thorne, 41 Utah 414, 126 P 286.

In People v Rogan, 1 Cal 2d 615, 36 P2d 631, 95 ALR 560, the prosecutor's argument to the jurors not to surrender their convictions by way of compromise and agree to a lesser penalty than death, in connection with which he referred to the parole system as offering an easy way to escape adequate punishment, and said that the average man served but a few years of a life sentence, was held not to have prejudiced the defendant, whose conviction of murder in the first degree was without recommendation (and who was also at the same trial found guilty of robbery in the first degree), and the trial judge having admonished the jury to disregard all improper allusions of counsel.

8. United States v Lotsch (CA2 NY) 102 F2d 35, cert den 307 US 622, 83 L Ed 1500, 59 S Ct 793; Taylor v State, 123 Fla 358, 166 So 825; People v Fielding, 158 NY 542, 53 NE 497.

Annotation: Counsels appeal in criminal case to self-interest of jurors as taxpayers, as grounds for mistrial, new trial, or reversal. 33 ALR2d 459.

9. Baker v Commonwealth, 184 Ky 207, 211 SW 566; State v Gulbrandsen, 238 Minn 508, 57 NW2d 419; State v Muskus, 158 Ohio St 276, 49 Ohio Ops 122, 109 NE2d 15, 33 ALR2d 452.

that the conviction was proper, or it appears that the trial judge took effective action to remove any improper consequence of the argument, it has been held not to amount to reversible error.

It is apparent from the cases that appeals to the jurors' interest as taxpayers which would otherwise be regarded as highly improper may be condoned where they have been provoked by improper conduct of the defense.[10]

Where the defendant's counsel made repeated attempts to object to improper argument of the prosecuting attorney, stating that the defendant's crime was against the poor taxpayers of the vicinity, and in trying to stop the argument, repeatedly took exception to the trial court's allowing it to continue, it was held that after having been told by the court that he was out of order, he was not obliged to run the risk of punishment for contempt by continuing to object as the improper argument continued, the appellate court saying that it would even allow an exception on appeal where counsel were prevented from excepting at the trial, and furthermore that the objections taken were to the general course pursued by the district attorney, and, when the trial judge had sanctioned this, no further objection or exception was necessary, and that in any event the trial court should have sternly interrupted the improper argument on its own motion.[11]

§ 544. Commenting on failure to produce witnesses

It is generally held not improper for the prosecutor to comment upon the failure of the defendant to produce witnesses on his behalf, if (1) the witnesses are more accessible to the accused than to the prosecution, and (2) they are or should be cognizant of material facts which

10. Gilbert v State, 19 Ala App 104, 95 So 502; People v Wynekoop, 359 Ill 124, 194 NE 276, cert den 295 US 758, 79 L Ed 1700, 55 S Ct 915; Sparkman v State, 128 Tex Crim 627, 82 SW2d 972.

11. People v Fielding, 158 NY 542, 53 NE 497.

would aid the defendant or substantiate his story.[12] The absence of either of the above two elements renders the prosecutor's comment improper.[13]

There are exceptions to the above rule. The prosecutor cannot under any circumstances make adverse comment upon the failure of a wife to testify for her husband where she is made incompetent to testify by statute[14] or, if competent to testify, where the privilege of testifying is hers alone[15] or depends upon the consent of both the husband and wife.[16]

Character witnesses constitute another exception. Where the defendant has not put his character in issue, it is improper for the prosecutor to comment upon the failure of the accused to produce character witnesses. "A defendant's character is presumed to be good until the contrary is proven, and no evidence to impeach character is admissible against the accused until he has opened the door for such evidence by adducing proof of good character. It follows that the state's attorney has no right to offer such proof, or to argue that the lack of such proof tends, under the facts of the case, to overcome the presumption of good character."[17] This rule has been extended to preclude the prosecutor's commenting upon the failure of the defendant to attempt to impeach the character of the complaining witness.[18]

12. State v Shackelford, 228 SC 9, 88 SE2d 778.

But see Lowery v State, 21 Ala App 352, 108 So 351, holding that any comment on the failure to produce witnesses violates due process of law.

Annotation: Comment or argument by court or counsel that prosecution evidence is uncontradicted as amounting to improper reference to accused's failure to testify. 14 ALR3d 723.

13. People v Rubin, 366 Ill 195, 7 NE2d 890; People v De Paulo, 235 NY 39, 138 NE 498; Cole v State, 92 Tex Crim 368, 243 SW 1100.

14. Graves v United States, 150 US 118, 37 L Ed 1021, 14 S Ct 40.

15. Zumwalt v State, 16 Ariz 82, 141 P 710.

16. Johnson v State, 63 Miss 313.

17. People v Haas, 293 Ill 274, 127 NE 740.

18. Pointer v State, 37 Ala App 670, 74 So 2d 615.

§ 545. Accusing defense of suppressing or distorting facts

Generally speaking, a remark by the prosecutor that defense counsel was attempting to or had suppressed facts is prejudicial and grounds for a new trial if the trial judge does not instruct the jury to disregard it.

Accordingly, the following remarks have been held to constitute reversible error: a comment by the prosecutor that he would have been able to prove much more on the defendant if the defendant's attorney had not objected so often;[19] the prosecutor's remark, "Where is the gun, why isn't it here? They suppressed it. They had the shotgun and did not bring it here. Why did they leave it out?";[20] repeated insinuations during the course of the trial that the defendant had made a prejudicial statement, followed by a comment during summation that defendant's counsel had hidden facts;[21] a charge that a witness who testified falsely was coached by defense counsel.[22]

§ 546. References to facts outside record

References by the prosecutor to facts not in evidence have been deemed error sufficient to call for a new trial. Thus, it has been held as reversible error to allow the prosecutor to refer to incriminating statements made to him by the accused, which are not in evidence;[23] to allow the prosecutor to remark that the defendant came to him and offered to plead guilty to a lesser offense;[24] to permit the prosecutor to say that a witness had testified to certain

19. Stallings v State, 129 Tex Crim 300, 87 SW2d 255.

See also, People v Munday, 280 Ill 32, 117 NE 286.

And see Fletcher v Commonwealth, 250 Ky 597, 63 SW2d 780.

20. Smith v State, 25 Ala App 183, 142 So 779.

21. People v Teiper, 186 App Div 830, 175 NYS 197, mod on reh on other grounds 188 App Div 949, 178 NYS 54.

22. Garrett v State, 74 Okla Crim 78, 123 P2d 283.

23. State v Cyty, 50 Nev 256, 256 P 793, 52 ALR 1015.

24. Lynch v State, 81 Tex Crim 64, 193 SW 667.

facts before a coroner's jury, but this testimony was omitted from the minutes through a stenographic error;[25] to allow the prosecutor to assert that a witness had recognized the defendant in a lineup and, although he failed to identify him at the time, there were good reasons for his failure; and then to allow him to add, "I will be more than happy to tell you why after this trial is over";[26] to allow the prosecutor, in response to a question from a juror, to say: "I could from the penal code give you at least a half dozen particular other crimes I know [the defendant] has committed that he is not charged with here. We did not charge it. I would have to stop *some* place or we would be talking here all day."[27]

§ 547. Raising new matter

Generally, the courts which have treated the propriety of a prosecutor's raising new matter or new points during closing summation have held such argument to be improper.[28]

25. People v McMahon, 244 Ill 45, 91 NE 104.

26. People v Jackson, 7 NY2d 142, 196 NYS2d 79, 164 NE2d 381.

27. People v Chessman, 38 Cal 2d 166, 238 P2d 1001, cert den 343 US 915, 96 L Ed 1330, 72 S Ct 650, reh den 343 US 937, 96 L Ed 1344, 72 S Ct 773 (judgment was not reversed because the defendant, appearing pro se, did not object).

28. In Moore v United States, 120 App DC 173, 344 F2d 558, the court remarked that the argument should have been made during the prosecutor's main argument, and explained that as a general rule, the prosecutor should not be allowed to develop new arguments on rebuttal, but should be restricted to answering the arguments put forth by defense counsel.

In People v Bundy, 295 Ill 322, 129 NE 189, the court said that the prosecutor, in his closing argument, is entitled only to reply to the arguments of the defendant and cannot introduce any new line of argument.

In State v Honig, 78 Mo 249, the court noted its disapproval of a prosecutor's technique in refusing to make an opening summary argument and "reserving his fire" for his closing argument.

In State v Hale (Mo) 371 SW2d 249, the court stated that in the trial of criminal cases, it is improper and unfair for the state's counsel, in final argument, to refer to points upon which the state relies which were not mentioned in opening argument, for the reason that the defense is thereby deprived of the opportunity to answer such new points.

In State v Peterson (Mo) 423 SW2d 825, 26 ALR3d 1400, the court stated, as a rule applicable to the trial of

However, objections to closing summations based on the alleged argument of new matter are sustained or denied in the discretion of the trial judge, and his ruling may ordinarily constitute reversible error only upon a finding of abuse of discretion.[29]

In determining whether trial judges' rulings in particular cases have constituted an abuse of discretion, the courts

criminal as well as civil cases, that counsel having the affirmative will be held to the requirement of fairly stating his essential points in the opening argument, at least to the extent that the defendant may fairly answer them, and that a failure to require this will ordinarily constitute error, if the point has been properly raised at the time and preserved, pointing out that in criminal cases it is not required that a warning be given in advance to the prosecutor that his concluding argument will be so limited.

In Johnson v State, 192 Wis 22, 211 NW 668, the court upheld the trial judge's finding that the prosecutor's final argument constituted a proper reply to defense counsel's argument in this case, but took "this occasion, however, to suggest to district attorneys and trial courts" that the closing address of the state should be limited strictly to a reply and should not be the "argument in chief", since the defendant is entitled to be able to meet the arguments of the state and "to analyze jury." The court explained that when a defendant claims he is not guilty, any argument tending to show his guilt may be said to be in reply, but that it was not in this sense that the contents of reply arguments should be construed, and that the state should not be permitted to "argue in chief" by way of reply.

Finally, compare King v State, 127 Tex Crim 120, 74 SW2d 1029, where the court did not seem to flatly reject the rule prohibiting the argument of new matter, but nevertheless stated that "we have never held any such rule applicable in criminal cases, and could not lay down or make a general rule that would fit all cases." However, the court's decision seemed to rest on the particular facts of this case, and it appears to be arguable whether the court's statement should be taken as an implication that the argument of new matter would be allowed in all instances.

Annotation: Propriety and prejudicial effect of prosecuting attorney's arguing new matter or points in his closing summation in criminal case. 26 ALR3d 1409.

29. Moore v United States, 120 App DC 173, 344 F2d 558; State v Shannon (Mo) 413 SW2d 198.

In State v Hale (Mo) 371 SW2d 249, it was said that where a prosecuting attorney argues new matter or points in his closing summation in a criminal case, whether the judgment should be reversed depends upon whether the trial judge, who has a large measure of discretion in such circumstances, abused his discretion, in the totality of the attendant circumstances.

In State v Peterson (Mo) 423 SW2d 825, 26 ALR3d 1400, the court stated that "the usual discretion" permitted to trial courts in ruling upon arguments was not broad enough to encompass and nullify the error.

have looked to such matters as the severity of the punishment assessed by the jury,[30] the presence or absence of a request by defendant for surrebuttal,[31] and the presence or absence of an assignment of error, in a motion for a new trial, calling the attention of the trial judge to the alleged impropriety.[32]

The failure of defense counsel to ask leave to argue in surrebuttal has been regarded as one indication that no real prejudice was suffered by defendant in the prosecutor's argument of alleged new matter.[33]

§ 548. Displaying of objects or items not introduced in evidence

Certain well-settled rules underlie an appellate court's consideration of error predicated upon misconduct of a prosecuting attorney's displaying to a jury objects or items not introduced in evidence and its determination of whether such misconduct was prejudicial so as to require a reversal or a new trial.

First, it is well established that in order to predicate error upon such misconduct, the accused must ordinarily make timely objection in the trial court at the time the misconduct occurs.[34]

30. State v Hale (Mo) 371 SW2d 249; State v Peterson (Mo) 423 SW2d 825, 26 ALR3d 1400.

31. State v Hale (Mo) 371 SW2d 249.

32. State v Shannon (Mo) 413 SW2d 198.

33. State v Hale (Mo) 371 SW2d 249.

34. Garcia v State, 26 Ariz 597, 229 P 103; People v Agnew, 16 Cal 2d 655, 107 P2d 601; People v Cox, 76 Cal 281, 18 P 232; People v Moore, 81 Cal App 2d 799, 185 P2d 32; People v Kelly, 69 Cal App 558, 231 P 767; Kelley v State, 210 Ind 8, 200 NE 634; Wichita v Hibbs, 158 Kan 185, 146 P2d 397; Thompson v State, 220 Miss 200, 70 So 2d 341; State v Schroetter, 317 Mo 408, 297 SW 368; State v Wilson (Mo) 237 SW 776; State v Garton, 3 NJ Misc 681, 129 A 480, revd on other grounds 102 NJL 318, 133 A 403; State v Hardamon, 29 Wash 2d 182, 186 P2d 634; State v Sibert, 113 W Va 717, 169 SE 410.

Annotation: Prejudicial effect of prosecuting attorney's misconduct in physically exhibiting to jury objects or items not introduced as evidence. 46 ALR2d 1423.

Secondly, unless the harmful effect of such misconduct cannot be eradicated by appropriate instructions of the trial court, error cannot be predicated thereon in the appellate court in the absence of a request to the trial court to instruct the jury to disregard it.[35]

Thirdly, in order to predicate error upon such misconduct, the accused must see to it that the record shows the occurrence of the misconduct.[36]

And finally the determination of whether or not misconduct of the prosecuting attorney warrants a new trial rests almost entirely within the discretion of the trial judge, and in the absence of an abuse of that discretion the appellate courts will not reverse his decision.[37]

§ 549. Discussing the punishment and possibility of clemency

Where punishment is imposed by the court and not by the jury, the duration of the imprisonment for the crime in question is not a proper subject of comment by counsel.[38]

Where, in a criminal prosecution, the law imposes upon the jury the duty of determining the penalty, it is entirely proper for counsel to discuss the question of punishment,[39] although an appeal to the jury for the death penalty, in a prosecution for homicide, as saving the expense of maintaining the defendant in a penal institution is improper and constitutes reversible error.[40] Where the accused is tried under a statute permitting the jury in its discretion

35. People v Kelly, 69 Cal App 558, 231 P 767; Thompson v State, 220 Miss 200, 70 So 2d 341; Brandon v State, 146 Tex Crim 480, 176 SW2d 323.

36. People v Agnew, 16 Cal 2d 655, 107 P2d 601; Blancett v Commonwealth, 281 Ky 686, 136 SW2d 1069.

37. People v Kelly, 69 Cal App 558, 231 P 767; Wichita v Hibbs, 158 Kan 185, 146 P2d 397; State v Posey, 347 Mo 1088, 152 SW2d 34; State v Harold, 45 Wash 2d 505, 275 P2d 895; State v Cohen, 72 Wash 109, 129 P 891.

38. State v Tetrault, 78 NH 14, 95 A 669.

39. Commonwealth v Brown, 309 Pa 515, 164 A 726, 86 ALR 892 (murder in the first degree).

40. People v Watson, 216 NY 565, 111 NE 243.

to recommend the defendant to mercy and thereby reduce his punishment, it is the right of counsel for the defendant to argue such a recommendation to the jury.[41]

It is the right and duty of counsel for the defendant in appealing for life imprisonment instead of the death penalty to discuss the defendant's age, his upbringing and environment, and all other matters appearing from the evidence which may assist the jury in choosing the appropriate penalty.[42] On the other hand, counsel for the state have the same right to argue that the recommendation should be withheld.[43]

§ 550. Mention of possibility of release from mental institution

It sometimes happens that a prosecutor will argue that a defendant acquitted on the ground of insanity will be discharged from the institution to which he would be committed and would be turned loose on the streets. This argument may or may not be held prejudicial, depending upon the circumstances.[44]

The following cases represent situations where a prosecuting attorney's argument or comment that the accused, if acquitted on the ground of insanity, would be discharged from the institution to which he would be committed held to be prejudicial.[45]

41. Commonwealth v Brown, 309 Pa 515, 164 A 726, 86 ALR 892.

42. Commonwealth v Brown, supra.

43. Allen v State, 187 Ga 178, 200 SE 109, 120 ALR 495; Howell v State, 102 Ohio St 411, 131 NE 706, 17 ALR 1108.

44. **Annotation:** Prejudicial effect of argument or comment that accused, if acquitted on ground of insanity, would be released from institution to which committed. 44 ALR2d 978.

45. Boyle v State, 229 Ala 212, 154 So 575.

In Williams v State (Fla) 68 So 2d 583, a murder prosecution in which the accused had entered pleas of not guilty and not guilty by reason of insanity, the prosecuting attorney in his closing argument made a statement to the effect that if the jury should find the accused not guilty by reason of insanity he would be sent to the insane asylum and soon after being confined there would be released to commit another homicide.

In State v Johnson (Mo) 267 SW2d

The following cases represent situations where a prosecuting attorney's argument or comment that the accused if acquitted, on the ground of insanity, would be discharged from the institution to which he would be committed was held not to be prejudicial.[46] Notice that in some of these cases, the trial court took prompt action to eradicate the effect of such argument.[47] And in other cases, it was deemed that the improper argument could not have affected the result of the trial.[48] Thus, although characterizing the argument as exceeding the bounds of proper commentary and not to be approved, the court stated that the error was not sufficient to work a reversal or to justify a reduction of the punishment assessed, because the evidence of the appellant's guilt was overwhelming and the evidence, both lay and expert, was practically undisputed that the appellant was not insane at the time of the commission of the crime or so intoxicated as not to be able to form an intent to commit the crime.[49] Broadly speaking, the courts

642, 44 ALR2d 973, cert den 351 US 957, 100 L Ed 1479, 76 S Ct 858, cert den 357 US 922, 2 L Ed 2d 1366, 78 S Ct 1364, a prosecution for rape, the accused, who had been adjudged insane and committed to an institution in another state, pleaded insanity, and there was substantial evidence that he was presently insane. His counsel, urging the jury to bring in a verdict of not guilty by reason of insanity, pointed out that such a verdict meant that the court would immediately commit the accused to the state hospital for the insane, where he would be confined. In rebuttal, the prosecuting attorney pointed out that the accused had been committed in another state, after which he had come to Missouri and raped three girls, and culminated his argument with the statement that sending the accused to another hospital would do no good and that he would be out in two months.

46. Bachelor v State, 216 Ala 356, 113 So 67; Anderson v State, 209 Ala 36, 95 So 171; Russell v State, 201 Ala 572, 78 So 916; State v Evans, 345 Mo 398, 133 SW2d 389; Mott v State, 94 Okla Crim 145, 232 P2d 166; State v McDonald, 184 SC 290, 192 SE 365.

47. Bachelor v State, 216 Ala 356, 113 So 67; Anderson v State, 209 Ala 36, 95 So 171; State v Evans, 345 Mo 398, 133 SW2d 389.

48. State v McDonald, 184 SC 290, 192 SE 365.

49. Mott v State, 94 Okla Crim 145, 232 P2d 166, wherein the appellant, who had pleaded insanity produced by intoxication but who was convicted of murder and sentenced to death, contended that he had been prejudiced by the prosecuting attorney's closing argument to the jury urging the imposition of the death penalty, which included a statement that "something ought to be done with this defendant.

generally deem a prosecuting attorney's argument that an accused, if acquitted on the ground of insanity, might be released from the institution to which he is committed is outside the bounds of legitimate argument but may be rendered harmless by prompt curative action by the trial court.[50]

§ 551. Mention of possibility of pardon, parole, commutation, or other shortening of sentence

Some courts have held that prejudicial error arose where the prosecutor's argument or comment brought to the attention of the jury the possibility that life imprisonment of the defendant might be affected by parole, probation, pardon, or commutation, where the reference was calculated, and probably operated, to cause the jury to inflict the penalty of death as the alternative to that of life imprisonment, in order to assure adequacy of punishment.[51] Other courts however, even though regarding the remarks as improper, have held that under the circumstances no prejudicial error requiring that a death sentence be set aside resulted from argument or comment on the possibility of parole or pardon, especially where the trial court admonished the jury to disregard such argument.[52]

The only thing they have attempted to do is to keep him out of the electric chair. They say he needs treatment. You find him [not] guilty by reason of insanity, say he is dangerous at large, he would be sent to Dr. Adams at Vinita. Dr. Adams would look at him, say 'Get out. You are sane.' That's what will happen. These same men that are helping him today would be there with habeas corpus."

50. State v Johnson (Mo) 267 SW2d 642, 44 ALR2d 973, cert den 351 US 957, 100 L Ed 1479, 76 S Ct 858, cert den 357 US 922, 2 L Ed 2d 1366, 78 S Ct 1364.

51. People v Morse, 60 Cal 2d 631, 36 Cal Rptr 201, 388 P2d 33, 12 ALR3d 810; Commonwealth v Algce, 420 Pa 198, 216 A2d 50, 16 ALR3d 1126.

Annotation: Prejudicial effect of statement of prosecutor as to possibility of pardon or parole. 16 ALR3d 1137.

52. James v State, 246 Ala 617, 21 So 2d 847; State v Coey, 82 Ariz 133, 309 P2d 260.

McNeil v State, 102 Ala 121, 15 So 352, wherein the court held nonprejudicial the prosecutor's argument to the jury that they ought not to impose life imprisonment because of the possibility of a pardon being granted through the influence of the defendant's friends, whereas by imposing

Even in cases not involving a possibility of capital punishment, argument or comment raising the issue of pardon or parole has sometimes been held to result in prejudicial error, where it appeared that the argument might have influenced the jury finding as to guilt or as to the amount of punishment to be imposed, and no effective corrective action was taken at the trial.[53] But other courts, even while disapproving of the argument, in cases involving noncapi-

the death penalty they would run no such risk. It was pointed out that no fact was stated by the prosecutor, but only his opinion or anticipation as to what might result from inflicting a penalty other than that of death. . . ."

Pilley v State, 247 Ala 523, 25 So 2d 57, wherein the court held that it was improper for the prosecutor to argue to the jury that if it should go out and give the defendant "a Christmas present of life imprisonment . . . you have told every young 24-year-old man that he can go out and rob and take a person's life with immunity and all he has got to do is to go down to the penitentiary and possibly get a parole . . . and get back out again," although it was thought not to require reversal of a conviction of first degree murder with the death penalty where the trial court strongly instructed the jury that they should decide the case on the evidence presented to them and not be concerned with any future action which might be taken by the authorities.

Peterson v State, 231 Ala 625, 166 So 20, wherein remarks of the prosecutor in his opening statement to the jury that no man had ever served out a life sentence in the penitentiary, that if they sentenced the defendant to the penitentiary "a mushy parole board would let him out in a little while," that it had been his experience "that murderers did not stay there long," and that while there convicts were made comfortable and their existence rendered easy if not luxurious, were highly improper and should not have been made, but were not reversible error where the trial court sustained the defendant's immediate objection and instructed the jury not to consider them in making up a verdict.

Sullivan v State, 47 Ariz 224, 55 P2d 312, wherein reversal was not required because the prosecutor in requesting the jury to fix the penalty at death rather than life imprisonment stated that the average life prisoner only serves 8 years, and that if the defendant received a life sentence he would probably be paroled in 8 years and thrown on society to kill again. The court said that the reference was to a fact so well known among all intelligent citizens that it would almost seem that judicial notice might be taken that the average sentence to life imprisonment is terminated in a few years by parole or pardon.

53. People v Lynn, 387 Ill 549, 56 NE2d 808, where the prosecutor stated that the pardon authority would "undoubtedly" give consideration to certain factors and reduce the accused's sentence.

Hudson v Commonwealth, 161 Ky 257, 170 SW 620, wherein the court held that in a prosecution for seduction, reference by the prosecutor, in the presence of the jury, to an application for a pardon "gotten up" by

tal offenses have found that no prejudicial error resulted from argument or comment by the prosecutor as to the possibility that defendant, if convicted, might be pardoned or paroled.[54]

§ 552. Statement that jury's error can be corrected by court or other authority

Where the prosecutor in a criminal case made a statement to or in the presence of the jury to the effect that if the jurors make a mistake in returning a verdict or finding of fact against the accused, it can be corrected by another authority, and the record was not inconsistent with the conclusion that the jurors, in all reasonable probability, thought that such mistake could be so corrected and made a finding against the defendant, it was held that the statement by the prosecutor constituted prejudicial error requiring a reversal or setting aside of the verdict or finding on the ground that the statement tended to influence the jury to act without exercising reasonable caution and deliberation and to shift the responsibility for a wrong determination of the facts, and the correction thereof, to some other tribunal.[55]

the county judge, was improper, and was, with other errors, ground for reversal.

Adams v Commonwealth (Ky) 263 SW2d 103, wherein there was error which, with others, produced a cumulative prejudicial effect calculated to improperly influence the jury, where the prosecutor in his closing argument said: "Give him twenty-one years, and he is out in six," and objection to this statement was overruled and exception taken, although at the close of the argument the trial judge on his own motion told the jury that "you will not consider that [statement] except insofar as it meant he would be eligible for parole in that time."

54. Thackston v State, 205 Ark 493, 169 SW2d 130; People v Marx, 291 Ill 40, 125 NE 719.

55. Taylor v State, 22 Ala App 428, 116 So 415; Plyler v State, 21 Ala App 320, 108 So 83; Beard v State, 19 Ala App 102, 95 So 333; Pait v State (Fla) 112 So 2d 380; Blackwell v State, 76 Fla 124, 79 So 731, 1 ALR 502; Hammond v State, 156 Ga 880, 120 SE 539; McDonald v People, 126 Ill 150, 18 NE 817; Kelley v State, 210 Ind 380, 3 NE2d 65; Davis v State, 200 Ind 88, 161 NE 375, ovrld on other grounds Stephenson v State, 205 Ind 194, 186 NE 293; Goff v Commonwealth, 241 Ky 428, 44 SW2d 306; State v Biggerstaff, 17 Mont 510, 43 P 709; People v Johnson, 284 NY 182, 30 NE2d 465, 132 ALR 675; People v Sherwood, 271 NY 427, 3 NE2d 581;

Comments by the prosecuting attorney in their argument to the jury on the power of the court to suspend sentence or to set the jury's verdict aside,[56] or statements that a higher court has the power to review the finding of the jury on the weight of evidence, are calculated to induce the jury to disregard their responsibility, and are improper.[57]

In the same connection, where one of the functions of the jury is to impose or make recommendations regarding the punishment of one convicted of crime, a reference by the prosecutor to the latter's right to appeal is more likely to be considered as constituting reversible error if a death penalty is imposed, since the considerations which may lead a jury to impose the death penalty as distinguished from a lesser penalty are so difficult to judge that in most instances it cannot be excluded from the record that a reasonable probability existed that the jury may have been influenced by the statement of the prosecutor to impose a harsher penalty than they would have otherwise given.[58]

People v Esposito, 224 NY 370, 121 NE 344; State v Hawley, 229 NC 167, 48 SE2d 35; State v Little, 228 NC 417, 45 SE2d 542; Deutsch v State, 46 Ohio App 223, 13 Ohio L Abs 456, 188 NE 399; Crobaugh v State, 45 Ohio App 410, 12 Ohio L Abs 404, 187 NE 243; Commonwealth v Smith (Pa) 10 Phila 189, 30 Phila Leg Int 201; Gray v State, 191 Tenn 526, 235 SW2d 20; Weige v State, 81 Tex Crim 476, 196 SW 524; Murmutt v State (Tex Crim) 67 SW 508; Brazell v State, 33 Tex Crim 333, 26 SW 723; Crow v State, 33 Tex Crim 264, 26 SW 209; Lyons v Commonwealth, 204 Va 375, 131 SE2d 407, 3 ALR3d 1443.

A remark by a prosecuting attorney in the course of his argument to the jury to the effect that if the jury makes a mistake in the verdict, some other tribunal will correct it, is improper as tending to influence them to shift the burden of their responsibility from themselves to an appellate court and refusal of the trial judge to strike such a statement is reversible error. Blackwell v State, 76 Fla 124, 79 So 731, 1 ALR 502.

Annotation: Prejudicial effect of statement of prosecutor that if jury makes mistake in convicting it can be corrected by other authorities. 3 ALR3d 1448.

56. State v Guffey, 39 SD 84, 163 NW 679; Lyons v Commonwealth, 204 Va 375, 131 SE2d 407, 3 ALR3d 1443.

57. McDonald v People, 126 Ill 150, 18 NE 817.

58. Pait v State (Fla) 112 So 2d 380; Blackwell v State, 76 Fla 124, 79 So 731, 1 ALR 502; People v Johnson, 284 NY 182, 30 NE2d 465, 132 ALR 675.

A reference by a prosecuting attorney during his argument to the right of the accused to appeal to a higher court or to apply for clemency or

Argument of a prosecuting attorney urging jurors in a prosecution for homicide to convict the defendant of murder on the ground that the state pardon board is turning out persons convicted of manslaughter at the end of two years is improper.[59]

§ 553. Expression by prosecutor of personal opinion as to guilt of accused

A prosecuting attorney has the right to state his views as to what the evidence shows.[60]

On the other hand, there are many holdings and statements to the effect that such an expression of belief, opinion, or knowledge is improper if based, either expressly or inferentially, on facts not shown by the evidence produced at the trial.[61] Such statements, it is said add to the probative force of the testimony adduced upon the trial the weight of the prosecutor's personal influence or knowledge,

parole, calculated to stress unduly the possibility or probability of subsequent escape by the defendant of the just consequences of his offense, is improper. Broyles v Commonwealth (Ky) 267 SW2d 73, 47 ALR2d 1252.

In a criminal prosecution, the district attorney's deliberate injection, during his address to the jury on the subject of penalty, of considerations of parole, is not only unfair and improper but is likely to prejudice the defendant. Commonwealth v Aljoe, 420 Pa 198, 216 A2d 50, 16 ALR3d 1126.

59. Pollard v State, 201 Ind 180, 166 NE 654, 84 ALR 779.

In McNeill v State, 102 Ala 121, 15 So 352, however, it was declared not error for a prosecuting attorney to state to the jury in a prosecution for homicide that if a verdict for a less crime than murder was returned, the defendant would probably be pardoned.

60. Henderson v United States (CA6 Tenn) 218 F2d 14, 50 ALR2d 754, cert den 349 US 920, 99 L Ed 1253, 75 S Ct 660, reh den 349 US 969, 99 L Ed 1290, 75 S Ct 879; Riggins v State, 125 Md 165, 93 A 437; State v Davis, 88 SC 229, 70 SE 811.

Annotation: Propriety and effect of prosecuting attorney's argument to jury indicating his belief or knowledge as to guilt of accused. 50 ALR2d 766.

61. State v Thayer, 124 Ohio St 1, 176 NE 656, 75 ALR 48.

Statements by a prosecuting attorney in argument to the effect that he would not prosecute a case, or the case at bar, unless he believed the defendant to be guilty, have generally been held objectionable. State v Gunderson, 26 ND 294, 144 SW 659; State v Thayer, 124 Ohio St 1, 176 NE 656, 75 ALR 48.

or of his professional opinion, or the influence of his official position.[62]

It is incumbent on the defendant, to entitle him to a mistrial, new trial, or the reversal of a judgment of conviction by reason of the statement in question, to bring the matter to the attention of the trial court by a timely objection or an assignment of misconduct, and to invoke its protection or corrective action, such as an admonishment or reprimand of counsel, or an instruction to the jury to disregard the statement, as indicated in the citations hereunder;[63] or, as stated disjunctively or alternatively in some cases, he must object to the statement,[64] or must invoke some corrective action;[65] or must take one or the other of

62. State v Gunderson, 26 ND 294, 144 NW 659.

63. People v Mora, 139 Cal App 2d 266, 293 P2d 522 (declaring that the failure to assign the statement as misconduct when it was made was entitled to some weight in determining its prejudicial effect); People v Le Beau, 136 Cal App 2d 69, 288 P2d 294; People v Johnson, 99 Cal App 2d 717, 222 P2d 335 (objection and assignment as misconduct); People v Cooper, 36 Cal App 2d 6, 96 P2d 1012 (assignment of statement as misconduct and request for instruction to jury to disregard it); People v Podwys, 6 Cal App 2d 71, 44 P2d 377 (objection and request to admonish jury); Commonwealth v Wilcox, 316 Pa 129, 173 A 653 (objection and request for withdrawal of juror); State v Egan, 47 SD 1, 195 NW 642 (declaring that it is incumbent on the defendant to call the objectionable statement to the attention of the court when it is made, and invoke its protection); Murmutt v State (Tex Crim) 67 SW 508 (objection and written request for instruction to disregard); Morrison v State, 40 Tex Crim 473, 51 SW 358 (holding that where counsel excepts to the remarks of the prosecuting attorney, he must, in addition to the exception, tender a special charge to the court telling the jury to disregard the statements).

64. People v Owens, 11 Cal App 2d 724, 54 P2d 728; State v Killion, 95 Kan 371, 148 P 643; State v Cook, 212 Minn 495, 4 NW2d 323; Reed v State, 66 Neb 184, 92 NW 321; State v Pisano, 33 NJ Super 559, 111 A2d 279; State v Nevius, 147 Ohio St 263, 34 Ohio Ops 210, 71 NE2d 258, cert den 331 US 839, 91 L Ed 1851, 67 S Ct 1521; Spangler v State, 42 Tex Crim 233, 61 SW 314, ovrld on another point Melton v State, 47 Tex Crim 451, 83 SW 822.

65. Norris v State, 236 Ala 281, 182 So 69 (holding that where the statement may be rendered harmless by an instruction to the jury to disregard it, but such instruction is not requested, a motion for a mistrial is properly overruled); People v Chilcott, 18 Cal App 2d 583, 64 P2d 450 (instruction to disregard); Wells v State, 75 Fla 229, 77 So 879 (appropriate corrective action); State v Mack, 45 La Ann 1155, 14 So 141; State v Jones, 331 Mo 601, 55 SW2d 960; Igo v State (Okla Crim) 267 P2d 1082

such steps;[66] and, in the event of an adverse ruling or a refusal or failure to act upon such objection, motion, or request, he must except thereto.[67]

But there is also some authority for the proposition that it is the duty of the court, under some circumstances, to act sua sponte or ex mero motu,[68] and in some jurisdictions,

(instruction to disregard); Williams v State, 4 Okla Crim 523, 114 P 1114 (request for instruction to disregard); Commonwealth v Arcuroso, 283 Pa 84, 128 A 668 (request for corrective action); Mangum v State, 139 Tex Crim 111, 139 SW2d 94 (request for instruction to disregard); Parrocini v State, 90 Tex Crim 320, 234 SW 671 (refusing reversal where no request for an instruction to disregard had been made); Davis v State, 57 Tex Crim 545, 124 SW 104 (in which the fact that no special charge as to the remarks complained of was requested was assigned as a reason, inter alia, for sustaining the judgment of conviction); Cross v State (Tex Crim) 91 SW 223 (written request for instruction to disregard); Adams v State, 47 Tex Crim 347, 84 SW 231 (holding that an objectionable statement of belief or opinion concerning the guilt of the defendant is not a ground for reversal in the absence of a request that the jury be instructed to disregard it and the refusal of such request); Hawkins v State (Tex Crim) 71 SW 756 (request for instruction to disregard); Habel v State, 28 Tex App 588, 13 SW 1001 (request for instruction to disregard); Kennedy v State, 19 Tex App 618 (request for instruction to disregard); Young v State, 19 Tex App 536 (request for instruction to disregard); State v Spencer, 15 Utah 149, 49 P 302; State v Taylor, 47 Wash 2d 213, 287 P2d 298; State v Lane, 36 Wash 2d 227, 217 P2d 322, mod on reh on other grounds 37 Wash 2d 145, 222 P2d 394 (request for instruction to disregard); State v McWhinney, 23 Wash 2d 334, 161 P2d 162 (request for instruction to disregard).

66. People v Kirkes, 39 Cal 2d 719, 249 P2d 1 (in which the court recognized the general rule that when a district attorney is guilty of misconduct in the trial of a criminal case, it is ordinarily the duty of counsel for the defense promptly to call the attention of the court thereto and assign it as misconduct, or request the court to instruct the jury to disregard it); Apple v State, 190 Md 661, 59 A2d 509 (holding that to entitle the defendant to have the point considered on appeal, it must be reserved in the lower court by timely objection and exception, or a request to have the jury instructed to disregard the statement).

67. State v Phillips, 233 Mo 299, 135 SW 4; Reed v State, 66 Neb 184, 92 NW 321; State v Nevius, 147 Ohio St 263, 34 Ohio Ops 210, 71 NE2d 258, cert den 331 US 839, 91 L Ed 1851, 67 S Ct 1521; Mangum v State, 139 Tex Crim 111, 139 SW2d 94; State v McWhinney, 23 Wash 2d 334, 161 P2d 162.

But see People v McGuire, 89 Mich 64, 50 NW 786, in which the court said, with respect to the contention that the error could not be taken advantage of on appeal because of the failure to except to the court's refusal to give the instruction, that this contention would be correct if the action were a civil action, but that in a criminal case the rule was different.

68. Steele v United States (CA5

this duty is imposed by statutory provision.

To entitle the defendant to have the question considered on appeal, it must appear from the record that the statement complained of was actually made.[69] Moreover, to entitle the defendant to a reversal, the record must contain a recital of facts sufficient to enable the appellate court to see wherein the statement complained of was, or may have been, prejudicial.[70]

§ 554. Appeal to racial, national, or religious prejudice

The primary requisites for the declaration of a mistrial, the granting of a new trial, or the reversal of a conviction, by reason of a statement by prosecuting counsel which is complained of as appealing to or evoking racial, national, or religious prejudice against the defendant, are that the

Tex) 222 F2d 628 (a prosecution for an income tax evasion, wherein certain statements by the United States attorney in his argument to the jury, including the assertion of his personal opinion that the defendant was guilty, although not objected to, were held to be "so far out of bounds as to put the district judge in error in not, of his own motion, admonishing the Government's counsel to desist from that kind of argument and directing the jury that the argument was incorrect and unfair, and that they should not consider it"); Hicks v State, 196 Ga 671, 27 SE2d 307; State v Gulbrandsen, 238 Minn 508, 57 NW2d 419.

See Hardy v State (Tex App) 13 SW 1008.

69. Rossi v United States (CA8 Colo) 9 F2d 362; Williams v State, 255 Ala 229, 51 So 2d 250 (holding that a request for a charge to the jury that the statement of the prosecutor that he was convinced that the defendant was guilty should be given no weight or consideration by the jury in making up their verdict was properly refused where there was nothing in the record to indicate that such argument had been made); Lawler v Commonwealth, 182 Ky 185, 206 SW 306.

70. Bustin v State, 184 Miss 1, 185 So 259 (holding that where the prejudicial character of the words complained of is dependent upon the connection in which they were used, such connection must be shown by the record); State v Barker, 68 NJL 19, 52 A 284; State v Nevius, 147 Ohio St 263, 34 Ohio Ops 210, 71 NE2d 258, cert den 331 US 839, 91 L Ed 1851, 67 S Ct 1521 (holding that where the question is raised for the first time in the appellate court, it must affirmatively appear from the record that defendant was deprived of a fair trial by the remarks complained of).

In Bingham v State, 82 Okla Crim 5, 165 P2d 646, the court stated that enough must appear in the record to enable the court to determine from an examination of the entire argument whether the particular statement complained of is prejudicial and improper.

statement must have been such as to be calculated, or to have a tendency, to engender such prejudice.[71] There are numerous holdings or statements to the effect that a reference to the race, color, nationality, or religion of the defendant or the injured person, or to the race, nationality, or religious group to which he belongs, is not necessarily improper or prejudicial.[72]

It is necessary that the defendant was, or may have been, thereby deprived of his right to a fair and impartial trial, to his injury. Thus, where any injury from the statement may be averted or counteracted by corrective action at the trial, it is usually required that such action should have been invoked by a timely objection, motion, or request, although it has been held or stated in some cases that it is the duty of the court to take such action ex mero motu, or sua sponte.

It has been declared that, to be objectionable, the refer-

71. **Annotation:** Counsel's appeal in criminal case to racial, national, or religious prejudice as ground for mistrial, new trial, or reversal. 45 ALR2d 303.

72. D'Aquino v United States (CA9 Cal) 192 F2d 338, reh den 203 F2d 390, cert den 343 US 935, 96 L Ed 1343, 72 S Ct 772, reh den 343 US 958, 96 L Ed 1358, 72 S Ct 1053, 345 US 931, 97 L Ed 1361, 73 S Ct 786; United States v Heitler (DC Ill) 274 F 401, error dismd 260 US 703, 67 L Ed 472, 43 S Ct 163, and affd (CA7) 289 F 1021, cert dismd 263 US 728, 68 L Ed 528, 44 S Ct 135; Daniels v State, 243 Ala 675, 11 So 2d 756, cert den 319 US 755, 87 L Ed 1708, 63 S Ct 1168; Davis v State, 233 Ala 202, 172 So 344; Owens v State, 215 Ala 42, 109 So 109 (mere casual or incidental reference not objectionable); Johnson v State, 35 Ala App 645, 51 So 2d 901; James v State, 18 Ala App 618, 92 So 909; Cauley v State, 156 Ark 577, 247 SW 772; People v Frost, 37 Cal App 120, 174 P 106; Honda v People, 111 Colo 279, 141 P2d 178; People v Harris, 391 Ill 358, 63 NE2d 398; Quarles v Commonwealth (Ky) 245 SW2d 947 (reference held improper but harmless); State v Webb, 149 La 93, 88 So 700; State v Dalcour, 145 La 1008, 83 So 223; State v Mangercino, 325 Mo 794, 30 SW2d 763; State v Lee, 288 Mo 41, 231 SW 619, ovrld on other grounds State v Burrell, 298 Mo 672, 252 SW 709; People v Pacuicca (Co Ct) 134 NYS2d 381, affd 286 App Div 996, 144 NYS2d 711; Camp v State, 95 Okla Crim 70, 239 P2d 1036; Golden v State, 23 Okla Crim 243, 214 P 946; Cedillos v State, 151 Tex Crim 459, 209 SW2d 770; White v State, 139 Tex Crim 660, 128 SW2d 51, revd on other grounds 309 US 631, 84 L Ed 989, 60 S Ct 706, reh den 310 US 530, 84 L Ed 1342, 60 S Ct 1032, conformed to 139 Tex Crim 674, 141 SW2d 951; Lacy v State, 137 Tex Crim 362, 128 SW2d 1165, cert den 308 US 551, 84 L Ed 463, 60 S Ct 87; Clements v State, 118 Tex Crim 37, 42 SW2d 67; State v Cohn, 155 Wash 644, 285 P 665.

ence should be so made as to emphasize the racial or other difference.[73] A reference of the kind in question may be justified by the fact that it has a legitimate factual bearing on the issues,[74] that it was made only for the purpose of illustrating a point,[75] or for the purpose of identifying the person referred to.[76]

Such statements may be justified if a similar reference or statement had previously been made by counsel for the defendant,[77] or if the matter referred to had otherwise been previously brought into the case by or at the insistence of the defendant, or without objection on his part.[78]

In most instances, at least where the statement complained of is not inflammatory or of such a character as to constitute flagrant misconduct, the prejudicial effect thereof may be removed or counteracted by corrective action at the trial by the court[79] or the offending counsel.[80]

73. Davis v State, 233 Ala 202, 172 So 344; Owens v State, 215 Ala 42, 109 So 109; Johnson v State, 35 Ala App 645, 51 So 2d 901.

74. Rosenthal v United States (CA8 Iowa) 45 F2d 1000, 78 ALR 1415; Hodgskin v United States (CA2 NY) 279 F 85; United States v Heitler (DC Ill) 274 F 401, error dismd 260 US 703, 67 L Ed 472, 43 S Ct 163, and affd (CA7) 289 F 1021, cert dismd 263 US 728, 68 L Ed 528, 44 S Ct 135; Daniels v State, 243 Ala 675, 11 So 2d 756, cert den 319 US 755, 87 L Ed 1708, 63 S Ct 1168; State v Howard, 120 La 311, 45 So 260; Tubb v State, 217 Miss 741, 64 So 2d 911; Jennings v State, 118 Miss 616, 79 So 813; State v Jackson, 336 Mo 1069, 83 SW2d 87, 103 ALR 339; State v Mangercino, 325 Mo 794, 30 SW2d 763; Lacy v State, 137 Tex Crim 362, 128 SW2d 1165, cert den 308 US 551, 84 L Ed 463, 60 S Ct 87; State v Unosawa, 29 Wash 2d 578, 188 P2d 104; State v Cohn, 155 Wash 644, 285 P 665 (reference made for purpose of identification).

75. State v Brinkman, 68 Utah 557, 251 P 364.

76. Gordon v State, 161 Tex Crim 594, 280 SW2d 267, cert den 350 US 924, 100 L Ed 809, 76 S Ct 214.

77. State v Dalcour, 145 La 1008, 83 So 223.

78. Honda v People, 111 Colo 279, 141 P2d 178.

79. See People v Maria, 359 Ill 231, 194 NE 510, in which the court, after observing that "there is no instrument that can be used to determine the effect of inflammatory remarks upon the minds of the jurors," said further that even if that effect could be determined, "there is no eraser available to the trial court to remove it."

80. See People v Jeans, 79 Cal App 464, 249 P 1089.

It is ordinarily held to be incumbent on the defense to call the matter to the attention of the court and invoke such corrective action by a timely objection, motion, or request,[81] although it has been stated in some cases that it is the duty of the court to take such action ex mero motu or sua sponte.[82]

In determining the effect of the statement complained of, it will be viewed and appraised by the court in the light of the context and of the circumstances under which it was made.[83] The prosecutor is allowed reasonable latitude in appealing to the emotions of the jury. However, comments calculated to create, arouse or inflame their sympathies or prejudices unduly against the accused are deemed improper. Thus, it has been held to be error to permit the prosecutor to refer to a black defendant as a "black gorilla",[84] to permit him to bring in issue the defendant's race by saying, "I do not ask you to convict the defendant merely because a white man was killed by a black. At the last court held here this very month I asked a jury to convict a black man who murdered a black girl in cold blood, and the jury found him guilty and he was sentenced to the electric chair";[85] to permit him to appeal to the members of the jury through their faith, by stating, "I would also be proud if I were a member of the Catholic Church. They stand for morals and morality and welfare of the community at large."[86]

The prosecutor's attempts to incite the jury with references to race or religion are objectionable and prejudicial even when they attain a certain level of sophistication. As a result, object if any references to race or religion are

81. Fontanello v United States (CA9 Wash) 19 F2d 921; Honda v People, 111 Colo 279, 141 P2d 178; State v Cabaudo, 83 Conn 160, 76 A 42; Gluck v State (Fla) 62 So 2d 71.

82. See Jones v State, 21 Ala App 234, 109 So 189; Collins v State, 100 Miss 435, 56 So 527.

83. Honda v People, 111 Colo 279, 141 P2d 178.

84. Harris v State, 209 Miss 141, 46 So 2d 91.

85. State v Hinton, 210 SC 480, 43 SE2d 360.

86. State v Leek, 152 Iowa 12, 130 NW 1062.

made at all, even if the remarks are not made with reference to the defendant's race or religion. The added subtlety will not validate this type of reference.

§ 555. Reference to prior conviction of accused for same or other offenses

Under the general rule that a defendant on trial charged with a particular crime may not be proved guilty thereof by evidence showing that he has committed other crimes, it is improper for counsel to allude, in the course of argument, to the fact that the accused has committed other crimes.[87]

Since, on a new trial, the former conviction is entirely outside the evidence, it is improper for a prosecuting attorney to remark on the fact that the defendant has previously been convicted of the same charge and the conviction reversed on appeal.[88]

However, where the accused has been indicted for a higher degree of crime than that of which he was convicted, a statement to the jury that a conviction upon a new trial must be limited to the lower degree of which the defendant was previously convicted is not improper.[89]

§ 556. Evoking prejudice against certain crimes

Statements designed to arouse prejudice against sexual

87. Rhodes v Commonwealth, 107 Ky 354, 54 SW 170; State v Reynolds, 41 NJ 163, 195 A2d 449, 1 ALR3d 1438, cert den 377 US 1000, 12 L Ed 2d 1050, 84 S Ct 1930, 1934, reh den 379 US 873, 13 L Ed 2d 80, 81, 85 S Ct 22, 23.

Annotation: Prejudicial effect of prosecuting attorney's argument or disclosure during trial that another defendant has been convicted or has pleaded guilty. 48 ALR2d 1016.

88. State v Matheson, 142 Iowa 414, 120 NW 1036; Whit v State, 87 Miss 564, 40 So 324 (statement by district attorney in closing argument that "every lawyer who deserves the name 'lawyer' knows that the case was reversed by the supreme court on the merest technicality"); State v Jackson, 336 Mo 1069, 83 SW2d 87, 103 ALR 339; Hatch v State, 8 Tex App 416 (statement that the defendant had case reversed "by dodge and technicality").

89. State v Smith, 49 La Ann 1515, 22 So 882.

crimes committed upon women, unless reasonably supported by the evidence or deductions drawn therefrom, are not within the scope of proper argument. Thus the prosecutor could not urge a conviction of rape to prevent the possibility of the commission of a similar offense against a member of a juryman's family.[90] On the other hand, another case held that it was proper for the prosecutor, in his argument to the jury in the prosecution of a minister of the gospel for statutory rape upon one of his parishioners, to comment upon the enormity of the crime committed under such circumstances.[91]

It is not proper for the prosecutor to appeal to prejudices of the jury against violations of liquor laws.[92]

§ 557. Denunciation of defendant or the defense tactics

Since a prosecuting attorney, in a criminal case, represents the people of the state, including the defendant, it is his duty not to lay aside the impartiality that should characterize his official actions in order to become a heated partisan, and by vituperation of the prisoner and appeals to prejudice seek to procure a conviction at all hazards.[93] It is therefore improper for a prosecuting attorney to denounce and vilify the defendant on account of the nature and character of his defense.[94]

It would seem that a matter which is proved by direct

90. Hemphill v State, 72 Tex Crim 638, 165 SW 462.

91. People v Buckner, 281 Ill 340, 117 NE 1023, 3 ALR 1323.

92. Pope v State, 22 Ala App 260, 114 So 565.

See State v Sheeler (Mo App) 300 SW 318, a 1927 case wherein an argument by the prosecutor urging the jury not to permit the government to be run by Italian bootleggers was held to be prejudicial error even though the prosecutor stated that the defendant was not an Italian and was not kin to one.

93. Goff v Commonwealth, 241 Ky 428, 44 SW2d 306; State v Warford, 106 Mo 55, 16 SW 886; People v Fielding, 158 NY 542, 53 NE 497; Bishop v State, 72 Tex Crim 1, 160 SW 705.

94. Ryan v People, 60 Colo 425, 153 P 756; McConnell v State, 22 Tex App 354, 3 SW 699.

testimony or is fairly inferable from facts and circumstances proved and which has a bearing upon the issues is a fair subject for comment by counsel, and if such deductions and inferences tend to fix upon a defendant the wickedness of the crime charged against him, it is within the scope of proper and fair argument to denounce him accordingly.[95] The line between denunciation and abuse which will reverse a conviction and that which will not, if one can be found other than that based on capacity to injure, seems to rest on the distinction between mere personal abuse and invective called forth by the character of the crime shown by the evidence. But to make vituperation and abuse grounds for reversing a judgment, it must appear that the remarks indulged in were unwarranted and grossly improper, and that they were of a material character and well calculated to affect injuriously the rights of the opposite party.[96]

The prosecutor is not allowed to comment on the personal appearance of the defendant, not as a witness or on account of his manner and bearing as such, but as indicating a probability of guilt.[97]

§ 558. Arguing law or reading lawbooks

In a number of instances, the question has arisen

95. Shushan v United States (CA5 La) 117 F2d 110, 133 ALR 1040, cert den 313 US 574, 85 L Ed 1531, 61 S Ct 1085, cert den 313 US 574, 85 L Ed 1532, 61 S Ct 1086, reh den 314 US 706, 86 L Ed 564, 62 S Ct 53; Haupt v State, 108 Ga 53, 34 SE 313; People v Preston, 341 Ill 407, 173 NE 383, 77 ALR 631; People v Strauch, 240 Ill 60, 88 NE 155.

96. Robinson v United States (CA8 Mo) 32 F2d 505, 66 ALR 468; Mobile & O. R. Co. v Carpenter, 104 Miss 706, 61 So 693; Hampton v State, 88 Miss 257, 40 So 545; People v Fielding, 158 NY 542, 53 NE 497; McConnell v State, 22 Tex App 354, 3 SW 699.

And see State v Turner (Mo) 272 SW2d 266, 48 ALR2d 1008, holding, in a prosecution for burglary in which two alleged confederates pleaded guilty, that a statement in the closing argument of prosecutor to the effect that the defendant and the alleged confederates are "birds of a feather" was justified by the evidence.

97. Annotation: Admissibility, in homicide prosecution, of deceased's clothing worn at time of killing. 68 ALR2d 903 at page 944.

whether counsel may argue law or read lawbooks to the jury.[98]

According to one line of cases, the law as laid down by standard authorities and contained in reported cases of courts of last resort may properly be read to the jury, provided that the law presented is not in conflict with the established law of the state.[99]

On the other hand, although there appears to be no case holding that counsel's reading of law to a jury in a criminal case, in and of itself, constitutes reversible error, there are a number of cases which apparently deny counsel the right to read law to a jury or which characterize the practice as being improper.[1] This view is based upon the

98. **Annotation:** Counsel's right in criminal prosecution to argue law or to read lawbooks to the jury. 67 ALR2d 245.

99. Richmond's Appeal, 59 Conn 226, 22 A 82 (rule limited to criminal cases involving issue of insanity); Rogers v State, 128 Ga 67, 57 SE 227; People v Preston, 341 Ill 407, 173 NE 383, 77 ALR 631; Palmer v People, 138 Ill 356, 28 NE 130; State v Whitmore, 53 Kan 343, 36 P 748.

In People v Preston, 341 Ill 407, 173 NE 383, 77 ALR 631, it was held that the state's attorney may read to the jury portions of the opinions of the supreme court of the state, in reply to argument of the defendant's counsel as to the legal effects of intoxication and insanity as a defense in a prosecution for murder, where the jury is by statute made the judges of the law in criminal cases, and only sufficient facts in the opinions are read to show the issues of fact and the application of the law thereto, and no facts are read which might have an evidentiary bearing on the issues of the present trial or which have no relevancy to the legal questions involved in the case on trial.

1. Kuhn v United States (CA9 Cal) 24 F2d 910, rearg den 26 F2d 463, cert den 278 US 605, 73 L Ed 533, 49 S Ct 11 (stating that the practice is not to be encouraged); Owen v People, 118 Colo 415, 195 P2d 953; Tindall v State, 99 Fla 1132, 128 So 494; Brownlee v State, 95 Fla 775, 116 So 618; People v De Lordo, 350 Ill 148, 182 NE 726; Reed v Commonwealth, 140 Ky 736, 131 SW 776.

But see People v Bote, 376 Ill 264, 33 NE2d 449, limiting this holding to the reading of state Supreme Court opinions. Duncan v Commonwealth, 13 Ky LR 195, 16 SW 584; Crane v Commonwealth, 8 Ky LR 515 (abstract), 1 SW 880; McDowell v Commonwealth, 4 Ky LR 353 (abstract); People v Smith, 177 Mich 358, 143 NW 12; State v Jones, 153 Mo 457, 55 SW 80; Mikolajsak v State, 96 Tex Crim 207, 256 SW 927; State v Hanna, 81 Utah 583, 21 P2d 537; State v Neel, 23 Utah 541, 65 P 494; State v Rholeder, 82 Wash 618, 144 P 914.

See Reed v Commonwealth, 140 Ky 736, 131 SW 776, wherein the appellate court, in remanding a man-

theory that in reading law to the jury, counsel is usurping the trial court's function.[2] Most of the courts which have deemed it improper for counsel to read law to the jury have nevertheless held or recognized that the fact that the prosecuting attorney was permitted to do so over the accused's objection would not constitute reversible error unless the accused's substantial rights were thereby prejudiced.[3]

In any event, even when it is allowed, the arguing or reading of law to the jury is subject to reasonable limitations. For example, counsel is not permitted to read cases which tend to distract the attention of the jury from the case in hand without throwing any light upon it.[4] Thus, counsel will not be permitted to read to the jury court decisions discussing principles of law which are irrelevant to the case and have no application to the facts and evidence.[5]

Likewise, the reading of facts for the purpose of prejudicing the jury should not be permitted, as, for example, the reading of facts for the purpose of contrasting them with

slaughter case for a new trial because of an erroneous instruction, directed the trial court to "further see to it that neither the counsel for the accused nor the Commonwealth's attorney is permitted to read to the jury any extracts from the Code, the statutes, or any other lawbook."

Also see Mikolajsak v State, 96 Tex Crim 207, 256 SW 927, wherein, although prevented from determining whether the accused had been injured by the action of the trial court in permitting the prosecuting attorney to read to the jury "law on the case from many law books" by the fact that the bills of exception failed to show what was read to the jury, the court declared that "after a charge of the court, under our present practice, has been submitted to attorneys and the court has read it to the jury before argument begins, we can see little occasion for the attorneys to read the law to the jury, other than as contained in the charge."

2. Owen v People, 118 Colo 415, 195 P2d 953; Brownlee v State, 95 Fla 775, 116 So 618; State v Hanna, 81 Utah 583, 21 P2d 537; State v Neel, 23 Utah 541, 65 P 494; State v Rholeder, 82 Wash 618, 144 P 914.

3. Kuhn v United States (CA9 Cal) 24 F2d 910, rearg den 26 F2d 463, cert den 278 US 605, 73 L Ed 533, 49 S Ct 11; Tindall v State, 99 Fla 1132, 128 So 494; Duncan v Commonwealth, 13 Ky LR 195, 16 SW 584; Crane v Commonwealth, 8 Ky LR 515 (abstract), 1 SW 880.

4. State v Crisp, 244 NC 407, 94 SE2d 402, 67 ALR2d 236.

5. State v Crisp, supra.

those of the case at bar.[6] Insofar as such matters are concerned, the right to permit the reading of lawbooks in criminal cases is left to the sound discretion of the trial court, which will not be interfered with on appeal unless it clearly appears that the rights of the accused have been prejudiced.[7] Notice however that the inhibition is not against reading facts at all, but only against reading such facts as may have an evidentiary bearing on the issues of the present case, and such as have no relevancy to legal questions involved in the case at trial.[8]

§ 559. Retaliatory statements

If counsel for a party litigant or for the defendant in a criminal prosecution pursues an improper line of argument, he thereby invites a reply, and statements made by opposing counsel or the prosecuting attorney by way of retaliation thereto have often been considered proper which would otherwise be objectionable.[9] This principle has been applied although the statements in reply were irrelevant, where they were in reply to irrelevant matter in the argument of opposing counsel.[10]

Although it is improper for counsel for the prosecution to comment in his argument upon the failure of the accused to produce evidence of good character unless the accused has put his character in issue, where counsel for the defendant has commented on the defendant's good character, in the absence of any evidence on which to base his

6. State v Corpening, 157 NC 621, 73 SE 214.

State v Whit, 50 NC (5 Jones L) 224, holding that it is improper for counsel to read the facts in an opinion on a former appeal for the purpose of contrasting them with the facts established by a witness at the present trial.

7. Askew v State, 94 Ala 4, 10 So 657; People v Wheeler, 60 Cal 581; State v O'Neil, 51 Kan 651, 33 P 287 (in prosecutions other than for libel).

8. People v Preston, 341 Ill 407, 173 NE 383, 77 ALR 631.

9. United States v De Vasto (CA2 NY) 52 F2d 26, 78 ALR 336, cert den 284 US 678, 76 L Ed 573, 52 S Ct 138; People v Izzo, 14 Ill 2d 203, 151 NE2d 329, 89 ALR2d 187, cert den and app dismd 362 US 403, 4 L Ed 2d 864, 80 S Ct 812.

10. State v Hilton, 87 SC 434, 69 SE 1077.

statements, retaliatory comment by counsel for the prosecution on the failure of the defendant to produce character witnesses has not been considered improper. Remarks made by prosecuting attorneys possibly improper in themselves as comments on a defendant's failure to testify have been held proper where they were made as replies to the statements of opposing counsel.

It has been held that an appeal to the jury by counsel for the defendant on the basis that a finding against the defendant would be tantamount to a finding that his witnesses had committed perjury justifies a statement by opposing counsel that the same argument had been repeatedly made by defendant's counsel to juries in the county for the past twenty-five years.[11]

C. CALLING ATTENTION TO DEFENDANTS FAILURE TO TESTIFY

§ 560. In general

Any comments by a prosecutor which refer to the fact that the defendant did not testify on his own behalf are objectionable and prejudicial as a matter of law.[12] It is doubtful that any admonition to the jury can cure this grave constitutional error.

11. Snowden v Webb, 217 Miss 664, 64 So 2d 745, 39 ALR2d 93, sugg of error overr 217 Misc 680, 65 So 2d 839, and sugg of error dismd in part and sustained in part 217 Miss 682, 67 So 2d 251.

12. It has been held that the self-incrimination guaranty of the Fifth Amendment, in its bearing on the states by reason of the Fourteenth Amendment, forbids either comment by the prosecution on an accused's silence or instructions by the court that such silence is evidence of guilt. Griffin v California, 380 US 609, 14 L Ed 2d 106, 85 S Ct 1229, reh den 381 US 957, 14 L Ed 2d 730, 85 S Ct 1797.

Annotations: Violation of federal constitutional rule (Griffin v California) prohibiting adverse comment by prosecutor or court upon accused's failure to testify, as constituting reversible or harmless error. 24 ALR3d 1093.

Comment on accused's failure to testify, by counsel for codefendant. 1 ALR3d 989.

Propriety and prejudicial effect of comment or evidence as to accused's willingness to take lie detector test. 95 ALR2d 819.

In many jurisdictions, the statutes expressly prohibit comment on the failure of the accused to testify; in others, the statutes provide that his failure to become a witness in his own behalf does not create a presumption against him; under other forms of statute it is improper for the prosecuting attorney to refer, in the presence of the jury, to the defendant's failure to testify.[13] On the other side of the coin, it has been held that a statute permitting the prosecuting attorney to comment on the failure of the accused to testify contravenes the constitutional right of the accused against self-incrimination.[14]

A recent case of first impression in the federal courts extended the Fifth Amendment protection against self-incrimination and the federal statute allowing a defendant to testify at his own request without adverse presumption if he remained silent, to cover the situation where a codefendant's attorney comments on the failure of a defendant to testify.[15]

13. Wilson v United States, 149 US 60, 37 L Ed 650, 13 S Ct 765; Jackson v State, 45 Fla 38, 34 So 243; Bennett v State, 86 Ga 401, 12 SE 806; People v Donaldson, 255 Ill 19, 99 NE 62; McDonald v People, 126 Ill 150, 18 NE 817; Watt v People, 126 Ill 9, 18 NE 340; Angelo v People, 96 Ill 209; Pollard v State, 201 Ind 180, 166 NE 654, 84 ALR 779; Long v State, 56 Ind 182; Commonwealth v Richmond, 207 Mass 240, 93 NE 816; Commonwealth v Scott, 123 Mass 239; People v Lay, 193 Mich 17, 159 NW 299; Smith v State, 90 Miss 111, 43 So 465; State v Larkin, 250 Mo 218, 157 SW 600; State v Weaver, 165 Mo 1, 65 SW 308; State v Ober, 52 NH 459; People v Watson, 216 NY 565, 111 NE 243; State v Carlisle, 28 SD 169, 132 NW 686 (decided prior to amendment changing rule); Haley v State, 84 Tex Crim 629, 209 SW 675, 3 ALR 779; Skidmore v State, 57 Tex Crim 497, 123 SW 1129; Hare v State, 56 Tex Crim 6, 118 SW 544; Sample v State, 52 Tex Crim 505, 108 SW 685; Barnard v State, 48 Tex Crim 111, 86 SW 760; Hunt v State, 28 Tex App 149, 12 SW 737; Powell v Commonwealth, 167 Va 558, 189 SE 433, 110 ALR 90.

It has been held that the federal statute (18 USCS § 3481) providing that in a federal criminal prosecution, the person charged shall, at his own request, be a competent witness, but that his failure to make such a request shall not create any presumption against him, was designed, inter alia, to bar counsel for the prosecution from commenting on the defendant's refusal to testify. Griffin v California, 380 US 609, 14 L Ed 2d 106, 85 S Ct 1229, reh den 381 US 957, 14 L Ed 2d 730, 85 S Ct 1797.

14. State v Wolfe, 64 SD 178, 266 NW 116, 104 ALR 464.

15. In a prosecution for violation of federal narcotics laws, it appeared that narcotics were thrown from a car

§ 561. Statement that prosecution testimony was uncontradicted

A reference by counsel for the state to the testimony of the state as uncontradicted and undenied are generally held not to be violations of statutory provisions forbidding comment upon the failure of the accused to testify.[16] Thus, to argue that no defense has been made to the state's case is not a violation of the rule forbidding reference to the failure of the accused to testify.[17] A general statement by a prosecuting attorney as to why certain testimony or evidence was not produced by the defendant, or why certain facts were not disproved, is not improper.[18] Such a statement is not improper as a comment on the failure of the defendants to testify, but is merely an argument that the

in which the two defendants were riding, and each of the defendants, represented by different counsel, sought to establish the other as the criminal offender. One of the defendants testified at the trial, and his counsel, in argument to the jury, made repeated adverse comments on the codefendant's failure to testify. With respect thereto, the jury was instructed by the court that a failure to testify cannot give rise to any inference against the nontestifying defendant. On appeal by the nontestifying defendant, the court, ruling that if an attorney's duty to his client should require him to draw the jury's attention to the possible inference of guilt from the codefendant's silence, the trial judge's duty is to order the defendants to be tried separately, held that the defendant's constitutionally guaranteed right of silence free from prejudicial comments had been violated. De Luna v United States (CA5 Tex) 308 F2d 140, 1 ALR3d 969, reh den 324 F2d 375.

16. Davis v State, 174 Ark 891, 298 SW 359; Davidson v State, 108 Ark 191, 158 SW 1103; People v Miller, 278 Ill 490, 116 NE 131; People v Donaldson, 255 Ill 19, 99 NE 62; State v Ruck, 194 Mo 416, 92 SW 706; Sample v State, 52 Tex Crim 505, 108 SW 685.

Annotation: Comment or argument by court or counsel that prosecution evidence is uncontradicted as amounting to improper reference to accused's failure to testify. 14 ALR3d 723.

17. People v Miller, 278 Ill 490, 116 NE 131; Clark v State, 91 Okla Crim 210, 218 P2d 410.

18. In People v Miller, 278 Ill 490, 116 NE 131, counsel for the state, in his argument to the jury, made statements to the effect that the defendant's counsel had not explained certain letters introduced by the state, and further stated: "What defense has been offered in answer to the state's case? Have you stopped to give that inquiry? I repeat, what defense has been made in this case?" It was held that this statement was not a comment on the defendant's failure to testify.

testimony of the witnesses should be believed because it was undisputed.[19]

On the other hand, if the evidence of the state could have been denied only by the defendant, or if the remarks of the prosecutor could only have referred to the defendant, the statement that certain evidence is uncontradicted or undenied is a reference to the failure of the defendant to testify, and improper.[20] Thus, the government's statement in final argument in a criminal prosecution that its witness' statement stood "unimpeached and uncontradicted" constitutes improper comment on the defendant's failure to testify, where the government's witness could have been contradicted only by the defendant or his codefendant, who could not have been put on the stand against his will.[21] However, in a few cases it has been held that it is not a violation of the statute for a prosecuting attorney to remark that certain evidence was uncontradicted, even though the defendant was the only person who could have contradicted it.[22]

§ 562. Reference to failure of accused to explain an incriminating fact

The failure of the accused to explain away incriminating facts and circumstances may be commented upon in argument.[23] Thus, the failure of the defendant to explain his

19. Davis v State, 174 Ark 891, 298 SW 359.

20. People v Watson, 216 NY 565, 111 NE 243; Barnard v State, 48 Tex Crim 111, 86 SW 760.

21. Desmond v United States (CA1 Mass) 345 F2d 225, 14 ALR3d 718.

22. Miller v Commonwealth, 153 Va 890, 149 SE 459, 68 ALR 1102.

In Miller v Commonwealth, supra, where the defendant was charged with seduction under promise of marriage, the attorney for the commonwealth, in his argument to the jury, said: "No witness has gone upon that stand to deny the statements made to Leo Honaker and Everett Honaker that the defendant had had intercourse with Hattie Lee Honaker." The court held that even though the defendant alone was in a position to deny such testimony, the language did not call the attention of the jury to the fact that the accused had failed to testify, and therefore was not in violation of the statute prohibiting comment by the prosecuting attorney on the failure of the defendant to testify.

23. State v Larkin, 250 Mo 218, 157 SW 600; Powell v Commonwealth, 167 Va 558, 189 SE 433, 110 ALR 90.

possession of stolen goods[24] or his whereabouts at the time of the crime[25] are proper subjects of comment. Likewise, references in the argument for the prosecution to the conduct of the defendant at the time of his arrest, as, for example, a remark by the prosecutor that the defendant, when accused, did not deny his guilt, are usually not considered improper.[26]

§ 563. What constitutes improper reference

You must listen carefully to the prosecutor's summation, as he may use subtle methods to accent the failure of your client to take the stand, since indirect and covert references to the neglect of the defendant to take the witness stand may be as prejudicial to your client's rights as a direct comment upon such neglect.[27] The rule forbidding counsel in argument to the jury in a criminal case to comment upon the failure of the defendant to testify is not limited to philippics against him, but extends to any mention of such failure.[28] So, for example, don't permit the

24. Commonwealth v Rizzo, 78 Pa Super 163.

25. In Mason v State, 74 Tex Crim 256, 168 SW 115, the defendant was charged with murder, and did not testify in his own behalf, but did produce testimony to show that between two certain hours of the evening of the murder, he was not at the place where it was committed. During his argument to the jury, the prosecuting attorney remarked that the testimony of the defendant did not show where he was prior to those two hours. The court held that such a remark was not improper as being a comment on the failure of the defendant to testify.

26. State v Schmidt, 136 Mo 644, 38 SW 719.

27. Watt v People, 126 Ill 9, 18 NE 340; State v Weaver, 165 Mo 1, 65 SW 308; Barnard v State, 48 Tex Crim 111, 86 SW 760.

28. Jackson v State, 45 Fla 38, 34 So 243; State v Weaver, 165 Mo 1, 65 SW 308; Hare v State, 56 Tex Crim 6, 118 SW 544; Hunt v State, 28 Tex App 149, 12 SW 737.

In Long v State, 56 Ind 182, where counsel for the state, in making the concluding argument to the jury, said: "It is true, gentlemen of the jury, the evidence in this case is not as clear as it might be. There were but two parties to this transaction. You have heard the evidence of one of them. We would have been pleased to have heard from the other, to see what light he could have thrown upon this transaction," the remarks of counsel were held to be a violation of the statute forbidding any comment on the defendant's failure to testify.

In Haley v State, 84 Tex Crim 629, 209 SW 675, 3 ALR 779, where the defendant was charged with murder,

prosecutor to make reference to "uncorroborated" or "undenied" evidence. These are merely attempts to do by indirection what cannot be done directly.

References to the defendant's failure to testify at the preliminary hearing,[29] or on a former trial[30] are included within the prohibition.

§ 564. Permitted or justified statements

Where the defendant in a criminal case elects to take the witness stand and to give testimony in his own behalf, or to testify on any one phase of the case, it is generally held that he places himself in the position of any other witness, and that the prosecuting attorney has the right to comment on his testimony or on his failure to deny or explain incriminating facts or statements.[31] And it has been held

the prosecuting attorney, referring to the counsel for the defendant, stated: "You said the facts of this case point just as much to the guilt of these men, Terry McKeller and John McKeller, as Irvin Haley. The state has seen fit to put the two McKellers upon the witness stand to deny their guilt, but you did not put Mr. Haley upon the witness stand to deny his guilt." The court held that such remarks were a plain disregard of the command of the statute forbidding any allusion or comment on the failure of the defendant to testify.

In State v Hull, 18 RI 207, 26 A 191, the court said that it was improper for a prosecuting attorney to state that the defendant does not dare put in her testimony, although the statement was preceded with the comment that, of course, it is not proper for him to remark upon her failure to testify.

29. Miller v Oklahoma (CA8 Okla) 149 F 330.

30. Stewart v United States, 366 US 1, 6 L Ed 2d 84, 81 S Ct 941; Smith v State, 90 Miss 111, 43 So 465; Hare v State, 56 Tex Crim 6, 118 SW 544.

In Hare v State, supra, the court said: "To construe the statutory inhibition as applying only to the present trial would render it dangerous to any citizen's case if his counsel decided not to put him on the stand, when, if a subsequent trial was had, the state's case might be stronger and require defendant's testimony, and his previous silence (when he had a right to be silent) be used as an indication of fabrication. Such a construction would destroy the presumption of innocence."

31. Johnson v United States, 318 US 189, 87 L Ed 704, 63 S Ct 549, reh den 318 US 801, 87 L Ed 1164, 63 S Ct 826; Caminetti v United States, 242 US 470, 61 L Ed 442, 37 S Ct 192; De Luna v United States (CA5 Tex) 308 F2d 140, 1 ALR3d 969, reh den 324 F2d 375; Hodge v State, 97 Ala 37, 12 So 164, ovrld on another point Avery v State, 124 Ala 20, 27 So 505; Watt v People, 126 Ill 9, 18 NE 340; State v Mosier (Mo) 102 SW2d 620;

that a prosecutor's comment on the failure of the accused to testify is justified, where counsel for the defendants, in his closing address to the jury, states that the jurors had heard all the testimony, that the defendants, if they had taken the stand, could not add anything, and that they had been interrogated thoroughly, and that he (counsel) knew all the testimony, these statements having the effect of inviting consideration of what the defendants would have testified to, and of surrendering any privilege they may have had not to testify.[32]

State v Larkin, 250 Mo 218, 157 SW 600; State v Ober, 52 NH 459; Hare v State, 56 Tex Crim 6, 118 SW 544.

32. United States v Feinberg (CA2 NY) 140 F2d 592, 154 ALR 272, cert den 322 US 726, 88 L Ed 1562, 64 S Ct 943.

CHAPTER EIGHTEEN

HOW TO HANDLE PREJUDICIAL CONDUCT OF TRIAL JUDGE

A. INTRODUCTION

§ 565. In general

The entire structure of our judicial system has, as its base, the supposed fairness and impartiality of the trial judge.[1] All too often, however, trial judges are guilty of the commission of deliberate or inadvertent prejudice.

In balancing your trial objectives, it is necessary to place your client's rights ahead of your desire not to offend the judge. Often, a judge who is prone to prejudice the cases of certain defendants will become cautious and meticulously fair when he realizes that you are not a person to be trifled with.

§ 566. Making a record

Since prejudicial conduct can occur at any stage of the proceeding, you must be constantly on the alert to protect your client's rights. Make certain that the record adequately reflects the events in the courtroom to ensure full appellate review.

One of the identifying features of the able and zealous defense attorney is his willingness to stand up and object to the prejudicial remarks or conduct of the trial judge. When you take a firm stand in defense of your client's rights and against prejudicial conduct, you will find, more often than not, that both the judge and the jury will begin to look at you in a new light and in a manner favorable to your client.

The failure to object to prejudicial misconduct may later be treated as a waiver. It is vital that you never lose your composure at trial. However, make certain that all of your objections get into the record.

If you have been zealous in the protection of your client, and you believe that in so doing you might have antagonized the judge, consider trying to neutralize that antagonism with the following type of statement at the time of

1. **Annotation:** Construction of provision in Federal Criminal Procedure Rule 42(b) that if contempt charges involve disrespect to or criticism of judge, he is disqualified from presiding at trial or hearing except with defendant's consent. 3 ALR Fed 420.

sentence, "Your Honor, the defendant genuinely appreciates the great patience which you have shown in permitting him to raise so many legal and constitutional questions. The defendant realizes that he may have to go to jail to serve a sentence, but as he goes away he is very thankful that we are in an American court of justice where Your Honor has listened so patiently, even though he didn't agree with all of Your Honor's rulings. I want Your Honor to at least have this defendant still feel that the system of American justice is wise and that Your Honor will impose the type of sentence which will give him hope to come back and be a decent citizen. I think Your Honor has been gracious and forebearing in the manner in which you permitted the interposition of so many objections."

A judge's prejudicial attitude may manifest itself with impatience toward your objections. If you are told, for example, to sit down and stop objecting, note for the record that you are merely attempting to protect your client's rights. While you should not object unnecessarily for "showboat" purposes, you do have the obligation to ensure that your defendant is given a fair trial.

Your problem as defense attorney is a thorny one. You must try to ensure your client a fair trial, "make a record," and try, if possible, not to antagonize the judge. At trial, some of the sting will be taken out of your objections if you state that "the defendant objects, rather than by saying, "I object."

B. PARTICULAR JUDICIAL MISCONDUCT

§ 567. In general

The range of possible prejudicial judicial misconduct is a broad one. It may entail outright disregard for your client's rights, remarks which indicate his belief in your client's guilt, sarcastic or vituperative remarks, or it may be his attitude, his facial expressions or the general manner in which he deals with you and the prosecutor.[2]

Prejudicial misconduct can manifest itself at any stage of the proceeding, from arraignment to sentence. For example, a judge may not, during the initial stages of the prosecution, refuse an adjournment to inexperienced counsel which is sought for the purpose of preparing for trial.[3] Indeed, if no good reason for haste appears in the record, the refusal to grant an adjournment has been held to have unduly prejudiced the defendant's rights to the extent that reversal of the subsequent conviction was warranted.[4]

The trial judge's obligation to conduct a fair and impartial trial does not end when the last witness has concluded his testimony. It continues throughout the summations, the charge to the jury and the imposition of sentence.

Once the jury has commenced its deliberations, it is error for the trial judge to reopen the case to admit further proof in order to bolster the prosecution's contentions and to overcome apparent inconsistencies in its case.[5]

§ 568. Interrupting or unduly interfering with examination of witnesses

It is improper for the court to interfere with your prerogative to develop the evidence as you see fit. Hence, the judge may not recall the defendant to the stand to interrogate him as to matters not touched upon in his original examination.[6]

2. **Annotation:** Violation of federal constitutional rule (Griffin v California) prohibiting adverse comment by prosecutor or court upon accused's failure to testify, as constituting reversible or harmless error. 24 ALR3d 1093.

3. People v Green, 19 App Div 2d 749, 242 NYS2d 881.

4. Johnson v Zerbst, 304 US 458, 82 L Ed 1461, 58 S Ct 1019, 146 ALR 357; Powell v Alabama, 287 US 45, 77 L Ed 158, 53 S Ct 55, 84 ALR 527; People v McLaughlin, 291 NY 480, 53 NE2d 356.

5. People v Gonzalez, 24 App Div 2d 989, 265 NYS2d 310.

6. People v Farrell, 7 App Div 2d 642, 179 NYS2d 540.

In People v Landy, 38 App Div 2d 962, 331 NYS2d 860, a new trial was required in the interest of justice because the trial judge at numerous crucial points in the trial improperly

A judge's prejudicial attitude may manifest itself with impatience toward the manner in which you examine witnesses. Insist on developing your testimony in a proper order. Do not allow the judge to take over either the direct or cross-examination of your client. If, during your direct and cross-examination of a witness, the judge tells you to "stop wasting time", to "move along onto something else", or if he attempts to take over the questioning himself, state, in a firm but respectful tone, "Your honor, the defendant has the right to develop his proof and conduct his examination in an orderly manner, which he is prepared to do."

If the judge persists in his conduct, you can add, "Your Honor, the defendant respectfully asserts that if he is not permitted to develop his proof (or conduct his cross-examination) in an orderly manner, he will be deprived of his right to effective assistance of counsel as guaranteed by the 6th Amendment of the United States Constitution and of due process of law under the Fourteenth Amendment."

If the judge interrupts your cross-examination of a prosecution witness and tries to rehabilitate him, as often happens, you must gently but firmly insist upon your rights. Say, "Your Honor, I would appreciate it if you would permit me to continue with my examination; I intend to cover the precise points which Your Honor is suggesting." If the judge continues in this vein, you can say, "Your Honor, the defendant excepts to this interruption of the cross-examination. These interruptions break counsel's train of thought and serve to deprive the defendant of his constitutional right to the effective assistance of counsel."

§ 569. Disparaging the defendant or his defense

A trial judge's conduct is prejudicial to your client if it intentionally or inadvertently indicates disbelief in the defense theory or a defense witness, if it tends to embar-

took over complete questioning of key witnesses and elicited from them evidence damaging to the defendant's case.

rass your client or you or if it indicates his feeling that your client is guilty. The trial judge must not only be impartial between parties, but must convey the sense of impartiality to the jury. The appearance of bias will provide a basis for reversal even if the trial judge is, in fact, completely impartial and detached.[7]

If, during the questioning of your client or of defendant witnesses, the judge intimates, either by the nature of the question or by tone, inflection, or facial expression that he disbelieves the testimony, always interpose an appropriate objection. For example, "Your honor, the defendant respectfully excepts to the tone and inflection in which Your Honor is putting questions to this witness. They suggest to the jury that his testimony is unworthy of belief. He respectfully suggests that the question is improper, as the jury must remain the sole judge of the credibility of witnesses."

It may be wise to ask permission to approach the bench to make such objections in order not to heighten the judge's disbelief in the witness' testimony in the minds of the jurors. In any event, make certain that all such objections are recorded, including those made to the use of gestures and facial expressions.[8]

Your objections on the record will alert them to the possibility that your client was deprived of a fair trial by reason of the judge's prejudicial misconduct. Even if this alone does not result in a reversal, it will cause them to examine other claimed errors with a view toward the possible prejudices suffered by your client and cause them to resolve close questions in his favor.

Witnesses for the defense may not be treated in a man-

7. Bollenbach v United States, 326 US 607, 90 L Ed 350, 66 S Ct 402; Wilson v United States (CA9 Cal) 250 F2d 312, reh den 254 F2d 391. See Rothblatt, Handbook of Evidence for Criminal Trials p 273.

Annotation: Remarks or acts of trial judge, criticizing, rebuking, or punishing defense counsel in criminal case, as requiring new trial or reversal. 62 ALR2d 166 at page 244.

8. Veal v State, 196 Tenn 443, 268 SW2d 345.

ner which conveys the impression that the trial judge does not believe their testimony.[9] Care must be taken in this regard, as such a disbelief can be conveyed indirectly.[10] For example, it is error for the trial judge to question witnesses in an incredulous manner which indicates his doubt as to the veracity of their testimony.[11] If the trial judge indicates his disbelief through the use of gestures or facial expressions, note his conduct for the record and object to it. Most judges will immediately deny any intention to convey a belief to the jurors and will immediately state that fact to them.

The trial judge must act even more scrupulously toward the defendant than he does toward defense witnesses. Object immediately if he commits error, either by showing his disbelief in your client's testimony or indicating a belief in his guilt.[12]

There are many ways in which disbelief in a defendant's testimony can be shown. For example, in a case in which an assistant district attorney had testified as to a pre-trial interrogation of the defendant, the defendant, in his testimony, denied that the interrogation had taken place. It was prejudicial error for the judge to thereafter comment that if the defendant was telling the truth, the prosecutor was a liar.[13] Similarly, in a prosecution for housebreaking which had allegedly occurred in the early morning, it was an error for the judge to comment, after the defendant admitted having been in the neighborhood at 3:00 A.M. that "honest people are in bed by 3:00 in the morning."[14]

9. Johnson v Zerbst, 304 US 458, 82 L Ed 1461, 58 S Ct 1019, 146 ALR 357; People v Mendes, 3 NY2d 120, 164 NYS2d 401, 143 NE2d 806; People v Adler, 274 App Div 820, 80 NYS2d 210; People v Shenk, 181 App Div 753, 168 NYS 886, affd without op 228 NY 574, 127 NE 918.

10. People v Ohanian, 245 NY 227, 157 NE 94.

11. People v Kenny, 20 App Div 2d 578, 246 NYS2d 92; People v Viscio, 241 App Div 499, 272 NYS 213.

12. People v Herman, 255 App Div 314, 7 NYS2d 560, People v Robins, 242 App Div 516; 275 NYS 940, Wilson v State, 85 Tex Crim 94, 210 SW 542; Hall v State, 250 Miss 253, 165 So 2d 345; Anderson v State, 27 Wyo 345, 196 P 1047.

13. People v Watts, 11 App Div 2d 1054, 206 NYS2d 157.

14. Cunningham v United States, 114 App DC 86, 311 F2d 772.

§ 570. Disparaging defense counsel

Any disparagement of defense counsel by the trial judge can have as prejudicial an effect upon the defendant as a direct indication of judicial bias against him. Bias or prejudice directed against you can provide ground for reversal in both jury and nonjury trials. Disparagement of defense counsel in the presence of the jurors will almost invariably tend to prejudice them against your client.

It is as much error for a trial judge to indicate disbelief in your statements as it is for him to indicate disbelief in the testimony of the defendant or of defense witnesses. So, for example, it was reversible error for a trial judge to imply in open court during the process of jury selection that defense counsel's affidavit in support of a motion for a continuance was false.[15]

An attempt to make an involuntary witness out of defense counsel has also been held to be reversible error. In one case when the defendant denied the testimony of prosecution witnesses as to admissions allegedly made by him, the trial court told defense counsel to consider himself under oath. He was then asked to stipulate to the correctness of the prosecution testimony.[16]

Harassment or disparagement of defense counsel can manifest itself in many ways. The trial judge may not embarrass the defense attorney in front of the jury by making disparaging remarks which demean him, nor should he make rulings which prevent defense counsel from making an effective presentation or from obtaining a full and fair consideration of the case by the jury.[17]

Some examples of prejudicial misconduct of this type which have led to reversals are comments in an ironic vein

15. Allen v United States (CA9 Alaska) 115 F 3.

16. People v Allen, 25 App Div 2d 955, 271 NYS2d 576.

17. People v Becker, 210 NY 274, 104 NE 396; People v Adler, 274 App Div 820, 80 NYS2d 210; People v Kepner, 267 App Div 838, 46 NYS2d 111.

when defense counsel offered to stipulate to a fact,[18] the characterization of a defense motion as "foolish" or "silly,"[19] or asking a defense attorney who interposes objections to certain testimony, whether or not he wants to keep the truth from coming out.[20]

Among other examples of such types of misconduct are the insinuation that defense counsel had sequestered a prosecution witness,[21] and the suggestion that defense counsel might have been responsible for the reluctance of a prosecution witness to answer questions.[22] Prejudice is clearly shown by references to defense motions as "shyster stuff,"[23] by constant admonitions to defense counsel to be brief,[24] by simply shutting off the examination on the ground that it is too prolix,[25] or by limiting the cross-examination of prosecution witnesses to protect them from being "bulldozed" or "browbeaten."[26] It is also manifested by warnings to defense attorneys to stop wasting the jury's time.[27]

Very often, individual attempts to limit or disparage defense counsel will not seem to offer sufficient basis for reversal. However, when the record is viewed in its entirety, a pattern of bias and hostility may emerge which clearly demonstrates the prejudicial misconduct of the trial

18. Jones v State, 166 Ark 290, 265 SW 974.

19. McAlister v State, 206 Ark 998, 178 SW2d 67.

20. Addis v United States (CA10 Kan) 62 F2d 329, cert den 289 US 744, 77 L Ed 1491, 53 S Ct 688; Cook v State, 36 Ala App 449, 57 So 2d 832.

21. People v Abbott, 4 Cal Unrep 276, 34 P 500.

22. State v Allen, 100 Iowa 7, 69 NW 274.

23. Moore v State, 147 Neb 390, 23 NW2d 552.

24. Sunderland v United States (CA8 Neb) 19 F2d 202.

25. People v Lewerenz, 24 Ill 2d 295, 181 NE2d 99, 93 ALR2d 1092; People v Barca, 9 App Div 2d 920, 194 NYS2d 991; State v Hedding, 122 Vt 379, 172 A2d 599.

26. Willis v Commonwealth, 183 Va 125, 31 SE2d 306.

27. People v Coli, 2 Ill 2d 186, 117 NE2d 777.

judge and requires a reversal of the judgment of conviction.[28]

Among the more extreme examples of hostile judicial conduct which prejudices the defendant is the fining of defense counsel or his commitment to jail in the presence of the jury.[29] The stigma this places upon defense counsel will also inevitably be attached to the defendant as well.[30] If censure of defense counsel is warranted for some reason, it should be administered out of the presence of the jury.[31] A statement to the defense attorney by the trial judge to the effect that he had deliberately caused a witness to swear to false statements is tantamount to a charge of subordination of perjury and is clearly highly prejudicial.[32]

As defense attorney, you are absolutely entitled to be treated by the trial judge in a manner which will not prejudice the rights of your client. You are entitled to this as a matter of right and not of indulgence.[33] Do not allow timidity to prevent you from standing up for your client's rights. Your failure to object to a trial judge's prejudicial misconduct may later be viewed as an intentional waiver of right and may also subject you to later attack for failure to render effective assistance.

§ 571. Cross-examination of defense witnesses

The cross-examination of defense witnesses is the function of the prosecutor. If the trial judge usurps the questioning, he may be held to have shed his cloak of impartiality. In the minds of the jurors he will henceforth be

28. Sunderland v United States (CA8 Neb) 19 F2d 202; People v Becker, 210 NY 274, 104 NE 396; Commonwealth v Field, 171 Pa Super 177, 90 A2d 391; Robertson v State, 38 Tex 187; State v Phillips, 59 Wash 252, 109 P 1047.

29. People v Black, 150 Cal App 2d 494, 310 P2d 472; People v Neal, 290 Mich 123, 287 NW 403; State v Loveless, 140 W Va 875, 87 SE2d 273, later app 142 W Va 809, 98 SE2d 773.

30. State v White, 10 Wash 611, 39 P 160, 41 P 442.

31. Smith v State, 12 Okla Crim 513, 159 P 941; Warren v State, 96 Tex Crim 627, 259 SW 575.

32. Withrow v United States (CA4 W Va) 1 F2d 858.

33. Grock v United States, 53 App DC 146, 289 F 544.

regarded as being on the side of the prosecution.[34] Do not permit the trial judge to follow such a course of conduct.

§ 572. Influencing the jury

The trial judge is obligated to properly answer all questions submitted to him by the jury.[35] His answers must be given in open court with an opportunity to the defense to interpose timely objections. The judge may not attempt to ease the burden upon the jury by telling them that if the defendant is found guilty his sentence will be suspended,[36] or that he has the right to take an appeal.[37] Such statements operate to facilitate guilty verdicts. It is also error to inform the jury that it may take prior crimes committed by the defendant into consideration,[38] if the fact of the commission of such prior crime is not properly before it.[39]

It has been determined to be error for a trial judge to tell the jury, in substance, that they would not be permitted to examine the indictment as there were things in it they should not see.[40] This statement implied that the indictment contained information unfavorable to the defendant.

§ 573. Manner of charging the jury

Prejudice can occur, of course, during the charge to the jury. Errors of law or misstatements of fact can be handled by means of the usual exceptions. Often, however, prejudice is the result of the manner in which the evidence was marshalled. So, for example, if the court overemphasized the prosecution's case to the detriment of the defense, you

34. United States v Hill (CA7 Ill) 332 F2d 105; Jackson v United States, 117 App DC 325, 329 F2d 893.

35. People v Jordan, 18 App Div 2d 923.

36. Bethel v State, 162 Ark 76, 257 SW 740, 31 ALR 402.

37. State v Clark, 227 Or 391, 362 P2d 335.

38. Polansky v United States (CA1 NH) 332 F2d 233; People v Spitzer, 294 NY 5, 60 NE2d 18.

39. People v Powers, 20 App Div 2d 662, 246 NYS2d 578.

40. Faust v State, 222 Ga 27, 148 SE2d 430, conformed to 113 Ga App 539, 149 SE2d 499.

can state, "Your Honor, the defendant objects to so much of the Court's charge as made reference in an animated manner to the testimony of the witnesses Smith, Brown, and Green, as developed on direct examination without an equally animated reference being made by Your Honor to the evidence elicited from these witnesses on cross-examination and to the contradictory statements made by those witnesses in statements taken from them."

A trial judge's reaction in abusive language to a defense suggestion that the charge be in writing also has been held unduly prejudicial.[41]

Error has been committed during the court's ruling on requests for charges when it stated, "Now the Court has heretofore advised counsel of action on fourteen special requests to charge and the defendants, of course, object to the Court's action in over-ruling each of the special requests denied."[42]

The charge itself may not raise collateral issues which are not relevant to the question of guilt or innocence[43] nor may it summarize the contentions of the prosecution without making reference to those of the defense.[44] In this respect, the marshalling of the evidence should refer to points brought out by the defense on cross-examination as well as evidence developed through defense witnesses during their direct testimony.

§ 574. Verdict and sentence

The trial judge generally has discretion with regard to the length of time within which a jury may be held together before it arrives at a determination. It is prejudicial misconduct however, to coerce the jury into reaching a

41. Moulton v State, 199 Ala 411, 74 So 454.

42. United States v Costner (CA6 Tenn) 359 F2d 969.

43. United States v Leggett (CA4 NC) 312 F2d 566.

44. Harding v United States (CA9 Cal) 335 F2d 515; State v Crawford, 261 NC 658, 135 SE2d 652.

verdict. So, for example, the judge may not imply that jurors are violating their oaths by not reaching a verdict.[45]

In non-jury cases, it is prejudicial to the defendant for the trial judge to arrive at a determination on the basis of matters not properly in evidence. He may not base his determination upon matters exclusively within his personal knowledge.[46] To do so effectively deprives the defense of its right of cross-examination. Similarly, the sentence may not be based upon any extraneous matters. A sentence in which the judge made it clear that the defendant was being punished for lying to the court rather than for the crime itself was reversed.[47] It is also error to deny the defendant the opportunity to show cause why sentence should not be imposed.[48]

Trial judges may not misuse the sentence procedure to impose greater punishment. Hence, it is improper to impose a reformatory sentence which is longer than the statutorily permitted sentence for the crime after making a finding that the defendant is not reformable.

45. Kesley v United States (CA5 Fla) 47 F2d 453, 85 ALR 1418; Pierce v Pierce, 38 Mich 412; People v Sheldon, 156 NY 268, 50 NE 840; People v Kincaid, 9 App Div 2d 954, 195 NYS2d 784; People v Dixon, 118 App Div 593, 103 NYS 186, app dismd 190 NY 540, 83 NE 1128; Green v Telfair (NY) 11 How Pr 260.

46. People v Wallenberg, 24 Ill 2d 350, 181 NE2d 143.

47. People v Sinkler, 9 App Div 2d 549, 190 NYS2d 835.

48. People v Nesce, 201 NY 111, 94 NE 655; People v Miles, 13 App Div 2d 509, 211 NYS2d 855.

CHAPTER NINETEEN

THE CHARGE TO THE JURY

A. INTRODUCTION

§ 575. Nature and purpose of charge

The accused has a right to have the jury properly instructed, and every essential part of the case should be covered by the instructions given.[1] In other words, the instructions to the jury should present the case in all of the phases and aspects in which the jury should consider it.[2]

More convictions are reversed because of errors in the charge than because of errors committed during other portions of the trial. Appellate courts often consider errors made in admitting evidence inconsequential. But when the

1. State v Hoot, 120 Iowa 238, 94 NW 564.

Annotations: Giving, in accused's absence, additional instruction to jury after submission of felony case. 94 ALR2d 270 at page 307.

Propriety and effect, in criminal case, of use of alias of accused in instructions to jury. 87 ALR2d 1217.

Procedure to be followed where jury requests information as to possibility of pardon or parole from sentence imposed. 35 ALR2d 769.

Propriety and effect of court's indication to jury that court would suspend sentence. 8 ALR2d 1001.

2. Woodbury v State, 69 Ala 242.

Appellate Court is faced with an improper charge, it will be quick to deem the error grave and serious.

§ 576. Duty of court to instruct on law

With respect to criminal cases, it is the rule in some states that whether requested or not, it is the duty of the court to instruct the jury upon all questions of law arising therein, or, under some statutes, upon all questions of law necessary for the information of the jury in giving their verdict,[3] whereas under the statutes of some states it is only in felony cases that the court is required to give the law applicable to the case irrespective of a request to do so.[4]

It has been held that the rules which obtain in civil cases in relation to the authority of the court to instruct the jury upon all matters of law arising upon the issues to be tried are usually applicable in the trial of criminal cases.[5]

In some jurisdictions, it is provided that the jury in criminal cases have the right to determine the law as well as the facts. In those states operating under such provisions, it is held that while it is proper for the court to give instructions to the jury, being careful to do so in advisory form,[6] the question of giving instructions rests in the judge's discretion.[7] On the other hand, some courts take the view that the court's obligation to explain the law is not

3. State v Dowell, 47 Idaho 457, 276 P 39, 68 ALR 1061; State v Baird, 288 Mo 62, 231 SW 625, 15 ALR 1035; State v Martin, 230 Mo 1, 129 SW 931; Mitchell v Bradstreet Co., 116 Mo 226, 22 SW 358, 724 (stating rule); Young v State, 74 Neb 346, 104 NW 867.

4. Miers v State, 34 Tex Crim 161, 29 SW 1074; Jones v State, 33 Tex Crim 492, 26 SW 1082.

5. Sparf v United States, 156 US 51, 39 L Ed 343, 15 S Ct 273.

6. Beard v State, 71 Md 275, 17 A 1044.

While the jury in a criminal case is the judge of the law as well as the facts, the trial court, pursuant to a state rule, may, and at the request of the defendant or the state shall, give such advisory instructions to the jury as may correctly state the applicable law. Barger v State, 235 Md 556, 202 A2d 344, 9 ALR3d 926.

7. Beard v State, 71 Md 275, 17 A 1044.

diminished by the right of the jury to judge of the law.[8] In this case it is made the duty of the court to instruct the jury as to the law in the case,[9] and at the same time to inform them that they are judges of the law,[10] and if he errs in so doing, the error may be reviewed on appeal as in other cases.[11]

The trial court in a murder prosecution did not err in failing to point instructions concerning reasonable doubt and circumstantial evidence specifically to the issue of the degree of the crime rather than to the defendant's right to acquittal, where the defendant's plea of not guilty remained before the court, and there were other instructions that the jury should consider not merely the issue of first degree murder or acquittal, but that the defendant should be given the benefit of any doubt in determining the degree of the crime.[12]

Instructions on the effect of circumstantial evidence, of testimony of accomplices, of wilfully false testimony, and of testimony elicited for impeachment, being merely cautionary in nature, the failure to give such instructions does not constitute error in the absence of a request therefor.[13]

§ 577. Written instructions

Unless constitution, statute, or rule of court so requires, instructions need not always be in writing,[14] although it has been declared to be better practice in all cases to have the charge in writing,[15] and in many states the statutes or

8. Posey v State, 234 Ind 696, 131 NE2d 145, 54 ALR2d 706; Commonwealth v Knapp, 27 Mass (10 Pick) 477.

9. Hudelson v State, 94 Ind 426; State v Syphrett, 27 SC 29, 2 SE 624 (libel case).

10. Hudelson v State, 94 Ind 426.

11. State v Syphrett, 27 SC 29, 2 SE 624.

12. People v Morse, 60 Cal 2d 631, 36 Cal Rptr 201, 388 P2d 33, 12 ALR3d 810.

13. State v Turner (Mo) 272 SW2d 266, 48 ALR2d 1008.

14. State v Woodrow, 58 W Va 527, 52 SE 545.

15. State v Woodrow, 58 W Va 527, 52 SE 545; Gardner v State, 27 Wyo 316, 196 P 750, 15 ALR 1040.

rules of practice in various terms require written instructions.

B. CAUTIONARY INSTRUCTIONS

§ 578. Testimony of witnesses

It is not a proper function of a court to classify witnesses to a jury and say that one class is to be viewed with caution because its vices are different in kind or degree from those of another class.[16] Thus, a jury may not be directed to view with caution the testimony of an abandoned woman.[17]

While it would be proper to tell the jury that it is their duty to consider whether the fact that a witness expected a reward in case of conviction affected the truthfulness of his testimony, it would be improper to tell the jury to receive his testimony with caution and distrust on this account.[18]

It is not prejudicial to give an instruction, applicable to witnesses for the prosecution, in effect stating that the testimony of persons convicted of a crime is to be examined with caution, and to be disregarded unless it produces in the jurors' minds positive conviction of its truth.[19]

§ 579. Testimony of detectives or police officers

There is some authority to the effect that the giving of instructions as to the caution to be observed in weighing the testimony of private detectives or persons employed to find evidence rests largely in the discretion of the trial

16. Hronek v People, 134 Ill 139, 24 NE 861; Jones v Casler, 139 Ind 382, 38 NE 812; State v Tuttle, 67 Ohio St 440, 66 NE 524.

Annotation: Admissibility of photograph of corpse in prosecution for homicide or civil action for causing death. 73 ALR2d 769 at page 800.

17. State v Tuttle, 67 Ohio St 440, 66 NE 524.

18. State v Wisnewski, 13 ND 649, 102 NW 883.

19. Marino v United States (CA9 Cal) 91 F2d 691, 113 ALR 975, cert den 302 US 764, 82 L Ed 593, 58 S Ct 410.

court.[20] Other authorities are to the effect that the defendant in a criminal action is entitled to such instruction when a detective's testimony is relied on by the state.[21]

In general, an instruction warning the jury to use great care in weighing the testimony of police officers should be refused.[22] There is authority, however, to the effect that such an instruction is proper when, and only when, the officer is a witness for the state in an endeavor to convict the accused.[23]

§ 580. Testimony of accomplice

In some jurisdictions it has been held that the giving of cautionary instructions regarding the testimony of an accomplice is a matter within the discretion of the trial court and that it is not reversible error to refuse such an instruction.[24]

In other jurisdictions the rule is that an accused on trial

20. Jaynes v People, 44 Colo 535, 99 P 325.

But compare Hronek v People, 134 Ill 139, 24 NE 861, holding that an instruction that the evidence of private detectives should be received with a large degree of caution is properly refused because not containing a correct proposition of law.

21. Sandage v State, 61 Neb 240, 85 NW 35.

22. Wilder v People, 86 Colo 35, 278 P 594, 65 ALR 1260; Hronek v People, 134 Ill 139, 24 NE 861.

See People v Mendelson, 264 Ill 453, 106 NE 249, holding improper instructions singling out policemen and stating the rule for determining their credibility.

23. Shellenberger v State, 97 Neb 498, 150 NW 643.

In Romero v State, 101 Neb 650, 164 NW 554, the court held the instruction proper but disapproved of a sentence to the effect that the instruction was not intended to impeach or discredit the testimony of police officers, but only as a reasonable caution to be borne in mind.

24. State v Simpson, 120 Utah 596, 236 P2d 1077.

Annotations: Propriety of specific jury instructions as to credibility of accomplices. 4 ALR3d 351.

Thief as accomplice of one charged with receiving stolen property, or vice versa, within rule requiring corroboration or cautionary instruction. 53 ALR2d 817.

Question as to who are accomplices, within rule requiring corroboration of their testimony, as one of law or fact. 19 ALR2d 1352 at page 1387.

is entitled to have the jury instructed as to the weight and consideration to be given the testimony of an accomplice, and specifically informed that the testimony of an accomplice should be received with care and caution.[25] However, requests may be refused where the subject matter is covered by instructions given,[26] or where there is circumstantial evidence of guilt as well as the testimony of an accomplice.[27] Nor should the instruction be given where the accomplice is called as a witness on behalf of the defendant.[28]

25. People v Berardi, 332 Ill 295, 163 NE 668, 62 ALR 274; Hoyt v People, 140 Ill 588, 30 NE 315; State v Richardson, 248 Mo 563, 154 SW 735 (recognizing rule); State v Kuhlman, 152 Mo 100, 53 SW 416; Dunn v People, 29 NY 523; Kern v Pullen, 138 Or 222, 6 P2d 224, 82 ALR 434 (overruled as to construction of statute involved in Fitze v American-Hawaiian S. S. Co. 167 Or 439, 117 P2d 825); Commonwealth v DeMasi, 234 Pa 570, 83 A 430.

See United States v Lancaster (CC Ga) 44 F 896, wherein the court instructed the jury that the credit to be given the accomplice was entirely for them, that they should anxiously and judiciously scan the evidence, and that to refuse to consider the accomplice's testimony merely because he was an accomplice would be to hold him incompetent.

See also State v Foster, 38 NM 540, 37 P2d 541, 95 ALR 1247, holding it proper to refuse an instruction as to a plea of guilty under a promise of clemency as affecting credibility, where the promise was not made to the codefendants personally.

In Hoyt v People, 140 Ill 588, 30 NE 315, it was held reversible error to refuse a request to instruct the jury that while a person accused of a crime may be convicted upon the uncorroborated testimony of an accomplice, a jury should always act upon such testimony with great care and caution, and subject it to careful examination, in the light of all other evidence in the case; and the jury ought not to convict upon such testimony alone, unless after a careful examination of such testimony they are satisfied beyond a reasonable doubt of its truth, and they can safely rely upon it.

26. People v Berardi, 332 Ill 295, 163 NE 668, 62 ALR 274.

The rule requiring the usual cautionary instructions in case of accomplices is satisfied, where each defendant seeks to cast the blame onto the other, by an instruction that neither of the defendants could be convicted on the unsupported testimony of the other, which is more favorable to the complaining defendant than a mere request for a cautionary instruction. State v Clark, 156 Wash 47, 286 P 69, 85 ALR 502.

27. State v Troiana, 129 Wash 228, 224 P 388; Cupps v State, 120 Wis 504, 97 NW 210, same result reached on reh 120 Wis 532, 98 NW 546.

28. Ainsworth v Munoskong Hunting & Fishing Club, 153 Mich 185, 116 NW 992; State v Mintz, 245 Mo 540, 150 SW 1042.

§ 581. Sexual offenses

In a prosecution for a sexual offense, according to some authorities the defendant should be afforded a cautionary instruction that the charge is easily made and difficult to disprove,[29] and that for that reason the testimony of the prosecuting witness should be examined with caution.[30] However, the failure to give such an instruction, although sometimes a ground for reversal,[31] is not necessarily so.[32]

Such failure may not be complained of where the giving of such instruction was not requested,[33] and the denial of a requested instruction is not error where it is in effect covered by the instructions given.[34] Moreover, there is authority to the effect that the matter of defending against the charge, although proper by way of argument of counsel, is not proper as an independent instruction,[35] and also to the effect that the propriety of giving or refusing a cautionary instruction on the subject generally rests in the trial court's discretion.[36]

C. SUBJECT MATTER

§ 582. In general

The court is duty bound in a criminal case to charge on every issue or theory having any support in the evidence.[37]

29. People v Lucas, 16 Cal 2d 178, 105 P2d 102, 130 ALR 1485.

30. People v Lucas, supra.

Annotation: Admissibility, in prosecution for sexual offense, as evidence of other similar offenses. 77 ALR2d 841 at page 906.

31. State v Clevenger, 27 NM 466, 202 P 687.

32. People v Lucas, 16 Cal 2d 178, 105 P2d 102, 130 ALR 1485; State v Loomer, 105 Kan 410, 184 P 723.

33. McQueary v People, 48 Colo 214, 110 P 210.

34. State v Trusty, 122 Iowa 82, 97 NW 989, wherein the court noted in connection with the instruction in question that the jury was otherwise adequately instructed as to their duties with regard to the evidence.

35. Doyle v State, 39 Fla 155, 22 So 272.

36. State v Lightheart, 153 Minn 40, 189 NW 408.

37. Stevenson v United States, 162 US 313, 40 L Ed 980, 16 S Ct 839; Judge v State, 58 Ala 406; State v Scheele, 57 Conn 307, 18 A 256; Vasquez v State, 54 Fla 127, 44 So 739;

An instruction should be given on circumstantial evidence, whether requested or not, where the defendant's guilt depends upon such evidence in whole or in part.[38]

The instructions should distinctly set forth the law applicable not only to the case as made by the evidence for the prosecution, but also to the case as made by all the evidence, and especially to any favorable evidence comprising defensive matter in behalf of the accused.[39] It has been observed that if a court attempts to summarize and declare the contentions made by either party, he should do it with great care, and only after being assured that he appreciates not only what those contentions are, but also their relative importance as viewed by the counsel.[40]

§ 583. Stating and defining the offense and its elements

Where time is not of the essence of the offense charged, it is not error to direct the jury that it is sufficient to find that the crime was committed "on or about" the time

Delk v State, 135 Ga 312, 69 SE 541; Davis v Commonwealth, 193 Ky 597, 237 SW 24, 23 ALR 1551; State v Martinez, 30 NM 178, 230 P 379; Commonwealth v McMurray, 198 Pa 51, 47 A 952; State v Turner, 29 SC 34, 6 SE 891; Monroe v State, 23 Tex 210.

Annotations: Prejudicial effect of statement or instruction of court as to possibility of parole or pardon. 12 ALR3d 832.

Instructions urging dissenting jurors in criminal case to give due consideration to opinion of majority. 100 ALR2d 177.

Identification of accused by his voice. 70 ALR2d 995 at page 1019.

Conviction of lesser offense, against which statute of limitations has run, where statute has not run against offense with which defendant is charged. 47 ALR2d 887 at pages 890 and 892.

Modern view as to propriety and correctness of instructions referable to maxim "falsus in uno, falsus in omnibus." 4 ALR2d 1077.

38. Lair v State (Okla Crim) 316 P2d 225, 71 ALR2d 856, stating that it is reversible error not to instruct on the fundamentals of a case.

39. Bird v United States, 180 US 356, 45 L Ed 570, 21 S Ct 403; Washington v State, 63 Ala 135; State v Budge, 126 Me 223, 137 A 244, 53 ALR 241; State v Baird, 288 Mo 62, 231 SW 625, 15 ALR 1035; State v Martinez, 39 NM 290, 46 P2d 657; Long v State, 59 Tex Crim 103, 127 SW 551; Meuly v State, 26 Tex App 274, 9 SW 563; State v Stenback, 78 Utah 350, 2 P2d 1050, 79 ALR 878.

40. Duthey v State, 131 Wis 178, 111 NW 222.

charged,[41] and to refuse instructions precluding conviction because of an immaterial variance as to time.[42]

It is the rule in many states that, whether requested to or not, it is the duty of the court in criminal cases to instruct the jury upon all questions of law arising therein, statutes frequently containing an express injunction to this effect. Where this is the situation, language frequently appears in the decisions indicating that, at least as an abstract proposition, it is the duty of the judge in a criminal case to define and explain the offense charged for the benefit of the jury. Stated differently, it is the duty of the court in its charge to give the law as to the offense charged and the elements thereof.[43]

In some, but not all, of the states in which the constitutions or statutes provide that the jury shall be judges of the

41. Ferguson v State, 52 Neb 432, 72 NW 590.

42. Commonwealth v Major, 198 Pa 290, 47 A 741.

43. People v McClintic, 193 Mich 589, 160 NW 461; Commonwealth v Paese, 220 Pa 371, 69 A 891 (approving definition of "manslaughter").

See Commonwealth v Di Stasio, 297 Mass 347, 8 NE2d 923, 113 ALR 1133, cert den 302 US 683, 759, 82 L Ed 527, 587, 58 S Ct 50, 370, a prosecution against an accessory, wherein an instruction as to first degree murder by the principal was held not to take the question of degree of murder from the jury.

In State v McGuire, 84 Conn 470, 80 A 761, a homicide case, the court observed that "in most cases a more practical and helpful charge can be given without any attempt to define the crime charged or the elements of it to the jury," and further, that the court can best perform its duty "by calling the jury's attention to the evidence and claims, and telling them what the conclusion of the law is upon each state of facts which they may be warranted in finding upon the evidence, and instructing them as to the verdict which they should render upon each of the states of fact which may be found."

Where an instruction gives details of all the elements of the crime charged, and as a condition to conviction requires proof thereof beyond a reasonable doubt, it is not incumbent on the court to instruct as to the necessity for proof beyond a reasonable doubt as to one element alone. Cahill v People, 111 Colo 29, 137 P2d 673, 148 ALR 536.

Annotations: Criminal conspiracies as to gambling. 91 ALR2d 1148 at page 1203.

Entrapment with respect to violation of fish and game laws. 75 ALR2d 709.

Effect of failure or refusal of court, in robbery prosecution, to instruct on assault and battery. 58 ALR2d 808.

law as well as the facts in criminal cases, the view is taken that although the judge in a criminal case may in his discretion give the jury advisory instructions, he is not required to do so. Where this view prevails the judge in a criminal case is under no duty to give instructions defining the offense charged or to instruct the jury as to the nature thereof.[44] Further, the judge need not instruct the jury that the defendant is not on trial for certain other designated offenses.[45]

In charging as to the elements of the crime, the court may use the language of the statute violated,[46] and may, indeed, quote the statute itself,[47] except for inapplicable parts,[48] such as the provision as to punishment where the jury have nothing to do therewith. So too, where the crime charged is defined in one subdivision of a statute, it is error to read to the jury the other subdivisions defining unrelated crimes.[49] But the failure to eliminate the inapplicable

44. In Beard v State, 71 Md 275, 17 A 1044, a prosecution for keeping a common nuisance, it was recognized that a constitutional provision that "in the trial of all criminal cases the jury shall be the judges of law as well as of fact" was merely declaratory of existing law at the time of its adoption; that both before and since it had been the practice of judges in some parts of the state to decline to give instructions to the jury in criminal cases under any circumstances, while in other parts of the state it had been the practice to give advisory instructions when requested to do so; that whether to do so or not was regarded as discretionary with the trial judge, there being no positive duty requiring him to pursue the one course or the other; that, in any event, instructions in criminal cases were advisory, and the judge could not thereby bind the jury as to the definition of the crime or as to the legal effect of the evidence before them.

45. State v Ryno, 68 Kan 348, 74 P 1114.

46. Cahill v People, 111 Colo 29, 137 P2d 673, 148 ALR 536; Alt v State, 88 Neb 259, 129 NW 432; Clark v State, 28 Tex App 189, 12 SW 729.

47. Alt v State, 88 Neb 259, 129 NW 432.

Where many acts of sexual intercourse between the defendant and the prosecutrix had been proved, the act of the court in reading the statute violated could not mislead the jury into believing that they might find the defendant guilty of any other offense than that on which the state elected to ask a conviction, where the jury were specifically instructed that they could not convict for acts at any other time. People v Turner, 265 Ill 594, 107 NE 162.

48. Hiller v State, 116 Neb 582, 218 NW 386, 58 ALR 1322.

49. In a prosecution for extortion by

portions of the definition is not ground for reversal where no prejudice results therefrom,[50] or where, reading the charge as a whole, the instruction upon the subject of the offense is limited to the allegations of the indictment or information.[51]

Instructions need not be couched in the same form or phraseology as the indictment or information.[52] Thus, although the word "feloniously" should be used in an indictment or information charging a felony, this is not necessary in instructions.[53]

Instructions as to the offense must include every element thereof.[54] Thus, if the crime is not defined in the language of the statute, the language used must set forth the essential constituents of the offense.[55] When a court attempts to gather the elements of the crime and tell the jury that if they are proved there must be a verdict of guilty, all the elements constituting the crime charged must be set out.[56] At least, this is the general rule where the trial judge attempts to state to the jury the elements of the offense charged.[57]

No further definition of the crime is necessary where the court in its charge requires the jury, as a condition to conviction, to find every fact necessary to constitute the offense.[58]

threat to accuse one of grand larceny, instructions defining larceny should be restricted to the kind of larceny referred to in the threat. Lee v State, 16 Ariz 291, 145 P 244.

50. Cahill v People, 111 Colo 29, 137 P2d 673, 148 ALR 536; Ferguson v State, 52 Neb 432, 72 NW 590.

51. State v Rodriguez, 23 NM 156, 167 P 426.

52. Whitaker v Commonwealth, 188 Ky 95, 221 SW 215, 10 ALR 145.

53. Stout v Commonwealth, 123 Ky 184, 94 SW 15.

54. State v Johnson, 8 Iowa 525; Jones v State, 95 Miss 121, 48 So 407; Hans v State, 72 Neb 288, 100 NW 419; State v Magill, 19 ND 131, 122 NW 330.

55. State v Magill, supra.

56. State v Sipes, 202 Iowa 173, 209 NW 458, 47 ALR 407.

57. State v Sipes, supra.

58. State v Keyes, 196 Mo 136, 93 SW 801.

A reference in the instructions to "the crime charged" is not improper.[59] But to use the disjunctive "or" instead of the conjunctive "and" in enumerating the elements of the crime is fatal error.[60]

One aspect of the broad question of the duty of the judge in a criminal case to define or explain the offense charged is his duty with respect to defining or explaining particular words or phrases appearing in the statutes or case law establishing the offense. The courts tend, in this connection, to distinguish between the unusual and technical words and phrases and words which are of common usage or self-explanatory in character, holding that while the trial judge may have some duty to define or explain technical words used in setting out the offense charged, he ordinarily has no duty to explain or define non-technical, self-explaining words or phrases which are of easy comprehension to the ordinary layman. The cases are by no means in agreement on the question whether certain specific words, such, for example, as "deliberation" and "premeditation," are to be regarded for the purpose under consideration as technical or non-technical terms.[61]

§ 584. Reasonable doubt

In a criminal case, the jury must be instructed that the crime must be proved beyond a reasonable doubt; otherwise the accused must be acquitted, and the court's failure or

59. State v Thornton, 10 SD 349, 73 NW 196.

60. State v Magill, 19 ND 131, 122 NW 330.

61. In State v Stenback, 78 Utah 350, 2 P2d 1050, 79 ALR 878, it is said, obiter regarding the failure of the trial court to define deliberation or premeditation: "It is of vital concern to the defendant and to the state that the jury be instructed as to the meaning of these terms, because unless they are understood the jury cannot intelligently distinguish murder in the first degree from murder in the second degree. The jury should have been instructed as to the meaning of these terms, because it cannot be assumed that a jury of laymen fully understand their meaning as applied to first degree murder."

refusal to do so will ordinarily constitute reversible error.[62] Moreover, it is the duty of the judge so to charge without a request.[63] The defendant is entitled to such an instruction in every case,[64] and a statute may expressly direct that such instruction be given.[65]

§ 585. Character or reputation of accused

Because of the generally accepted proposition that one of good character is less likely to commit crime than one of bad reputation, it has become appropriate and common for courts to charge the jury that good reputation, if proved, is a fact to be considered by the jury, together with all other facts and circumstances of the case, in reaching the ultimate conclusion of guilt or innocence.[66]

To charge, however, that evidence of good character is

62. Wilson v United States, 232 US 563, 58 L Ed 728, 34 S Ct 347 (holding that by the instruction given the court did instruct as to the rule); Agnew v United States, 165 US 36, 41 L Ed 624, 17 S Ct 235; Cochran v United States, 157 US 286, 39 L Ed 704, 15 S Ct 628; Marshall v State, 219 Ala 83, 121 So 72, 63 ALR 560; Letcher v State, 159 Ala 59, 48 So 805; Hall v State, 78 Fla 420, 83 So 513, 8 ALR 1034; Commonwealth v York, 50 Mass (9 Met) 93; State v Griffin, 98 SC 105, 82 SE 254.

63. Hamilton v State, 96 Ga 301, 22 SE 528.

64. Kaufman v United States (CA2 NY) 212 F 613; Monaghan v State, 10 Okla Crim 89, 134 P 77.

65. Kern v Pullen, 138 Or 222, 6 P2d 224, 82 ALR 434, ovrld in part Fitze v American-Hawaiian S. S. Co. 167 Or 439, 117 P2d 825.

66. Perara v United States (CA8 Ark) 235 F 515, 10 ALR 1; State v Cushing, 14 Wash 527, 45 P 145, later app 17 Wash 544, 50 P 512.

In Perara v United States (CA8 Ark) 235 F 515, 10 ALR 1, it was observed that a statement of the kind referred to in the text, without elaboration, was about all that could be profitably or safely said to a jury on the subject. But other courts have observed that such a statement added nothing to the mere fact of letting the testimony in. See quotations in opinion of Straup, J., in State v Brown, 39 Utah 140, 115 P 994.

In State v Cushing, 14 Wash 527, 45 P 145, later app 17 Wash 544, 50 P 512, it was held error to refuse a request for the following instruction: "You are instructed that the defendant is entitled to have the evidence touching the question of his reputation for peace and quietude considered by the jury in determining the question of his guilt, and especially in determining the question as to who was the aggressor in the affray in which K lost his life. In such cases, proof of good reputation for peace and quietude on the part of the defendant

proper to be considered as a circumstance tending to prove the defendant's guilt or innocence constitutes error.[67]

An instruction that since the law presumes that a person of good character is less likely to commit a crime than a person of a different reputation, the jury should consider evidence of the defendant's good character together with all other evidence in the case, was properly refused, because there was no such presumption, and because also, instead of leaving it to the jury to attach such importance to the evidence as they think proper, the instruction should inform them expressly of the scope of their power in the exercise of a sound discretion with respect to the evidence.[68]

§ 586. Instructing on knowledge, malice and intent

Although the statute defining a crime may not use the word "knowingly," yet where the element of knowledge is implied as an element of the offense, it is proper in instructions to require a finding thereof as a condition of conviction.[69]

is proper evidence to be considered by the jury in connection with all the other evidence. In determining the guilt or innocence of the accused, the weight to be attached to the fact of good character or reputation, like that to be attached to every other fact of the case, is for the jury alone to determine."

Annotations: Admissibility, in robbery prosecution, of evidence of other robberies. 42 ALR2d 854 at page 885.

Admissibility, in prosecution for illegal sale of intoxicating liquor, of other sales. 40 ALR2d 817 at page 863.

Admissibility, in prosecution for bribery or accepting bribes, of evidence tending to show commission of other bribery or acceptance of bribe. 20 ALR2d 1012 at page 1036.

Admissibility, in prosecution based on abortion, of evidence of commission of similar crimes by accused. 15 ALR2d 1080 at page 1113.

67. People v Fisher, 295 Ill 250, 129 NE 196.

68. Cahill v People, 111 Colo 29, 137 P2d 673, 148 ALR 536, but noting that some courts have approved instructions containing the words "the law presumes."

69. United States v Agueci (CA2 NY) 310 F2d 817, 99 ALR2d 478, cert den 372 US 959, 10 L Ed 2d 11, 83 S Ct 1013, cert den 372 US 959, 10 L Ed 2d 12, 83 S Ct 1016; State v Aschenbrenner, 171 Or 664, 138 P2d 911, 147 ALR 1052.

Annotations: Homicide: presump-

In every criminal prosecution, the court should instruct the jury as to the mental element which is a requisite of the crime charged,[70] and is guilty of error if in its instructions it authorizes a conviction without proof of such element.[71] Thus, an instruction making the question of guilt depend solely upon the intentional doing of an unlawful act constitutes error where a specific criminal intent is a material element of the crime charged.[72] However, a failure to charge in the precise language of a request is not prejudicial where the matter is covered in the instructions given.[73]

Where malice is an element of the crime charged, it must be included in the definition of the offense given to the jury,[74] or in a formula or hypothetical instruction as to guilt if the jury believe certain facts.[75]

On the other hand, an instruction requiring a finding of malice aforethought is erroneous where the statute merely provides that the act must be done maliciously.[76]

§ 587. Motive

Some courts are committed to the doctrine that the defendant is entitled to an instruction on the subject of motive.[77] Thus, the jury may be instructed that the failure

tion of deliberation and premeditation from circumstances attending the killing. 96 ALR2d 1435.

Homicide: presumption of deliberation or premeditation from the fact of killing. 86 ALR2d 656 at page 659.

70. State v Johnson, 8 Iowa 525.

71. Miller v Oklahoma (CA8 Okla) 149 F 330; People v Dole, 122 Cal 486, 55 P 581; State v Warren, 109 Mo 430, 19 SW 191; State v Gee Jon, 46 Nev 418, 211 P 676, 30 ALR 1443, reh den 46 Nev 438, 217 P 587, 30 ALR 1451.

72. People v Flack, 125 NY 324, 26 NE 267.

73. People v Katz, 209 NY 311, 103 NE 305.

74. Watkins v Commonwealth, 146 Ky 449, 142 SW 1035; Crow v State, 136 Tenn 333, 189 SW 687, 1 ALR 1160.

75. State v Gee Jon, 46 Nev 418, 211 P 676, 30 ALR 1443, reh den 46 Nev 438, 217 P 587, 30 ALR 1451, but holding the omission not prejudicial.

76. Green v State, 151 Ala 14, 44 So 194.

77. Trobough v State, 119 Neb 128, 227 NW 443, 64 ALR 1051.

Annotation: Necessity that trial

of the evidence to show any motive to commit the crime is a circumstance which the jury should consider;[78] but according to some authorities, it is not error to fail or to refuse to give such an instruction,[79] unless the court gives an instruction on behalf of the state authorizing a conviction whether or not any motive is apparent, in which case the defendant is entitled to the converse thereof.[80]

In a proper case a trial court may instruct the jury that proof of motive is not essential to enable them to find the defendant guilty.[81]

§ 588. Parties to crime; aiding and abetting

In proper cases the trial court should in its instructions state the law as to principals in crime,[82] as to principals

court charge upon motive in homicide case. 71 ALR2d 1025.

78. State v Logan, 344 Mo 351, 126 SW2d 256, 122 ALR 417; State v Vanella, 40 Mont 326, 106 P 364 (holding it proper to modify the request by substituting for the words "a circumstance in favor of his [accused's] innocence," the words "a circumstance which you should consider"); State v Lu Sing, 34 Mont 31, 85 P 521; Trobough v State, 119 Neb 128, 227 NW 443, 65 ALR 1051.

See People v Brown, 203 NY 44, 96 NE 367, holding nonprejudicial an instruction on motive, which assumed a fact.

79. Singh v State, 35 Ariz 432, 280 P 672, 67 ALR 129; People v Enright, 256 Ill 221, 99 NE 936; State v Logan, 344 Mo 351, 126 SW2d 256, 122 ALR 417; State v Feeley, 194 Mo 300, 92 SW 663.

See People v Enright, 256 Ill 221, 99 NE 936, holding that where there is no evidence as to relations between the defendant and the murdered person, an instruction as to the right of the jury to consider the absence of evidence showing motive is calculated to mislead them into understanding that the law requires evidence of a motive.

80. State v Logan, 344 Mo 351, 126 SW2d 256, 122 ALR 417.

81. Hotema v United States, 186 US 413, 46 L Ed 1225, 22 S Ct 895; Johnson v United States, 157 US 320, 39 L Ed 717, 15 S Ct 614.

In Johnson v United States, supra, it was held not error to modify an instruction as to motive by adding the observation "that the presence or absence of motive is not a necessary requisite to enable you to find the guilt of a party."

82. See McAlister v State, 45 Tex Crim 258, 76 SW 760, holding an instruction as to who are principals to be incorrect.

and accessories,[83] and as to guilt of persons acting together in the commission of a crime where either of them actually commits it,[84] although the court may refuse such a charge when it is not justified by the facts.[85]

It has been held that, in a prosecution for conspiracy to violate the federal narcotics law and for substantive violations of the law by the defendants individually, the trial judge has the burden of impressing upon the jury the need for judging each defendant separately upon each separate substantive count charged in the indictment.[86] Instructions on the subject of constructive presence are proper, where the evidence shows that a wound was inflicted by another person, while the defendant, although nearby, did not show himself until after the murder had been accomplished.[87]

Subject to the foregoing rules, where there is proof of an aiding and abetting, it is proper to predicate an instruction thereon.[88] An instruction on the subject should require the finding of the requisite intent,[89] and should use the conjunc-

83. See Commonwealth v Di Stasio, 297 Mass 347, 8 NE2d 923, 113 ALR 1133, cert den 302 US 683, 759, 82 L Ed 527, 587, 58 S Ct 50, 370.

84. In State v Tucker, 36 Or 291, 61 P 894, a burglary case, it was held that the instruction was warranted by proof of the breaking, that two persons were engaged in it, and that the defendant and another were shortly thereafter engaged in disposing of the propery stolen.

85. Bird v United States, 187 US 118, 47 L Ed 100, 23 S Ct 42.

86. United States v Agueci (CA2 NY) 310 F2d 817, 99 ALR2d 478, cert den 372 US 959, 10 L Ed 2d 11, 83 S Ct 1013, cert den 372 US 959, 10 L Ed 2d 12, 83 S Ct 1016.

87. Johnson v United States, 157 US 320, 39 L Ed 717, 15 S Ct 614.

88. Reed v Commonwealth, 273 Ky 607, 117 SW2d 589, 116 ALR 673; State v Clark, 156 Wash 47, 286 P 69, 85 ALR 502.

See Coffin v United States, 162 US 664, 40 L Ed 1109, 16 S Ct 943 (holding the instruction given not to be erroneous); Spies v People, 122 Ill 1, 12 NE 865, 17 NE 898, error dismd 123 US 131, 31 L Ed 80, 8 S Ct 22 (holding that an instruction as to advice to commit murder was not too broad in view of other instructions as to aiding and abetting); State v Carmody, 50 Or 1, 91 P 446, 1081 (holding the instruction stated a rule of statutory law); Campbell v State, 63 Tex Crim 595, 141 SW 232 (holding the refusal of the request was not error, in view of the instruction given).

89. Hicks v United States, 150 US 442, 37 L Ed 1137, 14 S Ct 144.

In Chapman v State, 43 Tex Crim 328, 65 SW 1098, it was held that

tive "aid and abet" instead of the disjunctive "aid or abet."[90] But there is a cure of the error in using the words "aid or abet" in an instruction as to aiders and abettors, where, from another instruction, the jury cannot fail to understand that merely aiding or assisting in the commission of a crime, without guilty knowledge, is not criminal.[91]

If there is no evidence to show a previous conspiracy between the accused and the person who killed the victim, it is error in effect to charge that where an accomplice is present for the purpose of aiding and abetting in a murder, but refrains from so aiding and abetting because it turns out not to be necessary, for the accomplishment of the common purpose, he is as guilty as if he had actively participated.[92]

after defining "principals," the trial court should have instructed the jury that if the defendant was present, knowing the unlawful intent of the other parties, naming them, and if he adopted said intent, and while present he aided by acts or encouraged by words or gestures and consented to the commission of the crime, then, in that event, he would be guilty as a principal.

If the actual doer of the offense may be guilty of one degree of felonious homicide, and the aider or abettor guilty of another, the case should be properly presented to the jury as to the person actually committing the offense, embracing his or her intent, and then the jury should be instructed that if the accused, knowing such intent of the actual committer of the offense, entered into it, and aided such doer, with some other intent on his part of a greater or less degree, they should find him guilty and assess his punishment accordingly. Red v State, 39 Tex Crim 667, 47 SW 1003.

A correct rule is stated in a requested instruction that in the absence of a conspiracy, oen who is present when a homicide is committed by another during a sudden quarrel, or in the heat of passion, is not guilty of aiding and abetting the homicide, although he may become involved in an independent fight with others of the party of the deceased, unless he does some overt act with a view to produce that result, or purposely incites the principal to do the act. And it is error to modify it by striking the words "with a view" and inserting instead the word "tending," thus authorizing a conviction of the accused without proof of a guilty purpose. Woolweaver v State, 50 Ohio St 277, 34 NE 352.

90. People v Dole, 122 Cal 486, 55 P 581.

But see Commonwealth v Macloon, 101 Mass 1.

91. People v Dole, 122 Cal 486, 55 P 581.

92. Hicks v United States, 150 US 442, 37 L Ed 1137, 14 S Ct 144.

§ 589. Incriminating circumstances; flight, concealment, attempted escape

Where, in a criminal case, there is evidence of the defendant's flight, the jury should be properly instructed as to the manner in which they should consider and weigh such evidence,[93] unless, it has been ruled, the only issue to be determined by the jury is one other than the defendant's commission of the crime, as where a number of eyewitnesses testify as to his having committed the crime, and especially where his counsel admits his participation therein.[94] Refusal to instruct a jury that they might consider that the defendant did not attempt to flee after the crime has been held not error, the court having given the usual instruction on the presumption of innocence.[95]

Evidence of an escape or attempt to escape from custody, although competent in connection with other facts and circumstances on the question of guilt, is generally considered as having only a slight tendency to prove guilt; and where there is evidence of an escape or attempted escape of an accused after months of confinement and comparatively without danger, it is proper to submit the act as a fact to be considered, not as determinative of guilt, and to state that in such circumstances the fact tends only slightly to prove guilt.[96]

It would seem that the court might properly instruct the jury to take into consideration such a fact as concealment, where there is evidence tending to prove it, as evidence bearing upon the question of guilt. But a charge which magnifies and distorts the inferences to be drawn from the concealment of a crime or the fact of concealment of the accused, as, for example, one which states in substance that no person conscious of innocence would resort to

93. Jenkins v Commonwealth, 132 Va 692, 111 SE 101, 25 ALR 882.

94. State v Foster, 130 NC 666, 41 SE 284.

95. State v Anderson, 207 Or 675, 298 P2d 195, 60 ALR2d 850.

96. Bird v United States, 187 US 118, 47 L Ed 100, 23 S Ct 42.

concealment, is erroneous.[97] Such an instruction ignores the fundamental truth that the innocent do often conceal through fear or other emotion.[98]

§ 590. Defenses and defense theories

All phases of the defense should be covered by instructions,[99] because the defendant has a right to have the jury instructed upon any theory that the testimony may reasonably present if it is not unreasonable or stamped with improbability.[1]

The defendant is entitled to charges correctly stating the law of his case, if they are supported by any evidence, however weak, insufficient, or doubtful in credibility it may be.[2] It is immaterial that the testimony may spring from persons deeply interested, or may be contradicted so as to

97. Hickory v United States, 160 US 408, 40 L Ed 474, 16 S Ct 327, holding it to be error to charge the jury in effect that the facts are, under both divine and human law, conclusive proof of guilt.

98. Hickory v United States, supra.

99. Cox v Commonwealth, 280 Ky 94, 132 SW2d 739, 131 ALR 478.

Annotations: Duty of trial court to instruct on self-defense, in absence of request by accused. 56 ALR2d 1170.

Entrapment to commit offense against laws regulating sales of liquor. 55 ALR2d 1322 at page 1382.

Entrapment to commit sexual offense. 52 ALR2d 1194.

Entrapment to commit offense with respect to narcotics law. 33 ALR2d 883 at page 902.

Presumption of continuing insanity as applied to accused in criminal case. 27 ALR2d 121.

1. Little v United States (CA10 Colo) 73 F2d 861, 96 ALR 889; People v Dole, 122 Cal 486, 55 P 581; State v Gallivan, 75 Conn 326, 53 A 731; Keener v State, 18 Ga 194; People v Strause, 290 Ill 259, 125 NE 339, 22 ALR 235; State v Brady, 121 Iowa 561, 97 NW 62; Cox v Commonwealth, 280 Ky 94, 132 SW2d 739, 131 ALR 478; Owens v State, 82 Miss 18, 33 So 718; State v Grugin, 147 Mo 39, 47 SW 1058; Russell v State, 77 Neb 519, 110 NW 380; State v Willberg, 45 Nev 183, 200 P 475; State v Hennessy, 29 Nev 320, 90 P 221; State v Hughes, 43 NM 109, 86 P2d 278; State v Martinez, 39 NM 290, 46 P2d 657; State v Martinez, 30 NM 178, 230 P 379; Skelly v State, 64 Okla Crim 112, 77 P2d 1162, reh den 65 Okla Crim 54, 82 P2d 843; Snell v State, 29 Tex App 236, 15 SW 722; Snowden v State, 12 Tex App 105; State v Legg, 59 W Va 315, 53 SE 545.

2. Gibson v State, 89 Ala 121, 8 So 98.

be entitled to but little weight in the estimation of the trial judge.[3]

A court may not ignore matters of fact submitted by the defendant by refusing to submit to the jury the law applicable thereto.[4] However, an instruction that certain facts will not constitute a defense is not misleading where the facts enumerated are not all that were relied on by the defense.[5]

As a general rule, the defendant is entitled to instructions properly presenting the defense of insanity or mental incapacity, self-defense, alibi,[6] abandonment of the conspiracy,[7] and the bar of the statute of limitations. Thus if there is evidence tending to show that the offense charged might be barred by the statute of limitations, the court should instruct the jury that before they can convict, they must find that the offense was committed within the limitation period.[8]

The defendant is entitled to a charge on the defense theory of former jeopardy or acquittal, although where no evidence in support of a plea of former acquittal is interposed, the court may decline to instruct on the issue,[9] and an instruction is erroneous and is properly refused where it requires the jury to acquit if they find that a former jury has been impaneled and sworn to try the defendant on the same charge, without regard to the facts which may have led to the discharge of such jury.[10]

Defendant is entitled to a proper instruction on the defense of entrapment,[11] although failure to instruct the

3. Gibson v State, supra.

4. Phillips v State, 26 Tex App 228, 9 SW 557.

5. State v Hartley, 22 Nev 342, 40 P 372.

6. § 591, infra.

7. Phillips v State, 26 Tex App 228, 9 SW 557.

8. Thorp v State, 59 Tex Crim 517, 129 SW 607.

9. Hartgraves v State, 5 Okla Crim 266, 114 P 343.

10. Welsh v State, 126 Ind 71, 25 NE 883.

11. Error has been held committed by the trial court in a prosecution for violation of the federal narcotics laws in declining to instruct the jury on the defense of entrapment, where the defendant's testimony reveals circum-

jury on the defense of entrapment in a criminal prosecution has been held not error where there was evidence supporting such defense.[12] A requested instruction on entrapment was properly refused in a prosecution for illegally selling whisky based on a sale where the sheriff was concealed in the purchaser's automobile;[13] and in a prosecution for selling morphine, a request to instruct on entrapment is properly refused where the officers merely furnished money for the making of the purchase.[14]

Filing a request to charge is a proper way of raising the issue of the defense theory upon which defendant wants an instruction.[15] Of course, where there is no evidence tending to support a plea, the jury may be directed not to consider the defense in arriving at their verdict.[16] While all issues should be fairly and clearly stated to the jury, the courts have ruled that the failure to instruct as to a theory of defense having support in the evidence is not error in the absence of a proper request.[17] Thus, it has been held that the failure to refer to an alleged alibi is not error where no request for an instruction was made.[18]

It has been held that while generally where one charged

stances constituting such defense, even though such testimony is contradicted by other evidence. Lutfy v United States (CA9 Ariz) 198 F2d 760, 33 ALR2d 879.

12. United States v Pisano (CA7 Ill) 193 F2d 355, 31 ALR2d 409.

An instruction with respect to entrapment has been held properly refused where there is no proof in the record to sustain the theory of entrapment. State v Parr, 129 Mont 175, 283 P2d 1086, 55 ALR2d 1313.

13. State v Rouner, 333 Mo 1236, 64 SW2d 916, 92 ALR 1099.

14. The refusal in a prosecution for selling morphine in violation of the Narcotic Drug Act, of a request to instruct on the law of entrapment, was not error, where the officers of the law did no affirmative act whatever to incite or persuade defendant to sell the morphine, but merely furnished marked money to an informer for the making of the purchase. People v Guagliata, 362 Ill 427, 200 NE 169, 103 ALR 1035.

15. State v Marquardt, 139 Conn 1, 89 A2d 219, 31 ALR2d 1206 (entrapment).

16. State v Burnette, 242 NC 164, 87 SE2d 191, 52 ALR2d 1181; Hartgraves v State, 5 Okla Crim 266, 114 P 343.

17. State v Hessenius, 165 Iowa 415, 146 NW 58.

18. Goldsby v United States, 160 US 70, 40 L Ed 343, 16 S Ct 216.

with crime admits the act but denies an essential element of the offense charged, he is entitled to a specific instruction that he is to be acquitted if such essential element is found lacking; yet if an instruction submitting the prosecution theory of the case is couched in such language as the ordinary juryman can easily and readily understand and comprehend, and its negative completely and adequately covers the defense of the accused, it is unnecessary to give an affirmative instruction on the theory of such defense.[19]

A court should avoid giving any instruction designed to cast discredit or suspicion on a defense which is recognized by law as legitimate, and which an accused person is making in good faith,[20] or on any class of legitimate evidence offered to support a defense.[21] It is even improper to refer to a defense the defendant attempted or claimed to set up, for the use of such words tends to intimate to the jury that the effort amounted to nothing more than an attempt.[22] But the use of the word "alleged" in referring to a defense does not render an instruction objectionable as disparaging it.[23]

§ 591. Alibi

If there is evidence to justify it, the accused is entitled to

19. Grigsby v Commonwealth, 299 Ky 721, 187 SW2d 259, 159 ALR 196, holding further that where the defendant in a criminal case proves facts or circumstances to excuse his act which otherwise would in and of itself be a crime, or the specific issue is one of criminal intent, such as where there is a claim of accident, self-defense or mental capacity, ordinarily an affirmative instruction should be given; but where the issue is as to a culpable overt act forming a constituent part of the crime, an affirmative defense instruction need not be given.

20. State v Johnson (Mo) 267 SW2d 642, 44 ALR2d 973, cert den 351 US 957, 100 L Ed 1479, 76 S Ct 858, cert den 357 US 922, 2 L Ed 2d 1366, 78 S Ct 1364; State v Crowe, 39 Mont 174, 102 P 579; State v King, 50 Wash 312, 97 P 247; Looney v Norfolk & W. R. Co. 102 W Va 40, 135 SE 262, 48 ALR 806, reh den 102 W Va 59, 137 SE 756.

21. Asher v State, 201 Ind 353, 168 NE 456, 67 ALR 118.

22. See People v McGinnis, 234 Ill 68, 84 NE 687, where the court held that to refer to a defense as "what is claimed to be this self-defense" constitutes error.

23. Green v State, 154 Ga 394, 114 SE 361.

have the court, upon request, give proper and adequate instructions upon the defense of alibi.[24] To justify the giving of an instruction on alibi, the evidence should show or tend to show that the defendant was elsewhere when the crime charged against him was committed.[25]

The defendant is not entitled to instructions on an alibi theory if the crime charged does not require his presence at the time and place of its commission, as where he is charged as an aider and abettor.[26]

According to the weight of authority, any instruction which tends to belittle or disparage the claim of alibi is erroneous.[27] A statement by the court that it does not think it necessary to instruct the jury upon alibi tends to disparage the claim in the mind of the jury.[28]

It is error for a court in its instruction to say that alibi is a well-worn defense,[29] or to term it a rogue's defense.[30]

In general, the defense of alibi is not one requiring that the evidence given in support of it be scrutinized otherwise or differently from that given in support of any other issue in the case,[31] and any instruction that the evidence should be tested differently from other evidence is erroneous.[32]

A defendant in a criminal case seeking to prove an alibi

24. Falgout v United States (CA5 La) 279 F 513, 29 ALR 1115; Anderson v State, 34 Tex Crim 546, 31 SW 673; State v King, 50 Wash 312, 97 P 247.

25. Singh v State, 35 Ariz 432, 280 P 672, 67 ALR 129; State v Steffen, 210 Iowa 196, 230 NW 536, 78 ALR 748, ovrld on another point Grismore v Consolidated Products Co. 232 Iowa 328, 5 NW2d 646; Schultz v State, 88 Neb 613, 130 NW 105.

26. Tomlinson v United States, 68 App DC 106, 93 F2d 652, 114 ALR 1315, cert den 303 US 642, 646, 82 L Ed 1102, 1107, 58 S Ct 645; State v Wolkow, 110 Kan 722, 205 P 639, 42 ALR 265.

27. Asher v State, 201 Ind 353, 168 NE 456, 67 ALR 118; State v Crowell, 149 Mo 391, 50 SW 893; Henry v State, 51 Neb 149, 70 NW 924.

28. State v King, 50 Wash 312, 97 P 247.

29. State v Crowell, 149 Mo 391, 50 SW 893.

30. State v Danelly, 116 SC 113, 107 SE 149, 14 ALR 1420.

31. State v Crowell, 149 Mo 391, 50 SW 893.

32. Williams v State, 47 Ala 659.

is entitled to have the jury correctly instructed as to the burden of proof, and an instruction that "the burden of proof is not upon an accused to establish an alibi by a preponderance of evidence" is not covered by a statement in a charge that the defendant is presumed to be innocent and that the burden is on the government to prove guilt beyond all reasonable doubt.[33]

D. INSANITY OR MENTAL INCAPACITY

§ 592. In general

It is always the duty of the court to instruct upon insanity where evidence tending to establish it is introduced and there is a proper request. Of course, a court may properly refuse to charge upon the subject where there is no proof of insanity offered by the defense or disclosed by the circumstances established by the prosecution.[34] In this regard, it has been said that mere proof that the defendant was grief-stricken, that he was intoxicated one half the time, and that he had a "wild look" in his eyes, does not necessitate instructions as to insanity.[35] An error on the part of the court by giving an insanity instruction where there is no evidence on the point, cannot be just cause of complaint.[36] In accord with the general rule, the court may refuse requests covered by instructions given.[37] For exam-

33. Falgout v United States (CA5 La) 279 F 513, 29 ALR 1115.

34. Battle v United States, 209 US 36, 52 L Ed 670, 28 S Ct 422 (holding that an instruction as to the burden on the government to prove sanity sufficed where there was a mere shadow of proof of insanity); Hankins v State, 133 Ark 38, 201 SW 832; People v Hubert, 119 Cal 216, 51 P 329; Singleton v State, 71 Miss 782, 16 So 295; State v Roy, 40 NM 397, 60 P2d 646, 110 ALR 1; State v Kidwell, 62 W Va 466, 59 SE 494.

Annotations: Instructions, in criminal case in which defendant pleads insanity, as to his hospital confinement in the event of acquittal. 11 ALR3d 737.

Presumption of continuing insanity as applied to accused in criminal case. 27 ALR2d 121.

35. State v Roy, 40 NM 397, 60 P2d 646, 110 ALR 1.

36. State v Hartley, 22 Nev 342, 40 P 372.

37. Ryan v People, 50 Colo 99, 114 P 306; People v Garbutt, 17 Mich 9 (recognizing rule).

ple, failure to give a submitted instruction as to the defense of insanity is not error where the charges given with respect thereto are lengthy, adequate, and complete, recognize insanity as a legal defense, and cover any implications which might properly be inferred from the type of disease claimed to be suffered by the accused.[38] Further in this regard, an instruction requiring an acquittal in case of reasonable doubt as to sanity is covered by an instruction to acquit in case of a reasonable doubt as to whether the defendant is so insane or distracted in mind as to be incapable of intending all natural, provable, and usual consequences of his acts.[39]

§ 593. Definitions and criteria of insanity

Where there is an issue of insanity in a criminal case, the court should properly define the term.[40]

In this regard, it is proper to instruct the jury that "insanity is either partial or general. General alienation always excuses. Partial insanity does not always excuse. . . . The law does not excuse unless the derangement is so great that it actually renders the person incapable, at the time of its commission, of distinguishing between right and wrong in respect to the particular act charged and proved

38. State v Bunk, 4 NJ 461, 73 A2d 249, 19 ALR2d 1316, cert den 340 US 839, 95 L Ed 615, 71 S Ct 25, disapproved on other grounds State v Reynolds, 41 NJ 163, 195 A2d 449, 1 ALR3d 1438, cert den 377 US 1000, 12 L Ed 2d 1050, 84 S Ct 1930, 1934, reh den 379 US 873, 13 L Ed 2d 80, 81, 85 S Ct 22, 23.

39. Ryan v People, 50 Colo 99, 114 P 306.

40. State v Knight, 95 Me 467, 50 A 276.

An instruction that insanity is a physical disease, located in the brain, which disease so perverts and deranges one of the mental and moral faculties as to render the person suffering therefrom incapable of distinguishing right from wrong in reference to the particular act charged against him and incapable of understanding that the particular act in question was a violation of the laws of God and society, is proper. State v Porter, 213 Mo 43, 111 SW 529.

An instruction that frenzy arising solely from the passions of anger and jealousy, no matter how furious, is not insanity is harmless. Guetig v State, 66 Ind 94.

against him."[41] And it has been held to be proper to instruct the jury that insanity as a defense to prosecution "means such a diseased and deranged condition of the mental faculties as to render the person incapable of distinguishing between right and wrong in relation to the act with which he is charged."[42]

In an adequate and proper instruction, the court should always set forth the proper test of insanity to be applied.[43] It has been held that the jury should be instructed that it must be clearly proved that at the time of committing the act the party accused was laboring under such a defect of reason from disease of the mind as not to know the nature and quality of the act he was doing, or, if he did not know it, that he did not know that what he was doing was wrong.[44]

An instruction that the jury should find the defendant not guilty if they find that he was unable to know that the act was wrongful, and was not able to comprehend and understand the consequences of the act, is not objectionable as adding a second condition to acquittal, where the condition of a verdict of guilty is a finding that the prisoner knew and understood that the act was wrongful and "was able to comprehend, and understood the consequences of such act," and was thus favorable to him.[45]

41. State v Porter, 213 Mo 43, 111 SW 529.

42. People v Hoin, 62 Cal 120.

43. James v State, 193 Ala 55, 69 So 569; Stevens v State, 31 Ind 485 (disapproving an instruction which was not clear, which did not fix the test of a knowledge of right and wrong, but which recognized the necessity of a mental power sufficient to apply that knowledge and act accordingly); State v James, 96 NJL 132, 114 A 553, 16 ALR 1141 (holding request properly refused because erroneous).

See Hamblin v State, 81 Neb 148, 115 NW 850, holding an instruction not erroneous as applied to the evidence, although in the abstract it was objectionable as requiring the jury to find that the defendant was laboring under a mental aberration and that his intellectual powers were obliterated to the extent that he had no will, and no purpose, and no consciousness of right or wrong.

An instruction requiring an acquittal of the defendant "was so mentally unbalanced that he did not know the consequences of his acts" is properly refused. James v State, 193 Ala 55, 69 So 569.

44. Freeman v People (NY) 4 Denio 9.

45. Queenan v Oklahoma, 190 US

§ 594. Cautionary instructions

A court may not disparage the defense of insanity in its charge,[46] and, according to some authorities, should not instruct the jury to examine the evidence with respect thereto with care, lest an ingenious counterfeit of the disease should furnish protection to guilt.[47] Nor should a court indulge in such cautionary expressions as that the jury "would be doing an injustice to society and to law to permit him to escape punishment" if the defendant possesses the mental faculties referred to.[48]

§ 595. Irresistible impulse

In some jurisdictions, the rule exists that even if the accused was able to comprehend the nature and consequences of his act, and to know that it was wrong, nevertheless, if he was forced to its execution by an impulse which he was powerless to control in consequence of an actual disease of the mind, he will be excused.[49] Where such an irresistible impulse is recognized as an excuse for crime, it is error to refuse to instruct upon the subject if the facts call for an application of the rule.[50]

But there must be evidence to sustain such a defense, and an instruction on irresistible impulse which is purely drawn in the abstract will be refused.[51] Thus where instructions reviewed were well suited to the facts of the case,

548, 47 L Ed 1175, 23 S Ct 762, aff'g 11 Okla 261, 71 P 218.

46. Asher v State, 201 Ind 353, 168 NE 456, 67 ALR 118.

47. Aszman v State, 123 Ind 347, 24 NE 123; State v Crowe, 39 Mont 174, 102 P 579.

48. Hamblin v State, 81 Neb 148, 115 NW 850.

49. Practice Aids: The doctrine of "irresistible impulse" is discussed in detail in 21 Am Jur 2d, CRIMINAL LAW §§ 36 et seq.

50. Smith v United States, 59 App DC 144, 36 F2d 548, 70 ALR 654; Jolly v Commonwealth, 110 Ky 190, 61 SW 49.

51. State v Bundy, 24 SC 439.

they were not objectionable purely on the basis that they failed to explain the doctrine of irresistible impulse.[52]

E. PRESUMPTIONS AND BURDEN OF PROOF

§ 596. In general

Unless specifically provided for by statute, the jury in a criminal case should not be instructed that any evidence raises a presumption against the defendant, nor should the words "prima facie case" be used unless they are found in the language of an applicable statute.[53]

In criminal cases, the jury should be instructed that the burden rests upon the state to prove the guilt of the accused beyond a reasonable doubt,[54] and on request, that the burden of proof never shifts from the state to the defendant.[55] The defendant may be entitled also to instructions on the burden of proof as to particular elements of the offense.[56]

Since the burden of establishing guilt does not shift, an instruction which has the effect of shifting the burden of proof is erroneous.[57]

Prefacing an instruction as to a matter of defense with the words "if the jury find and believe"[58] or "if proved,"[59] or requiring that the jury be satisfied as to a defensive mat-

52. State v Peel, 23 Mont 358, 59 P 169.

53. State v Kulow, 255 Iowa 789, 123 NW2d 872, 16 ALR3d 1085.

54. Marshall v State, 219 Ala 83, 121 So 72, 63 ALR 560.

55. Phillips v State, 26 Tex App 228, 9 SW 557.

56. State v McBee, 52 W Va 257, 43 SE 121.

57. Coffin v United States, 156 US 432, 39 L Ed 481, 15 S Ct 394; People v Powell, 87 Cal 348, 25 P 481; McNish v State, 45 Fla 83, 34 So 219; State v Strawther, 342 Mo 618, 116 SW2d 133, 120 ALR 583; State v Hickam, 95 Mo 322, 8 SW 252; Perkins v State, 35 Okla Crim 279, 250 P 544, 49 ALR 1129; Huddleston v State, 54 Tex Crim 93, 112 SW 64; Vann v State, 45 Tex Crim 434, 77 SW 813; State v Hatfield, 65 Wash 550, 118 P 735; State v Pilling, 53 Wash 464, 102 P 230.

58. Flege v State, 93 Neb 610, 142 NW 276.

59. State v Green, 86 Utah 192, 40 P2d 961.

ter,[60] or referring to a matter of defense "when satisfactorily established,"[61] makes the instruction subject to the objection that it casts or tends to cast upon the defendant the burden of proving the fact in question. However, despite such words, an instruction may not be subject to objection on this account when it is considered as a whole,[62] or when the instruction is considered with other proper instructions relating to the defensive matter.[63]

It has been ruled that in a criminal case it is fatal error to give an instruction which in effect requires the defendant to prove by a preponderance of the evidence a matter going to the essence of the crime and negativing the commission of any crime.[64] So too, in homicide cases it has been held to be error to instruct that the defendant has the burden of proving circumstances of mitigation or justification.[65]

An instruction is self-contradictory and misleading where it informs the jury that if they find that the defendant killed the deceased, then the burden of proving circumstances of mitigation or justification is upon him; but if after consideration of the evidence they have a reasonable doubt as to whether he killed in the lawful defense of his son, they should acquit.[66]

But it is proper to instruct that when the killing is proved or admitted, it devolves upon the defendant to show any circumstances of mitigation to excuse or justify it by some proof strong enough to create in the minds of the jury a reasonable doubt.[67]

60. Post v United States (CA5 Fla) 135 F 1, 1022; Wacaser v People, 134 Ill 438, 25 NE 564.

61. State v Crowe, 39 Mont 174, 102 P 579.

62. Snow v State, 91 Tex Crim 1, 237 SW 563, 20 ALR 1180.

63. Painter v Commonwealth, 140 Va 459, 124 SE 431.

64. State v Matheson, 130 Iowa 440, 103 NW 137.

65. State v Strawther, 342 Mo 618, 116 SW 2d 133, 120 ALR 583; Huddleston v State, 54 Tex Crim 93, 112 SW 64.

66. State v Strawther, 342 Mo 618, 116 SW2d 133, 120 ALR 583.

67. Culpepper v State, 4 Okla Crim 103, 111 P 679.

§ 597. Presumptions of innocence

The defendant in a criminal case is entitled to an instruction as to the presumption of innocence which exists in his favor. While it has been declared that such an instruction should be given in every criminal case,[68] and in some states it is the duty of the court to state the presumption irrespective of any request,[69] there is authority to the effect that the failure to instruct as to the presumption of innocence or to give specific instructions involving the presumption is not reversible error in the absence of a request.[70]

An instruction on the presumption of innocence, that the presumption is not intended to prevent the conviction of any person who is in fact guilty, or to aid the guilty to escape punishment was prejudicial.[71]

While it is the rule in some states that a defendant in a criminal case is entitled to an instruction that he is presumed to be innocent at the outset of the trial,[72] it is generally recognized that, if requested, the court must not only charge the jury in effect that the defendant enters a criminal trial with the presumption of innocence, or that he is presumed to be innocent, but also that this presumption remains with him until overcome by evidence convincing the jury of his guilt beyond a reasonable doubt.[73] It has

68. People v Hardwick, 204 Cal 582, 269 P 427, 59 ALR 1480; People v McClintic, 193 Mich 589, 160 NW 461; People v De Fore, 64 Mich 693, 31 NW 585.

69. See Coffin v United States, 156 US 432, 39 L Ed 431, 15 S Ct 394 (referring to the rule in Texas).

70. Bowman v State, 207 Ind 358, 192 NE 755, 96 ALR 522 (applying rule to instruction as to duty to reconcile evidence with the presumption of innocence); State v Donahue, 75 Or 409, 144 P 755, 5 ALR 1121, adhered to on reh 75 Or 420, 147 P 548, 5 ALR 1126.

71. Reynolds v United States (CA9 Alaska) 238 F2d 460.

72. Commonwealth v Madeiros, 255 Mass 304, 151 NE 297, 47 ALR 962, later app 257 Mass 1, 152 NE 745; Commonwealth v De Francesco, 248 Mass 9, 142 NE 749, 34 ALR 937.

See Holt v United States, 218 US 245, 54 L Ed 1021, 31 S Ct 2, holding correct an instruction stating in effect that the criminal prosecution begins with the presumption of innocence.

73. Agnew v United States, 165 US 36, 41 L Ed 624, 17 S Ct 235 (instruction as to presumption of innocence

been declared that the jury should be instructed that a presumption of innocence continues with the defendant through the trial and the deliberations of the jury.[74] However, the rule according to other authorities is that the presumption does not run with the accused throughout the trial, and continue with him through all its stages, and hence, a request stating the contrary is properly denied.[75]

An instruction which makes it clear that the prosecution has the burden of proving guilt beyond a reasonable doubt, but states that the presumption of innocence is intended for the protection of the innocent and not as a bulwark behind which the guilty may hide, does not require the reversal of a conviction as tending to lead the jury to

held correct); Coffin v United States, 156 US 432, 39 L Ed 481, 15 S Ct 394; Aszman v State, 123 Ind 347, 24 NE 123; State v Furney, 41 Kan 115, 21 P 213; People v McClintic, 193 Mich 589, 160 NW 461; Edwards v State, 69 Neb 386, 95 NW 1038; Berry v State, 4 Okla Crim 202, 111 P 676 (holding instruction to be correct).

In Agnew v United States, 165 US 36, 41 L Ed 624, 17 S Ct 235, it was held that the following instruction was correct: "the defendant is presumed to be innocent of all the charges against him until he is proved guilty by the evidence submitted to you. This presumption remains with the defendant until such time in the progress of the case that you are satisfied of the guilt beyond a reasonable doubt."

In People v McClintic, 193 Mich 589, 160 NW 461, it was held that it was error to charge that the defendant stands innocent until the people, through the prosecuting attorney, have convinced the jury of his guilt beyond a reasonable doubt.

The judge must make plain that the presumption of innocence is to be considered by the jury along with the evidence in the case, and that it continues until the evidence satisfies the jury of the guilt of the accused beyond a reasonable doubt. Lisansky v United States (CA4 Md) 31 F2d 846, 67 ALR 67, cert den 279 US 873, 73 L Ed 1008, 49 S Ct 514.

74. People v Hardwick, 204 Cal 582, 269 P 427, 59 ALR 1480.

75. Commonwealth v Madeiros, 255 Mass 304, 151 NE 297, 47 ALR 962; Culpepper v State, 4 Okla Crim 103, 111 P 679.

In State ex rel. Carmons v Woods, 102 Kan 499, 170 P 986, a bastardy proceeding, the court held correct an instruction which stated that the defendant was presumed to be innocent of the charge against him, and that the presumption remained with him through all stages of the trial and until overcome by the evidence of the state by a preponderance of the credible evidence.

In homicide cases it is proper to instruct that the presumption of innocence is a presumption of law that remains with the defendant up to the moment when the killing is proved or admitted. Culpepper v State, 4 Okla Crim 103, 111 P 679.

suppose that the defendant could not invoke the presumption until he has dispelled proof of his guilt.[76]

§ 598. Nonproduction of evidence; failure to testify

A statute forbidding reference to or comment upon the neglect or refusal of an accused to testify does not preclude a court from instructing the jury that such failure does not relieve the state from the obligation to establish guilt beyond a reasonable doubt, nor—unless the statute in terms prohibits, or by construction is deemed to prohibit, reference to the matter by the court—does it preclude the court from instructing that because of such failure nothing shall be taken against the defendant.[77] Some statutes, while forbidding reference to the failure to testify by the prosecuting attorney, do not in terms prohibit such reference by the court.[78]

In some jurisdictions, where an accused voluntarily testifying fails to explain incriminating circumstances and events already in evidence in which he participated, and concerning which he is fully informed, the court may charge to the effect that the jury may take this omission into consideration in reaching a verdict.[79] However, it is error to give an instruction that the defendant's failure to deny any material fact proved in the case and within his personal knowledge constitutes an admission thereof.[80]

76. United States v Farina (CA2 NY) 184 F2d 18, cert den 340 US 875, 95 L Ed 636, 71 S Ct 121, reh den 341 US 928, 95 L Ed 1359, 71 S Ct 795.

77. Ferguson v State, 52 Neb 432, 72 NW 590; State v Carlisle, 28 SD 169, 132 NW 686.

Annotations: Propriety under Griffin v California and prejudicial effect of unrequested instruction that no inferences against accused should be drawn from his failure to testify. 18 ALR3d 1335.

Inferences arising from refusal of witness other than accused to answer questions on the ground that answer would tend to incriminate him. 24 ALR2d 895.

78. See State v Wisnewski, 13 ND 649, 102 NW 883.

79. Raffel v United States, 271 US 494, 70 L Ed 1054, 46 S Ct 566; Caminetti v United States, 242 US 470, 61 L Ed 442, 37 S Ct 192.

80. Russell v State, 77 Neb 519, 110 NW 380.

In general it is error in a criminal case to authorize the jury to consider the failure of the accused to produce his wife as a witness as a circumstance against him, or authorize the drawing of an adverse inference therefrom.[81] However, a charge that no inference is to be drawn from the fact that the defendant's wife availed herself of the privilege against testifying may be refused where she was not called as a witness and had not refused to testify.[82]

§ 599. Character of accused

With substantial unanimity it is held that when evidence of the good character of an accused has been introduced, the court on request should instruct the jury as to the application of and the weight they may attach to the evidence.[83]

Where an accused has testified in his own behalf and put his character in issue by offering evidence thereon, it is proper for the court to instruct the jury (1) that evidence of the accused's character may be considered as substantive evidence on the question of his guilt or innocence and also as evidence bearing on his credibility as a witness, (2) but the evidence of the character of any other witness is to be considered simply as going to his credibility.[84]

In Mississippi, it is held that in view of the prohibition against charges on the weight of the testimony, it is proper to refuse an instruction that evidence of good character may itself raise a reasonable doubt, the rule being that

81. In a bigamy prosecution, the court may properly refuse an instruction based upon the statute as to the effect of failure of a husband or wife to testify, and declaring that the failure of two named persons, the defendant's wife and alleged second wife, to testify creates no presumption against him, for it would invade the province of the jury by assuming that the second named is the defendant's wife. Corvin v Commonwealth, 131 Va 649, 108 SE 651, 39 ALR 592.

82. Commonwealth v Spencer, 212 Mass 438, 99 NE 266.

83. State v McGuire, 84 Conn 470, 80 A 761; State v Brown, 39 Utah 140, 115 P 994; State v Cushing, 14 Wash 527, 45 P 145, later app 17 Wash 544, 50 P 512.

84. State v Minton, 234 NC 716, 68 SE2d 844, 31 ALR2d 682.

such evidence should go to the jury without intimation from the court touching its value.[85]

F. VERDICT AND PUNISHMENT

§ 600. Form and nature of verdict

If a party desires an instruction as to a form of verdict, he should prepare an instruction indicating such form as he deems correct.[86] A requested instruction that the jury may render a general verdict or a special one is properly refused in the absence of a request to submit any special findings upon any branch of the case.[87]

In instructing as to verdicts that may be found, the court should cover all the verdicts that the jury might render.[88] Thus, instructions which did not permit the jury to pass upon the question of whether the accused had been convicted twice before of similar offenses involving violations of the local option law, and which permitted conviction of a third violation charge upon a finding of guilt only of the particular crime presently charged, was prejudicially erroneous; instructions should properly permit the jury to return possible verdicts of guilty or not guilty of the primary crime, or of the second or third offense violations, or of any combination of the three,[89] and where the defendant relies upon the defense of insanity, there should be a proper charge on the verdict of not guilty by reason of insanity.[90]

On the other hand, the court in its charge should not

85. Singleton v State, 71 Miss 782, 16 So 295.

Practice Aids: As to application of rules in homicide cases, see 40 Am Jur 2d, Homicide § 503.

86. Spies v People, 122 Ill 1, 12 NE 865, 17 NE 898, error dismd 123 US 131, 31 L Ed 80, 8 S Ct 22.

Annotation: Prejudicial effect of statement or instruction of court as to possibility of parole or pardon. 12 ALR3d 832.

87. Prosser v Montana C. R. Co., 17 Mont 372, 43 P 81.

88. Kearney v State, 101 Ga 803, 29 SE 127.

89. Brown v Commonwealth (Ky) 378 SW2d 608, 14 ALR3d 1330.

90. State v Crowe, 39 Mont 174, 102 P 579.

indicate what verdict to render.[91] And since the jury have nothing to do with costs, it is better practice not to refer thereto in instructions.[92]

§ 601. Assessment of punishment

In criminal cases where the assessment of the punishment is by the court and not the jury, any instruction as to the punishment is unnecessary and should not be given, because it can be of no aid to the jury in determining the issue of guilt.[93]

Where the right to fix the penalty for the crime or the right to make recommendations in this respect rests with the jury, the court may and should instruct as to the punishment or the effect of the recommendation on the punishment.[94] However, in some cases the failure to do so may not be error. Thus an instruction that the jury had the discretion to fine the defendant or not to fine him is properly refused where the statute prescribes a fine in all cases of guilt.[95]

§ 602. Recommendation of clemency

In any prosecution in which the jury may properly recommend the punishment to be imposed or recommend the accused to the mercy of the court or to executive clemency, it is proper for the court to charge in regard thereto.[96] In some jurisdictions, the court is under no duty to give such instruction in the absence of a request,[97]

91. McCurdy v Hughes, 63 ND 435, 248 NW 512, 87 ALR 683.

92. Dorn v Cooper, 139 Iowa 742, 117 NW 1, 118 NW 35.

93. Hiller v State, 116 Neb 582, 218 NW 386, 58 ALR 1322; Edwards v State, 69 Neb 386, 95 NW 1038; State v Inlow, 44 Utah 485, 141 P 530.

Annotation: Prejudicial effect of statement or instruction of court as to possibility of parole or pardon. 12 ALR3d 832.

94. Commonwealth v Brown, 309 Pa 515, 164 A 726, 86 ALR 892.

95. Welsh v State, 126 Ind 71, 25 NE 883.

96. Calton v Utah, 130 US 83, 32 L Ed 870, 9 S Ct 435.

97. Garner v State, 28 Fla 113, 9 So 835.

whereas in other jurisdictions the duty exists irrespective of request.[98]

The refusal of a request to instruct as to the right to make a recommendation of mercy is error.[99]

98. Calton v Utah, 130 US 83, 32 L Ed 870, 9 S Ct 435.

99. State v Martin, 92 NJL 436, 106 A 385, 17 ALR 1090, later app 94 NJL 139, 109 A 350, ovrld on other grounds State v White, 27 NJ 158, 142 A2d 65.

CHAPTER TWENTY

REQUESTS TO CHARGE

A. INTRODUCTION

§ 603. In general

At the close of the evidence, or at such earlier time as the Court may direct, you file your requests to charge. As the term implies, a "request" asks the court to instruct the jury on the law as set forth in your request. The Court should inform you of its proposed action upon the request prior to the arguments to the jury. The jury will be instructed after the arguments are completed. Your exceptions must be taken before the jury retires to consider its verdict.

In some jurisdictions, it is customary for the trial judge to hold a conference with the attorneys to "settle" his instructions. In certain other jurisdictions, such conferences may be held at the request of counsel. When such conferences are held, it is proper to submit requests and take exceptions at that time. The conferees then discuss and analyze the proposed charge.

B. PREPARATION AND SUBMISSION OF REQUESTS

§ 604. In general

Prepare your basic requests before the trial. Such preparation will pinpoint the key trial issues in your mind, as well as direct the course of your defense during the trial. Many of your requests can then be cast in the form of questions and used when you select your jury. You will be emphasizing the important principles for the accused to the jury from the beginning of the trial to the end.

Of course, always be ready to revamp and prepare supplemental requests to meet the evidence as it unfolds at the trial.

Always prepare your requests for instructions in writing. As a courtesy to the court, submit them as far in advance of closing argument as possible. Do not, however, hand them up in advance of the presentation, when doing so may remove the element of surprise by revealing a previously undisclosed theory of defense to the prosecutor.

§ 605. Language of requests

Where you have found appellate authority for your request, make the most of it. But do not use the precise language of the decision. The language in most cases is unintelligible to the jury. You must paraphrase the decision's complex language into simple terms, without changing the meaning. Be prepared, if necessary, to have an appropriate case to lend authority to your statement of the law.

Have prepared an accurately and simply worded set of instructions to help the Judge submit to the jury the principles you are urging. State each request as clearly and briefly as the legal proposition permits. Limit each request to a single issue or proposition. Each request should be complete within itself and contain all the necessary instructions on that particular issue. Avoid technical terms wherever possible. Similarly, avoid involved, complicated and dependent sentences. The simple declarative sentence is always best.

§ 606. Form of request

Group your requests according to categories. Have each request follow naturally from the preceding one. For example, you might submit your requests to charge in the following order:

a. The purpose of the court's instructions.

b. The nature of the charges brought against the accused.

c. The issues for the jury's determination.

d. The elements that the prosecution must prove to establish the crime charged.

e. The principles of burden of proof and reasonable doubt.

f. Credibility of witnesses.

g. Particular items of evidence.

h. Cautioning the jury to confine their deliberations to the evidence.

i. Cautioning the jury to exclude prejudice from their consideration.

§ 607. Submission of alternate charges to judge

You should often try to have the court instruct the jury in a bolder fashion than is usually done. This is particularly important if you believe that decisional law may soon make advances which would help in your case. In these instances prepare a series of charges in order, ranging from the best possible instruction down to the one you are absolutely entitled to. Clearly designate the alternative instructions. You will thereby have reserved for appeal the Judge's failure to charge in the best possible manner, but you will nevertheless have received the advantage of some instruction of your choosing.

§ 608. Anticipate and counter prosecutor's requests

Anticipate the instructions normally submitted by the prosecutor, by submitting counter-instructions. For example, if the defendant fled from the police, the prosecutor will request instructions that the flight of the accused may be considered by the jury in determining guilt. Counter it by requesting instructions clearly defining what does or does not constitute flight. If the prosecutor requests instructions that proof of a motive weakens the presumption of innocence and strengthens other evidence of guilt, counter it with a request that "motive alone is not sufficient to prove the commission of the crime, unless supported by other evidence which clearly establishes the defendant's participation in the crime charged."

§ 609. Exceptions

Your exceptions to the charge must be taken before the jury retires to consider its verdict.

You must be certain to except to every portion of the Judge's charge which you believe to be erroneous. You must specifically request that the Judge correct his charge and instruct the jury as to the law set forth in your carefully prepared requests to charge. The following are common grounds for exception:

(a) Bias. If the Judge's charge is biased, partial and replete with an animated discussion of the prosecution's evidence, do not hesitate to except to the entire charge upon this ground.

I would suggest the following form of exception: "Now, may it please the Court, the defendant excepts to the charge in its entirety, in that it is not an impartial charge, free from bias, but an animated discussion of the evidence, and a second summation for the prosecution."

If the charge dealt overwhelmingly with the testimony of particular prosecution witnesses, here is an effective exception: "We except to the Court's charge, or so much thereof which makes reference, in the animated discussion, to the witnesses Smith, Brown and Green as developed on the direct examination without an equally animated reference being made by the Court as to the evidence elicited from these witnesses on the cross-examination and the contradictory statements made by those witnesses in statements taken from them by the prosecutor."

(b) Error of Law. If you object to what you consider an erroneous instruction, except as follows: "The defendant excepts to so much of the Court's charge as states that (here insert the text or substance of objectionable portion of charge). I request the Court to charge in words or substance the (here insert desired charge)."

(c) Refusal to Charge as per Written Request. If your objection is based upon the Court's refusal to give a requested instruction, except as follows: "The defendant excepts to the Court's refusal to charge my requests to charge numbered 2, 4, 6 and 7. The defendant requests that our requests to charge, as submitted to the Court in writing, be marked and made part of the record."

In the Federal Courts, the Judge is required to permit you to object, out of the presence of the jury, to his charge. If your exceptions will be lengthy, it is best to take advantage of that right. Where you determine to except in the jury's presence, do so in a routine manner. Do not let it appear as if you are disagreeing too violently with the Judge, because the jury tends to feel that the Court is omnipotent and cannot be in error.

Pay close attention to the charge when it is delivered. Even if you discussed it in conference or were given the opportunity to read it in advance, there is always the possibility that the Judge has amended it or that he will change it during the reading.

Make your objections to the charge specific. Appellate courts apply a much stricter rule in finding error when a general exception to the charge has been taken than they do when a specific exception has been taken. Therefore, do not say, "Your honor, I take exception to the charge as an unfair one." Rather, you should state, "Your honor, Defendant excepts to your failure to properly marshal the evidence on behalf of the defense. While you discussed at length the direct testimony of prosecution witnesses, you did not discuss the contradictions developed in their cross-examination. Nor did your honor do more than skim over the testimony adduced on behalf of the defendant without clarifying its importance in relation to the issue of scienter."

You should, of course, note with particularity any objections you have toward the demeanor of the court during the charge. Be certain, however, that you are correct, as this type of exception is a serious one. If the Judge, for example, speaks in a loud, clear tone of voice when marshalling the prosecution's evidence, but mumbles when marshalling the defense's evidence, note your exception. Note your exception any time you are certain that through tone or gesture the Judge is seeking to inform the jury of his belief in your client's guilt.

JUDGMENT AND SENTENCE

E. COUNSEL'S FUNCTION AND TECHNIQUES AT SENTENCING

F. VALIDITY AND EFFECT OF SENTENCE

A. INTRODUCTION

§ 610. In general

This discussion involves the sentencing and punishment of the defendant after his conviction.[1] In a legal sense,

1. **Annotations:** Length of sentence as violation of constitutional provisions prohibiting cruel and unusual punishment. 33 ALR3d 335.

Propriety of increased punishment on new trial for same offense. 12 ALR3d 978.

What is "harm" within provisions of statutes increasing penalty for kidnapping where victim suffers harm. 11 ALR3d 1053.

When criminal case becomes moot, so as to preclude review of or attack on conviction or sentence. 9 ALR3d 462.

Unanimity as to punishment in criminal case where jury can recommend lesser penalty. 1 ALR3d 1461.

Court's right, in imposing sentence, to hear evidence of, or to consider, other offenses committed by defendant. 96 ALR2d 768.

Criminal conspiracies as to gambling. 91 ALR2d 1148 at page 1205.

Validity and construction of Federal Bank Robbery Act. 59 ALR2d 946 at page 990.

Sentences by different courts as concurrent. 57 ALR2d 1410.

Propriety and effect of prosecuting attorney's argument to jury indicating his belief or knowledge as to guilt of accused. 50 ALR2d 766 at page 803.

Power of court to impose sentence providing for intermittent incarceration. 39 ALR2d 985.

Right to notice and hearing before revocation of suspension of sentence, parole, or probation. 29 ALR2d 1074.

Reference by counsel for prosecution in opening statement to matters which he does not later attempt to prove as ground for new trial, reversal, or modification. 28 ALR2d 972.

Determination of character of for-

sentence is ordinarily synonymous with judgment and denotes the action of a court of criminal jurisdiction formally declaring to the accused the legal consequences of the guilt which he has confessed or of which he has been convicted. Where there is a general verdict of guilty on two or more indictments consolidated for trial, or on two or more counts of a single indictment, the court is authorized to impose a sentence or judgment on each separate indictment or on each separate count that is supported by evidence.[2]

It is said that a formal judgment of acquittal is not required where the jury has returned a verdict of not guilty, since the record and the case against the defendant end with the verdict.[3]

§ 611. Time of sentencing

If sentence is not pronounced on a verdict during the term when the verdict was rendered, the cause continues on the docket and necessarily passes over to a succeeding term for final judgment or other appropriate action.[4] Even though a convicted defendant is not sentenced during the current term of court, and the failure or omission to pass sentence is due to the inaction or oversight of the court, the court during the succeeding term or terms does not lose jurisdiction of the case or of the person of the defendant, and he may be required to appear before the court during any subsequent term and be sentenced the same as

mer crime as a felony, so as to warrant punishment of an accused as a second offender. 19 ALR2d 227 at page 261.

Evidence of identity for purposes of statute as to enhance punishment in case of prior conviction. 11 ALR2d 870 at page 880.

Effect of voluntary statements damaging to accused, not proper subject of testimony, uttered by testifying police or peace officer. 8 ALR2d 1013 at page 1085.

Propriety and effect of court's indication to jury that court would suspend sentence. 8 ALR2d 1001.

2. State v Austin, 241 NC 548, 85 SE2d 924.

3. Arnold v State, 76 Wyo 445, 306 P2d 368, 65 ALR2d 839.

4. Miller v Aderhold, 288 US 206, 77 L Ed 702, 53 S Ct 325.

if sentence were being passed during the term current with the trial.[5]

In the absence of a statute or rule, the court may impose sentence on the defendant before a motion for arrest of judgment or a motion for a new trial has been acted on, and before the time allowed for filing any motion has expired.[6]

Where a statute provides that sentence shall be imposed not less than 2 nor more than 10 days after a verdict or finding of guilt, it has been held that the time is not jurisdictional and that the statute is merely directory, and that the judgment should be rendered within a reasonable time after the determination of guilt, during which period the court will determine whether or not the prisoner is capable of rehabilitation.[7]

It has been held that the court may properly refuse to sentence a defendant on the main charge before determining an habitual-criminal charge.[8]

§ 612. Waiver and estoppel

The accused may waive a statutory right to have sentence pronounced at or within a set time.[9] And a defendant who secures a delay in the pronouncement of sentence is estopped to claim that the court has lost jurisdiction to render judgment.[10]

§ 613. Presence of defendant

As a general rule the record must show that the defend-

5. Davis v State, 192 Ga 648, 16 SE2d 428, ans conformed to 66 Ga App 107, 16 SE2d 913; Commonwealth ex rel. Holly v Ashe, 368 Pa 211, 82 A2d 244, cert den 342 US 862, 96 L Ed 649, 72 S Ct 90.

6. State v De Grace, 144 Or 159, 22 P2d 896, 90 ALR 232, ovrld on other grounds State v Jackson, 228 Or 371, 365 P2d 294, 89 ALR2d 1225.

7. State v Fedder, 1 Utah 2d 117, 262 P2d 753.

8. State v Durham, 177 Or 574, 164 P2d 448, 162 ALR 422.

9. People v Manriquez, 188 Cal 602, 206 P 63, 20 ALR 1441; State v Sorenson, 75 Mont 30, 241 P 616.

10. McLaughlin v State, 207 Ind 484, 192 NE 753, 97 ALR 800.

ant was personally present in court when judgment was entered.[11] A defendant has the right to be present at the time sentence or judgment is pronounced against him,[12] and generally a sentence passed in his absence is invalid,[13] even though he voluntarily absents himself from the courtroom.[14]

A sentence in absentia may not validly be imposed unless the record shows that diligent effort was made to find the defendant and also shows the reason for the defendant's absence.[15]

Although a defendant must be present when sentence is orally pronounced, he need not be present when the sentence is later written out and signed or when it is filed.[16]

B. PROCEEDING SUBSEQUENT TO GUILTY VERDICT

§ 614 In general

We hope your job will end with a verdict of not-guilty, the gratitude of your client and your own personal satisfac-

11. Re Clark, 24 Wash 2d 105, 163 P2d 577.

Annotations: Necessity and sufficiency of question to defendant as to whether he has anything to say why sentence should not be pronounced against him. 96 ALR2d 1292.

Absence of accused at return of verdict in felony case. 23 ALR2d 456 at pages 497–514.

Absence of counsel for accused at time of sentence as requiring vacation thereof or other relief. 20 ALR2d 1240.

12. Joseph v State, 236 Ind 529, 141 NE2d 109, 69 ALR2d 824, cert dismd 359 US 117, 3 L Ed 2d 673, 79 S Ct 720.

13. State v Stephenson, 41 NJ Super 315, 125 A2d 157 (sentence is void); State v Brooks, 211 NC 702, 191 SE 749 (defendant's presence is essential).

14. State ex rel. Shetsky v Utecht, 228 Minn 44, 36 NW2d 126, 6 ALR2d 988.

Annotation: Voluntary absence of accused when sentence is pronounced. 6 ALR2d 997.

15. People v Brown, 102 Cal App 2d 60, 226 P2d 609, further holding that due process of law does not forbid a state to pronounce judgment in a criminal case when a defendant absconds and is not in court at the time set for sentence.

16. United States v Bell, 15 Alaska 401.

tion of a job well done. However, a very important phase of your work still lies ahead of you if the jury's verdict was unfavorable or if you decide to enter a plea of guilty. If the handling of the sentence is carried out competently, you can still have your client's gratitude and your own feeling of personal satisfaction.

§ 615. Delaying the sentence

Sentence, particularly in felony cases, will not immediately follow upon a jury's verdict of guilty. Local procedures will usually provide for either the discretionary or absolute right to a deferral sentence, pending a pre-sentence investigation by the Probation Department. Unless you have an express agreement with the Judge as to sentence, or unless the nature of the case and the Judge's attitude make it clear that your client will be given lenient treatment, seek a deferral of sentence. This deferral will give you time to plan and formulate a strategy for sentence in accordance with the suggestions contained herein.[17]

§ 616. Seek to have defendant continued on bail

If the time of sentence is deferred, move to have your client continued on bail pending the imposition of sentence. Point out to the Judge that your client always attended promptly and that there is no reason to assume that he will not appear for sentence. Note also the necessity of having your client wind up his affairs in the event he is to receive a sentence of imprisonment. Many of the arguments first used to achieve a low bail can again be asserted to assure a continuation of bail.

C. POST-VERDICT MOTIONS

§ 617. In general

Check the local statute to determine which post-verdict

17. **Annotation:** Effect of delay in taking defendant into custody after conviction and sentence. 98 ALR2d 687.

motions are available and the time within which the motions are to be made. The local practices should be followed with regard to the form of the motion—either oral or in writing. If such motions are made orally, make certain that they are transcribed so that they may be preserved for an eventual appeal.

The motions enumerated herein should be made only if there is some reasonable basis for them or unless they are required if certain claims of error are to be preserved for appeal. The making of baseless motions may have the negative effect of antagonizing the Judge prior to sentence.

§ 618. Motion to set aside the verdict, for judgment N. O. V. or for a judgment of acquittal

This is usually a routine post-verdict motion and is seldom granted. The motion is necessary in some states in order to preserve the right to question the sufficiency of the evidence on appeal.

You should always argue the motion strenuously in a proper case. If, after crediting all the prosecution's evidence and drawing every reasonable inference from it in favor of the prosecution, reasonable jurors could not find guilt beyond a reasonable doubt, the motion should be granted.

In certain instances the motion must be granted when, for example, the defendant was convicted on the basis of the uncorroborated testimony of an accomplice or the uncorroborated testimony of the alleged victim of rape.

§ 619. Motion in arrest of judgment

This motion is generally used to challenge basic errors in the verdict or the indictment.

Among the more common grounds used in this motion are that the conviction rests upon an unconstitutional statute; that the indictment fails to state a crime; that the court lacks jurisdiction; that the verdict does not conform to the indictment; that one or more jurors had an unauthorized view of the scene of the crime, etc.

§ 620. Motion for a new trial

There are various grounds upon which this motion may be made.

The most common of these is newly discovered evidence. In order to properly avail yourself of this ground, you must show both that even with due diligence the evidence was not available to you at trial and that it is material rather than cumulative and, as such, was likely to have produced a different result if introduced at trial.

In theory you can also seek a new trial on the ground of the legal insufficiency of the evidence. Such ground, however, is better used in a motion to set aside the verdict or for judgment N.O.V, as the granting of such a motion would result in a dismissal of the charge rather than in a new trial. If the evidence was legally sufficient, but the preponderance of evidence favored your client, you should move for a new trial in the interests of justice on the ground that the verdict was against the preponderance of the evidence. This motion, in effect, gives the judge the opportunity to sit as a juror and to assess the weight of the evidence and the credibility of witnesses.

The motion can also be made on the ground of errors committed either at trial or in pre-trial proceedings. This motion gives the court the opportunity to review and correct erroneous rulings or decisions. You must show that the error is material, in that a different result would have likely ensued had the error not been committed.

D. FACTORS DETERMINING SENTENCE

§ 621. Pre-sentence report

The pre-sentence report is rendered by probation authorities to the Judge between conviction and sentence. Theoretically, it gives the Judge a complete picture of the defendant. It should tell the Judge what the pros and cons are in the defendant's past. It is an aid to him in determining sentence.[18]

Quite often the investigating officer obtains his information from very biased sources, and a distorted picture of the defendant's background results. Moreover, probation departments are overworked and understaffed.[19]

Unfortunately, the pre-sentence report is a big factor in the sentencing machinery. It is your job to supplement a favorable report or offset one that is unfavorable.

§ 622. Nature of the crime

Understandably, the nature and degree of the crime are related directly to the type of sentence imposed. However, there is far more involved. The Judge will not merely determine what the crime is, look to the statute for the penalty imposed, and act accordingly—he is interested in the motivating circumstances of the crime. Was it part of an emotional explosion that happened once and may never happen again, or was it part of a general criminal pattern? Was the defendant cooperative after he was apprehended? Has he a sense of guilt concerning the crime or is he oblivious to what he did? Was he under the influence of others stronger than he? Was he armed during the crime?

The answers to these questions will have as great a bearing on the sentence as does the nature and degree of the crime itself.[20]

18. Right of state or Federal prisoner to credit for time served in another jurisdiction before delivery to state or Federal authorities. 18 ALR2d 511.

Annotations: Right to credit for time served under erroneous or void sentence or invalid judgment of conviction necessitating new trial. 35 ALR2d 1283.

19. See generally Note, Right to Counsel at the Time of Sentence: New York's Forgotten Guarantee, 27 Brooklyn L Rev 110, 123–124 (1960).

20. Annotation: Mistaken belief in existence, validity, or effect of divorce or separation as mitigating punishment for bigamy or allied offense. 56 ALR2d 915 at page 938.

§ 623. Predilection of the judge

Another important factor is the attitude of the Judge. The Judge's attitude may often depend on his social, religious and professional background as well as his outlook on the particular crime.

Some are particularly prejudiced against crimes of violence, the use of guns and the like. Others are horrified by sexual offenses. Still others blame society for the frequency of sexual crimes. There are some judges who believe crimes of violence occur because of some particular stress on the defendant, and are unlikely to reoccur.

To better understand the predilection of judges, you should know something about the different "schools of punishment." Most judges belong to one or another.

Some judges belong to the retributive school. They consider the convicted defendant an evil person, an enemy of the people. Punishment is a form of vengeance to them. The defendant has wronged society so he must pay.

Other judges belong to the deterrent school. The members of this school look upon punishment as a deterrent to crime both as to the defendant and to others. Members of this school are governed by the fear of crime. They hope that punishment of the defendant will prevent the future occurrence of similar crimes.

Still others are members of the rehabilitation school. Most conscientious students of crime and punishment belong to this school. It is certainly the most modern school of thought. It contemplates the welfare of the defendant. It seeks to protect the defendant from himself, and society from the defendant, not by punishment but by rehabilitation. Emphasis is placed upon the defendant's useful role in the community; punishment is imposed only until the defendant is ready to resume that role. When punishment has served to rehabilitate him to society, he is restored to the community.

§ 624. Atmosphere of the community

The sentencing judge reacts keenly to the feeling of the community. The community's malice may be directed at a particular defendant or at the specific nature of the crime he has committed. His crime may have shocked the public and brought a stream of abusive language from press, radio, and television. Because of such an atmosphere, a judge may be compelled to impose a maximum sentence despite his inner dictates.

The more unfortunate situation is where the newspapers have embarked on a general campaign against one type of crime. These campaigns stir up community emotion. The Judge, being sensitive to these waves of public opinion, must lash out at *any* defendant unlucky enough to have committed the crime being campaigned against.

E. COUNSEL'S FUNCTION AND TECHNIQUES AT SENTENCING

§ 625. In general

Sentencing is not the time to dwell upon the innocence of your client; he has pleaded guilty or has been convicted. If you argue his innocence, it will only irritate the sentencing judge. At sentence your job is to convince the Court that the defendant will not commit a crime again, not that the defendant did not commit any crime at all.

Impress upon the Judge that the defendant can and will become a law-abiding person under the advice and help of the probation officer; that he need not be isolated as a menace to the community. You must convince the Judge that the imposition of a suspended or light sentence is merited by the defendant's history and the nature of the crime. Urge that probation, and not imprisonment, is most sensible in view of the circumstances.

If the seriousness of the crime excludes probation, point out to the Judge that the minimum penalty is consistent with the defendant's history and present outlook.

§ 626. Presence of counsel

In some jurisdictions it constitutes a violation of his constitutional right to counsel to sentence him without counsel being present,[21] at least if the defendant requests counsel at the time of sentencing.[22]

The constitutional right of the accused to assistance of counsel at the time of sentence applies whether there has been a trial or not.[23]

Sentencing procedures are fundamentally unfair where the defendant is not represented by counsel, and the judge assumes facts respecting defendant's criminal record that are materially untrue, and which counsel would have been dutybound to call to the court's attention.[24]

§ 627. Preparing for sentencing

Preparing for sentencing is not unlike preparing your case for trial. In fact, much of the information you gathered for the trial will be useful at sentence.

In order to adequately prepare your defense, you certainly must have studied the circumstances surrounding the crime. You looked into the defendant's background, his homelife, where he grew up, who his friends were, how far

21. Houston v Ellis (CA5 Tex) 252 F2d 186; Ex parte Sabongy, 18 NJ Super 334, 87 A2d 59; People v Hannigan, 7 NY2d 317, 197 NYS2d 152, 165 NE2d 172.

Absence, at the time of the imposition of sentence, of counsel appointed for the accused, though excused by the trial judge on the retirement of the jury pursuant to an arrangement between counsel and the United States attorney, required the vacation of the sentence in order to preserve the accused's constitutional right to assistance of counsel, because there is a real need for counsel at such time in order to determine the advisability of an appeal, and to present explanatory or extenuating facts to the court which may result in mitigation, or even suspension, of the penalty. Martin v United States (CA5 Tex) 182 F2d 225, 20 ALR2d 1236, cert den 340 US 892, 95 L Ed 647, 71 S Ct 200.

22. State v Crow (Mo) 377 SW2d 129, cert den 379 US 861, 13 L Ed 2d 65, 85 S Ct 124.

23. Evans v Rives, 75 App DC 242, 126 F2d 633.

24. Townsend v Burke, 334 US 736, 92 L Ed 1690, 68 S Ct 1252.

Annotation: Imposing sentence and procedural due process—Federal cases. 93 L Ed 1345.

he went in school, what kind of work he does. All of these facts are definitely important to the trial of a case; they are equally important, if not more so, to the sentence.

There are, however, additional facts that may or may not have been important to the trial of your case—the defendant's married life, his physical and mental condition, his monetary problems, and his social and religious activity in the community. This information is necessary; without it you cannot be really prepared to present your client's cause to the sentencing judge.

When you have gathered all of the above information, you will be in a position to ask and argue for a minimum or a suspended sentence. You will be able to show the Court why imprisonment may not be proper for this particular defendant. The sentencing judge should then be able to impose a fair and just sentence.

§ 628. Analyze types of possible sentences

Except for the serious felonies, the possible sentences for a particular offense generally vary. In many jurisdictions there is an alternative for the straight prison-term sentence. The defendant may receive an indeterminate sentence to a reformatory or some other correctional institution.

The type of sentence imposed may be significant in terms of rehabilitation and length of imprisonment. For example, in New York City, a sentence to a city prison—or what is known as the workhouse—for a fixed term of months entitles the defendant to five days off for good behavior for each month served. This amounts to approximately a one-sixth reduction of the sentence, for good behavior.

On the other hand, a sentence to a definite term in the New York City Penitentiary entitles the defendant to one-third (10 days per month) off the balance of his term, for good behavior.

Very often the Judge is not fully aware of the types of

sentences available and the different treatment afforded the defendant under each. He may inadvertently mistreat the defendant through the imposition of a harsh sentence.

Remind the Court of each possible sentence. Point out that the less severe sentence would be fair and just for your client.

§ 629. Pleading the defendant's case

In pleading for leniency for your client, address yourself to the following issues:

(a) *Consequences of arrest.* Show that the defendant has suffered great emotional strain from his arrest and incarceration; that he has become aware of the error of his ways; that his family has endured great hardship.

(b) *Defendant's previous criminal record.* Highlight a clean record. If the defendant has a record, however, be prepared to explain the circumstances surrounding every previous arrest and conviction.

(c) *Defendant's Employment Record.* Stress that a good employment record implies a good employment future. Explain the reasons for a poor employment record.

(d) *Defendant's Marital History.* If the defendant has tried to repair a broken home, stress these efforts. If he is divorced or separated, emphasize his efforts to meet his support obligations.

(e) *Defendant's Family Background.* Emphasize that defendant's family feels guilty and anxious to help him.

(f) *Defendant's Personality Traits.* Unfavorable personality traits will be highlighted in the pre-sentence report. Point out that since the commission of the crime, the defendant's standards or behavior are much higher. He has gained a respect for authority, and his goals in life are normal.

(g) *Alcoholism and Drug Addiction.* If there is a connection between your client's alcoholism or drug addiction and the crime he committed, tell the judge.

(h) *Defendant's Military Record.* Emphasize a good military record. Say little about a poor military record. If the pre-sentence report mentions it, explain that the defendant has changed since his army days.

(i) *Voice of Community Leaders.* Most judges will be influenced by pleas for the defendant that come from respected members of the community.

In short. Present to the Judge a picture of the defendant ready to take his place in lawful society and ready to fulfill his obligations to the community. Show that his imprisonment will defeat his rehabilitation and compel the community to do for his family what he could better do himself with no expense to the community.

F. VALIDITY AND EFFECT OF SENTENCE

§ 630. In general

Where the trial court has jurisdiction of the offense charged and of the defendant,[25] it has authority to impose

25. Bowen v Johnston, 306 US 19, 83 L Ed 455, 59 S Ct 442; Re Eckart, 166 US 481, 41 L Ed 1085, 17 S Ct 638; Adams Exp. Co. v Bradley, 179 Ky 238, 200 SW 340.

Annotations: Length of sentence as violation of constitutional provisions prohibiting cruel and unusual punishment. 33 ALR3d 335.

Inconsistency of criminal verdict as between different courts of indictment or information. 18 ALR3d 259.

Inconsistency of criminal verdict with verdict on another indictment or information tried at same time. 16 ALR3d 866.

Propriety of general sentence covering several counts in information or indictment, not exceeding in aggregate the sentences which might have been imposed cumulatively under the several counts. 91 ALR2d 511.

Effect of invalidation of sentence upon separate sentence which runs consecutively. 68 ALR2d 712.

Validity, under indeterminate sentence law, of sentence fixing identical minimum and maximum terms of imprisonment. 29 ALR2d 1344.

Construction of Federal statute (28 USC § 2255) dealing with vacation, by direct attack, of sentence in criminal case on ground that it violated Constitution or laws, or exceeded jurisdiction, or is otherwise subject to collateral attack. 20 ALR2d 976.

Necessity of notice of application or

sentence; its judgment remains in force until reversed[26] and is immune from collateral attack.[27]

A sentence imposed by a court without jurisdiction to pass such a sentence is deemed to be void and not merely irregular or erroneous.[28] Likewise a judgment of conviction under an unconstitutional law has also been held to be void.[29]

The imposition of an unauthorized or merely erroneous sentence does not require vacation of the entire judgment or granting of a new trial, but is a ground for reversing the erroneous portion of the judgment or sentence, leaving the verdict to stand as the basis for a new and proper sentence,[30] or in the case of a divisible sentence, the appellate court may modify it by striking out the illegal part and affirming the balance.[31]

§ 631. Definiteness and certainty

A high degree of exactitude is required in the pronouncement of judgments imposing penal servitude.[32] A sentence should be so definite as to need no construction to ascertain its import. The punishment inflicted upon the worst crimi-

intention to correct error in judgment entry. 14 ALR2d 224.

Former jeopardy as ground for habeas corpus. 8 ALR2d 285.

26. Ex parte Watkins (US) 3 Pet 193, 7 L Ed 650.

27. Adams Exp. Co. v Bradley, 179 Ky 238, 200 SW 340; Turbessi v Oliver Iron Min. Co. 250 Mich 110, 229 NW 454, 69 ALR 1059; Capos v Clatsop County, 144 Or 510, 25 P2d 903, 90 ALR 289; Eagle, Star & B. D. Ins. Co. v Heller, 149 Va 82, 140 SE 314, 57 ALR 490.

28. Nation v District of Columbia, 34 App DC 453.

A judgment of a court without jurisdiction of the subject matter is void. Wedmore v State, 233 Ind 545, 122 NE2d 1.

29. State v Williams, 146 NC 618, 61 SE 61; Kelley v Meyers, 124 Or 322, 263 P 903, 56 ALR 661; Ex parte Hollman, 79 SC 9, 60 SE 19; State v Dove, 75 SD 460, 67 NW2d 917.

30. State v Lindsey, 194 Wash 129, 77 P2d 596, cert den 304 US 559, 82 L Ed 1526, 58 S Ct 947, cert den 305 US 637, 83 L Ed 410, 59 S Ct 108.

31. Wahl v State, 39 Ariz 62, 3 P2d 1052; State v Herzoff, 200 Iowa 889, 205 NW 500; Pressly v State, 114 Tenn 534, 86 SW 378; State v Feilen, 70 Wash 65, 126 P 75.

32. Re Swink, 243 NC 86, 89 SE2d 792.

nal must be legal, and when this is not so, however unintentional, an offense is being committed in the name of the law against the person.[33] Accordingly, a sentence should be definite, certain, and not dependent on any contingency or condition.[34] Where the contrary is the case, the benefit of any doubt should be in favor of the defendant.[35]

The sentence should be stated with sufficient certainty to enable the officer to execute it.[36] It should clearly reveal the intention of the court as to the punishment to be inflicted.[37] For example, a sentence in a homicide case of "not to exceed seventy years" lacks certainty and gives the officers of the state penitentiary an insufficient knowledge of what the sentence really is.[38] In the case of an ambiguity, the intention of the court should not be sought through evidence dehors the record.[39]

An omission to specify the duration of imprisonment, where required, is generally held to be a defect which renders the sentence void for indefiniteness.[40] However, an uncertainty in the judgment of the court pronounced on the verdict in a criminal case does not always vacate or set

33. Ex parte Lamar (CA2d) 274 F 160, 24 ALR 864, affd 260 US 711, 67 L Ed 476, 43 S Ct 251, stating that society does not want to have an unlawful or indefinite sentence imposed against anyone, because if it is done against one person, it may be done against another and no man can say whose turn will come next.

34. State v Sturgis, 110 Me 96, 85 A 474.

35. Downey v United States, 67 App DC 192, 91 F2d 223; Cross v Huff, 208 Ga 392, 67 SE2d 124.

36. United States v Daugherty, 269 US 360, 70 L Ed 309, 46 S Ct 156; Sinner v State, 128 Neb 759, 260 NW 275.

37. United States v Daugherty, 269 US 360, 70 L Ed 309, 46 S Ct 156.

38. State v Jackson, 251 Iowa 537, 101 NW2d 731, pointing out that any term of years from 70 down meets the sentence of "not to exceed seventy years."

39. Re Parker, 225 NC 369, 35 SE2d 169, further stating that a sentence is not merely a directive from which those who are to execute it may obtain information as to the extent of that duty, but when put on the official court record it is a guaranty to the prisoner that prosecution will not again be attempted within its scope and that punishment shall not exceed its reasonably definite limits.

40. Lee Lim v Davis, 75 Utah 245, 284 P 323, 76 ALR 460.

aside the verdict of conviction.[41] A reviewing court will only remand the cause with directions to impose a lawful sentence.[42] Thus if judgment pronounced in a criminal case is ambiguous as to the basis for the sentence, the most that the defendant may successfully ask is to have the case remanded for a proper judgment, and not for a dismissal of the action.[43]

41. Emmertson v State Tax Com. 93 Utah 219, 72 P2d 467, 113 ALR 1174.

42. Lee Lim v Davis, 75 Utah 245, 284 P 323, 76 ALR 460.

43. State v Batson, 220 NC 411, 17 SE2d 511, 139 ALR 614.

INDEX